Soul
of the
Tiger

Soul

of the

Tiger

Searching for Nature's Answers
in Exotic Southeast Asia

Jeffrey A. McNeely
and
Paul Spencer Wachtel

Doubleday
NEW YORK

A portion of the income earned from SOUL OF THE TIGER will be donated to the World Wide Fund for Nature (WWF) and the International Union for Conservation of Nature and Natural Resources to support nature conservation in Southeast Asia.

Portions of this book have appeared in other forms in the following:
"Adu domba: Java's Holy Gladitorial Rams." *Orientations*, February 1977.
"Karapan Sapi: Bull Racing of Madura." *Seasons*, Winter 1978.
"Return to the Wild." *Silver Kris*, October 1978.
"The Universal Apothecary." *Winds*, July 1980.
"They Use Everything but the Cat's Meow." *International Wildlife*, May/June 1981.
"Malaysia's Rainforest: A Journey of Discovery." *Reader's Digest*, July 1982.
"Can We Talk to the Animals?" *Silver Kris*, July 1982.
"Oh, Rats." *International Wildlife*, January/February 1985.
"The Cobra King." *International Wildlife*, January/February 1986.

Library of Congress Cataloging-in-Publication Data

McNeely, Jeffrey A.
　Soul of the tiger.

　Bibliography: p. 355
　Includes index.
　1. Animals and civilization—Asia, Southeastern. 2. Man—Influence on nature—Asia, Southeastern. 3. Asia, Southeastern—Social life and customs. 4. Asia, Southeastern—Description and travel. I. Wachtel, Paul Spencer. II. Title.
QL85.M36　1988　　333.95'0959　　87-13687

To the memory of my father
— PAUL SPENCER WACHTEL

To Dr. Boonsong Lekagul, mentor and friend
— JEFFREY A. MCNEELY

Acknowledgments

We thank the people of Southeast Asia who have let us into their lives.

Pote, Mike, and Joey for incredible patience while Daddy was distracted by the exotic East.

Sue Rallo, Liz Edelman, Joanna Erfani, and Madlen Tschopp for working on their own time to help prepare the manuscript.

Numerous friends and colleagues who have shared our adventures, sharpened our perceptions, and offered advice and encouragement: Julian Bach, Jon Barzdo, John Blower, Pamina Blum, Jill Bolingbroke, George Bowden, John Cartwright, T. T. Chang, Lucas Chin, Jim Clad, Ted Cronin, Chuck Darsono, Bob Dobias, Pat Dugan, Michelle Edwards, Steve Edwards, Danny Elder, Chris Elliot, Sandie Ellis, Richard Englehardt, Taghi Farvar, Jon Fisher, George Frame, Lory Frame, Jose Furtado, Guy Goh, Monica Goh, Dennis Gray, Mark Halle, David Hallmark, Richard Hamilton, K. R. T. Hardjonagoro, Jerry Harrison, Peter Jackson, Peter Kedit, Mohamad Khan, Peter Kum, David Labang, S. K. Lau, Andrew Laurie, Warren Lindner, Diane Lorraine, Richard Luxmore, John MacKinnon, Kathy MacKinnon, Esmond Bradley Martin, Tom Millikin, Dan Navid, Pisit na Patalung, Ron Petocz, Pong Leng-Ee, Urs Ramseyer, Lynne Rich, Norman Rolnick, Darry Salim, Partha Sarathy, Mimes Sasmoyo, Jeff Sayer, George Schaller, Curt Schneider, John Seidensticker, Samar Singh, Bob Sitharam, William J. Stone, Effendi Sumardja, Julius Tahija, Lee Talbot, Jim Thorsell, Willem van Liere, Tony Whitten, Helen Wolfson, and Mike Woodford.

Kenton R. Miller, Director General of IUCN, and Charles de

Haes, Director General of WWF, who gave this project their full support, which helped in many ways.

Serge Beck, Nicole Gyggax, and Judy Mutziger of Vert Pomme, Montricher, Switzerland, who produced the maps.

And Ganesh, who we hope is pleased.

Contents

Preface

We left Southeast Asia at the end of 1980, having savored the area's diverse pleasures for a combined twenty-five years. We now live in Switzerland with no regrets, yet we miss the distinctive oriental sights, smells, and sounds—the thousand shades of green in the forest, the fragrance of sizzling *satay,* the choruses of singing gibbons. We admired the ability of the people to find peace unto themselves in the middle of chaos of Dantean proportions, and every time we return to visit Thailand, Malaysia, or Indonesia we are impressed anew at the diversity of approaches to earning a living in seemingly impossible circumstances. Perhaps above all we marvel at how strong and pervasive are beliefs relating people with nature.

This book is the result of our inquiry into the relationship between people and animals in Southeast Asia, what this relationship meant in the past, how it is changing, and what relevance it might have for the future. We record our personal impressions, supported by a varied literature and conversations with many of the key individuals involved in the region. We feel that the mammals, birds, and reptiles on which we have concentrated provide convincing evidence of the human concern with nature. A similar book could be written about the plants, or the insects.

Soul of the Tiger is set in Southeast Asia, the region from Burma east to Thailand and the Indochinese states of Laos, Kampuchea, and Vietnam, south through the Malay peninsula and the Indonesian archipelago which leads north and east to the Philippines and Papua New Guinea. But understanding the history of human-animal relationships in Southeast Asia also means looking to India and China, where many of the more sophisticated current beliefs originated. The Chinese have colonized much of Southeast Asia, particularly the commercial centers and areas where plantation agriculture and tin mining required outside labor. India has sent fewer people, but many of Southeast Asia's mainstream cultural ideas are based on Hindu, Buddhist, and Islamic beliefs which arrived via the subcontinent.

We have lived or worked in virtually every country in the region east of India, south of China, and north of Australia, but we were not always in the same place at the same time. We did not *both* go on all the adventures recounted, but since the book is not intended to be autobiographical we have combined our experiences and have consistently used "we" to refer to either or both of us.

Jeffrey A. McNeely is an anthropologist and zoologist whose professional interest in wildlife started while he was working his way through UCLA graduate school as a zookeeper at the Los Angeles Zoo. Joining the Peace Corps in 1968, he was sent to Thailand, where he worked for five years with Dr. Boonsong Lekagul, then Southeast Asia's leading conservationist. Together they wrote *Mammals of Thailand* and traveled throughout the region searching for oddities such as the world's smallest mammal. McNeely spent two years with the Mekong Committee of the United Nations designing a system of national parks for Laos, Cambodia, Vietnam, and part of Thailand, and was coleader of a two-year scientific expedition to the Tibetan border region of northeastern Nepal. From 1977 to 1980, he worked with the World Wildlife Fund in Indonesia, administering conservation projects aimed at securing the habitat of everything from Javan rhinos to proboscis monkeys to tree kangaroos. In late 1980, he joined the International Union for Conservation of Nature and Natural Resources (IUCN) in Switzerland as executive officer of the Commission on National Parks and Protected Areas. In that capacity, he organized the World National Parks Congress held in Bali in 1982 and carried out missions to advise on conservation in Burma, Sri Lanka, Malaysia, and the Philippines. Since 1983, he has served IUCN as director of its Programme and Policy Division, advising governments and conservation organizations worldwide on the actions needed to save nature.

Paul Spencer Wachtel is a journalist and retired playwright who first went to Asia in 1969 as a Peace Corps volunteer assigned to Sarawak, in Malaysian Borneo. There he advised teachers in remote primary schools on new instructional methods. Living in the forests of Borneo, he studied the wildlife and people, an interest he maintained after he started working in Singapore for an international advertising agency. This position allowed him to travel throughout the region directing TV commercials for a living and writing magazine articles for personal satisfaction. Moving to Indonesia in 1973, he managed an advertising agency and wrote about and photographed many of the country's more unusual aspects—royal mystics in the Javanese city of Solo, the importance of volcanoes, faith healers, marriage bureaus, and the culinary delights of itinerant food vendors who carry their restaurants on their shoulders and their cooking oil in recycled insecticide tins. Although a psychologist by education, Wachtel has learned more about people by combing much of the region in search of the unusual, spending time in the Philippines, Thailand, Malaysia, Laos, and Kampuchea. Early in 1981, he accepted a position with the World Wildlife Fund International headquarters in Switzerland, where he was responsible for WWF's international campaigns to save tropical rain forests, threatened plants, and wetlands. He is now head of the WWF Department of Creative Services, a unit which prepares fund-raising and marketing presentations.

We both come from ordinary Western backgrounds, and now work for organizations that are leaders in the international conservation field. Yet this book is our own, and does not necessarily represent the views or positions of IUCN or WWF. We have tried to understand the views of Southeast Asian people as objectively as possible, though we have inevitably brought a Western bias to our interpretations and our conclusions may not be greeted with approbation by all in the region.

We have often felt daunted by the enormity of trying to comprehend and explain the complex relationships between people and animals in one of the most culturally and naturally diverse regions of the globe. We have sometimes wished that Asians themselves had taken on the investigation. We are disappointed that so few of those in power in the region seem either to appreciate traditional knowledge or to care particularly about its being conserved. In the rush to build politically viable nations, government leaders have tended to ignore how traditional knowledge about nature could help make their countries more ecologically viable.

We hope that this book, incomplete though it certainly is, may help to foster a greater appreciation in Western audiences of the cultural and natural wealth of traditional tropical Asia. At the same time, it might arouse a renewed appreciation among Southeast Asia's urban elites of the importance of the traditional knowledge held by their own rural relatives.

Virtually all the world's rural societies relate to animals in ways that, while different in details, might be recognizable to a Southeast Asian. A book of this type could have been written about the people of East Africa, Central America, the Andes, or rural Europe. We have chosen Southeast Asia for two reasons: life's happy accidents put us there, and the region proved to be particularly rich in relationships between people and wildlife.

While we have profound respect for the traditions, history, and survival tactics of the past, we do not expect things ever to be the same again. But the systems that worked for thousands of years can teach us how to live better in the future, and that forward-looking perspective has guided our investigation.

We share responsibility for the book, settling the question of first author by a coin toss after the book was finished. The book is intended for a general audience, so we have avoided using footnotes in the interest of narrative continuity. However, numerous books, articles, and reports have contributed to our work so we have included a list of further readings for each chapter and a complete bibliography.

The rural people of Southeast Asia have given us much, and we consider this book a gift to friends. Our hope is that documenting the ways people and wildlife relate to each other in Southeast Asia will show that conservation is not just a fad of the wealthy. Rather, nature has been the foundation of all human cultures in the region and any healthy society of the future will need to incorporate ways and means of linking people with the natural world. If our book helps maintain the cultural and ecological diversity of Southeast Asia, and thereby contributes to new ways of life that are both biologically productive and emotionally satisfying, then we will have at least begun to repay the people of the region for all they gave to us.

Givrins and Mont-sur-Rolle, Switzerland   Paul Spencer Wachtel
10 April 1987   Jeffrey A. McNeely

Soul
of the
Tiger

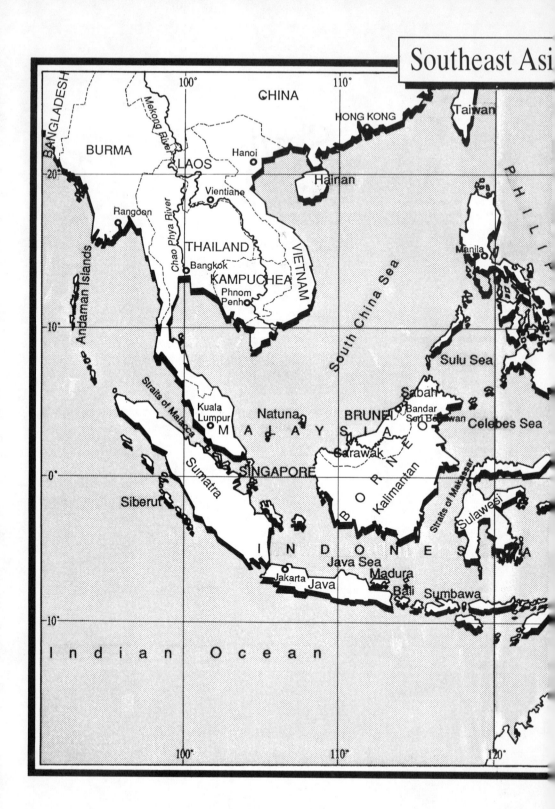

Southeast Asi

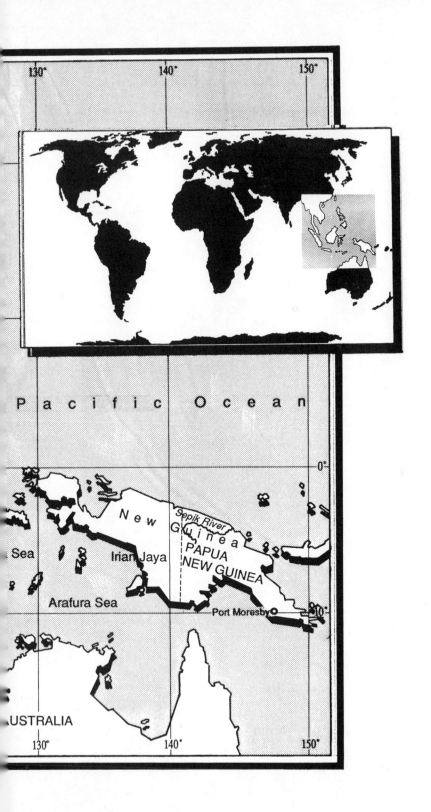

1

Searching for Natural Answers

The relationship between rural people and wildlife in Southeast Asia has stood the test of time and may point the way to a more productive future.

- A buffalo, a monkey, a crocodile, a puppy, a scorpion and an eagle were among the animals ritually slaughtered in 1979 as part of a once-a-century religious ceremony held to appease the nature gods who live in Bali's active Mount Agung volcano.
- Men in Malaysia and Indonesia are thought to transform into tigers, sometimes at death, other times at will. A village in Sumatra, under siege by a man-eating tiger, pools its resources and brings in an outside "hired gun" to sing the cat into a cage.
- A farmer from the Kelabit tribe in Borneo, a strict evangelical Christian, waits to begin planting his rice crop until he sees the arrival of the yellow wagtail from China. He uses other bird omens to help him decide when to weed his fields and harvest his crop.

- A young engineering graduate from Bangkok's Chulalongkorn University is ordained as a Buddhist monk. A key part of the ritual occurs when the abbot asks the neophyte, "Are you a man or a snake?"
- The breeding rate of pigs in Papua New Guinea determines when the women get a break from housework and the men go to war.
- Guards in Java's Ujung Kulon National Park use their handkerchiefs to soak up rhinoceros urine, which they use to prevent infection from leech bites and to cure earaches.
- Fishermen in eastern Indonesia believe their ancestors arrived on the back of a whale; today they hunt sperm whales by leaping into the sea and sinking a spear deep into the animal's back.
- Early religious leaders co-opted an elephant-god to promote their cause, and kings claimed the elephant's power to consolidate their positions.

FROM THE PARCHED HILLS of Burma to the sticky rain forests of Sulawesi and the frigid mountains of New Guinea, we have been both charmed and intrigued by the ways in which animals are entwined with the diverse human societies in the region. Wherever we have gone in Southeast Asia, whichever of the hundreds of different cultural groups we visited, animals were part of human life.

For the 80 percent of the population which remains in the countryside, animals are omens, powerful mythological symbols, meat, ancestors, tractors, thugs, gladiators, apothecaries, leather, and competitors. Animals are constant companions which cannot be ignored, and villagers have developed strategies for living in balance with nature which are often quite different from those of the government officials, intellectuals, and environmental activists living in the cities.

This intimate relationship often survives because the simple technology available to the rural people limits their impact on the environment. The people who live in best harmony with nature often survive at a subsistence level with few diversions and outside contacts. Given the choice, most rural people would prefer to have a car, a refrigerator, and a university education for their children rather than maintain their ecologically sound subsistence agriculture. Many of them are now being given a chance to choose the seductive option of worldly goods.

◆ ◆ ◆

Bangkok is notorious for having the worst traffic in Asia. Once considered "the Venice of the East" because of the hundreds of canals that provided the means to travel from home to market, the capital's transportation system has now become terrestrial. Modern Bangkok is a rabbit warren of streets and alleys clogged with noisy pedestrians trying to dodge a madhouse of vehicles—bicyclists carrying squealing pigs, modern Mercedes and decrepit Datsuns fighting for space on the street, buses crammed with uniformed book-laden students, portable restaurants constructed on pushcarts, ten-wheeled trucks belching black smoke, three-wheeled motor scooters that scare the hell out of us, and mufflerless motorcycles somehow accommodating families of five.

We were in Bangkok for a short visit in the hot season of 1970, taking a break after building eighteen small water systems for rural schools in the remote southern Thai province of Phangnga. "Phangnga," as we learned shortly after we had arrived the year before, means "to lean the elephant tusk." It seems that the first farmers in the region were victimized by elephants raiding their crops, so a great hunter attacked the elephant-king. After a fierce battle, the hunter killed the animal, cut off its tusks, and placed them against the elephant's side. But this was no ordinary elephant —he was an elephant-god and the huge carcass immediately turned to stone. Today, a massive limestone mountain with two vertical outcroppings looms over the provincial capital and is said to be in the form of an elephant with its butchered tusks leaning against its body.

We had spent our spare time in Phangnga's forests, trying to see *real* elephants and reveling in the incredible diversity of the tropical rain forest, a wondrous experience after having been brought up in American cities where the wildlife was mostly to be found in the zoo or on the streets.

We had wanted to learn about more Thai wildlife so we wrote to Dr. Boonsong Lekagul, the secretary general of the Association for the Conservation of Wildlife and Thailand's grand old man of natural history. Dr. Boonsong invited us to stop by the next time we visited the capital.

We had assumed that his "Dr." was a Ph.D. in some field of natural history, so we were a bit surprised to find Dr. Boonsong at a medical clinic. While waiting for our appointment, we chatted with the young receptionist, who told us that Dr. Boonsong innovated the concept of uniting under one roof several medical specialists and laboratory facilities. Dr. Boonsong had been a medical pioneer in Thailand, developing a number of new drugs and willingly traveling to remote areas to bring Western medical care to villagers.

Dr. Boonsong finally finished treating his patient and came out to see us. He was small, with an outdoorsman's healthy glow, narrow shoulders, and a rather hawklike face. Dr. Boonsong was sixty-three but seemed much younger.

"Come in, come in," he said, ushering us through his clinic and back into his private natural history museum. It was a single large high-ceilinged room attached to his house. Bookshelves and specimen drawers lined the lower part of the walls, overshadowed by dozens of sets of antlers and horns from all over the world. The table in the center was piled high with papers and stuffed birds. Inviting us to sit down, he called to a servant to bring cold drinks.

"I am very pleased to talk with young people who are keen naturalists," he told us. "Things are very difficult for wildlife in my country. Loggers are everywhere, and most of the politicians and government officials live in the cities and have forgotten their roots in the countryside. With the wars going on in all of our neighboring countries, the government is very nervous about the loyalties of Thai villagers. Nobody wants to do anything that the villagers might not like, such as stopping poaching or arresting people for illegally clearing the forest."

We asked him what could be done.

"I'm trying to make Thai people appreciate their wildlife more. This is one of my efforts," he explained as he handed us his *Bird Guide of Thailand*. He had spent ten years collecting specimens and painting each of Thailand's 850 species of birds, one tenth of all the birds in the world and as many as are found in all of North America. As the first such field guide prepared by a Southeast Asian, it was an important achievement.

"My problem is that I don't have enough time, money, or help," Dr. Boonsong continued. "I try to give as much time as I can to conservation, but I still have to run my clinic. Two of my sons are physicians, but they are both practicing in America and I can't retire until at least one of them returns. What I want to do now is write a book on the mammals of Thailand, another one on the reptiles and amphibians, and one on the butterflies." We learned later that he did not mention that he also would continue giving talks at schools, making wildlife films, writing letters to the government, and pushing for more funds for Thailand's national parks.

We told Dr. Boonsong about what we had been doing in Phangnga, asked him to help us identify a few of the more obscure birds we had seen, and discussed how we might be able to keep in touch. A servant quietly slipped into the museum, and respectfully informed Dr. Boonsong that lunch was ready.

"My friends will be taking rice with me," he murmured to her in Thai. "Please join me for lunch," he invited, in his careful and precise English. Also at Dr. Boonsong's table were his wife, who was the brains behind the business side of his clinic, his stepson, who was a dentist at the clinic, and two newspaper reporters. The middle of the table was spread with dishes of sweet and sour fried fish, chicken fried with quail eggs and mushrooms, shredded pork, four kinds of fresh vegetables, a green curry that was so spicy we feared for the serving spoon, and a large pot of fluffy white rice.

As at so many of the thousand or so other meals we were to share with Dr. Boonsong over the next few years, wildlife was the topic of conversation. Dr. Boonsong always gave good copy and the newspaper reporters sought his views on the destruction of the Thai forests and their wildlife.

"When I was a boy, the forests covered the land," Dr. Boonsong began, with the professional communicator's knack of explaining things clearly to the press. "People had been here for thousands of years. The early hunters used fire for cooking and to burn the vegetation in order to attract game to fresh new grass growing in the ashes. Later on, people domesticated animals and became farmers and started clearing the forest. But still plenty of forest was left for the animals. Then irrigation arrived, rice fields claimed the best wildlife habitat, and the wild animals started to suffer. Since World War II, things have been getting much worse. Villagers now have powerful firearms and jeeps. The trees are being felled to send timber overseas. Forests are being cleared to grow maize, sugarcane, and cassava to send to Japan and Europe. The real problem is not that we have too many people, or that the starving poor are clearing the forest. The problem is that we want the money that comes from selling our resources overseas. It's nice to be wealthier, but the cost is our forests and wildlife, and that's making us poorer."

The reporters left after the main course and we continued talking with Dr. Boonsong as dessert was served: sliced fresh pineapple, dark pink papaya, and peeled grapefruit-like pomelo. After the spicy meal, our palates welcomed the cool fruit. Over coffee, Dr. Boonsong asked us a question that was to change our lives: "How would you like to come and work with me to write a book on the mammals of Thailand?"

"Yes," we immediately responded. And that was the start of many years of seeking an understanding about people and wildlife in Southeast Asia.

◆ ◆ ◆

Our discussions with Dr. Boonsong introduced us to the idea that people's relationship with nature has been, and always will be, changing. We soon came to realize that four stages of human development have increasingly affected the natural world: control of fire, domestication of plants and animals, irrigation, and development of the world marketplace. These four stages involved changes that were so profound that they might better be considered "ecocultural revolutions." Each was constructed on the foundations of cultural innovation and involved ecological, social, religious and political changes which led to significant increases in the human population. Each has had a profound effect on people and nature in Southeast Asia.

These ecocultural revolutions underline the cyclical nature of life in Asia. In the West we say that the only things you can count on are death and taxes. Many Asians would add rebirth to the list. Periods of stability are temporary intersections in a maze of change, which is why we should not view our current way of life as permanent, any more than we should imagine that our current corporeal incarnation will last much beyond the biblical three score and ten years. If we apply this concept of continual change to a broader social context, we can expect the structure of industrial society to take on a new form, and when that happens the relationship between people and nature will embark on yet another uncharted course.

We each spent over twelve years in Southeast Asia. During this time we saw people living with wildlife in ways that were so enduring and so important to the social, psychological, and physical well-being of villagers that these relationships would surely be important factors in any new and sustainable relationship between people and nature. A fifth ecocultural revolution for humanity will certainly be built on the enduring beliefs of the people who live closest to their natural resources.

◆ ◆ ◆

Why look to Southeast Asia when seeking a sustainable relationship between people and wildlife?

Europe languished in the dark ages while great cities and sophisticated empires flourished in the rich rice-growing river valleys of Indochina, Thailand, Burma, Sumatra, and Java. At the same time, the remote hills and islands supported hundreds of tribal cultures based on shifting cultivation or hunting and gathering, each with its own customs and language, and each affected to various degrees by the rice-growing civilizations in the river valleys. Only in Southeast Asia does such a rich mixture of major religions flourish —Animism, Buddhism, Chinese syncretism, Christianity, Confucianism, Hinduism, and Islam are all important forces in modern life.

Southeast Asia is not the most populous region on earth, nor the most powerful. While it has been strategically important for centuries, linking India, China, Australia, and the Pacific, and has been an important source of natural products for much of the world, the region's real strength is the spirit of the people. While they are not necessarily paragons of virtue, Southeast Asians have maintained deeply held and ancient beliefs about people's relationship with nature. Only recently have these relationships been losing ground to modern approaches to life that divorce people from nature.

In our quest for understanding the factors that create a productive relationship between people and animals, we have ranged far beyond the usual approach of concentrating on the animals. Instead, we have delved into the worlds of religion, art, anthropology, psychology, sociology, history, biography, travel, literature, and mythology to learn how humans and animals have coexisted. Rather than concentrating on a single village or one country—both of which would have been valid approaches—we have treated the region as a whole, seeking the common threads which are woven through numerous cultures and life-styles.

How have animals contributed to Asian culture? What means have rural people used to conserve wildlife? What changes are coming with the modern world? How can contemporary science contribute to a better relationship between people and nature?

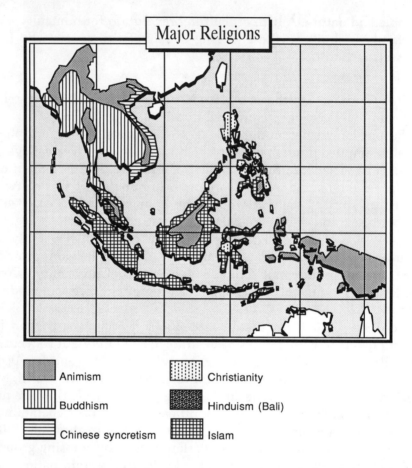

Major Religions

Animism		Christianity
Buddhism		Hinduism (Bali)
Chinese syncretism		Islam

How can government leaders use nature to help them stay in power? What lessons learned about the man-animal relationship in the past might be applied in the future?

If answers are to be found to the critical questions of how people adapt to nature, and how nature puts order and meaning into human life, then Southeast Asia may be the best place to look. This book records what we found.

SOUTHEAST ASIA AT A GLANCE

Country	Area (1,000 sq.mi.)	Population (million)	Per Capita GNP (U.S. $)	Major Religions (Official)	Government System
Brunei	2.3	.2 20% rural	21,140	Islam 63% Buddhist 14%	Monarchy
Burma	261.2	37.6 76% rural	180	Buddhist 87% Christian 6%	People's republic
Indonesia	741.1	167.5 78% rural	560	Islamic 84% Christian 8%	Multiparty republic
Kampuchea	69.9	7.2 86% rural	159	Buddhist 88% Islamic 2%	People's republic
Laos	91.4	4.1 84% rural	152	Buddhist 58% Animist 34%	People's republic
Malaysia	127.3	15.6 66% rural	1,870	Islamic 53% Buddhist 17%	Federal constitutional monarchy
Papua New Guinea	178.3	3.3 87% rural	790	Christian (nominal) 95% Animist 3%	Multiparty republic
Philippines	115.8	54.7 64% rural	300	Christian 94% Islamic 4%	Federal republic
Singapore	.2	2.5 0% rural	7,100	Taoist 29% Buddhist 27%	Multiparty republic
Thailand	198.5	51.3 81% rural	812	Buddhist 95% Islamic 4%	Constitutional monarchy
Vietnam	127.2	60.4 81% rural	170	Buddhist 55% Christian 12%	People's republic

Population estimated as of 1985. GNP as of 1983.

2

Seas of Immortality, Voices of Fire

Natural cycles—life and death, changing sea levels, volcanic eruptions—are the certainties, and surprises, of Asian existence.

WHEN WE FIRST ARRIVED in Southeast Asia in the late 1960s, we were fresh out of university and full of the self-confidence that knowing everything worth knowing brings to the young. We knew, for example, that time has a beginning and an end—it's a straight line, inexorably moving ahead. We were pushy and in a hurry, eager to make our mark. Peace Corps training in the late 1960s had convinced us that everyone working together could bring progress to the world, and that the individual can make a difference.

It didn't take us long to learn how things really worked. A group of us had booked passage on the *Rajah Mas*, a small cargo boat plying between the Sarawak cities of Kuching and Sibu. Eager to visit the Iban hill tribes we had heard so much about, and to see the fabulous Iban "longhouses"—single raised dwellings up to a hundred yards long resembling rustic motels on stilts and housing dozens of families—we went to the harbor two hours before sailing, not wanting to miss the departure. We installed ourselves on the deck, and promptly got in the way of the crew members, who were still loading Japanese motorcycles and boxes of tinned curry from China. We tried to get comfortable amid crates of Tiger beer. The appointed hour of departure came, and went. We smiled at the Malay crew and tested our few words of Malay. They smiled back and tried out their English. Finally, we assigned the best of our Malay speakers to find out the problem. She came back shaking her head. "The captain says we might leave later. He said maybe tonight, maybe tomorrow."

We didn't know then that a "maybe tomorrow" verdict was a sure sign that we should get off the boat and wander around Kuching for a couple of days, since the Malay word *esok* is the equivalent of *mañana* but without the same sense of urgency. An opportunity missed today will certainly come again tomorrow.

In Southeast Asia, people often think of time as a circle, without a beginning and an end, with cycles endlessly repeating themselves regardless of how hard humans may try to resist. The idea of cyclical time leads naturally to the idea that everything is connected— all is one, and animals, people, and the gods are parts of the same cosmic whole. Souls are immortal, so life is eternal; after death comes rebirth. In the words of the Hindu epic, the *Bhagavad Gita*, "Even as worn out clothes are cast off and others put on that are new, so worn out bodies are cast off by the dweller in the body and others put on that are new." Souls are everywhere and in everything, and souls of people can be reincarnated as animals, and vice versa.

Sacred and profane, yin and yang, male and female, fire and water are complementary aspects of the same thing; each is meaningless without its complement. Good and evil certainly exist, but as different aspects of the same entity—surely a closer reflection of modern life than the traditional Western conception of good and evil as absolute and separate qualities.

Asia's vibrancy and resilience derive at least partially from the ideas that time is cyclical and that all forms of life are connected with each other. As we were to learn, these two fundamental concepts also provide the key to understanding the relationship between people and nature.

Some cycles are easily experienced. Birth, life, and death form the foundation. The alternating monsoon rains and dry seasons bring inevitable floods and droughts. People plan their lives on the basis of the cycles of clearing and burning the land, planting, growth, harvesting, and regeneration of the natural vegetation. The tides, both daily and seasonal, influence the migrations of fish and sea turtles and thereby affect the fortunes of fishermen. The daily passage of the sun and moon, and the longer cycles of lunar months and solar years, are related to the movements of birds and elephants, as well as the breeding seasons of animals, both wild and domestic.

Cycles apply not only to the life of the individual, but also to the very course of the cosmos. While cosmic cycles are too long for any individual to experience directly, they form part of the mythology of creation which, perhaps not too surprisingly, is a reasonably accurate representation of what scientists think really happened. These cycles include floods that would have impressed Noah, and cataclysmic bouts of volcanic creation and destruction that would have made the gods on Valhalla or Mount Olympus nod with understanding.

Hindu mythology permeates Southeast Asia, and most parts of the region have been touched by the Hindu concept that the world itself moves through a cycle of four ages. The first age lasts the longest and is the most moral. Things degenerate from there until the last age, the shortest and least moral, destroys itself in fire, brimstone, and a cosmic rainstorm. Then all is quiescent until the inevitable cycle starts once again, with life arising anew out of the water.

◆ ◆ ◆

Virtually every ethnic group in Southeast Asia believes that its creation involved water, usually in the form of a flood which followed the cosmic fire. The most sophisticated story, and one which we were to find had influenced all of Southeast Asia, comes from Hindu India, where Vishnu is the cosmic water itself, the Supreme Deity out of which all the elements of the universe arise, and back into which they must ultimately dissolve.

During one rebirth of the universe the gods were dismayed because the *amrita*, the ambrosia that gives them immortality, failed to reappear after the cataclysmic flood. Without the amrita the gods would quickly become powerless, and the world would be in chaos. The deities asked Vishnu to help. He agreed and told the lesser gods how to concoct a new batch of the precious essence.

"Take Mount Meru for your churning stick, use the giant *naga*-serpent for rope, and churn the ocean for the amrita," Vishnu directed. Working together, both gods and demons churned the sea of milk by coiling the naga-serpent around the mountain, the gods at the tail, the demons at the head. Vishnu transformed himself into a tortoise to become the pivot of the mountain as it whirled.

As the milk sea was churned, precious items floated to the surface, including sacred cows, the tree of life, and troupes of *apsaras*, nymphs of entrancing loveliness and grace. Then rose the moon, followed by the goddess of prosperity, a white elephant, and everything else that made life on earth worth living. It was a harvest that lives on in the form of the Buddhist serpent-kings of Indochina and the popular elephant-gods. It explains the Balinese concept of the earth resting on a giant turtle and the extraordinarily beautiful, but ever-so-dangerous Javanese Queen of the Southern Ocean. It provides a basic theme for the architecture of almost all the Hindu and Buddhist temples and their geographical placement in relation to holy Mount Meru.

Finally the churning resulted in a single golden cup of amrita. During a monumental struggle between the gods and the demons over who would possess the amrita, Vishnu transformed himself into a seductive beauty and set the demons to fighting among themselves for his/her favors. With the demons distracted, the gods captured the prized amrita and drank deep from the cup of life. Invigorated with immortality, they drove the demons to the regions beneath the sea. The gods rejoiced and worshiped Vishnu, the sun shone brightly, and the world again prospered.

◆ ◆ ◆

Far from the Cosmic Sea, the exotic aromas of Bain de Soleil and Camembert hang heavy over the Club Med on the white beach at Kuantan, Malaysia. The picture-book beach is well sheltered to avoid outraging the conservative sensitivities of devout Muslim villagers who do not understand the importance of a good suntan to a Westerner's spiritual well-being.

At night, a few miles north, a six-foot-long leatherback turtle, weighing over a thousand pounds, crawls through the sparkling phosphorescence of the breakers and lumbers up the beach; she returns every breeding season to the sandy spot where she was hatched. The moon is small and it is a sultry velvet evening. Distant heat lightning casts a brief, eerie green glow that brings a moment's illumination to the turtle as she laboriously lays seventy eggs. These protein-rich, billiard-ball-sized spheres (which will not harden no matter how long you boil them) are dug up immediately by a wizened Malay fisherman who has the concession to collect turtle eggs along part of the 150-mile stretch of sand. In the morning the government official in charge of turtle breeding will buy back half the eggs and rebury them in a protected hatchery. The rest will be sold by Chinese shop owners in the local market to customers who believe the eggs can stimulate conjugal bliss.

Although the Club Med holiday-makers don't share the culinary habits of the permanent residents, they do share the beach. But that beach was high and dry as recently as 10,000 years ago. In fact much of the South China Sea didn't exist in those days and it was possible to walk from Kuantan to Kuching, Bangkok to Brunei, or Singapore to Surabaya. During the most recent ice age, at its coldest just 18,000 years ago, the low temperatures locked up so much water in the polar regions that the tropical sea level was lowered by about 350 feet, exposing dry land where today the shallow South China Sea covers colorful coral gardens.

But the low sea level was just part of a long cycle of shifting coasts. When the great polar ice caps melted, as they have some twenty times over the past 2 million years, the subsequent raising of the sea flooded most of the land, isolating the large islands of Borneo, Sumatra, and Java along with thousands of smaller islands. Today the sea level is about as high as it has ever been, and Southeast Asia has only half as much land as it had when the poles were at their iciest.

Part of the diversity of wildlife in the region is due to this cycle of sea level changes. The animals isolated on each island evolved new characteristics and, in some cases, became new species. Then the cycle repeated itself, the ice caps refroze, the sea levels dropped, and land bridges were re-created. New migrations took place, followed in turn by yet another sequence of isolation and evolution. The smaller, rapidly reproducing mammals were most affected; each of the larger offshore islands has its own forms of rats, squirrels, tree shrews, and mouse deer.

Even at its lowest, the sea separated Asia from Australia. Asian animals such as cats and weasels stopped at the edge of the land which was connected to Asia, a boundary extending from Borneo to Bali which has become famous in biogeography as "Wallace's Line," after the Victorian biologist Alfred Russel Wallace. On the

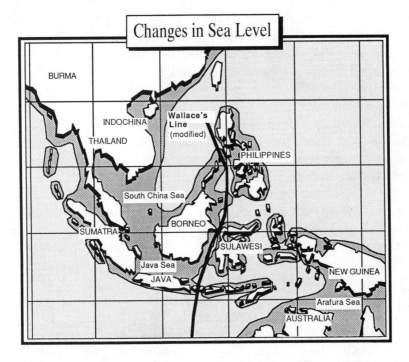

Changes in Sea Level

18,000 years ago mammals could walk through much of Southeast Asia but could not swim across the imaginary Wallace's line, which marks the eastern boundary of the exposed land. Wildlife to the west of the line is therefore considerably different from species east of the line.

Currently sea, this area was dry land as recently as 18,000 years ago.

eastern side of this line, Australian forms such as marsupials and eucalyptus trees extend slightly beyond New Guinea to the Indonesian island of Sulawesi.

The cycle of changing sea levels affected the movements of the people living in the region. Judging from fossil remains of *Homo erectus*, humans must have arrived in Java at least a million years ago, and it appears that they evolved into modern *Homo sapiens* while the sea levels changed around them. The early people were hunters and gatherers, like their African cousins, and the hunting was best when the sea levels were lowest. Most scientists agree that during those times the climate was cooler and drier and that most of the exposed land was covered with savanna grassland and monsoon forest. Because most of the vegetation in such habitats is within the easy reach of rhinos, elephants, deer, wild cattle, and other grazing animals, the savannas have far more large mammals than the lusher, taller, and more diverse tropical rain forest, which conceals most of its productivity in the tops of trees where it can be reached only by insects, birds, and tree-climbing mammals.

Fossils found with early man in Java include numerous animals which would have provided a hearty meal to a hungry big-game hunter. They include no less than ten large grazing animals (now Java has just four), five species of elephants (none survive today), and, in competition with man the predator, a dozen or so big carnivores (instead of the present leopard and wild dog). But as the sea level cycle shifted again and the islands were re-created, tropical rain forests expanded and the length of coastline increased. The hunting and gathering life-style became more challenging as many of the best sources of meat died out. In the tropical forests, men hunted monkeys, mouse deer, and birds instead of large game. The women may have reduced their hunting, instead making a far more important contribution to the diet by collecting a much wider range of plants, thereby setting the stage for agriculture.

By about 8,000 years ago, the climate and sea level had temporarily stabilized at the conditions we find today. Water, in the form of the life-bestowing sea, had played out another part of its megacycle.

◆ ◆ ◆

While sea level changes occur over hundreds of generations and figure in the folklore of the people of the region, the cycle of volcanic fire is often painfully immediate and obvious. But as most things are in Asia, these two cycles are intimately intertwined. New Zealand geologist J. R. Bray has discovered that major volcanic eruptions seem to accompany most of the periods when the climate is hottest, just before the cycle starts its cooling phase, which leads to larger glaciers and lower sea levels. The intensity of the eruptions appears to be related to the intensity of climatic cooling; the smoke and dust ejected from volcanoes screen out the sunlight (a phenomenon similar to the "nuclear winter" that many scientists fear would follow the mushroom clouds which would be produced by even a limited nuclear war).

In addition to the awesome impact an eruption has on the people living around an exploding volcano, the whole pattern of the regional climate may be changed, triggering the cycle of destruction and rebirth of large expanses of land filled with habitat for large grazing animals. Nowhere is this link more clear than in Indonesia, where a string of eighty active volcanoes extends in a scimitar-shaped curve from Sumatra, through Java, Bali, and Lombok and eventually curls around the eastern edge of the Lesser Sundas as far as Ceram, an arc roughly as long as Las Vegas to Miami, or Karachi to Hong Kong.

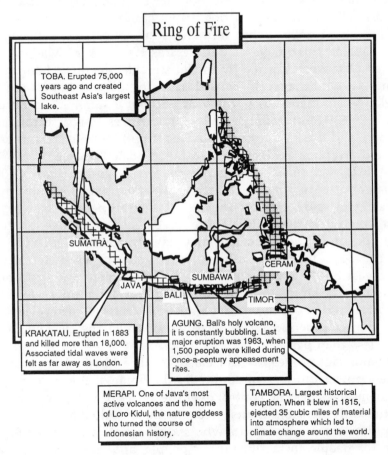

Ring of Fire

TOBA. Erupted 75,000 years ago and created Southeast Asia's largest lake.

SUMATRA

CERAM

SUMBAWA

JAVA

BALI

TIMOR

KRAKATAU. Erupted in 1883 and killed more than 18,000. Associated tidal waves were felt as far away as London.

AGUNG. Bali's holy volcano, it is constantly bubbling. Last major eruption was 1963, when 1,500 people were killed during once-a-century appeasement rites.

MERAPI. One of Java's most active volcanoes and the home of Loro Kidul, the nature goddess who turned the course of Indonesian history.

TAMBORA. Largest historical eruption. When it blew in 1815, ejected 35 cubic miles of material into atmosphere which led to climate change around the world.

More than 80 active volcanoes and dozens of earthquakes each year make Indonesia one of the world's most active geological zones.

When an Indonesian volcano erupts, the whole world takes notice. On the island of Sumbawa, two islands to the east of Bali, the volcanic eruption of Mount Tambora in 1815 vomited ten times more geologic rubbish than the more famous Krakatau eruption almost seventy years later, and one hundred and fifty times more than either the eruption of Vesuvius in 79 A.D. or Mount St. Helens in Washington State in 1980. Tambora killed more than 90,000 people on Sumbawa and the neighboring islands, at a time when the total population of Indonesia was just 5 or 6 million—less than 3 percent of its current population. Such a destructive event required an explanation, and Javanese claimed that the eruption signified that the Queen of the Southern Ocean, Loro Kidul, was celebrating the marriage of one of her children.

The dust Tambora shot into the stratosphere blocked out the sun, causing three days of darkness as far away as Madura, 300 miles to the west. Carried by the jet streams, the dust changed the climate around the world, caused frosts in July and August in New England, and made 1816 "the year without a summer" in Europe. The resulting crop failures caused food prices to soar throughout Europe, and the famine that followed crop failure in Ireland exacerbated a typhus epidemic which killed 65,000 people.

At least ten times more powerful than Tambora was Mount Toba in northern Sumatra, which threw more than 450 cubic miles of ash, dust, and rocks into the air 75,000 years ago. Such an explosion would have been sufficient to screen out the sun over a significant portion of the globe, and may have triggered another ice age. Mount Toba has since calmed down, and in its crater nestles Southeast Asia's largest lake. Lake Toba is big enough that one of its islands is larger than Singapore, a fact Indonesian President Suharto pointed out to visiting Singapore Prime Minister Lee Kuan Yew during a period when relations between the two neighbors were less than perfect.

From ancient times it was clear to local residents that volcanoes were a powerful force, undoubtedly the home of the gods. People, by themselves, had no control over the cycles of volcanic eruptions so the only sensible course was to make valuable offerings to propitiate the mighty spirits who spoke in fire. It was not uncommon for people to sacrifice other people, and some experts claim that as recently as early in this century the spirits residing deep within Java's Bromo-Tenger crater accepted a child a year. But people are not always willing to sacrifice their own kind.

Dressed in a white Nehru jacket, an elderly priest puffed his way to the crater edge of the 10,309-foot Gunung Agung, the highest, holiest and most active volcano on Bali. Following, and breathing harder, other holy men and honored farmers carried a live buffalo calf. The midday sun blazed down on the sweating men as they reached a precipitous edge. The buffalo gave a low moo before it was quickly dumped over the side into the sulphur-spurting maelstrom.

The buffalo was the last of a menagerie of animals offered to the Hindu gods—an eagle, a monkey, a crocodile, a puppy, and a scorpion and dozens of chickens, pigs and ducks were among the creatures ritually slaughtered in an enclosed area dubbed "God's kitchen" by Western journalists. There were some disappointments, however, for the priests. Their attempts to "borrow" an elephant from the Surabaya Zoo were politely ignored. The head priest argued that a tiger, too, was necessary to do the job properly but, following last-minute negotiations that threatened to disrupt the ceremony, conservationists managed to substitute a more common leopard cat.

The 1979 event was called *Eka Dasa Rudra* (the Great Rite of the Eleven Directions), a ceremony designed to restore balance between the forces of good and evil, with animal sacrifices necessary to secure peace and prosperity "for the government and the world," according to Wayan Surpha, chairman of Indonesia's Hindu Association. It is normally held on a once-a-century cycle, but seers determined that an extraordinary Eka Dasa Rudra needed to be held in 1963 to cleanse the world of man's impure actions during World War II and the Indonesian revolution. Unfortunately, the priests did not move fast enough, for one month before the great sacrifice was to have started (the whole activity was scheduled to last over six months), Mount Agung erupted, killing more than 1,500 people and causing widespread damage to farmlands. The Indonesian Ministry of Foreign Affairs officially announced that the eruption was a sign from the gods that "men have not yet succeeded in restoring the balance of nature in purification and renewal which bring harmony and happiness to mankind."

Mount Agung ("King of Mountains") is the home of the gods of Bali, including the dominant Hindu deities Siva, Brahma, and Vishnu, as well as the more ancient ancestral gods who are worshiped at every house-temple on the island. Agung is just one of several active volcanoes on Bali, but it has pride of place because of its impressive temper. Seers determined that the 1963 eruption was caused by the fury of the volcanic gods, since the Balinese had gone several centuries without staging proper ceremonies to appease the sensitive deities. Further, people had been pillaging the mountain, taking sulphur from the crater, wood from the forests, and building materials from the mountain itself. Retribution would surely come to all who had stolen from the high gods of Agung.

Anna Mathews, a British writer who was living on Agung when it erupted, reported that a holy woman in the village of Karangasem foretold the disaster, went to the authorities, and exhorted them to make proper offerings. The old woman claimed that unless a white goat, a white hen and a white duck were thrown into the river before 11 A.M. on March 16, the gods would send a terrible affliction. The official in charge thought her story ridiculous, and sent her away. Two days later, the doubting bureaucrat's village house was destroyed by the volcano. He did manage to rescue a few belongings and take them to Bali's capital of Denpasar, where ill-fortune caught up with him once again—the house he stayed in at Denpasar burned to the ground and he lost everything he had managed to save.

Devout Hindu Balinese calmly accepted the judgment of the gods. In one village the local priest, wanting to save his young son, ordered the confused youngster to flee. After running a short distance the boy turned to look back. He watched his father prepare himself for the coming flow of lava by dressing in the most sacred regalia of the temple, which included a headdress of crimson cloth with a plaque of antique gold carved in the shape of a mythological sunbird—the Garuda. He made his preparations deliberately and with care, even though the lava was coming closer by the minute.

Soon the temple was filled with villagers, the boy related to Mathews. The men wore their batiks, their ceremonial overskirts, and turbans in the sacred colors of scarlet, plum, purple, and dark moss-green. The women were also dressed in their best sarongs and jewelry, and had stuck into the loops of their thick black hair the trembling gold flowers they wore for temple festivals. Little girls, bare-shouldered, held their heads like sunbursts, each adorned with a golden headpiece that shimmered in the lamplight. The families lay down around their priest. Each man took his eldest son next to him and placed the women of his household behind him, some with babies at their breasts. Then they covered themselves with new white cotton cloth, a sign of purity. The high priest sang the praises of the Lord Brahma and rang his little bell to welcome the visiting god, who was coming as flowing lava.

The lava boiled over the temple wall and covered the temple and all its devotees. Not even a baby cried. The lamps disappeared in the uprush of poisonous black smoke. The boy knew that all of his family and friends were dead when the bell stopped ringing.

◆ ◆ ◆

The surviving Balinese realized that they had erred in ignoring the importance of regular cycles on which they rely, as do all farmers and rural people. It took sixteen years for the island to recover from the Gunung Agung eruption and to become properly prepared for the ceremony finally held in 1979. The power of the volcano had reasserted itself, and the gods had again proven why they inspire awe in the hearts of the villagers.

But Asian gods create as well as destroy. Krakatau, a moderate explosion by Southeast Asian standards, erupted in 1883 with a noise that the police chief of Rodriguez Island, 3,000 miles to the southwest, likened to "heavy guns from eastward." It caused a *tsunami* (tidal wave) 120 feet high and generated waves that smashed docks and boats in Japan and Australia, rolled by Cape Horn at 400 miles per hour and, the day following the disaster, caused ships in the English Channel to yank at their anchor chains. Scientists were amazed by the speed with which life returned to the charred island, in some places blanketed with a 200-foot-thick blanket of ash. Less than a year after the eruption a botanist discovered only a tiny spider, which presumably had been blown to the island from the adjacent mainland. But just three years after the explosion there was a Garden of Eden, of sorts, including fifteen species of flowering plants, eleven of ferns, and two of mosses. Airborne, swimming and hitchhiking on pieces of flotsam, often from great distances, birds, reptiles, and insects made a home on this unpromising chunk of rock and ash. Fifty years after the explosion there were few signs of the disturbance, and today parts of the island are covered by a luxuriant forest.

Volcanoes kill, but their fertile slopes are often the best place to grow crops. Each year Jakarta newspapers report dozens, sometimes hundreds of people dying from lava, landslides, and poison gas from Indonesia's active volcanoes. Indonesian officials are kept busy evacuating villagers off the hillsides of these volatile volcanoes, but some people, even when they have been moved off Java entirely, still straggle back to their dangerous but productive homeland.

◆ ◆ ◆

Southeast Asian villagers know from experience that nature often speaks in violent tongues. Volcanos erupt, floods wash away years of patient construction of rice field, temple, and house, drought kills carefully nurtured crops, or armies wipe out family and fortune. People cannot accept that these actions are totally random—surely the gods have some *reason* for displaying their anger. But humble farmers are not expected to comprehend the logic of the gods. That task is left to specialists—the priests who interpret the messages of the gods and help the village people take the proper steps, often with animal intermediaries, to appease the powers of the earth, sky and ocean. The village priest is a cosmic psychologist who explains the big natural cycles in a way that takes responsibility off the shoulders of the individual and puts the villager's mind to rest.

Anna Mathews described how her houseboy, Rami, responded as the lava advanced on their village of Iseh during the 1963 Mount Agung explosion. "We're all right in Iseh," he said with a contented smile. "The priest says so. This is the coming of the Lord Brahma. He comes as fire." This was true enough, as the banks of the stream that ran through Iseh had dried out and the banks were flaming. "Brahma will protect Iseh. The priest says so. He says, if any man is afraid, it is because he does not truly believe. Brahma shows himself as fire to show his might, so that men will believe in him."

Not long after dark, although fires were still burning below her house, Mathews again heard the sound of water in the streambed. The river had found its way through the lava and ash and was flowing again—a mere trickle, yet in Mathews' eyes a resurrection. She remarked on this to Rami. "Of course," he replied. "Now comes the god Vishnu. He comes as water."

3

Flames
and Farmers

Using fire to burn the vegetation to attract animals and later to grow crops caused fundamental shifts in people's relation with wildlife.

WE WERE WALKING through Phu Kheo Game Sanctuary in northeastern Thailand looking for signs of the country's last remaining Asian two-horned rhinos. It was March, the height of the dry season, and a good time to search because tracks are concentrated along the watercourses where the animals gather, revealing what species are present and in what numbers. We arrived at the edge of an elevated sandstone plateau covered with grassy glades interspersed with open forest. Our guide, a local hunter named Prasan Chantasen, stopped to roll a fat cigarette.

We gratefully sat down, leaning our backs against a tree that had lost all its leaves in the heat, and gazed across the cinder-dry brown savanna crisscrossed by the trails of elephants, the wild ox called gaur, and sambar deer. Prasan lit his *burii* and joined us.

Answering our unspoken question, he explained, "There used to be a village up here. The farmers cleared the forest and planted dry rice in these clearings. But after a few years, the soil proved too poor. So, when Phu Kheo was declared a reserve and the government offered the people better land down by the new reservoir, they were glad to leave. Now only animals live on the plateau."

A smile flashed across his wizened, nut-brown face as he took a puff on his cigarette. "And this is now by far the best place in the province to hunt. Unless you get caught." As Prasan's cigarette neared its end, we shouldered our rucksacks and wearily clambered to our feet. We hoped to reach the cooler and more densely forested hills before nightfall, so we were anxious to start off quickly. Prasan reached down to stub out his butt, carefully pinching out the ash. We approved. High fire hazard, so be especially careful, we thought, having been brought up on Smoky the Bear's "Only *you* can prevent forest fires." But to our surprise, Prasan then whipped out his Zippo lighter and *purposely* set the grass on fire!

We immediately began to chastise him, using the gentle Thai approach of asking questions rather than offering criticism. Why did you set the fire? Aren't you worried that the whole plateau will go up in smoke? "*Mai pen rai*," he responded. "Never mind. The fire is good. It burns off the old dead grass that few animals want to eat. The ashes help the new grass to grow, and if we don't burn the old grass, the forest will start to come back and the animals won't be able to find the food they need."

We set off in a swirl of smoke, not entirely convinced but unable to do anything about the blaze. By the time we reached the forest edge, the fire had covered much of the glade. Long-tailed drongos swooped through the smoke, hawking flying insects fleeing the flames.

We spent a week up in the limestone mountains, finding cave-dwelling langur monkeys, counting tracks of tigers and gaur, seeing a few elephants and pig-tailed macaques, and, on the last day, finding one very clear print of a rhino in the mud by the edge of a stream far up in the mountains. Satisfied by our success, however modest, we headed back to the reserve headquarters, concerned only about the destruction the brushfire must have caused.

Reaching the plateau, we found that the patch of savanna covering several acres had been burned, but the fire had barely touched the surrounding forest. And, to our surprise, new grass buds had already appeared and several sambar deer were grazing at the far side of the savanna. Prasan gave us an "I told you so" glance, but was far too polite to point out the obvious.

This trip was a revelation. It opened our eyes to the role of fire in Southeast Asia, and particularly about how important fire can be for the large grazing animals. Prasan's use of fire, multiplied by thousands of hunters over thousands of years, has modified the natural world to such a dramatic extent that it can be considered humanity's first "ecocultural revolution."

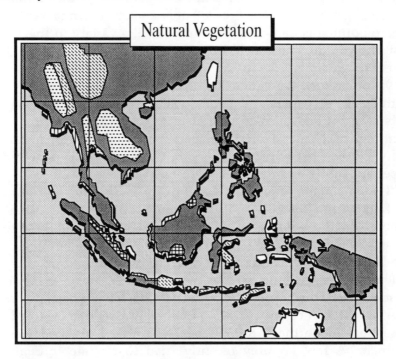

Natural Vegetation

This map illustrates the natural vegetation that is likely to have grown before agriculture widely altered habitats.

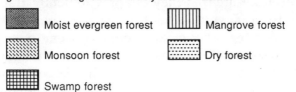

Moist evergreen forest   Mangrove forest

Monsoon forest   Dry forest

Swamp forest

When we arrived back in Bangkok after a bouncy, sweaty eight-hour bus ride, we asked Dr. Boonsong about how people use fire to improve grazing for animals. "Back in the old days, when I was a hunter," he explained, "I always went out in the dry season and followed the smoke. The big grazing animals—gaur, banteng, wild water buffalo, sambar, Eld's deer, wild pigs, and even elephants—are attracted by the new shoots, and the tigers are attracted by the grazers."

But what about the forest-dwelling animals? Aren't they affected? "The only big mammals up there that really need a continuous closed-canopy forest," Dr. Boonsong told us, "are gibbons and leaf monkeys, and they don't live in the dry forests that are burned. And anyway, the fires are only spotty, leaving lots of areas where nothing is damaged. The animals like variety in their lives, just like you do," he concluded as we headed out for a quick bath and massage down the street.

On our return we found Dr. Boonsong at his big work table, with stacks of papers and books pushed aside to make room for pots of paint and piles of stuffed birds. He was trying to get his paintings of Thailand's sixteen species of willow warblers exactly right for the next edition of his *Bird Guide of Thailand*—the differences are subtle and need a discerning eye.

"I hope you are now relaxed and ready to do some more work," he said with a tolerant smile. "If you want to start writing the chapter on the wild cattle, you had better take a look at these papers by my old friend Charles Wharton. He came out here from the University of Georgia a few years ago to study the kouprey."

The kouprey, a large species of wild cattle, was the last large mammal to be discovered in Southeast Asia, having been described by Western science only in 1937. Extremely rare, it is confined to a few spots in northern Kampuchea, southern Laos, and western Vietnam. A few kouprey recently tried to migrate through the steep escarpment which separates Kampuchea from northeast Thailand, but indications are that they fell prey to booby-traps set to prevent people from moving across this war-torn border.

Kouprey, along with the other grazing animals, seem to particularly favor areas of frequent fires. Wharton discovered that the best habitats in Southeast Asia for kouprey and other large mammals are found where abandoned rice fields were left by the ancient Khmer civilization whose capital was Angkor Wat. Small villages in northern Kampuchea are the last vestige of the grandeur that was Angkor civilization. The hardy people are subsistence shifting cultivators during the rainy season, but during the six long months of the dry season they revert to hunting and gathering, radiating in ever-widening circles to forage through the countryside. They travel in ox carts, and set fires wherever they go.

In an area which was originally dry forest, fire is the essential tool for maintaining suitably large areas of savanna which are exploited by both wild herbivores and by a very small population of rugged Khmers. One reason kouprey continue to survive in this insecure corner of Indochina is because the seasonal hunters still burn the land the way their Khmer ancestors did centuries ago.

The relationship between people, fire, and wild herbivores still seen in northern Kampuchea may well be ancient. Remains of *Homo erectus*, the ancestor of modern man who survived until perhaps 100,000 years ago, have been found alongside clear evidence of fire, and since their fossilized bones have been discovered as far apart as northern China and Java, it seems reasonable to assume that early people occupied areas of suitable habitat throughout this range. Based on evidence of the distribution of stone tools and the faunal remains found with the human fossils, the favored habitats, as in east Africa, were river valleys, seasonal swamps, open forests, and grasslands, where fire would have been an important means of keeping dangerous beasts at bay and improving hunting conditions.

At the earliest hunting and gathering stage of human existence, people probably had little more impact on the ecosystem than did any other predator. But as technology improved, the ecological niche of early man steadily expanded. As people learned to control fire, they began to change their habitat to suit their needs, particularly by burning grasslands. And, as their social organization and hunting technology became more complex, they were able to hunt even very large mammals.

◆ ◆ ◆

A few weeks after introducing us to the work of Charles Wharton, Dr. Boonsong took us to western Thailand, far up the Kwae Noi River in Kanchanaburi Province (the site of the infamous World War II "death railway" and the bridge over the River Kwai). As we drove through miles of sugarcane, all planted within the past decade or so, Dr. Boonsong pointed out the places where he had hunted in the late 1940s and 1950s. "This was all forest in those days, but with excellent habitat for gaur and elephant along the rivers, streams, and swamps.

"It used to take me two weeks of walking to get to this village," he told us wistfully, as he pulled his seemingly immortal tan Fiat up in front of the teak, bamboo, and thatch house of one of his old guides. After a cup of tea, mangosteens, a papaya, and some sweetened sticky rice, we all climbed up a small hill just behind the village. Twenty minutes of vigorous scrambling left us sweaty and breathless, but the view at the top was worth it. The mountains on the Burmese border dominated the horizon to the west, and spread out below us was a vast sugarcane-covered plain, dotted with little swamps.

"When I was your age, I used to climb up here to see where the animals were. During the dry season, they would come to drink at those swamps," Dr. Boonsong recalled, looking out over a landscape whose character had changed to pander to the craving for sugar in distant lands. "But I was not the first to use this place as a spying post. Look here." Dr. Boonsong got down on his hands and knees and started poking through the rocky rubble on the ground. We too squatted down, mystified but confident that we were going to see something interesting. After a minute or so, he picked up a rather nondescript piece of rock. "Look carefully. See how the edge is sharp, with lots of little nicks? This is a stone tool made by our early ancestors."

Quickly getting into the spirit of discovery, we too started searching and within a quarter of an hour had found a dozen stone tools. The hunters who made these tools were preying on large mammals which would have delighted Dr. Boonsong—nearby caves have yielded 10,000-year-old remains of stegodons, mammoths, and hippos. As the large mammals died out (perhaps helped on their way by hunters who used new, more effective weapons and hunting strategies), the adaptable *Homo sapiens* of that period began to develop more complex tools for hunting small and medium-sized animals, including the bow and arrow and various sorts of traps. Digging sticks, cordage, baskets, and other gathering tools were also being used during this period, as the people learned to use a greater variety of plants and aquatic life.

The next major step in human cultural development was the move from gathering wild plants to cultivating them. Dr. Boonsong pointed to the north. "Up there," he said, "in Mae Hong Son Province, my friend Chester Gorman has been working in one of the places I used to go to catch bats. It's called 'Spirit Cave,' and he is making some important discoveries."

Dated at about 10,000 years ago, just at the end of the Pleistocene Epoch, the evidence from Spirit Cave was revolutionary, indicating that agriculture, previously thought to have originated in the Middle East, may have been discovered first in Southeast Asia. According to anthropologist Wilhelm Solheim, "Some of the most technologically advanced cultures in the world in the period from about 13,000 B.C. to 4,000 B.C. flourished not in the Middle East or the adjacent Mediterranean, but in the northern reaches of mainland Southeast Asia."

Building on the increased use of plants, agriculture was inevitable. The people at Spirit Cave had a varied menu that included several varieties of beans, cucumbers, water chestnuts, almonds, peppers, and bottle gourds which were served with numerous kinds of meat—turtles, fish, bats, rats, squirrels, deer, pigs, and monkeys. Gorman had found that even the earliest cultivators in Southeast Asia enjoyed a varied and balanced diet. Many of the ingredients used in the old days are important components of the tastiest dishes in the finest Thai restaurants today.

◆ ◆ ◆

When the *Rajah Mas* finally pulled out of Kuching, we were in a festive mood, eager for the new experiences that awaited us far upstream. Little did we know that our first weeks in Sarawak, in the Malaysian part of Borneo, would be a trial by fire. After growing up in cities, we suddenly became hill farmers of the most basic sort. To learn how people lived in the rural communities where we were to introduce new teaching methods, we helped clear the jungle to plant crops. Our hosts were Iban who lived four hours by dugout *prahu* outside Kanowit. Most of the heavy work—felling large trees and lopping branches—had been done several months before. We were the burn team, and the result was spectacular as the hillsides were put to the torch. Flames leaped upward, producing smoke as thick as a London fog. For days, people's eyes smarted as badly as if they lived in Los Angeles, copious tears formed tracks down plump dirty cheeks, children coughed continuously, and ash covered everything in a fine dusty coating which lasted until the cleansing rains came a few weeks later.

Once the ground cooled down, it was time to plant the rice. The hillside was still smoldering in spots and the footing was made treacherous by bayonet-like unburned branches, so we watched with admiration as a barefooted farmer "dibbled"—used a sharpened stick to make holes in the scorched earth—while his wife followed a few steps behind and expertly tossed several grains of rice into each hole, then covered the opening by stamping her foot on the earth. In coming years, we were to show the people of many longhouses that we were better basketball players than they were, but, to the amusement of our hosts, we were never able to plant hill padi without having to crouch to accurately drop the rice seeds into the tiny hole.

This is "slash and burn" agriculture, which has been attacked by Western conservationists in recent years because vast areas of rain forest are destroyed in the process. But this blanket condemnation is hardly justified, as we were to learn.

The complex system of slash and burn—sometimes called "shifting cultivation" or "swidden"—is based on cutting living vegetation in the less humid "winter," letting it dry, burning it late in the dry season, and then planting a crop in the ashes early in the wet season. In the most stable and productive systems, the fields are rotated on a ten- to fifteen-year cycle. The field is abandoned after one year of growing crops, and the decade of fallow allows nutrients to be returned to the soil. A wide range of crops can be grown in such fields; groups such as the Lua in northern Thailand cultivate over 100 species. According to anthropologist Peter Kunstadter, an additional 300 plants are gathered from the fallow fields of the Lua, which are also good grazing and browsing areas for the wild herbivores which are hunted by the farmers. This agricultural diversity far surpasses that in the average supermarket—only 80 species are generally grown by modern market gardeners, and 95 percent of human nutrition is derived from just 30 plants. The subsistence-level hill farmers of northern Thailand enjoy a far more varied diet than the wealthiest industrialist.

Growing important food plants and domesticating certain animals do not simply replace hunting and gathering, but rather supplement it and allow people to wrest more productivity from nature, and to occupy more diverse habitats. The human population can grow through more intensive use of the land—shifting cultivation can support up to 150 people per square mile, while hunting requires at least 600 times as much land to support the same number of people. The domestication of plants changed forever the relationship between people and their environment, representing mankind's second "ecocultural revolution."

❖ ❖ ❖

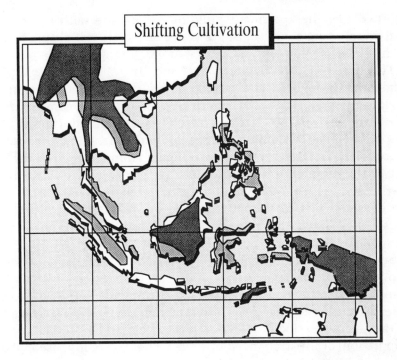

Shifting Cultivation

Man's learning to burn the forests to plant crops was a revolution in his relationship with nature. Shifting cultivation is environmentally beneficial when population pressures are low, harmful when there are too many people.

 Shifting cultivation is dominant

 Shifting cultivation is common, but not dominant

One of the first words you learn in Sarawak is *"ulu,"* Malay for the upper reaches of a river. It refers to far more than geography. To many people it describes a way of life that gets more primitive, alien and unattractive the farther inland you go. Ulu is a concept that depends on your perspective. To the urbane engineer in the small town of Marudi, the people who live in communal long-houses thirty miles away are country bumpkins, regardless of the fact that they too may speak English and have electricity, running water and television. The perceived difference between "us" (civilized and modern and handsome) and "them" (none of the above) gets wider the farther upriver one goes. It is considered "modern" to live in an apartment building with one family perched on *top* of another. Lay the apartment building on its side with up to fifty individual apartments sharing a common porch and sitting *next* to each other and you get an "old-fashioned" longhouse.

This differentiation between "us" and "them" is an age-old phenomenon throughout the world. In Southeast Asia, it stretches back to the prehistoric movements of people, adding complexity to the term "melting pot." A careful observer spending time in cosmopolitan Jakarta might well see individuals calling themselves Indonesians bearing complexions ranging from the lightest café au lait to thick freshly brewed Robusta, as our secretary liked to remark. She was from Menado in northern Sulawesi, and most people consider girls from that region to be Indonesia's prettiest because they have the fairest complexions. She did not try to dissuade anyone from that opinion.

Southeast Asia's original inhabitants—those who had apparently evolved into the first *Homo sapiens* in the region—were dark-skinned, frizzy-haired, broad-nosed australoids, some of whom spread from Southeast Asia into Australia some 40,000 years ago during a low period in the sea level cycle and founded today's population of Australian Aborigines. They certainly used plants extensively, but they were not farmers. They had a complex array of stone tools, but no pottery or woven cloth. The australoids were pushed into isolated corners of the region because they were unable to compete with later immigrants who arrived with cultural and ecological innovations that enabled them to support much higher populations on the same amount of land. The numbers of hunters and gatherers declined but they survive today as the *Orang Asli* (or "original people") of Malaysia and southern Thailand, the main inhabitants of the Andaman islands, small groups in the Philippines, and larger groups in eastern Indonesia and New Guinea (where they subsequently learned to cultivate yams and sweet potatoes). These descendants of the real natives of the region are treated with disdain and worse by the more sophisticated hill tribes and the even more sophisticated people who conquered the valleys and coasts.

The earliest farmers first made life miserable for the australoids 7,000 years ago. They came into Thailand and Indochina, moving into Indonesia even later. Called "Proto-Malays," they came overland from northwest India or Burma and had rich brown skin, a long head with wavy hair, and rather caucasoid facial features. They pioneered domestication of plants. But cultural sophistication does not always move forward, since some groups, such as the Yumbri of Thailand, the Punen of Borneo, and several others, have lost the skills of agriculture and have reverted to hunting and gathering. Others, such as the Mentawaian islanders from western Sumatra, supplement their hunting and gathering with simple agriculture. The best-known of the Proto-Malays—the Gajo of Sumatra, the Tenggerese of Java's eastern uplands, the Sasak of Lombok, the Dayak of Kalimantan and Sarawak, and the Toradja of Sulawesi—have mixed economies dominated by shifting cultivation. Invading shifting cultivators can move quickly; in one well-known case from recent times, an Iban group in central Borneo is known to have moved 200 miles in a single generation.

The most recent arrivals were the most successful settlers. The "Deutero-Malays" came from southern China and traveled mainly by sea down the Indochinese coast to Malaysia, and via the Philippines to Indonesia. With yellow-brown skin, a broad head and flat face, straight black hair, and distinctly Mongoloid features, they are today the dominant people of Southeast Asia. Over the relatively short period from 3,000 to 1,000 B.C., these agriculturalists used their knowledge of rice cultivation, pottery, and improved stone tools to settle throughout Southeast Asia. In the process they split into numerous local groups and adapted to local conditions. The Proto-Malays and Deutero-Malays, often lumped together and called "Austronesians" by anthropologists, later took to the sea in outrigger sailing canoes and eventually settled new lands as far away as New Zealand, Easter Island, Hawaii, and Madagascar— one of the world's greatest conquests of nature.

Although the Austronesians can be roughly categorized into two broad groups, the settlers roamed far throughout Southeast Asia, often becoming isolated, interbreeding with the australoids, and developing their own characteristics and languages. How many? The people who count these things estimate about 400, give or take a few dozen. But, they are quick to add, that doesn't include the hidden villages of New Guinea, the island equivalent of Babel, where you could easily add another 700 or so to the total. People with different languages are inclined to dislike, or at least distrust, each other.

Yet despite this great diversity, people share many beliefs which define their relationship with nature. Based on their reverence for spirits and ancestors, most groups have supported shamans—inspirational priests who claim the ability to communicate with spirits through trances. Virtually all Austronesian societies have divided their main deities into male sky-gods (often represented by birds) and female earth-gods (usually in the form of snakes). Most Austronesian cultures practiced head-hunting as a means of capturing "soul energy," which could be transferred from one body to another. We were to find that this soul energy was also harnessed as a hunting tool, and used to transform people into animals.

The Austronesian farmers were efficient immigrants. They expanded into fertile new environments that were occupied by sparse populations of australoid hunters and gatherers, who generally were pushed further into the forest.

Population growth rates during the period of expansion could well have exceeded 3 percent per year, comparable to the rapid growth of the past few decades. The growth of the Mongoloid population at the expense of the australoid continues today, as Javan migrants move into Irian Jaya and Malays and Chinese move into the forested interior of peninsular Malaysia occupied by the Orang Asli.

◆ ◆ ◆

The Austronesians quickly spread the innovative upland slash-and-burn technique throughout all suitable areas in Southeast Asia. Dr. J. E. Spencer of the University of California came to the startling conclusion that there is virtually no virgin forest in all of monsoon Southeast Asia. All the drier forests have been cleared by people at one time, and the surviving wildlife has adapted to this very powerful human influence.

As long as the human population remained relatively low, traditional shifting cultivation permitted local self-sufficiency and resulted in great cultural diversity as groups adapted to the local resources. Most shifting cultivation took place in the hills, where the soils and vegetation dried out more quickly and updrafts helped fan the flames among the cut vegetation. The lowlands, many of which were seasonally flooded, remained relatively intact and were used mostly for hunting and for gathering of tubers.

But perhaps 2,500 years ago came another ecocultural revolution. The coming of irrigation was to be as significant a turning point for the people of Southeast Asia as the industrial revolution was for Europe and America in the nineteenth century.

4

Rice
and Royalty

Irrigation brought another revolutionary change in the relationship between people and wildlife, and between people and their rulers.

WE OFTEN ENJOYED leaving behind the heat and dust of Jakarta by flying to Bali for the weekend. We contributed to the pollution of Bali by renting motorcycles for $5.00 a day, belching, noisy 125cc Hondas that gave us a feeling of freedom and energy, and provided a respite from the pressures of doing business in Indonesia. Late one evening in the rainy season of 1979, after spending the day with friends in the center of the island, we were driving back to our inexpensive accommodations in Kuta Beach. We often bounced into potholes as we dodged scrawny, snarling dogs which rested on the warm road. Outside the village of Sukawati we passed a group of men sitting on the road, chatting and smoking. We were in no hurry, so when they waved we stopped and hunkered down with them.

The cool night air settled on the warm water of the paddy fields, creating an eerie mist within which fireflies sparkled like errant nocturnal spirits over the still dark ponds. The ten men were dressed in well-worn shorts and once-white shirts, and their shovels and hoes leaned against a nearby tree. Someone had brought a radio, which was transmitting a Radio Indonesia shortwave broadcast of part of the mammoth *Mahabharata* epic sung in classical Javanese, a tongue as unintelligible to the Balinese as it was to us.

We dug some chocolate bars out of our shoulder bags and shared chunks with the farmers. They reciprocated with *kreteks*, cigarettes spiced with cloves, and we all sat quietly chatting, telling jokes, and listening to the clack of crickets and the burping of frogs. The men, we learned, comprised the village's civil engineering contingent, known as the *subak*. Since an individual farmer would be incapable of building and maintaining an elaborate irrigation system, groups of village men had organized themselves into these cooperative water societies governed by an elected headman. All villagers who own rice fields are members of the subak, they told us, and must abide by its rules and contribute work in proportion to the amount of water received.

The water came from the Batur volcano through a system of canals and bamboo pipes, controlled by a series of dikes along the way. Shortly before midnight, the subak members moved into action and diverted the water from one side of the hill to the other, from the neighboring village's terraces to their own. Water is the essence of rice, and hence of life, and it must be shared equitably.

◆ ◆ ◆

It's hard to overestimate the importance of rice to the life of Southeast Asians. In Thai, "eating" is translated as *"than khao,"* or "to eat rice," and a common greeting to a visitor to your house is *"than khao laew ru yang?"* or "have you eaten rice yet?" The hundreds of curries, vegetables, stews, and other delicacies of the Thai menu are grouped together under the category *"gap khao,"* or "with rice." Rice fields present a full palette of colors during their cycle: the red-gray mud during plowing, the intense emerald-green of densely packed seed beds, the lighter green of waving grass, the rich golden buds ready to burst with grain, the scorched brown of the burned stubble, and the dark reflections of the newly flooded fields that signal the start of a new cycle. But rice is far more than just a crop or a carbohydrate or scenery—it's an entire way of life and has formed the basis of all the great civilizations of Southeast Asia.

◆ ◆ ◆

We were far up the Huay Kha Khaeng, one of the larger streams leading into the famous River Kwai, looking for the last of the Thai wild water buffalo. Unlike the rather stupid, slow-moving, hard-working *khwai,* which are cared for and bossed around by Thai farm children, the wild water buffalo is a truly magnificent beast, much larger, more agile, and considerably more aggressive than its domesticated descendants.

Wild water buffalo were once common throughout Southeast Asia, living in the lush river valleys where people hunted animals and gathered wild plants. But 2,500 years ago, the idea of irrigated agriculture began moving across Southeast Asia. Irrigation led a cultural revolution that changed the landscape, domesticated the wild water buffalo, and enabled humans to take over the fertile lowlands. Many of the grasslands that were flooded every year by fierce rainstorms brought by the monsoon winds were transformed by irrigation works from dry-season hunting grounds to year-round farmlands.

Unlike shifting cultivation, which seems to have come into the region along with the wave of Austronesian immigrants, the concept of irrigation was carried by just a few foreign experts from India. This is reflected in a legend from Cambodia, where some of Southeast Asia's earliest irrigated rice was grown. The royal lineage in this part of the lower Mekong River was started, the story goes, by giant cobra-like snakes known as *nagas,* which had assumed human form and mated with female humans. An Indian Brahmin named Kaundinya arrived in the kingdom, uninvited. Dragged in front of the Naga-King by multiheaded snake guards, Kaundinya was asked the purpose of his visit. Swallowing his fear, the young man looked the gruesome reptilian chief in the eye and explained that the Hindu god Siva had taken his young wife and destroyed his crops.

"My grief overwhelmed me, so I departed to find a new land," he continued. "I traveled eastwards across high mountains, deep valleys, and wide rivers. After many weeks I met a magician who gave me a talisman in the form of rice. If it is your will that I settle here and make use of this talisman to raise up a nation of servants to the high gods, I will gladly do so. If not, then kill me, for I can go no further."

While the Naga-Chief considered this proposition, his daughter, Soma, fell in love with the handsome visitor from India and successfully pleaded for his life. They married and settled in the area around the Tonle Sap, the great lake of Cambodia, starting a new kingdom which soon dominated all of Indochina.

Like the best such stories, this one carries a grain of truth. The historical Kaundinya, the Brahmin bringer of rice, is known to have come from India and founded Funan, the first Cambodian state, around the time the Romans were taking over much of Europe. Along with rice that would grow in water, Kaundinya brought irrigation, monumental architecture, a Hindu/Buddhist state religion, and a royal system of government based on god-kings. Together, these new ideas changed the face of Southeast Asia.

But people could not do it alone. They needed a powerful plowing partner, a preindustrial tractor. For this too, Kaundinya had an answer: co-opt one of the wild beasts of the swamps. The water buffalo, a dangerous wild animal which was common in the wetlands of Indochina, had long been domesticated in India. Why not turn the feared wild animal into a docile beast of burden?

With the help of the buffalo, irrigation, and new forms of government, development projects converted grassy flood plains and marshes into highly productive rice bowls. The large grass-eating mammals—elephants, Javan rhinos, water buffalo, and several species of deer—lost their best habitat and were forced to retreat to the more remote swamps or to the hills. The only wild mammal to really win in this deal was the rat, which shared the human's fondness for rice.

One place where many displaced animals have survived is Huay Kha Khaeng, and Dr. Boonsong wanted us to search this part of western Thailand's Uthai Thani Province to investigate reports that it held the last remaining Thai herd of wild water buffalo. Domesticated water buffalo are common today—estimates of their numbers run upward of 130 million—and they have been introduced into countries as far from Asia as Italy, where they supply the milk that is made into mozzarella cheese. But their wild swamp-dwelling cousins survive in just a few scattered herds ranging from India to the Mekong Valley. These wild buffalo are usually larger, more vigorous, and more resistant to disease than the domestic forms, and scientifically controlled crossbreeds between wild and domestic buffalo could produce offspring with the valuable characteristics of both. Dr. Boonsong was worried that the wild herd might be losing some of its genetic qualities through inbreeding; if the population was too small, buffalo brothers and sisters might be mating.

After two weeks of roaming through one of Thailand's largest remaining wildernesses with John Seidensticker, a biologist at the Smithsonian Institution, we reported back to Dr. Boonsong with bad news. We had found few signs of buffalo and estimated that no more than forty wild buffalo survived in the nature reserve. We had talked to some of the Karen farmers in the village of Baan Rai. "Yes," we were told, "wild buffalo are there along the river, but they are very dangerous. We sometimes try to shoot them, but they are tricky and last year a hunter from another village was killed by a wounded buffalo. We send our female buffalo into the forest when they are ready to breed, so they can gain the strength of the wild ones. But if the calf is a male, we slaughter it before it grows up because it would be too hard to handle."

Reaching the far end of the reserve, we constructed a flimsy bamboo raft to float down the river to the road head and the bus that would take us to the provincial town of Kanchanaburi. Along the way, we saw small children taking their buffalo down to the river for a bath. The huge slate-gray draft animal, which we had secretly dreaded meeting face to face in the forest, has been converted into an amiable plaything being used as a diving board by tiny humans who were no taller than a buffalo's leg. The buffalo has survived, even prospered, as a beast of burden, but it is no longer a majestic animal, merely a useful one.

◆ ◆ ◆

The "wet rice" revolution was the third major ecocultural advance for people in Asia, and led to mankind's permanent conquest of the lowlands. Its impact was so profound because irrigated rice can support fifteen to thirty times the number of people as shifting cultivation on the same area of land. Unlike the ten- to fifteen-year fallow cycle of dry rice fields used by shifting cultivators, irrigated rice fields do not lose their fertility from one year to the next. The flooded fields can produce reasonable yields continuously for hundreds of years without chemical fertilizers because the shallow water soup in which the plants are grown also supports blue-green

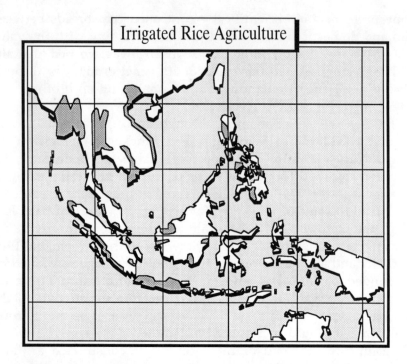

Irrigated Rice Agriculture

Wet rice allowed massive population growth and supported
the great state religions.

Major irrigated rice-growing areas. Small irrigated holdings
are distributed throughout the region.

algae which take nitrogen from the air and provide a natural fertilizer. While artificial fertilizers can increase the yield, they are not
necessary to provide a sufficient harvest to support the farmer and
his family, with some left over for the temple.

◆ ◆ ◆

More rice meant more people, and the surpluses produced by the
farmers supported Hindu and Buddhist temples and the god-kings
who went along with the new systems of agriculture. The rituals
and architecture of these major religions were reinterpreted and
integrated with existing traditional beliefs involving nature deities.
Instead of opposing each other, as they did in India, Hinduism and
Buddhism in Southeast Asia blended together, borrowed from each
other, and became the state religion. "Indianized" states first appeared in the region around the second century A.D. and eventually
became established in the lowlands, coastal regions, and fertile

river valleys of Burma, Cambodia, Thailand, eastern Borneo, Sumatra, the Malay Peninsula, Java, Bali, and Lombok.

An essential element in these early civilizations was that the king became a god, or at least a semigod. Understandably, many local chieftains seized the chance to make this dramatic leap in their status and warmly welcomed the Brahmin priests who brought such interesting new ideas from India. The sycophantic royal families and hangers-on, eager to bask in reflected godliness, lost little time in also adopting the trappings of Hinduism and Buddhism.

This was a challenging time to be a king. While Hinduism and Buddhism, as interpreted, made the rulers living gods, with this honor came some responsibilities that were sometimes difficult to carry out. The Hindu and Buddhist rulers of Southeast Asia were not bureaucrats in charge of a ponderous government structure—in fact, they tended to stay aloof from the mundane problems the farmers faced. Instead, surrounding themselves with pomp, ornate regalia, fawning priests, and complex mythology, the kings claimed to offer a link between the people and their gods. But with such high connections it fell on the kings' shoulders to ensure the benevolence of nature: good weather, productive crops, calm volcanoes, and healthy living conditions.

"In setting out to reign," says Australian historian David Chandler, "the king was expected to mediate among his subjects; among sky, earth, and underworld; Vishnu, man, and Siva; gods, people and ancestors. But the authorization *per se* was no guarantee for success; this depended on his merit, his performance, and on his exemplary re-enactment of ceremonies over a length of time."

In other words, the king was judged like any modern politician —on the basis of what he could *produce*, in terms of general welfare, weather, peace (or victories), good harvests, and the absence of disease. But unlike modern politicians, his performance was not designed to impress the public but the gods, through prearranged, repeated dealings with moments of the agricultural year, and with ceremonies and rites directed toward the numerous Hindu gods and local spirits.

The greatly improved crop yields resulting from irrigation were absorbed by public expenditure on ceremonies, cities with monumental architecture, and eventually standing armies fighting wars of status with neighboring kingdoms. Anthropologist E. R. Leach of Cambridge University says, "Those who are now remembered as great Kings were practitioners of banditry on a grand scale whose fame rests solely on their short-term success in carrying fire and slaughter into the territory of their more prosperous neighbors." Military success was a manifestation of the monarch's personal power. Establishing authority or altering political frontiers was just a symbol of this power.

Even with the spiritual and symbolic assistance of a temple devoted to Siva or a naga-serpent curling around his family tree, a king sometimes failed to deliver military conquests, a good monsoon or the plentiful sunshine needed for a good harvest. Obviously, he was not effectively arguing the case of his people with the gods, making him vulnerable to the many potential usurpers waiting for just such an opportunity. A challenger who succeeded in removing a ruler from the throne immediately claimed all of the semidivine connections of his defeated opponent, well aware that no common man could pretend to reach the gods who controlled the cycles of life.

In short, the precolonial kings of the "Indianized" states of Southeast Asia were given semidivine status in return for taking responsibility for maintaining a healthy environment within which the farmers could prosper. Royalty's right to bear this responsibility was reinforced by Hindu and Buddhist beliefs that included symbolic relationships with perceived animal ancestors such as crocodiles, elephants, or cobras which could guarantee access to the powers that controlled the cycles of the weather, the sun, and the floods.

◆ ◆ ◆

In the lowlands, the semidivine status of kings lasted for hundreds of years; vestiges of these beliefs survive today. We have been with the King of Gianyar, Bali, and the Sultan of Yogyakarta as their subjects crawled to approach the rulers. The Sultans of the various Malaysian states (who take turns being King of Malaysia) maintain their elegant ceremonial life-styles, and the royal family of Thailand is treated with considerable reverence and adulation by the Thai public. Kampuchea's Prince Norodom Sihanouk, now in exile in China, is worshiped as a contemporary god-king and he somewhat unrealistically identifies his downtrodden Kampuchea with the glories of Angkor, the first great wet rice kingdom.

Sukarno, Indonesia's first president (served 1949–67), was a commoner by birth but a god-king by proclivity. Just as Hindu gods were incarnate and possessed mystical powers, some said Sukarno had been clairvoyant at seven and that he had brought rain when he visited drought-stricken Bali. Leading a blessed life, he survived two attempted coups d'état, five major uprisings, a palace bombing, and five or six miscellaneous assassination attempts at close quarters. Journalist Dennis Bloodworth notes that people thought "his bathwater would cure the sick, the dish from which he ate ended barrenness . . . people say they have seen his profile in the moon." As befitted a self-appointed god-ruler Sukarno placed himself in the company of Christ and Mohammed. He followed the ways of the virile Hindu gods by selecting many women to share his bed, and most were honored to be chosen.

According to Indonesian author Mochtar Lubis, "The Sukarno regime was the ideal model of a situation in which it would be very difficult, if not impossible, to ascertain where the political leader ends and the *dukun* (medicine man, the fortune teller, the mystic guru) begins. . . . He was all wisdom and justice, all magnanimity. He was the father; he was god. Anybody who dared to disagree with him, let alone oppose him, was evil. He was Krishna, he was Vishnu."

◆ ◆ ◆

While the transformation from chief to demigod was a revolutionary change in status for the leaders, the mainstream religious beliefs of the farmers continued to be based on the solid Austronesian foundation that had been in place for millennia. They just added Hindu and Buddhist ideas to their belief in spirits, souls, and magic. The additional spices changed the flavor of the curry but not the basic recipe, so when a king decided to build a temple to honor the Hindu god Siva, the site chosen was often a mountain or other special place already sacred to local people. Instead of putting the animals which dominated rural mythology out to pasture, clever priests linked them with Hindu gods and literature. Ancestor cults were strengthened, not displaced, by the construction of temples dedicated to the new gods. Buddhist priests and Hindu Brahmins existed side by side with the village shamen. And nature spirits, essential players in preirrigation agricultural societies, were ingeniously decked with Hindu or Buddhist trappings.

5

Traders
and Invaders

Selling the products of field and forest to customers in foreign lands created a fourth ecocultural revolution that threatens the traditional harmony between people and wildlife.

IT WAS A RAINY JULY DAY in Bangkok in the middle of the 1974 monsoon. We had waded through the flooded streets from the bus stop to the office, rolling up our pants as high as our knees, tying our shoes and socks around our necks, and sheltering ourselves as best we could under our *rom Chiengmai*, a gaily painted bamboo-framed waxed-paper umbrella that looked a little frilly but which did a reasonable job of keeping the driving rain off our backs. After the mugginess of the summer rainstorm, the office air conditioning was frigid and we were certain that pneumonia was just a few more shivers away.

We were sitting in the office of Willem J. (Bill) van Liere, a Dutch soil scientist and senior agricultural adviser to the Committee for the Coordination of Investigations of the Lower Mekong Basin.

Better known as the Mekong Committee, the group had been set up by the governments of Laos, Cambodia, Thailand, and Vietnam to oversee the cooperative activities involved in building dams, planning irrigation projects, and otherwise developing the shared water resources of the Mekong River. Bangkok was the logical choice as the headquarters city, since it was the capital where you were least likely to have your dictation interrupted by a hand grenade lobbed through the window.

The plan Bill had hired us to prepare would have been ambitious even in peacetime: to design a system of national parks for the entire drainage of the Mekong River south of China. Bill van Liere had the vision to recognize that conservation, when integrated with the huge dams and agricultural development programs that were being supported by massive foreign aid, could be a peaceful way to counter the roughshod tactics of the Khmer Rouge, Viet Cong, and Pathet Lao. We were going to win the hearts and minds of the village farmers by protecting the forests that would in turn protect their supply of life-giving water.

We had almost finished the book on the mammals of Thailand that we were writing with Dr. Boonsong, and since the fauna of the four countries does not differ a great deal, we were reasonably familiar with the wildlife. But like many conservationists, we had tended to consider people the biggest problem rather than part of the solution; we had ignored the idea that wildlife conservation should also bring some direct benefits to villagers. But now we were expected to look at conservation from a broader perspective. We quickly found that by looking primarily at animals, we were missing the most important point for conservation: People and wildlife must be considered together, not separately. This basic, simple insight would change our perception of both people and nature in some surprising ways.

Bill van Liere immediately pointed us in the right direction. "As you know, most of the rural people are still hunters and gatherers to some extent, though nobody totally depends on this life-style any more," he explained, leaning back in his chair and lighting up a Sumatran cigar. "Shifting cultivation still turns the hills into a holocaust every dry season, but that system is beginning to break down because too many landless lowlanders are moving into the hills and disrupting the age-old cycle of cultivation and fallow. Irrigation has been a great boon, especially in the past hundred years, and has provided a full dish of rice to everybody in the region. With the basic needs for food well met, aid programs are now helping farmers clear new land to grow market crops like cassava, maize, and sugarcane, which they can then sell to Japan, Europe, and North America. With the money they earn they can buy televisions and motorcycles from the industrialized countries. Everybody wins." Everybody, that is, except the animals which used to live in the new land which is being cleared to feed the industrialized countries.

Working with the engineers and agriculturalists of the Mekong Committee taught us how development projects, often funded from foreign aid, were affecting both the environment and the farming practices of traditional people throughout the region. "Development" generally means improving the material welfare of the people by increasing their productivity, which in turn ties them into the world marketplace as both producers of export crops and consumers of imported manufactured goods.

The term "development" had a powerful and positive ring, and we persisted in our work. Despite the challenges of implementing development projects in the middle of a war, Bill took us into the field to inspect dam sites, agricultural experiment stations, and areas with potential for national parks. One evening, as we sat around the dinner table in an Agriculture Department bungalow in northeastern Thailand eating sticky rice and barbecued chicken that we dipped into a pungent chili sauce with our fingers, Bill reminded us that the earlier approaches of people manipulating nature—burning, agriculture, and irrigation—led to major increases in population but did not really change the fact that farmers were basically growing crops for local consumption. All that was changed by the international marketplace. "Foreign trade places far greater demands on both the land and the people," Bill pointed out, sipping a cup of Nescafé. "The farmers now grow things they can sell, not just things they can eat. You can't really blame the farmers, of course. They've joined the rest of the world in their desire to be acquisitive."

Once a farmer has a bit of cash, he immediately buys a bicycle and a radio, which open the world to him and begin to weaken his ties to his local environment. His options are vast, since the world output of goods and services has nearly quadrupled during the past generation. With more money, a farmer might buy a Japanese-made sewing machine for his wife and an Indian-made tractor for himself to plow the additional land he has purchased. The thread for the sewing machine might come from England, while the fuel for the tractor comes from Saudi Arabia. He will buy fertilizers and pesticides to further increase productivity, mortgaging his farm to raise the capital if necessary. Greater productivity means more tax revenue for the government, so more is spent for health, education, and transport. And so the development cycle churns, fed ultimately by the world marketplace.

It soon became apparent to us that entering the global marketplace was Southeast Asia's fourth ecocultural revolution. Just as the concept of irrigation, the third revolution, was instituted through development of new technology, the idea of significantly expanded trade became a reality as technology became more available and more sophisticated with the arrival of the European colonialists. Over the past fifty years, oil has further accelerated the expansion of the global economy by making international transport both fast and inexpensive, and fueling the vastly increased industrial production.

◆ ◆ ◆

In Sarawak we witnessed the first generation of rural folk to be fully involved in a cash economy. Our requests to take photos in Iban longhouses were met by squeals of laughter by the women who rushed inside to get dressed up, which usually meant putting on a bra. Methodist missionaries had converted the Iban to Christianity and had convinced the women it was immoral to walk around bare-breasted. Rumor has it that the missionaries were immediately followed by opportunistic Chinese traders whose overstocked boats offered the newly modest women brassieres, in addition to tinned corned beef, beer, and soap. With cash earned from farming, hunting, or collecting forest products such as *illepe* nuts, used in the manufacture of chewing gum, people could buy outboard engines and go to the big towns perhaps once a year instead of once a lifetime. They carried with them surplus medicinal plants, marketable feathers, antlers, horns, furs, and other animal products, along with anything else of value they had collected since their previous visit to the market. Today, forest products from even the most remote parts of rural Asia can reach the capital city in just a few days.

The trade in animals and animal by-products has threatened some creatures. The various species of Asian rhinos, for example, have long been slaughtered for their horns, skin, and blood, all thought to have medicinal properties. A recent trend in international fashion has led to a significant increase in the trade in crocodile skins, encouraging hunters to exterminate these massive reptiles from many of their former haunts. And the export of vast numbers of live monkeys for medical experiments has caused so much controversy that several governments have banned the trade.

But perhaps more pervasive and pernicious than the direct exploitation of wildlife has been the destruction of their habitats. The tropical forests are by far the richest habitats for animals, with vast numbers of birds, mammals, and reptiles supported by countless species of herbs, shrubs, and trees—including many that are highly prized for their wood. Unfortunately for the wildlife, tropical hardwood trees, which in a sense *are* the rain forest, are the world's most commercially important wild plants. They generate a world trade in tropical hardwood estimated at $8 billion annually, of which Southeast Asia is the largest supplier. Virtually uncontrolled logging to meet this demand has destroyed extensive areas of the forests of Thailand, Malaysia, the Philippines, and Indonesia. The indications are that logging will continue until all marketable trees have been harvested, except in a few of the most successful national parks.

While monkeys and browsing animals may prosper in logged forests, healthy populations of some of the most interesting and important species—such as orangutans—need mature forest to provide the necessary variety of food and the continuous canopy of interlinked branches for transportation. But timber operations are usually followed immediately by an influx of farmers who move unhindered along logging roads to plant their crops in virgin soil. They "slash and burn" the remaining forest and get a few harvests out of the generally poor soil. It takes decades for the forest to reclaim the land.

◆ ◆ ◆

The timber trade in Southeast Asia has been going on since the early long-distance traders from China and India first dealt in exotic timbers like sandalwood. The early Hindu and Buddhist merchants represented distant powers with different ways of controlling natural resources, and brought revolutionary ideas like irrigation and god-kings with them. The ecocultural revolution of greatly expanded international trade was accompanied by other religions and cultural influences. Chinese ancestor worshipers, who generally kept their religious beliefs to themselves, and Indian

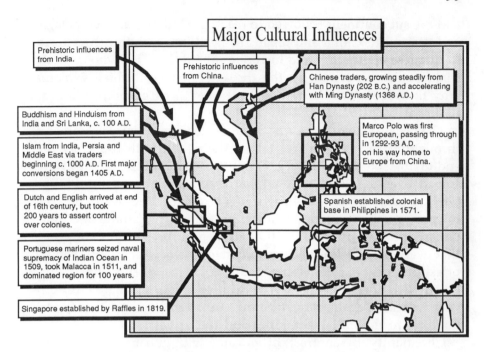

Major Cultural Influences

Prehistoric influences from India.

Prehistoric influences from China.

Chinese traders, growing steadily from Han Dynasty (202 B.C.) and accelerating with Ming Dynasty (1368 A.D.)

Buddhism and Hinduism from India and Sri Lanka, c. 100 A.D.

Marco Polo was first European, passing through in 1292-93 A.D. on his way home to Europe from China.

Islam from India, Persia and Middle East via traders beginning c. 1000 A.D. First major conversions began 1405 A.D.

Dutch and English arrived at end of 16th century, but took 200 years to assert control over colonies.

Spanish established colonial base in Philippines in 1571.

Portuguese mariners seized naval supremacy of Indian Ocean in 1509, took Malacca in 1511, and dominated region for 100 years.

Singapore established by Raffles in 1819.

Southeast Asia has long been a crossroads between east (China and Japan) and west (India, the Middle East, and Europe). Cultural influences were always reinterpreted and synthesized to fit in with local history, beliefs, and approaches; foreign cultures were never adopted wholesale.

Muslims and European Christians, who did not, arrived several hundred years after the wave of Hindu and Buddhist influence and facilitated the opening up of Southeast Asia to international commerce.

The first Islamic traders, coming to Southeast Asia from India in the eleventh century, were concentrated in Malacca in peninsular Malaysia. After several hundred years in power, the Muslim traders lost their dominant position to Catholic Portuguese, the first of the European adventurers who sailed around the Cape of Good Hope to the "Indies." The Europeans sought and fought for the fortune and fame that came when they returned to Lisbon, Madrid, Venice, or Amsterdam with a leaky galleon filled to the gunwales with nutmeg, cardamom, cloves, and pepper.

The key to wealth and power was the port of Malacca, which guards the strategically vital Straits of Malacca between the Malay Peninsula and Sumatra. This is the route that traders from Europe and the subcontinent followed to reach the Indonesian archipelago, and beyond to China and Japan. Tomes Pires, a sixteenth-century Portuguese apothecary and historian, noted that "He who controls Malacca has his hands on the throat of Venice," which explains why the acquisitive Portuguese unleashed their cannons and captured the town in 1511.

The Muslim merchants who were ousted from Malacca scattered throughout the archipelago, taking their faith with them. By the end of the sixteenth century, about 20 Muslim principalities were spread over the 20,000 islands between Sumatra and the Philippines. Islam was an excellent trader's religion because it put the buyer and seller on more or less equal footing. It stimulated individual initiative by teaching that all men in Allah's eyes are peers, that everyone has direct access to Him even without an intervening priest or an expensive temple, and that He can be worshiped anywhere, even on the wind-swept deck of a ship during a storm. It was radically egalitarian, offering an alternative to the feudal bondage to the Indianized kings and their priests.

Christianity, by contrast, often came with gun-bearing soldiers. When St. Francis Xavier arrived in Amboina (today Ambon) in the sixteenth century to try to convert the inhabitants to Christianity, he found that the knowledge of the Portuguese language in the Moluccas was limited to the conjugation of the verb *rapio* (steal), for which, he noted, there appeared "an amazing capacity for inventing new tenses and participles."

The Catholic missionaries had to live down the reputations of the European traders and adventurers who had preceded them. They did their best, but their religion had more appeal among the previously Animist hill tribes rather than in the centers of coastal civilization where Islam had finally taken root. Some historians speculate that the aggressive Christianity of the Europeans actually helped to promote Islam, by giving the indigenous government leaders a non-European alternative with which to counterbalance the power of the colonialists. Where Christianity has remained a minor religion, as in Indonesia, it is tolerated by the Islamic-oriented governments and even welcomed as a means of bringing pork-eating Animistic tribal people into the national mainstream. But where Christianity is an important force, as in the Philippines and the Malaysian states of Sabah and Sarawak, conflicts with Islam often arise.

◆ ◆ ◆

European traders have been coming to Southeast Asia for almost four centuries. Once the door was opened to the white men, the tradition-bound kings were unable to resist the flood of foreigners who invited themselves to the party. At the beginning of the eighteenth century, Southeast Asia still followed a way of life that had altered little for many centuries. "Outside the ranks of the rulers (and their hangers-on), there was little if any buffer between those who governed and the cultivator, the fisherman, and the petty trader," says historian Milton Osborne. "This was a world that placed a high value on order, the observance of proper relationships, and the maintenance of due respect for traditional procedures. It was a world, as a result, that was also vulnerable to the men of the West [who] frequently did not work by the Southeast Asian rules."

By the time the dust had settled, Southeast Asia had been carved into colonies and spheres of influence. After their brief attempt at regional dominance, the Portuguese settled for East Timor. The French took Indochina, the Spanish (and later the Americans) got the Philippines, the Dutch grabbed the East Indies, the Germans settled for a piece of New Guinea, and the British claimed Burma, Malaya, and the northern part of Borneo. Only Thailand, by playing the British and French off against each other and judiciously shedding some remote provinces, was able to maintain its independence.

Throughout this process, the Chinese played a characteristically low-key role. Chinese traders had a lesser religious influence, but they were not to be outdone when it came to commerce. They quietly spread throughout the region, trading glass beads and iron tools for an eclectic shopping list that included peacock feathers, the ivory-like bill (casque) of the helmeted hornbill, edible bird nests, and rhinoceros horn, a trade that continues today. The Chinese commercial influence began as long ago as the second century A.D., when traders set sail from the maritime provinces of Kwangtung and Fukien. Chinese influence has remained pervasive over the years and has reached even the most isolated corners of Southeast Asia—far upriver in Sarawak, Kelabit tribesmen today proudly exhibit Ming Dynasty pickle jars. The shops in almost every town and hamlet throughout the region are owned by dili-

Colonial Empires Before World War I

Note that only Thailand was not colonized. Some boundary changes have taken place since World War I, but this map indicates the way the colonial powers sliced the Southeast Asian cake.

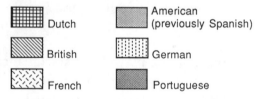

Dutch

British

French

American
(previously Spanish)

German

Portuguese

gent Chinese who open the premises at dawn and close the shop late at night and who make more money than any other group of people. It is not surprising that Chinese describe coming of age as "being able to earn money."

Today, the Chinese rule the economic life of Southeast Asia, much to the consternation of many non-Chinese. But the subtle form of Chinese colonialism is now forced to compete with the more blatant Japanese, American, and European commercial endeavors.

◆ ◆ ◆

The demands of the global marketplace have changed the face of the land throughout the region. In the East Indies (now Indonesia), farmers were encouraged by the Dutch colonials, sometimes through virtual slavery, to raise cash crops to satisfy the desires of distant people for such commodities as cloves, sugar, coffee, and tea. More farmers were needed to grow more export crops, so the human population on fertile soils in places like Java grew quickly. Then the land became too crowded, and farmers were forced into more and more intensive forms of agriculture, a process American anthropologist Clifford Geertz has termed "agricultural involution."

Even where the process of intensification of agriculture has been relatively voluntary, as in Thailand, the effects on wildlife have often been devastating. While irrigated rice took over many of the swampy areas along the Chao Phya River 2,000 years earlier, it was not until 1856 that Thailand opened treaty relationships with foreign countries, with accompanying commercial agreements. Rice, previously cultivated primarily for local consumption, soon became the most important earner of foreign exchange, and by the early 1900s practically all grasslands and swamps available for wet rice agriculture had come under cultivation. Rice exports from Bangkok increased tenfold from 1860 to 1910 and from Saigon increased twentyfold over the same period. The grazing animals which had survived the coming of irrigation could not meet the new threat from foreign demand for food, and Southeast Asia's most spectacular species of deer, the swamp-dwelling Schomburgk's deer (stags sometimes carried racks of antlers with over thirty points), was exterminated in 1938. Other large grazing animals, including elephants, Javan rhinos, and wild water buffalo, retreated to their last refuges in the hills.

Since 1950, rice yields in Asia have doubled, partly because of high-yielding varieties developed by the International Rice Research Institute in the Philippines. These new varieties have led the "green revolution," but they require heavy doses of fertilizer and pesticides, and mechanical pumps to provide water. Loaded on trucks, trains, barges, and ships, rice from Southeast Asia reaches markets from Saudi Arabia to South America. The bottom line is more food and more wealth, which usually results in more people, which in turn means less land available for wildlife.

The most severe impact of trade on agriculture came in the hills, where shifting cultivation had previously been designed simply to feed the farmer's family. In the Thai uplands, for example, new roads, machinery, and access to markets have led to massive habitat alteration, with the area under cash crops increasing thirty times from 1950 to 1984. The soils in the hills are usually so poor that the upland crops can be grown for only a few years before declining yields force farmers to abandon the fields. The total area of forest which has been cleared has been so substantial that little shelter is left for the wildlife. In the wetter areas of southern Thailand, the introduction of rubber in 1901 in many areas caused the disappearance of tropical rain forest.

Similar conversion is taking place throughout the region: rubber in Vietnam, Kampuchea, Malaysia, Sumatra, and Java; timber exploitation everywhere there are forests; oil palm in Malaysia; plantation crops like sugarcane on the fertile soils of Java, western Thailand, and the Philippines; and other export crops ranging from corn to pineapples to opium on the most suitable soils in every country. All are providing much-wanted foreign exchange, and most are playing havoc with the natural ecosystems.

◆ ◆ ◆

Our final report to the Mekong Committee recommended a system of protected areas that would cover roughly 7 percent of the land area of the Mekong Basin (the United States safeguards about 4 percent of its land in protected areas). Most of these national parks were to be located in the hilly areas unsuitable for permanent agriculture, but able to protect the forests surrounding the proposed dams. They would lengthen the life of the dams by slowing down siltation and soil erosion, and ensuring a regular flow of water throughout the year. Because the planners could see the relevance of protected areas and wildlife conservation to the overall development plan of the Mekong Basin, they willingly incorporated the system into the overall land-use plan for the region.

Dr. Boonsong put our recommendations into perspective. "The big problem we are facing," he observed, "is that the crops being grown for international trade all require lots of oil. They need pesticides, fertilizers, pumps, tractors, refrigeration, trucks for transportation, and so on. Almost all of them end up consuming more energy than they produce. Our supply of energy is very fragile and depends on many influences which are far beyond the control of the farmers, or even the central government. The farmers grow cash crops, but this cannot last. Worse, they are destroying the forests upon which the long-term future of the region will depend. I hope that the national parks you are recommending will help people see how important are their forests and wildlife for their survival in the long run."

Shortly after our report was issued, the Western-supported governments of Laos, the Republic of Vietnam, and Cambodia became the People's Democratic Republic of Laos, the Socialist Republic of Vietnam, and Democratic Kampuchea. The considerable international funds required to support the development program dried up and the plans were shelved. Parts of Kampuchea are still at war, much of rural Laos remains insecure, and the Thai countryside has been invaded by hundreds of thousands of refugees. Outside forces continue to threaten the forests and wildlife of Southeast Asia.

6

Stairways to Heaven

The arts serve the gods and reflect man's relationship with the natural world; they establish standards for the behavior of both people and nature.

THE BEST MONKEYS are almost like people, according to the *Ramayana*, the Hindu epic which came into Southeast Asia from India and became the region's best-loved and most influential piece of literature, matched in the West only by the Bible. The stars in the *Ramayana* each represent, in a graphic and dramatic way, the important moral values which hold Asian society together. Rama, the hero, is an incarnation of the god Vishnu, who embodies the ideal masculine virtues of strength, fortitude, and devotion to truth, although sometimes tinged with jealousy. Sita, his wife, while at times scatterbrained, is the feminine ideal of beauty and devotion. Rawana, the demon-king, personifies all that is bad—lust, deceit, violence, hatred, and visible emotions.

In the monumental story, recounted in various forms and on

many occasions throughout Southeast Asia, the faithful white monkey general Hanuman helps his friend Rama rescue Sita, who is held in the clutches of the many-headed Rawana. Hanuman is a useful ally. He's the general of all the monkeys and can fly as fast as the wind, has the strength to uproot trees and mountains, and can change his size at will, even to the point of making himself disappear. On behalf of Rama, Hanuman sneaks into Rawana's kingdom, rescues Sita, and goes on a monkey rampage. He knocks down people, buildings, and even an elephant before he is finally caught and sentenced to death on a burning pyre. Hanuman manages to escape in the final act and, his tail ablaze, ignites the entire evil kingdom, fighting, screeching, and having a merry time along the way.

When Hanuman bows to pay respect to Rama as he reports the success of his mission, he is a symbolic meeting point between early nature worship and the great state religious systems which were to sway the region's political future. "In this one figure," says art historian Ananda Coomaraswamy, "those early systems have achieved a spiritual quality and made a lasting contribution to the idealism of man."

Coomaraswamy adds, "It may be questioned whether there is in the whole of literature another apotheosis of loyalty and self-surrender like that of Hanuman. He is the Hindu ideal of the perfect servant, the servant who finds full realization of manhood, of faithfulness, in his obedience—the subordinate whose glory is in his own inferiority."

Hanuman's victory is a victory for the common man. Small wonder that he is venerated throughout the Southeast Asian nations where the *Ramayana* illuminates the ethics of human relationships. Among many cultures in the region, hunting monkeys is taboo and, because Hanuman is such a great hero, monkeys are given sacred groves and temples throughout Asia. In Thailand, a temple devoted to Hanuman in the city of Lopburi is overpopulated by hordes of two species of medium-sized, brown macaque monkeys surviving on handouts from visitors and nearby merchants. Lopburi was founded, the story goes, when Rama wanted to reward Hanuman by giving him a city. Rama shot an arrow into the air, saying that Hanuman's city would be built where the arrow fell. It landed in what is now Lopburi, and the spot is marked by a green post that represents Rama's arrow. This is the centerpiece of a shrine which is revered as the residence of the town's guardian spirits.

◆ ◆ ◆

It is twilight on the island of Bali, in the tropics a brief moment of mystery when the open masculine power of the sun relinquishes control to the mysterious feminine spirits of the moon. The sun plunges quickly into the sea, abandoning the earth, while 150 men silently drift into the temple courtyard. Clad only in black-and-white-checked sarongs, the men form concentric circles around a branched torch, which is lit by an elderly priest in white, his wisp of a beard fluttering gently in the ocean breeze. An urgent piercing shout breaks the tension, the men begin chattering like excited monkeys, and the *kecak* dance begins, for many the most powerful and unnerving dance in all of Asia.

The 150 men are Hanuman's troops, farmers acting as the monkey chorus to a reenactment of scenes from the *Ramayana* in which Hanuman is the star. They begin by murmuring a soft, repetitive "chak-a-chak" for several minutes (not easy, try it), then, as counterpoint to the action raging around the central torch, they screech, whine, and exalt, never breaking character, always enhancing the action, never commanding it. They are a collective force in the sense that a swarm of locusts is a collective force—the individual by himself has little impact on the outcome, the coordinated effort of the group *is* the outcome.

Rawana prances onto the stage. The men gently wave their arms and emit an unearthly hiss to simulate the villain's ability to fly. When Hanuman goes on his rampage they lie on their backs and thrust their arms in the air while clucking and chattering in approval.

The chorus is more than a stage device. The hypnotically swaying, sweating mass is reaffirming loyalty to the leader (in this case the monkey general), illustrating the principle that sublimating the needs of the individual to the power of the group helps hold Balinese society together.

Ethnologist Urs Ramseyer traces the modern kecak dance to the men's chorus of the *Sanghyang Bedari* trance dance. "These early dances related to a chorus of frogs," he told us one day in his office at the Museum of Ethnology in Basel. "If a frog sings out of tune, the Balinese say, the others attack him and bite off his head. In Balinese music and dance there is no improvisation. Everybody has his carefully defined role and anyone who doesn't precisely follow the script is ostracized."

The kecak (the name derives from both the Indonesian verb "to keep one's arms akimbo" and from the sound made by the monkey chorus) is primarily a dance of exorcism, driving evil from the group through continuous incantation. Rather than human words, the power-giving sounds are from the animal world: monkey jabberings and angry squawks, reiterated bird-like cries, and lonely wails. Just as the Monkey King conquered Rawana on behalf of Rama, so the monkey chorus conquers, through the unity of the dancers, any evil threatening the village. Earning money from tourists who come to appreciate the spectacle is just an added benefit.

◆ ◆ ◆

When we lived in West Java we liked to escape to Bali on occasion to breathe fresh air and be soothed by the rich green of the rice terraces, perhaps the most psychologically soothing color of all. Bali is home to what may be the most artistic culture in Asia, and perhaps in the world. In the garden of painter Ida Bagus Gede Djika in Sanur, we were impressed by a painting that he said represented the creation.

Contrary to our preconceptions about how the origin of life should be portrayed, there was no omnipotent bearded old man discharging the electricity of life. Pak Ida had instead painted a turtle and two snakes.

"What do you think the creation was, anyway?" he laughed. "In the beginning there was absolutely nothing. I think your Bible agrees with us on that. But then a universal serpent named Antaboga appeared, which in turn created the turtle we call Bedawang. Look at the painting. On the turtle's shell are two coiled snakes, nagas, and together they form the foundation of the world. The island of Bali rests on the turtle, which floats on the ocean."

Which makes sense in a way. Separated from nearby Java on the west by a shallow strait and from Lombok on the east by a deep and treacherous channel, Bali sits like a sea turtle amid dangerous tidal currents. Its fertile rice fields face the turbulent Indian Ocean to the south, rather than the tranquil Java Sea to the north. With good reason, many Balinese fear the sea. All of the island's coasts are exposed to the full force of the monsoons and its beaches are either fringed with coral reefs that make boating hazardous or are backed by steep cliffs. Anchorage at sea is all but impossible and there are no large natural harbors—the current harbor at Benoa was constructed by the Dutch. These geographical limitations isolated Bali from the maritime trade that helped homogenize most coastal settlements in the region, allowing it to evolve far more independently than most other parts of Indonesia.

One of Bali's four major temples, and perhaps the most impressive, is perched on a cliff ninety yards above spray-splashed rocks. The blue water far below the Ulu Watu temple is the playground for green turtles, which have been there for ages but which are now rapidly decreasing in number, and daredevil Australian surfers, new arrivals who are multiplying prodigiously. Obviously, Bali isn't the same place it was a generation ago. It suffers from tourist pollution. Some visitors stay in luxury hotels and through their package tours sense a bit of Bali, enough to understand, very quickly, that this is a special place. Other visitors frequent the less expensive and more relaxed resort of Kuta Beach, where the motorcycles are noisy and available, "magic mushroom" omelettes are featured on some menus, and pirate cassettes of Dire Straits and David Bowie cost $1.50 each. Lining the noisy main street of Kuta are a dozen or so travel bureaus, with handmade posters announcing "Tonight, Barong dance in Tampaksiring" or "Big cremation Saturday in Bangli, sign up now."

Yet even though it is under pressure, Bali's culture today is remarkably intact and offers an insight into a previous era. Clifford Geertz notes that the Balinese system of belief was formerly widespread throughout Southeast Asia. An understanding of the organization of the Balinese state may help clarify the history of the entire Southeast Asian region, he argues, particularly as it relates to the responsibilities of the kings and the related ceremonies and spectacles.

Geertz learned that the traditional Balinese state was patterned after the structure of the cosmos, a concept repeated in the royal palaces and Buddhist temples of Thailand, Cambodia, Laos, and Burma. The king was an earthly incarnation of Siva and the king's palace, like Siva's home at Mount Meru, was the center of the terrestrial universe around which orbited his ministers and outlying towns and territories.

The Kings of Bali, like the Sultans of Java, still wield considerable power even though the numerous royal families have agreed with the Jakarta government to relinquish their historic roles in order to establish a unified republic. But as recently as the nineteenth century, the royal government of Bali, like that of Thailand and precolonial Burma, Java, and Cambodia, was concerned above all with spectacle, not administration.

Today tourists can sit in the jasmine-scented gardens of the new luxury hotels and watch a Balinese dance performance that reflects the traditional state ceremonials of classical Bali. The Balinese dance and drama "were metaphysical theater," says Geertz, "designed to express a view of the ultimate nature of reality and, at the same time, to shape the existing conditions of life to be consonant with that reality." The ceremonials took the form of public dramatization of the power of the gods and their earthly representatives, the kings. "It was a theater state in which the kings and princes were the impresarios, the priests the directors, and the peasants the supporting cast, stage crew and audience," Geertz explains. "The stupendous cremations, tooth filings, temple dedications, pilgrimages and blood sacrifices, mobilizing thousands of people and great wealth, were not means to political ends: they were the ends themselves, they were what the state was for. Court ceremonialism was the driving force of court politics, and mass ritual was not a device to shore up the state, but rather the state, even in its final gasp, was a device for the enactment of mass ritual. Power served pomp, not pomp power."

What does this pompous approach to political philosophy have to do with nature? The literature, dances, songs, paintings, and architecture depict the governing principles of the universe: people are separated from the gods by a basic and irrevocable difference in status, and the ups and downs of human life are but low-level approximations of divine dramas. The earthly status of the kings and priests is related to the major natural cycles. This in turn generates a logic which structures everyday life. Equally important, including animals as essential elements of art, literature, and ceremonials demonstrates that people and nature are all part of the same whole, and that animals are often more appreciated by the gods than people are.

◆ ◆ ◆

Many human societies have used art to try to control their environment. Much so-called primitive art is used in magical rituals to affect the behavior of the animals which are most important to the community, sometimes through a spiritual intermediary. Although the carvings, decorations, and dances may be of subsequent interest to anthropologists, museum curators, and tourists, the value of the art to the people is in its function, not necessarily its existence.

On the remote Indonesian island of Siberut, we saw men carving elaborate monkey images to appease the souls of the monkeys they were about to hunt. Using art to ensure hunting success is one of the most pervasive uses of "primitive" art and perhaps one of the most ancient.

In Sarawak each year at the opening of the fishing season, a Melanau headman built on the beach an image of Raja Gamiling, the lord of the fish, and surrounded it with offerings of fish and chickens. Tiny rafts made of the stems of nipa palms were piled high with offerings of colored rice and eggs, then launched out to sea. "The idea of this ceremony is the propitiation of the Spirits, but there is more to it than that," wrote turn-of-the-century British naturalist Charles Hose. "Boom [a local chief] used to take up his position on the shore and watch carefully which way the rafts floated and which way any current might be setting. The course of the nipa stems, which were dispatched daily for some ten days, was carefully marked by a sort of channel of leaf-topped casuarina stakes planted in the shallow water; along these in the course of time, the fish would be guided along the swift in-coming tide into fish-traps set for them. It is therefore easy to see that Boom, as a Tribal Chief, Village Artist, and Magician, was a person of some importance to the fisher-folk."

But Boom's art was temporary—once it had served its purpose, it was no longer valuable. Hose once found an abandoned image of Raja Gamiling and recognized it as Boom's creation. Boom acknowledged that it might have been his handiwork, but refused to take it back. It had served its purpose, he said, and implied that it had never been intended as a thing of beauty and a joy forever.

In Sarawak's interior we were invited to participate in a ceremony in honor of the goddess Bungan, a deity created early in this century which combines respect for the tradition of headhunting with the concept of fertility and rebirth, symbolized by a hen and her eggs. We watched with admiration as many of the males of Uma Aging, a Kayan longhouse one kilometer upriver from the tiny town of Belaga, cut palm leaves into narrow strips and wove elaborate decorations for their shotguns and their persons. We lined up with others as a village elder, Lato Satong, wearing a blue

Hawaiian shirt and gray trousers, tied an elaborate plaited palm leaf bracelet on our wrists, ostensibly indicating that we had taken heads. This initiated us into the male society of half the longhouse (the other half of the longhouse is fundamentalist Christian and was not amused to see Europeans getting involved in pagan ceremonies) and we shouted and ate and drank in an exercise of male bonding, Sarawak style. The next morning, when we went down to the river to bathe, a secondary school student asked why we were still wearing our *leku.* "We thought you should wear it until it falls off, or maybe longer," we hesitatingly answered, afraid of having broken a taboo. The other men, we then realized, had thrown away their bracelets soon after the ceremony had finished.

Most of the best art of Southeast Asia is discarded after it has been used, like a no-deposit bottle. As Swiss anthropologist Urs Ramseyer points out about Balinese art, "The volcanic tuff of which much of the statues are made crumbles relatively quickly. The animal sacrifices are eaten by the public. The decorations of temple offerings are made of materials which cannot last long in the tropical climate. The delicately crafted sarcophagi in which the dead lie are burned during cremations. The figures cut with watchmaker-like precision from lontar palm leaves must crumble in a short time. All this contrasts with Borobudur, Angkor, the pyramids, Christian cathedrals. For the Balinese, life is like that; Bali has no 'great' art to offer, perhaps because it does not need the majestic permanence of the Gothic cathedral, for art is just everyday living."

◆ ◆ ◆

For some, however, art is *eternal* living. We were in Chiengmai, which most visitors, and in fact most Thais, consider to be Thailand's most pleasant city. Nestled in a broad valley in the northern hills, the city is reputed to have the most beautiful women, the most refined culture, and the most elegant temples. Chiengmai is also the entrepôt for opium, jade, and other valuable goods smuggled out of neighboring Laos and Burma.

Dr. Boonsong wanted to show us how animals have influenced Thai traditional art, and particularly the architecture of the Buddhist temples. He took us to meet the Abbot of Wat Doi Suthep, the temple of Suthep mountain overlooking Chiengmai. The Abbot was a scholar who had spent many years as a professor at Chiengmai University before taking his vows and withdrawing to a life of reflection. In his mid-fifties, he was still energetic, and his lively eyes gleamed as he gave us a basic course in cosmic architecture.

"The first thing to remember," he told us, "is that our temples are based on the sacred Buddhist texts known as the *Traiphum*, which describe heaven, earth, and the netherworld. Our temples are designed to resemble heaven as closely as possible, so that we can ensure an intimate harmony between heaven and the more immediate world of our land and its people."

After sipping a glass of sugar-laced tea in his small, tidy office, we were dazzled by the bright midday sun bouncing off the white walls of the main temple. "When you walked up the long flight of stairs to our temple, you certainly noticed that the railing was in the form of a giant snake. We call this animal naga, and he symbolizes the link between the lower earth and our celestial temple here at the top of the mountain."

We started walking around the massive enclosed temple, with the inside walls lined with statues of Buddha in a wide variety of forms, as tiny hill-tribe children dodged around us seeking tourists who would pay to use them as models in their photographs. "The moats you see around many temples, or the ponds filled with turtles, represent the Cosmic Ocean," the Abbot explained. "The temple walls, with their many small but evenly spaced peaks, are the mystical mountains, and the temple itself is Mount Meru.

"Look here," he suggested as he took several steps back from the temple and cast his eyes upward to draw our attention to the overall structure of the building (pointing with a finger would have been impolite). "Our temple complex is particularly fortunate in being located here on the mountain, because we can more closely represent the differences between the levels of heaven. You see that the *mondop* [main temple] has seven tiers, representing the seven subordinate mountains leading up to Mount Meru, which is represented by the temple's highest spire. And as long as you are looking up, notice that our roof, like most temple roofs, is the most decorative part of the temple." We did as we were told and gaped like schoolboys at the golden gables and ridge posts inlaid with tiny mirrors. The structure dramatically swept out and up toward the unrelenting sun.

"You might find this part interesting since you work with animals. Notice the boards which cover the temple's gables," he suggested. "You'll see that they undulate and end in likenesses of the head of the giant naga who represents the earth and its waters—in other words, fertility. Now compare the serpent form with the form of the ridgeposts. They symbolize the head of Garuda, the sacred bird of the sun, something like a holy eagle, and the sweeping roof might be thought of as Garuda's wings. Garuda and naga are opposites, representing sun and earth, fire and water. But each defines the other and they always need to stay together as parts of the cosmic whole."

We didn't realize at the time just how important naga and Garuda are to the people of Southeast Asia. For the moment we were simply awed by the majesty of the temple buildings and the tranquillity we felt in spite of impending dehydration.

We passed through a courtyard which had several plaques of twelve animals each, encrusted with gold leaf applied by pious worshipers. The rhinos, tigers, elephants, dragons, rats and so forth, "are the creatures that are said to inhabit Mount Meru," the Abbot explained, answering the question that was apparent in our wondering eyes. "All Buddhist temples are based on the same holy scriptures. You will find the same creatures again and again, whether you go to Pagan in Burma or Angkor Wat in Cambodia."

This is not to say that each temple we saw from Burma to Bali was identical—far from it. But each had the same elements and purpose. The temple is the earthly equivalent of the divine cosmos and the architecture is magical. Its sacred function is to reflect a united world of which animals, people, and gods are all part.

Clearly the artists who can build these structures are very special men. French art historian René Huyghe notes that the Asian architect must have both outstanding technical skill and moral qualities. But we were surprised that these men do not engrave their names on the cornerstones. As we thanked the Abbot and made a small contribution to the temple maintenance fund, we asked him about the architects and artists who were responsible for this important contribution to Thai culture. "Unlike Westerners, we are not very concerned about individual credit," he replied. "Our artists, at least in more traditional times, had no desire to be remembered by posterity because, like all of us, they were only temporarily inhabiting a body and their soul would be reincarnated in another body depending on the quality of the life they led. Seeking personal credit would be contrary to the ideals of the Buddha."

◆ ◆ ◆

The Asian arts give form to peoples' attempts to come to grips with the complexity of nature. Art reflects nature, and an understanding of the relationship between people and nature can be enhanced by looking at dances, body tattoos, weaving, wood carvings, ceremonial sacrifices, paintings, music, stone carvings, and all the other forms art can take. The art is often decorative, but rarely is decoration the sole reason for its existence. It serves to guide human behavior and to show respect to the gods, not to bring glory to the artist.

7

Protector
of the Buddha

*The king cobra, among the world's deadliest snakes and a sym-
bol of danger in the West, is considered a powerful and positive
religious symbol in the East.*

THE MOST DARING SNAKE CHARMER in the world practices her skill in a
Burmese cave. On the chosen morning the snake priestess—in
daily life a farmer's wife who has been given the assignment to
ensure the coming of the monsoon rains—leads a long, slow procession of villagers up the steep slopes of Mount Popa, several
days by steamer up the Irrawaddy River from Rangoon. Her face,
neck, and arms are dusted white with rice powder, she wears a
loose-fitting thick muslin robe of ancient design, she has said her
prayers to the gods, and her soul has been blessed by the local
Buddhist abbot. She is about to need all the help she can get.

Approaching the shallow cave where a king cobra is lurking, she
moves slowly and respectfully, murmuring apologies for disturbing
the snake's rest. She kneels in front of the reptile and touches her

forehead to the ground three times, as the snake rears up and spreads its hood in alarm. The priestess serenely rises and undulates her body in slow, sensuous rhythms, like an Indian snake charmer with his flute in the Rangoon marketplace.

After several minutes of her trance-like dance, the priestess induces the cobra to strike. But the direction of the strike is predictable, and the woman steps back so that the cobra's half-inch-long fangs, ejaculating a teaspoonful of deadly venom, hit only her loose robe. The dance continues. The cobra strikes again and again, but the amount of venom that drips down the front of the woman's robe lessens with each strike. After fifteen minutes the snake is thoroughly confused, weary, and frustrated, and exhausted of venom.

Approaching the cobra, whose head is still reared three feet off the ground, the woman gives the snake three kisses on the top of its head. Bowing low, she murmurs her thanks to the Lord Naga, and backs away slowly, as a commoner always takes leave of a king. The crowd, their tension relieved at last, follows the priestess back down the mountain, small boys laughing and kicking up dust and villagers singing. In the distance, storm clouds gather over the Gulf of Martaban, soon to release their life-giving liquid to the parched rice fields below.

◆ ◆ ◆

The king cobra ceremony is obviously more than a little phallic, which starts to explain part of the Asian fascination with nagas (from the Sanskrit word for serpent, now referring to both living cobras and to various mythical serpents). The rearing stance and spread hood of the cobra represent phallic tumescence to villagers from India to Indonesia. In Hindu temples, the cobra is considered a manifestation of Siva, god of destruction and creation; the altars of Siva temples, with the phallic *lingam* set in the *yoni*, its female counterpart, are often guarded by carved stone cobras, and living snakes sometimes make the temples their home.

Nagas above all symbolize water, guarding the life-energy stored in springs, wells, and ponds. In the periods between cosmic ages, the great Hindu god Vishnu sleeps in the Sea of Milk dreaming of the next age of earth. His mattress is the huge naga Ananta, whose name means "endless," and the giant cobra rears his seven heads over Vishnu's sleeping face to protect him from the elements. "The anthropomorphic figure, the serpent coils that form his bed, and the water on which this serpent floats, are triune manifestations of the single divine, imperishable, cosmic substance, the energy underlying and inhabiting all the forms of life," says historian Heinrich Zimmer.

Because of this powerful link with life, snakes have been involved with women in fertility rites since ancient times. Often described by outsiders as barbarous and obscene, the ceremonies were in fact serious religious rites considered essential for human welfare. According to the American herpetologist Sherman Minton, during the annual festival of the snakes along India's Malabar Coast in the nineteenth century, women encouraged living cobras to penetrate their vaginas in a graphic simulation of the activities of Siva and the Hindu mother goddess Shakti. In the 1880s a visitor to Nagpur said: "Rough pictures of snakes in all sorts of shapes and positions are sold and distributed, something after the manner of valentines. In the one I have seen in days gone by, the position of the women with the snakes were of a most indecent description and left no doubt that, so far as the idea in these sketches was concerned, the cobra was regarded as a phallus."

But symbolism in Asia is seldom entirely straightforward. Hindu and Buddhist beliefs have ancient roots from many sources and the same symbol may have several meanings. Italian anthropologist Gabriella Eichinger Ferro-Luzzi points out that the snake in India has ambivalent male/female associations. "If its shape, movement, and the fact that it lives in holes in the ground are considered, it tends to become a phallic symbol. The latter habit, however, may also be viewed from a different angle. The snake, living in the earth, may be seen not as opposed to the earth, but as its representative, and hence tends to become a female symbol." Many of the naga images found in temples are door guardians, often with a male naga on one side and a female naga, complete with breasts, on the other side. These pairs of nagas represent the yin and yang, male and female, elements and thereby symbolize the dynamic balance between the two. By protecting waters and guarding doors against evil influences, nagas serve Mother Earth.

To Westerners, nurtured on the Christian association of serpents with the devil, and typically afflicted with snake phobia, the Asian veneration of cobras seems difficult to understand. After all, the naga's earthly form is the king cobra, which grows up to eighteen feet long and is the world's largest poisonous snake. When it rears up, its head is high enough to look a startled villager right in the eye, radiating menace and fathomless mystery. It injects a considerable amount of venom when it strikes, pumping in the poison with a tenacious chewing motion of its jaws. Death can come to a human within twenty minutes. Its poison is so deadly that the snake has even killed elephants by sinking its fangs into the tips of their trunks or the vulnerable soft spot between their toes. The king cobra's smaller cousin, the common or Asian cobra, is an even greater threat to people because it is far more common. In Burma alone, hundreds of people each year die of its bite.

And yet from India to the Philippines, cobras have been raised to the status of life-giving gods, powerful symbols whose phallic shape and periodic shedding of the skin symbolize fertility, the seasonal rebirth of nature, and immortality. Although male in structure, the cobra also represents the earth goddess, and its feminine attributes often overwhelm the more obvious phallic symbolism.

The religious and mythological significance of the cobra in Asia probably arose from the nature of the creatures themselves. The king cobra is one of the most fearless reptiles. It feeds on other snakes, eating an average of twenty feet of serpent per month, and has few natural enemies, one reason why many Asians regard it as the master of all species. Yet it is also one of only a few snakes to build a nest and watch over its eggs. Perhaps most important, the young of both king and common cobras emerge from their eggs just before the rainy season in many parts of Asia, and the first rains flush even adults from their holes. As a result, the snakes' annual appearance, coming as it does with the monsoon rains, reinforces its symbolism of the rebirth of the earth.

◆ ◆ ◆

Serpent worship was well established when the evangelical school of Buddhism started spreading from Nepal into Hindu India and Animist Southeast Asia 2,500 years ago. But the wise Buddhist missionaries did not try to replace the ancient snake cults, rather they pressed the nagas into the service of the Buddha. According to the Buddhist *Jataka Tales*, when Siddhartha, the Nepalese prince who became the Buddha, was about to be born, nagas gathered in the garden of his mother, Queen Maya, and assisted at his birth; when no hot water was available for the prince's first bath, the snakes caused a warm spring to gush forth.

This link between the Buddha and nagas was easy to forge. "Between the Buddha and the naga there is no such antagonism as we are used to in the savior-versus-serpent symbolism of the west," says Heinrich Zimmer. According to the Buddhist view, all of nature's creatures rejoice upon the appearance of the Incarnate Redeemer. The serpent, as the principal personification of the waters of terrestrial life, is eager to serve the Buddha, and solicitously watches his progress toward final enlightenment.

While not particularly successful in India, where it had to compete with firmly entrenched Hinduism, Buddhism spread rapidly among the Animists of Southeast Asia. In Cambodian and Thai temple art, the Buddha is often pictured seated on the coils of the Naga-King, with the snake's seven great hoods rearing over the Buddha as a protective umbrella.

The Abbot of Nakhon Ratchasima temple in northeast Thailand told us about the significance of this theme. "After seven days at the foot of the Bo tree and another seven days under a great banyan tree, the Buddha moved to a third tree, belonging to the Serpent King, Muchalinda. The Enlightened One was deep in profound meditation, seeking the truth that would free mankind from the ropes tying humans to their material goods." An ironical smile flashed across the Abbot's wizened face as he looked at the tourists who passed by, festooned with cameras and Walkman stereos.

"An evil demon attacked the Buddha by sending down a great rainstorm, but the Buddha was completely oblivious of the danger. The King of the Nagas, however, saw what was happening to his master, and he quickly coiled his body under the Buddha, who was seated in the sacred lotus position, and lifted him above the floodwaters. Then the Naga-King spread his hoods over the Master's head to protect him from the fierce rain sent by the demon.

"For seven days the rain pounded down and the cold winds whipped around the Buddha, but the Merciful Teacher remained in deep meditation. On the seventh day, the demon tired and the storm retreated. Muchalinda unloosed his coils, transformed himself into a gentle youth, and with joined hands to his forehead bowed in devotion to the Master."

The naga who guarded the sleeping Hindu god Vishnu was recruited by the Buddhists to protect the Buddha during his nap as well, thereby linking Hindu deities directly with Buddhism. But the naga's service to the Buddha does not end there. The ordination of new monks is called in Thai, *Khwan Nag*, the "gift of the naga." The naga-king was so devoted to the Buddha's compassion-

ate philosophy of charitable relations among all living things, the
story goes, that he was ordained into the monkhood while he was
still in human form. But one day, during a deep sleep, the naga-
monk turned back into a snake and was seen by brother monks,
who reported the awful sight to the Lord Buddha. The Buddha
gently explained to Naga that no creature except a human can
become a monk. The naga was contrite and relinquished his monkhood, but asked if his name could be given to neophyte monks in
recognition that Naga had indeed once been a monk. The Serene
One consented, and since then all prospective monks have had to
first wear white robes and be called "naga" for two days. On the
morning of the third day, the "naga" has his head shaved, and he
approaches the Abbot. "Are you a naga or a man?" the abbot asks
at the beginning of the ordination ceremony. Only when the neophyte answers that he is a man is he allowed to put on the yellow
robe and be ordained into the monkhood.

The Buddha no doubt would be appalled at this story, for his
original teaching rejected all spirits, gods, and the worship of idols,
stating that the true path to contentment can be discovered only
through self-denial, self-knowledge, rejection of attachment to
material goods, and meditation. But for Thai youths who enter the
monkhood, the question also symbolizes that the attributes of naga
—virility, sexuality, and productivity—are being left behind.

The reality faced by Buddha's proselytizers was that the naga
cult was so powerful among the Southeast Asian rice farmers—
whose crops were at the mercy of nature—that nagas had to be
incorporated into the new religion if converts were to be made.
Once the nagas were co-opted as supporters, Buddhism took hold
and ultimately thrived in the rich lowland Indochinese valleys of
the Mekong, Irrawaddy, and Chao Phya rivers, as well as in what
are now peninsular Malaysia, Sumatra, and Java.

But the coming of Islam in the fourteenth century brought an
even more powerful threat to the naga deities, particularly in the
coastal areas of Indonesia and the Malay Peninsula. According to
the fifteenth-century *Keddah Annals*, one of the great early history
books of Malaysia, most Hindu and Buddhist images were destroyed when Islamic proselytizers arrived, since the teachings of
Allah strictly prohibit all forms of idolatry. But the nagas survived
even this supreme peril, living on symbolically in the most important totem coveted by Indonesian and Malaysian males: the decorative but deadly knife known as the *kris*.

The kris is much more than a weapon. "Every great leader must have a kris," notes K. R. T. Hardjonagoro, chairman of the Kris Association of Indonesia and Regent and museum keeper for the Susuhunan of Solo. "A kris is a symbol of power, the symbol of life—Life with a great L. It's what keeps our political system strong." For his kris, President Suharto offered a $5,000 "tip" (you debase the magic by purchasing a special kris) to the brother of Pak Suyono, a venerable kris maker in Yogyakarta.

Some kris blades are wavy, others are straight, but the naga is the prototype for both. The wavy-bladed form depicts a naga in motion, while the naga is in repose in the straight-bladed form. For a Javanese man, the relationship between the kris and snake is so close that he may wash the blade in the entrails and brain of a cobra to enhance the knife's mystical power.

When crafted by an expert and finished with the proper spiritual incantations, the ceremonial serpent-shaped blade is thought to be embodied with its own spirit and able to destroy distant enemies while its owner remains safely at home. The best krises, such as those made by Pak Jeno outside Yogyakarta, contain iron, steel, and nickel from a meteorite. "A kris will foil a robber—he approaches the house, he is overwhelmed, he cannot go in," says Pak Jeno, who distributes calling cards, advertises, and has two models of the Eiffel Tower in the cupboard of his living room. "A kris can foil a murderer: He can't bend his trigger finger. It can hold back floodwaters, extinguish fires, and divert volcano flows. A woman can marry a kris: Legally, it's the same as marrying the kris's master."

Even today, in the unique bouillabaisse of religions and cultures that comprise Javanese society, a warrior (in mind, if not in deed) places his kris in a prominent place in his house, makes offerings to its spirit, and assuages the totem's need for blood by pricking his finger with the blade whenever the knife is taken out of its scabbard.

The kris plays a prominent role in a number of the myths and legends of Southeast Asia. One macabre story tells of the unfortunate honeymoons of Nyai (Queen) Loro Kidul, the Javanese Queen of the Southern Ocean (also known as the nature goddess who founded the current Javanese royal line). She married eight times—and eight times her bridegroom was dead by breakfast. Her ninth husband differed from his predecessors in being a *wali*, or holy man, and abstained from consummating the marriage. Instead he stayed awake on his wedding night, deep in prayer. Halfway through the night, he witnessed a sobering spectacle: out of his bride's vagina crawled a deadly snake. When the *wali* grabbed the serpent and threw it to the ground it turned into a kris, which is today venerated in central Java as a holy relic.

◆ ◆ ◆

The coming of Hinduism and Buddhism, overlaying the existing naga tradition, linked Indochinese royalty with fertility. Throughout Cambodia, the phallic *lingam* symbol of the Hindu god Siva came to represent the very essence of royal power. And at the temple city of Angkor Wat, the jewel of Cambodian civilization, four long causeways 100 yards long are bordered by rows of squatting stone giants who hold huge nagas that form the balustrade, each rearing up at the entrance with a huge seven-headed cobra fan. These causeways were considered sacred bridges to Mount Meru, the abode of the gods, and passing down the causeway of the naga was said to lead to the holy dwelling place of the Lord Buddha.

The Cambodian naga-kings had very astutely turned the common man's veneration of nagas into a powerful means of justifying their sometimes arbitrary and outrageous rule. Huge stone temples covered with ornate carvings, built at an incredible cost of material and manpower, were necessary for the naga-kings to keep the irrigation waters flowing to nourish the rice—and doubled as impressive monuments to the rulers themselves.

Several of the temples in the one-square-mile Angkor complex were devoted especially to the nagas. As described by the thirteenth century Chinese traveler Chou Ta-Kuan, the Phimeanakas temple, built in the tenth century, had a golden tower where the royal naga changed into a beautiful woman as darkness fell each evening. The King of Cambodia was required to mate with her before visiting any of his hundreds of other wives and concubines. If either party failed to keep the nightly appointment, the King would die or disaster would overtake the kingdom.

One of them must have become weary, because shortly after Chou Ta-Kuan returned to China, the naga-kings were conquered by the more vigorous Thai warrior kings to the west. The fabled temples of Angkor Wat were abandoned and forgotten for 400 years until they were rediscovered by French explorer Henri

Mouhot in 1858. The naga-kings became extinct, but the belief of the common man in nagas continued.

◆ ◆ ◆

In modern times, nagas have continued to rear their powerful heads to confront authority. In 1937, as the French were beginning to lose their colonial grip on Vietnam, belief in a new naga-god in the form of a python spread over the central highlands. Villagers stopped work, animals were sacrificed, people barricaded them-selves in their villages and refused visitors, and, worst of all, the men refused to report to their French masters for corvée.

This messianic movement, led by a powerful leader from the Jarai tribe named Sam Bram, was based on the legend that a Jarai woman living in the Ayun River valley had given birth to a naga that could "talk like a man." The naga at times appeared in human form as a dashing young man with bronze skin and large round eyes, but spent most of his time in the forest, returning to the village from time to time to make pronouncements. He later moved to the depths of the sea, and from there he surfaced to visit distant places by moving through the air like the wind. The naga-god issued commandments through his Jarai friend, specifying, for ex-ample, that the people must avoid fornication and rough behavior and could not eat snakes, crustaceans, or aquatic birds.

The naga let it be known that during the seventh month in a future year a fierce typhoon would uproot all the trees in the for-est, split mountains, and shatter the land. All foreigners in the highlands—French, Vietnamese, and Lao—would be destroyed and the believers in the naga-god would share the goods left behind by the foreigners. From that day on, says American anthropologist Gerald Hickey, the people believed they would be free of outside controls. The naga would bring them independence.

This idea was far too revolutionary for the French to accept, so they quickly arrested Sam Bram. Even the naga-god could not save him from a life sentence in a French prison near Khe Sanh, where he remained until the Japanese released him in 1945.

◆ ◆ ◆

Nagas live on in the hearts of the Khmer people. On the night of January 30, 1972, Cambodian troops guarding the capital, Phnom Penh, went into a frenzy of activity, firing artillery, machine guns, and mortars in a barrage so intense that two of their own troops were accidentally killed and eighty-five innocent bystanders were wounded. An invasion of the Khmer Rouge or the hated Vietnamese? No. It was something even more fearsome than insurgents. That night a giant evil naga, named Reahou, ate the moon. The fusillade was aimed at appeasing the evil serpent, and, at great expense and no little loss of international dignity, it worked. The moon returned to the sky and Cambodia was saved from the malevolent cosmic serpent who occasionally tries to disrupt human affairs by eating the sun and the moon.

Scientists described the event as a lunar eclipse, caused by the earth casting its shadow over the moon. The Cambodians knew otherwise.

8

Garuda,
the Power of the Sun

Representing the sun, the Hindu deity Garuda is the symbol of predominantly Muslim Indonesia and supports the most sacred Buddhist temples.

ONE OF THE FIRST PRIORITIES Indonesia addressed after declaring her independence from the Dutch in the closing days of World War II was to find a symbol for the new nation. After careful consideration the leaders chose the Garuda, a giant golden sun-bird which is the mount of Vishnu, considered by many Hindus as the supreme deity. Garuda is famed for his supernatural powers, invulnerability, and creative energy. Garuda also hates *nagas*, his earth-bound competitors.

It might seem strange that a Hindu deity would become the emblem of a vigorous young country where over 80 percent of the population consider themselves Muslims. But the Garuda, as King of Birds, is also a symbol of the important role that birds have played in Indonesia from the dawn of human society. Birds have served Indonesians as fortune-tellers, guided missiles, and transportation to heaven, and the waving forms of wings are the most pervasive motif in Indonesian folk art. "There is little doubt," says historian Claire Holt, "that Garuda's ascendancy was facilitated by the old Indonesian veneration of birds."

As Australian artist Donald Friend observed of Garuda, "We had best prepare his welcome with marked respect, for *this* is not one of those modern permissive birds with whom anything goes: the Garuda upholds absolute values and is a divine creature of quite impeccable antecedents."

Garuda is far more than just another bird of prey. Originally he was the sun itself, which was conceived by some early Asians as a bird flying across the sky. Today he represents the heavens, the home of the stars, the sun, the moon, the gods, and the birds. Garuda is the polar opposite of the earthbound nagas, which represent the life-giving terrestrial waters. Garuda and Naga are an archetypical pair of symbolic antagonists who are respectively the champions of heaven and earth, day and night, male and female. In this natural antipathy the blazing tropical sun of the Garuda continuously attacks the liquid energy of Naga's earthly waters, evaporating the moisture of the land. But Asian gods have many faces. They create as well as destroy. Both Garuda's light and warmth *and* Naga's soil and water are essential for growing crops.

Garuda also attacks and eats snakes, as do many of the hawks, eagles, and falcons found in Southeast Asia. Being a relentless hunter of nagas, whether real snakes or the stylized king cobra-naga, Garuda possesses mystical power against the effects of poison, which enhances his popularity in folklore and daily worship.

The Garuda-Naga antipathy started out as a family quarrel involving an evil aunt. According to the *Garudeya*, a history book dating from the early days of Indian influence in Indonesia 1,500 years ago, Garuda inherited his hatred of snakes because his mother had become enslaved by her sister, the mother of the naga-serpents. Garuda tried to free his mother, but the nagas demanded a ransom of the gods' immortality-inducing *amrita*. The loyal son flew to the flaming mountain where the precious liquid was stored and, after the usual series of heroic battles with gods who were reluctant to give up their favorite tipple, delivered the nectar to the nagas. Garuda's mother was released.

Vishnu, who subsequently teamed up with Garuda to double-cross the nagas and regain the priceless ambrosia, was so impressed by Garuda's exploits that he made the sun-bird immortal and chose Garuda as his steed. Garuda's victory over the snakes made him their enemy forever. Friend considered that as a result of these noble actions "Garuda was, and is, a by-word for filial devotion. His role has been the rescuer," which takes many forms, including the character of Jetayu, the sun-bird who attempts to rescue Rama's wife Sita in the *Ramayana.*

Several of the societies of Sumatra and Borneo which retain pre-Hindu cultures still believe that the rivals of the birds of the air are the snakes who live as deities of the earth, rivers and streams. Serpents teach knowledge of special plants, including sources of medicines and dyes for weaving, and are closely linked with women—dyeing and weaving are considered "women's warfare" by the Iban of Borneo and in many societies collecting medicinal herbs is woman's work. The dark, the secretive, the enclosed, and female is symbolized by the earthbound snake, in opposition to the bright, open, visible, and male, which is symbolized by the sky and the birds of the air.

Small wonder Garuda was an obvious choice for the Indonesian nation-builders looking for a potent symbol. And political subtleties reinforced their decision—the Malay states that now form Malaysia and Indonesia have historically been at odds with the naga cultures of the north, initially Cambodia and, more recently, dragon-dominated China.

◆ ◆ ◆

Garuda in its current form came to the Indonesian archipelago as part of a powerful group of Indian ideas that transformed the country—human god-kings, irrigation systems, status hierarchies, monumental architecture, and a priesthood. In places with rich soil, like Java and Bali, Indianized states were established and the forests pushed back, along with the forest-dwelling human tribes and wildlife. The new civilization brought with it stylized bird-gods like Garuda to replace the rustic sky and sun deities represented by naturalistic birds.

While relics of Hindu and Buddhist cities dot the forests of Sumatra, and, to a lesser extent, Borneo, large land-based civilizations did not really catch on in these areas because the soils could not maintain the level of surplus productivity required to support a top-heavy religious and government bureaucracy. Instead, hunting and shifting cultivation continued as the main way of life, and as a result the ancient bird beliefs have continued to flourish.

Borneo is foremost among the islands where birds help mold behavior. Tom Harrisson, who encouraged a brief reintroduction of head-hunting as an important tactic in his mobilization of the Bornean tribes against the Japanese in World War II, spent most of his life after the war in Borneo as curator of the Sarawak Museum. "There is probably no other part of the world," he says, "where birds and men are more intimately intermixed than in Borneo. Here birds are interwoven into the whole texture of thought and belief. For some three quarters of the population they are major determinants of conduct. For nine tenths they play a large part in mythology and in perpetuating ideas surviving out of the past."

The model for the Garuda-like sun-bird in Borneo is the Brahminy kite. Sometimes called *Burong Apui* (fire bird), this native Bornean bird-god is capable of great miracles. The Kelabit hill tribe of central Borneo, once a warring and generally inebriated group that has now been almost entirely converted into a group of teetotaling, fundamentalist Christians, have told Burong Apui's entertaining story around longhouse fires for generations.

A villager named Tama Agar was suffering from leprosy, a disease that still afflicts many throughout the region. At a stream he met the kindly sunbird. "Come and sit near me," the bird said, "and I will give you a special cure for your disease." The bird then relieved himself all over the man, who was immediately cured. Impressed by the man's confidence in him, the bird continued his fecal magic, enriching the man with valuable gems, beads and feathers. Transformed from a pitied wretch to a wealthy and healthy man, Tama Agar made a triumphant return to his longhouse, accompanied by the sunbird.

Given an honored place in the rafters, Burong Apui repeated his anointing act and cured Tama's leprous wife. The family prospered from then on, until one fateful day a chieftain from a longhouse over the hill came to visit and became curious about the suddenly improved fortunes of the family. While Tama Agar was far downriver trading some of his new wealth for presents for his wife, the visitor seduced Madame Tama. During an impassioned moment she revealed the secret of Burong Apui.

The visitor quietly took up his blowpipe and shot Burong Apui through the eye, killing it instantly; he set the bird to roast and returned to his new paramour. Shortly after, Tama Agar's two sons returned from a hunting trip. The younger son, famished from the morning's hunt, quickly ate the cooked bird. The visiting chieftain, seeing the bird disappear, was so enraged that he reached for his blowpipe and threatened to kill the boys, who ran away into the forest.

The visiting chieftain realized the importance of Burong Apui, so he set out to find the young hunters. Sensing that he could never catch them in the jungle, he decided to entice the young men back to their longhouse by using an irresistible bait: he sent his nubile daughter into the forest. The lovely virgin walked for hours, then sat down and wept in frustration. The younger son, who had developed the ability to fly after eating Burong Apui, soared to the young lady's side and, using the sweet words that suddenly sprang to his lips, soon seduced the girl.

Being a somewhat traditional young lady, she demanded some gifts in return for her favors. The boy boxed his ears and out poured gold. This miraculous performance convinced the girl that she should steal the heart of the Burong Apui out of the boy's stomach. Out of her woven shoulder bag she pulled a bottle of *arak*, a potent rice moonshine enjoyed throughout the island, and made him so drunk that he vomited up the bird's heart. She immediately popped it into her mouth and swallowed it.

Self-satisfied and filled with a new feeling of power, she magnanimously agreed to have a few drinks with her new lover to console him for his loss. Soon she became so drunk that she too vomited up the Burong Apui heart, and the youth quickly returned it to his stomach. Sobered by this turn of events, the girl joined the youth for the long walk back to the longhouse. Soon they were joined by the elder brother, who had been keeping an eye on the longhouse from the edge of the forest.

Leaving the girl sitting under a tree, the two brothers approached the longhouse, the elder on foot to attract the attention of the adulterous visiting chieftain, the younger flying out of the sun to attack, ripping out the man's eyes with his talons. Blinded, the interloper returned in shame to his longhouse, leaving behind his no-longer-virgin daughter, who had fallen in love with Tama's younger son. Tama himself returned from his shopping trip just in time for a glorious wedding.

This story, still repeated with uproarious embellishments between sips of rice wine in longhouses in remote regions of Borneo not yet reached by television, reinforces the power of birds and cautions people to be careful in their use of wealth and power—especially when they are not earned through hard work.

Christian missionaries of the Evangelical Church of Borneo have turned the same tale into a parable aimed at promoting moderation in strong drink.

◆ ◆ ◆

Singalang Burong, generally based on a Brahminy kite, is assisted by the *kenyalang,* usually a rhinoceros hornbill, which helps the Iban in times of war. Singalang Burong and the *kenyalang* were important players in the most masculine pastime of the tribes of Borneo: head-hunting. One day, according to an Iban story, a handsome young man named Ketupong shot a strange red-eyed bird with his blowpipe. As he bent down to pick up his prey, the carcass of the bird changed into a beautiful robe made of feathers. Nonplussed, the hunter carefully folded the garment and put it into his bamboo dart quiver.

As he started heading home, he heard a woman's gentle voice ask him, "Have you seen my dress?" Ketupong turned and saw a beautiful, and quite naked, young girl. Startled, he blurted, "Yes, I have it here in my quiver." And, with sufficient presence of mind to remember his mother's constant admonitions to start a family, he impulsively added: "But I won't give it to you until you promise to marry me."

The girl, named Inchin Temaga, agreed. They wed, had a son, and lived happily, although Ketupong often observed his wife looking wistfully at the sky. One day Ketupong noticed his wife weaving two bright coats with an unusual pattern that resembled a bird's plumage. "Who are you making those coats for?" he inquired. "They are for you and our son," she responded. "When they are finished you can wear them to fly up into the heavens." She went on to explain that she was the daughter of Singalang Burong (whose name means "lion-eagle bird"), the god of war and foremost deity of the Iban, whose longhouse was in the sky. When the coats were finished, Inchin grew feathers and her arms turned into wings. Without a word, she stepped off the longhouse veranda and soared into the air. Indignantly, Ketupong yelled for her to return and fix his dinner. "If you want to visit me, wear the coats I have made for you," she called back.

Ketupong, being a man of limited imagination, eventually forgot about his strange wife and remarried, this time to a woman who kept her feet on the ground. But the son could not forget his mother and constantly pestered his father to take him to visit her. Finally the boy reminded Ketupong of the feathered coats. They donned the magical garments and took off into the air.

They eventually came to a great longhouse in the sky. The gates opened and they were welcomed by a splendid warrior in Iban war dress—Singalang Burong himself. Then Inchin Temaga appeared. Upset that her husband had remarried, she told him that while their son could remain, he must return to earth to be with his new family.

Singalang Burong taught his grandson the mysteries of his kingdom. One day one of the king's warriors was killed by a giant. As was the custom, Singalang Burong taught his grandson how to pack all the dead man's belongings into a box, adding, "The box cannot be opened and the warrior's spirit set free until we have taught the giant a lesson he won't forget. We must cut off his head."

After a long journey they reached the giant's longhouse. Waiting until dark, Singalang Burong rushed into the house with a terrible shout and skewered the giant with his spear. With one slice of his *parang*, he lopped off the giant's head.

When the two returned home there was a great feast which lasted three days. During the festivities Singalang Burong pointed out the figure of a strange bird atop a tall pole. Its beak was pointed in the direction of the giant's house. "What's that, Grandfather?" the boy asked. "It's a hornbill, one of our most sacred birds," the wise deity explained. "It helps us defeat our enemies in battle by capturing their spirits."

Eventually the time came for the boy to return to earth, where he taught his fellow Iban all that he had learned in his grandfather's aerie longhouse. The Iban enlisted the bird as their god of war and were thereafter successful in bringing home many heads from their far-ranging battles.

Iban explicitly attribute much of their success in war to an ingenious weapon learned from Singalang Burong: the guided hornbill. Their weapon, called the *kenyalang*, is intricately carved from specially selected fresh, green wood. Launching this weapon requires a set of rituals that spans a four-day period, beginning with long chants about the perceived wrongs that must be avenged. These justify the planned attack on enemy territory and convince the warhead-hornbill of the justice of the action. Then young girls make offerings to the hornbill. Ritual experts, chanting verses explaining the traditional responsibilities of each family, carry the wooden image to all the private apartments of the longhouse. It is a pep talk for the warriors as much as an appeal to the gods.

Finally the chief, wearing a clouded leopard skin robe generously decorated with black and white hornbill feathers, cuts out the tongue of the wooden statue, and the hornbill spirit is launched on its way to kill the spirits of the enemies, thus ensuring victory when the actual attack is made.

"For a bellicose people convinced that all material objects possess soul counterparts," says anthropologist J. D. Freeman, "the creation of a spiritual weapon like the kenyalang is ingenious tactically—a primitive precursor of the guided missiles of the modern west. Inasmuch as the Iban had the greatest faith in the efficacy of their hornbill ritual, it was of considerable value to them psychologically, as warriors."

The great hornbill celebration survives. Now, however, it is a five-day party called *Gawai Kenyalang* held once a decade or so, to highlight really big occasions, such as the election of a tribal chief to the Malaysian Parliament. The energy once devoted to headhunting is now directed to eating, drinking, singing, cockfighting, and courting.

According to Harrisson, the preeminence of hornbills can be traced back, "into the bowels of Asia, the mythology of China and India, Phoenix and Garuda. And it is quite easy to compare, side by side, ancient Asian mainland art forms in bronze, silk, lacquer, ivory and hornbill ivory itself, which vanished centuries ago there but survive in the closest [hornbill design] parallels carved into a Kayan man's canoe paddle or tattooed upon the buttocks of a Kalimantan lady in Borneo today."

As the largest birds in the forest, with outrageously long bills and striking black and white tail feathers, hornbills make good models for myths. In the rain forest the hornbill is the king of the treetops, with a bellicose screech that sometimes sounds like a runaway steam engine containing a litter of yelping puppies. The whoosh of its wings can be heard a half mile away. Nine of the world's forty-four hornbill species are found in Borneo. The rhinoceros hornbill is the most outrageous of all with its huge, upturned casque the size of a banana.

Far back into prehistory, the hornbill has been a special bird in Indonesia and Malaysia. On bronze-age funeral drums, the hornbill often appears as the figurehead on the stern of a ship, guiding souls of the deceased to the hereafter. And even today, stylized hornbill heads symbolizing death and resurrection appear as carved figureheads on boats plying Sumatra's Lake Toba.

At least part of the hornbill's link with ancient conceptions about the liberation of the soul after death is due to its strange breeding habits: the female imprisons herself during the four- to six-week incubation period and subsequent six-week rearing period. She seeks a large, hollow tree, dropping sticks and debris into the cavity to raise its floor to a comfortable level. She then spends several days plastering up the entrance with mud and her own droppings, which harden into an impenetrable clay. The male helps from the outside, using the flat sides of his bill like a trowel until only a narrow slit remains, through which the male serves food. This breeding practice clearly relates to the concept of the Iban people that links females with dark and enclosed places. The female hornbill's emergence from the prison with her young symbolizes the freeing of the soul after death. It also points out, once again, the dual nature of Asian symbols. Just as the cobra-naga has both feminine and masculine attributes, the hornbill-Garuda, while primarily male, also relates to female actions and concepts.

◆ ◆ ◆

Garuda in all of his manifestations is among the most powerful animal symbols in Southeast Asia, serving Animist, Buddhist, Christian, Hindu, and Muslim alike. At Angkor Wat, the bas-reliefs depicting celestial palaces are held aloft by Garudas. Bangkok's Temple of the Emerald Buddha, the most revered shrine in Thailand, is kept "afloat" by a ring of golden Garudas grasping nagas in their claws. Vishnu mounted on Garuda is a common motif on the gables of Thai Buddhist monasteries, and the distinctive soaring roofs of Thai architecture are thought to represent Garuda's head and wings.

The current dynasty of Buddhist Thai kings is named after Rama, a popular incarnation of Vishnu, the universal god of the Hindus—the current monarch, King Bhumibol Adulyadej, is Rama IX. Given the close relationship between Vishnu and Garuda, it is logical that the great sunbird, called *Krut* in Thai, has been adopted as the personal emblem of the king. It is the only creature allowed to be above the king's head and appears on the royal banner and elsewhere as a symbol of divine royalty.

While few Western-educated Thais would today say that King Bhumibol is an incarnation of Vishnu, the people are obviously comfortable in having the King associated with Garuda, the ancient symbol of the sun and the deadly enemy of nagas. In this case fire is stronger than water, and Thais believe that even a powerful Chinese dragon can be frightened into producing rain when it is threatened by the even more powerful Garuda. Associating the king with the sun gives the state power over the monsoon, that most fickle of all the requirements of wet rice agriculture. His Majesty's emblem is the Garuda holding a naga in both talons, similar in appearance if not meaning to the American eagle gripping a snake. Garuda and Naga. Sun and water. Male and female. Open and closed. They are the opposites which, by maintaining the productivity of nature, keep society functioning.

9

Ganesh, the Potbellied Elephant God

The most beloved deity in Asia is a rotund jungle elephant who touches the common person.

IN THE VILLAGE of Air Sugihan in South Sumatra, everyone was weary after a long day of keeping the elephants out of the ripening cornfields that represented the community's first crop. A long night was ahead for the "transmigrants," poor farmers from over-crowded Java who had been offered free land and a new start in the sparsely populated parts of Sumatra. We were in the village to interview these settlers for a magazine article, and found that some of them were pioneers against their will who wished they were back on Java. One problem: the central government in Jakarta had placed their village in the middle of an ancient elephant migration route. The elephants were there first, and weren't about to let a few Javanese farmers block their way.

Night falls quickly in the tropics, and the distant tiger roars and nearby calls of owls and nightjars took over from the gibbon whoops and hornbill screeches of the day. After a simple meal of rice, overly fragrant *pete* broad beans (we sweated their powerful essence for days) and *rendang*, spicy beef simmered for hours in coconut milk, we prepared for bed. We laid our sleeping bags out on the dirt floor, and lit a Double Rabbit brand mosquito coil while humming the jingle we had composed for its advertising ("kills mosquitoes 'til they're dead"). We tried to ignore the "regional dances" television show blaring from the nearby community center, gave the curious children a chocolate bar to share between them and promised to teach them a song in the morning, and settled in. A light drizzle tapped on the red-tiled roof of our hut and lulled us into a dreamless sleep.

Shortly after midnight, the hut began to vibrate gently, a feeling not unlike a minor earth tremor. Suddenly the peaceful night was shattered by human screams of *"Gajah! Gajah!"* followed by trumpeting elephant screams that probably meant "People! People!" Elephants stampeded through the village, knocked over huts, broke open the buffalo and goat pens, and tore a swath through the cornfield. We all sprang into hopeless and helpless action, running around like the chickens that had been sprung from their coops.

Minutes later, calm returned to the village as the elephants got bored with their revenge. Days of reconstruction were required to return the village to its preraid state, and there was no guarantee that the elephants would pay any attention to the government's concerted efforts to move them to another stomping ground. One part of the Indonesian government was charged with supporting the transmigration program, another ministry with conserving elephants. The elephants were ignoring all the bureaucrats by doing whatever they felt like.

◆ ◆ ◆

It is no surprise that the jungle elephant is held in awe by people of the forest and has been revered for thousands of years. It is immense, strong, intelligent, and potentially devastating. In most years, more rural Asians are killed by elephants than tigers, averaging 200 to 300 human deaths per year in India alone. It is difficult to ignore a presence like that and elephants have long been important players, if not the stars, in the folklore of the forests of tropical Asia.

It is just a single elephant-step from folklore to basic religion.

Alfred Foucher of the University of Paris has pointed out that long before organized religion, villagers worshiped a stout, goblin-like elephant-god to prevent unreasonable attacks on crops, people, or dwellings by the real thing.

In Aceh, at the northern tip of Sumatra, the elephant is a sacred animal whose use was confined to the king. When a group of Dutch soldiers captured a young elephant in the 1920s and escorted it down to the coast where it could be shipped back to a zoo in Holland, a group of Acehnese men ambushed the party and let the god escape, risking their liberty to prevent blasphemy.

The elephant-god, and other deities based on animals, such as Garuda and Naga, met the needs of villagers reasonably well for thousands of years. But 3,000 years ago a new concept uniting politics and the spiritual, generally an unholy alliance, started to make its mark on Asia. The appearance of the state religions changed the rules.

When Hinduism, with its strict caste system, was introduced the rural farmers may well have felt that the full benefits of the new religion's ceremonies were accessible only to Brahmin priests. There were too many levels of religious bureaucracy between him and Him—the Him in this case being the personification of the most powerful animal in the forest, a being the farmer had come to understand and respect on his own terms. The state religion required the support of the farmers for its long-term prosperity. How could they be brought into the fold?

Ancient Sanskrit had no term for "marketing consultant" but the religious promotors of the time knew their business. In an attempt to fight consumer apathy, the early Hindu multinationals invented a miraculous elephant called *Airavata,* who was created out of the Sea of Milk, and made him the mount of Lord Brahma, the creator of the universe. According to German scholar Heinrich Zimmer, Airavata represents both the rainbow—which is regarded as a weapon of the gods—and a certain type of lightning, thereby linking the elephant with the luminous manifestations of thunderstorms.

The Hindu image-builders merely built on existing beliefs. Even today, in rural villages of Sumatra, elephants are thought to cause lightning, though opinions of how it is done vary. In the Batak lands around Lake Toba, elephants are said to simply hurl the lightning from their trunks. In Palembang, it is supposed to be caused when elephants sharpen their tusks. In the Kampar region a slightly more sophisticated story is told which reflects awareness of the static electricity generated before a storm—as soon as a storm approaches, the elephants begin to tremble in every limb, their hair stands on end, and the lightning flashes then jump from these hairs.

The canny Brahmins built on such widespread folk beliefs to give their divine elephant characteristics which would be familiar to the simple rural folk. It was then relatively easy for the priests to promote the elephant to the new countries to the east. In Laos and Thailand he became *Erawan*, whose three heads represent the three major gods in the Hindu pantheon—Brahma, Vishnu, and Siva—and statues, paintings, and decorations of the three-headed elephant are common throughout rural Thailand and Laos. Erawan still reposes on the Lao flag, years after the royal family has been deposed and a non-religious communist regime has taken over.

◆ ◆ ◆

The early Buddhists were Hindus who took their religion in a different direction, rejecting the multiple gods and focusing on the psychological well-being of the individual. In splitting from the Hindu beliefs 2,500 years ago, the upstart Buddhist proselytizers were faced with the dilemma of building affiliations between ancient and contemporary beliefs. They too used folklore for their own aims, particularly the Jataka Tales that tell of the earlier incarnations *(boddhisatvas)* of the Buddha. One such Buddhist boddhisatva absorbed one of the Hindu Airavata's qualities and was positioned as a rainmaker.

Another boddhisatva was an elephant named Chadanta, who had a silvery trunk and six tusks of various heavenly colors. Living by the side of a lake, he was a king with 800 elephant subjects and two lovely elephant consorts. As might be expected in such a *ménage à trois*, the ladies had a falling out and Chadanta wound up as the scape-pachyderm. Imagining she had been gravely insulted, one of the elephant consorts became determined to teach Chadanta a lesson. With the aid of a holy man, she succeeded in marrying another king. She now had the power to take the revenge she lusted after. In a feminine application of power worthy of Lady Macbeth, she ordered the kingdom's most skillful hunter to track the six-tusked elephant and bring back the ivory.

After a long journey, the hunter reached Chadanta's palace, dug a pitfall, and captured the elephant-king. But the hunter's arrows were unable to kill the royal prey. The elephant-king gently asked his attacker why he was trying to kill him, and was told the story. Chadanta, being an incarnate Buddha, was not angry, having only compassion for the hunter and his former wife. He himself broke off his tusks and handed them to the hunter to give to the Queen, dying in the process. The Queen, when told the story, died of a broken heart.

◆ ◆ ◆

Airavata and Chadanta were miraculous elephants indeed, but even they were not good enough since the state religions were still not having the desired impact among the rural people. The elephant-god of the people was quite a different sort of character from the holier-than-thou clergyman's version; the villagers' down-home stomp-in-the-mud elephant-god related directly to the people's knowledge of the massive gray apparition which tears down trees in the forest and ravages the crops.

Around the fifth century A.D., somebody had a flash of genius: Create a kindly new god with the head of an elephant. His name was Ganesh, and he was a huge hit.

Presaging modern public relations strategies by fifteen centuries, Ganesh's supporters packaged him in a humorous, accessible form which appealed to the masses, and gave him attributes which were highly relevant to the needs of the man in the forest path. Incorporating the accepted double-edged nature of Asian deities, Ganesh was designed to bestow or withdraw success, remove or cause obstacles, and fulfill or ignore desires, depending on how he was approached.

The Hindu priests realized that to be accepted the new elephant-god had to have a worthy family tree. No problem. They simply rewrote the history books, as countless subsequent power brokers have done. Ganesh was retroactively fitted into the classical pantheon by making him a son of Siva, the Lord of Creation and Destruction. Colorful tales were devised to explain his ugly elephant head, so different from the fabulous beauty of most Hindu deities.

In one story, Siva's wife Parvathi accused her husband of infidelity. Enraged and embarrassed because the accusation was true, Siva attacked his wife with a golden sword. Their handsome young son, Ganesh, intervened to save his mother and had his head chopped off. Siva and Parvathi were appalled, so Siva ordered his soldiers to cut off the head of the first creature they met to replace that of Ganesh. They soon found an innocent elephant ambling down the road. They removed his head and took it to Siva, who placed it on the shoulders of his once-elegant son. Ganesh was miraculously restored to life, but forever after had the head of an elephant.

Siva himself is said to have told his son a rather more self-enobling story: "Parvathi and I once retired to the forest on the slopes of the Himalayas to enjoy each other's company, when we saw a female elephant making herself happy with a male elephant. This excited our passion and we decided to amuse ourselves in the form of elephants. I became a male elephant and Parvathi became a female elephant, and we pleased ourselves. As a result, you were born with the face of an elephant."

Arriving late on the scene, Ganesh missed the chance to land even a supporting role in the two classics of Hindu-Buddhist literature, the *Mahabharata* and the *Ramayana*. In order to explain his absence from these seminal works, Ganesh was given credit for the secretarial work—he is said to have written the great 5,000-stanza epic *Mahabharata* at the dictation of the sage Vyasa. The epic is considered such a harmonious work because before agreeing to write it down Ganesh stipulated that the dictation should never falter and that he should at all times be able to understand the story's meaning.

As literacy spread, Ganesh, the remover of obstacles, also gained the reputation of being a patron of letters. His patronage is still valued today—no Hindu author would dream of attempting to publish a major work without prior obeisance to the elephant-faced god.

Imaginatively packaged, well promoted, well connected, and clearly striking a responsive chord in the common person, the elephant-god Ganesh was so popular that he quickly rose through the ranks to take his place at Siva's elbow at the top of the Hindu pantheon.

"Ganesh is not the deity of a people who fear their god," says the art historian Ananda Coomaraswamy. "He is gentle, calm and friendly, a god who loves man and is loved by him. A genuine kindliness and a certain wise craft are written on his visage. But neither is he the god of any theoretic conception. He is obvious, simple, capable of a slight grossness, full of rude vigour and primal masculinity, destined from his birth to a marvellous future, both in faith and art, as the forefront of all undertakings that are to make for success. . . . Above all, he is the god neither of priests nor of kings, neither of theocracies nor of nations, but in all probability of that old diffusive mercantile culture. . . . To this day he is the god pre-eminently of merchants, and it is a curious fact that in the Indian city, when a merchant is made bankrupt, the event is notified to all comers to the office by Ganesh being turned upside down."

The merchants provided the distribution network for Ganesh's availability in every major market. Carried eastward by Indian merchants seeking the solace of a benevolent deity on their risky trading missions, images of Ganesh from India were distributed widely among the villages of Burma, Thailand, Cambodia, Sumatra, and Java. The locals quickly reinterpreted the exotic forms and the "native" versions feature their own characteristics. The Javan Ganesh, for example, usually has the soles of his feet touching each other, and he is often draped with Siva-like skull ornaments —two features seldom found anywhere else.

Ganesh was particularly popular in Java during the Hindu-Buddhist period that ran roughly from the first to the fifteenth centuries A.D. Since he was revered by travelers as remover of obstacles in their perilous trips, his images are often found in places of danger such as steep slopes, river crossings, or dense forests.

Some of these images wielded their considerable power well into the Muslim period of "modern" Java. The most famous *punden*, or holy place, in the east Javan town of Modjokerto is a foot-high stone statue of Ganesh, enclosed by a solid white fence at the foot of a massive banyan tree. When Java was still Buddhist, explains American anthropologist Clifford Geertz, the King of Solo, the great court city of Central Java, was chasing the King of Madura north and east toward the latter's homeland. Along the way, he stopped at Modjokerto—then still an unsettled forest lying between the two kingdoms—to rest his troops. To commemorate the place under the great banyan tree where he rested, he left the statue of Ganesh. This Ganesh in the town square is today believed by the local people to be occupied by a *demit*, a spirit who may support the wishes of people.

Extraordinary powers are claimed for this demit, says Geertz. Once when the Ganesh was taken to Bragkal, some fifteen miles away, it returned under its own power, presumably carried by the demit. On another occasion a Dutch controller (the lowest-ranking European official in the colonial bureaucracy) stationed in Modjokerto kicked the Ganesh to show his disdain for the devices of the heathen; he died within a week of a broken neck, and within the year his whole family followed him to the grave. The local people do not quickly forget such coincidences, so the Ganesh statue is well respected even by those who profess a belief in only one Allah.

◆ ◆ ◆

Though Ganesh originally belonged to the Hindu pantheon, he is equally revered by the Buddhists, who claim that a mystic mantra in praise of Ganesh was disclosed by the Buddha himself to Anand, his great disciple and proselytizer. This too is clearly revisionist history, as Ganesh was still a wild elephant-god living among jungle people when Buddha finally reached nirvana.

Since Buddhism formally rejects all gods, Ganesh is never allowed in Buddhist temples in Thailand, but is confined to the temple courtyard. Though officially banned, the elephant-god has sneaked into the temple through the back door and has infiltrated the very heart and soul of the Buddhist liturgy.

The essence of Buddhism is captured by a hum, a word, an idea, an ethereal sound called "om" that starts from a man's soul and filters out to encompass the universe. It is the first sound of the classic Buddhist mantra *om mani padme hum*, "hail to the jewel in the lotus." You can hear it in a mountain village in Nepal and amid the chaos of modern Bangkok.

Wat Benjamabopitr, Bangkok's famous and much-visited "Marble Temple," is a small haven of serenity, filled with acolytes and the faithful strolling among the lush green gardens and graceful statues of the Buddha. Inside the main building of the wat, seven elderly saffron-robed priests sit quietly in a line, eyes closed, chanting Pali prayers and oblivious of the tourists walking by. These "prayers" are far more than the usual requests for wealth, happiness, or successful exam results—they are *mantras*, a sort of nucleus or gathering point for energy, a concentrated form of cosmic power. To utter one properly requires patient study and effort, but once mastered, a mantra is said to evoke a powerful force from the combined structure of human and cosmos.

Most of the mantras begin with the sacred syllable *om*, a pure sound of ancient Vedic origin composed of three sounds merging together: a-u-m, beginning at the back of the throat with a soft a, filling the whole mouth cavity with the u, and closing with the m at the lips. When pronounced this way, om is said to contain the sounds of all the vowels of speech. And since the consonants are but interruptions of these sounds, the holy syllable contains in itself the seed sounds of all words and thus the names of all things and relationships. The three sounds also call forth the three gods symbolized by Erawan, the three-headed elephant—a for Brahma, u for Vishnu, and m for Siva.

More relevant here, om also links Erawan with Ganesh. Historian Alice Getty, perhaps the world's leading expert on Ganesh, has pointed out that the Sanskrit sign for om looks like the numeral 3 with a hook coming out of the right side; the hook is called "Ganesh's trunk." Ganesh is thus powerfully linked with Brahma, Vishnu, and Siva, since no rite may be performed without his invocation.

◆ ◆ ◆

By the time of Ganesh's elevation to the pantheon, says French art historian Alfred Foucher, "the Elephant-god had already behind him century upon century, if not thousands of years, of silent waiting at the foot of the sacred tree of the pre-Aryan village, standing on the roughly built platform which he shared with the other rustic deities: with the snakes which were to give birth to many Naga-kings, with the monkey which was to become Hanuman, with the bird which would later grow into Garuda. . . . For those more or less shapeless stones, those roughly carved pieces of wood or summarily outlined figures in clay, all those totems or fetishes—once bathed in the blood of human victims and today still smeared with minium (red ochre)—were so deeply rooted in an unfathomable past that the aristocracy of the new gods, introduced by the immigrant Aryans, were compelled to adopt them in some form or other. Had they not come to terms with them they would soon have found themselves estranged from the worship of the populace, and their priests deprived of gifts and followers."

Elephants remain an omnipresent, and often destructive, force in the lives of many villagers in Southeast Asia. You ignore the elephant at your peril, which is why Ganesh the elephant-god continues to serve the common man—whether Animist, Hindu, Buddhist, Muslim, communist—throughout the region, helping provide the strength, confidence, and fortitude of the Lord of the

Jungle to those in need. An image that has proven its worth as Ganesh has doesn't need the sanction of an official religion. On the contrary, the state religions of the region desperately need the support of the common person's elephant-god if they want to win the hearts of the people.

10

The White Elephant

As a reincarnation of the Buddha and birthright of the ruler, this animal has altered the history of Burma, Thailand, and Cambodia.

IT'S A LONG, HOT WALK up the steep stairs climbing Rangoon's Singuttara Hill, which was created, according to legend, when a giant centipede seized and ate elephants on the spot, piling their tusks to make the hill. At the summit you get a reward. The polished marble courtyard paving is cool on your bare feet and the Shwedagon Pagoda dazzles you with its golden splendor.

Shwedagon is Burma's most important religious edifice, and is said to enshrine eight sacred hairs from the head of Gautama, the most recent Buddha. The courtyard is lined with shrines, hundreds of statues of the Buddha, adoration halls, stone lions, sacred bells, and prayer posts. No expense has been spared to ensure that only the finest religious art surrounds the temple's masterpiece: a gigantic 326-foot golden-domed stupa crowned by a 76-carat diamond atop a gem-encrusted globe; together they create a dramatic flame burning in the bright sunlight.

Shwedagon dominates Rangoon as proudly as any man-made edifice dominates any of the world's major cities. Rudyard Kipling described Shwedagon as "a golden mystery on the horizon—a beautiful winking wonder that blazed in the sun." The stupa is plated with 8,688 solid gold slabs. Each is worth more than $500 and it is said that there is more gold on the Shwedagon Pagoda than in the vaults of the Bank of England. Much of the gold that gilds the holy spire, which W. Somerset Maugham compared to "a sudden hope in the dark night of the soul," was liberated from Thailand during wars fought among Burma, Thailand, and Cambodia in the sixteenth, seventeenth, and eighteenth centuries. One reason for the three centuries of violence was to determine which king could possess the most white elephants, an animal that represents the peace-loving Buddha.

◆ ◆ ◆

A white elephant is clearly serious business in Southeast Asia, and something quite different from the item of unwanted junk the term signifies in the West. Hindus had many reasons for revering white elephants. In ancient times, a white elephant was associated with rain clouds and, like the cobra-*nagas,* was a symbol of life and prosperity. It made sense for the Hindu priests to build on this time-proven perception, and elephants were built into their mythology. Four-tusked *Airavata,* who rose to the surface when the celestial Sea of Milk was churned, was an elephant Adam and begat all the elephants which followed. Just as Garuda became the mount of Vishnu, the elephant became the steed of Indra, the Hindu god of the heavens.

The white elephant is even more important for Buddhists. U Toke Gale, Burma's leading elephant expert, explains: "The white elephant has always been a symbol of Buddhism, of prestige, prosperity and political power, and has, at the same time, been for centuries one of the chief causes of invasions and plunder among some countries of the East."

Several elephants had been incarnate Buddhas *(boddhisatvas),* including Airavata and Chadanta. But the most important was the white elephant, which was the last animal incarnation of the Buddha before he was born again as a man to bring peace and contentment to the earth. The sacred white elephant is said to have appeared in a dream to Buddha's mother-to-be, Maya. The future Buddha, in his elephant form, held in his silvery trunk a white lotus flower (the symbol of the *yoni*, female genitalia). He uttered a long, drawn-out cry, bowed three times, and touched his forehead to the floor. Then he gently struck Maya's right side, and entered her womb. The Queen reported this extraordinary vision to the court astrologers, who divined that she would bring forth a great king or a great seer. Nine months later, Prince Siddhartha was born.

Since that time, white elephants have been closely linked with the Buddha and are still believed by some people to be reincarnated Buddhas. Small wonder that such animals were treated with respect, used as lures or diplomatic ploys, and even fought over.

Actually, a white elephant is not really white, and it takes an expert to distinguish one from the run-of-the-mill gray variety. According to the Thai "Law of the Conservation of Elephants 1921," seven special characteristics define a white elephant: white eyes, white palate, white nails, white hairs, white or pink skin, white hairs of tail, and a white prepuce. An elephant with all seven characteristics would be so fabulous as to be beyond price; any elephant with even one of them is considered a white elephant and therefore property of the king. Some authorities even say that white elephants should not snore noisily, but should emit the gentle sounds of Thai classical musical instruments, while the Burmese say its skin must turn red, not black, when sprayed with water.

These rare animals are well treated. A white elephant captured near the ceremonial capital at Pegu in 1806 spurred the Burmese royal court into action. A golden barge escorted by gilded canoes filled with dancers and musicians was sent down the Irrawaddy River (named after Burma's version of the sacred white elephant Airavata) to fetch it. The trip back upstream, white elephant on board, took months because the barge had to stop for several days at each major village along the river so that the people could see the miraculous white elephant and offer gifts.

When the barge finally reached the island of Mingun, a temporary palace with five-tiered golden spires inlaid with rubies and other precious stones had been built for the elephant.

The court astrologers and Brahmins arranged the appropriate ceremonies. Holy water from the Ganges and Irrawaddy rivers was splashed on the elephant to exorcise any evil spirits. All the elephant's regalia were fashioned out of pure gold, studded with rubies and emeralds. He wore flowing robes of silk and velvet, embroidered with threads of gold. These royal trappings were valued then at 707,088 ticals of silver (the average workman's wage being 1 tical a day). The king made the white elephant an honorary human being, and he was given a royal title roughly equivalent to Secretary of State or Foreign Minister.

For the rest of his days, he lived a life of leisure, feeding from vessels of silver and gold on the greenest, most tender grass, the lushest sugarcane, and the sweetest bananas. His drinking and bathing water was perfumed with the fragrance of jasmine flowers.

U Toke Gale quotes the seventeenth-century English traveler Ralph Fitch as saying that when a white elephant goes to the river to take his daily bath, he "goeth under a canopy of cloth of golde or of silke carried over him by sixe or eight men, and eight or ten men goe before him playing on drummes, shawmes, or other instruments, and when he is washed and commeth out of the river, there is a gentleman which doth wash his feet in a silver basin, which is his office given him by the king."

White elephant calves receive even better treatment. In the 1850s, according to U Toke Gale, a baby white elephant in Burma was suckled by ladies who "stood in a long row outside his palace, and the honour was eagerly sought after, for the creature was a national pride and not merely a royal monopoly. . . . Troupes of the palace coryphees danced for his pleasure, and there were choruses of sweet-voiced singers to lull him to sleep."

Besides providing a symbol of the state upon which the populace can heap their adulation, white elephants also have their practical uses. They are carefully scrutinized by the court astrologers for indications of what decisions should be made by the king. White elephants, with their ancient symbolic link with the clouds, are considered excellent predictors of a monsoon's arrival, a matter of considerable concern to the rice farmers of Thailand, Cambodia, and Burma. They are also weather vanes for deciding on the merit of national strategies. One Thai ruler is reported to have quietly dropped plans to invade a neighbor after learning that one of his white elephants had broken a tusk while fighting another elephant in the royal stables.

◆ ◆ ◆

From the sixteenth to the eighteenth centuries, a series of fierce "White Elephant Wars" was fought among Thailand, Cambodia, and Burma. They were filled with palace intrigues, shifting alliances, the flow of rich booty, and power struggles.

During this period one of the most prominent Thai kings, Mahachakrapat (reigned 1549–69), was elevated to the monarchy by an assassination plot in which a white elephant played an important supporting role.

Prince Mahachakrapat was the younger brother of King Prajai, who was poisoned by the Queen so she could install her commoner lover, Khun Worawongsa, on the throne. Worawongsa had few friends among the royal family and staff. According to Manich Jumsai, a member of the modern Thai royal family, the angry supporters of Mahachakrapat conceived a ploy to get Worawongsa away from his palace guards. They knew he was desperate to acquire a white elephant and thereby legitimize his hold on the throne in the eyes of the public. The nobles therefore told the usurper that a white elephant had been captured a short distance upriver from the capital of Ayutthaya. The royal family, traveling in a conspicuously ornate barge up the Chao Phya River, provided an easy target for Mahachakrapat loyalists and they were all assassinated during their procession to see the alleged sacred animal. Mahachakrapat, who had been innocently meditating in a distant monastery, discarded his saffron robe and ascended the throne.

Before Worawongsa was killed, however, King Ang Chan of Cambodia sensed weakness in the commoner king and invaded Thailand from the east. After sacking the provincial capital of Prachinburi, Ang Chan quickly retreated when he learned that Mahachakrapat had become the new king.

Mahachakrapat knew, as do most politicians, that the best way to consolidate your power is to attack a hated enemy. Mahachakrapat demanded that Ang Chan give him a white elephant as reparation for the destruction of Prachinburi, a gift that would have symbolized Cambodia's vassalage to Thailand. When Ang Chan indignantly refused, Mahachakrapat sent in the elephant tanks. But the Thais were soundly defeated in the battle and Ang Chan gloatingly called the site of the victory "Siem Reap," meaning "the defeat of Siam."

Mahachakrapat was not one to give up easily. He counterattacked in force and captured one of Ang Chan's brothers, 3,000 men, and the coveted white elephant. The new animal joined his

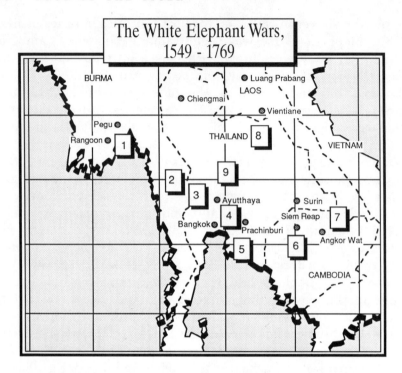

The White Elephant Wars, 1549 - 1769

Major conflicts are mentioned in the text. Boundaries indicated are modern; there were no borders in the days of the White Elephant Wars, merely spheres of influence.

1 Rangoon's fabulous Shwedagon Pagoda was greatly enriched by booty liberated from Thailand during the White Elephant Wars.

2 King Naresuan defeats Burmese Crown Prince on elephant-back in 1599, bringing decades-long pause to White Elephant Wars.

3 King Bayin Naung demands two white elephants, attacks Mahachakrapat in 1549. Queen Suriyothai is killed in battle.

4 In 1767 Burma attacks King Boromoraja, sacks Ayutthaya. Thais decide to start afresh, move capital to Bangkok.

5 In 1549, Cambodia's King Ang Chan sacks Prachinburi, withdraws when he learns Mahachakrapat has taken throne.

6 Mahachakrapat sends army to demanc white elephant from Cambodian king Ang Chan, who rejects demand and defeats Thai army at Siem Reap.

7 Immediately following defeat, Mahachakrapat sends stronger army to Angkor in 1556, defeats Ang Chan, returns with white elephant.

8 In 1763, white elephant of King Boromoraja escapes to northeast, is captured by Khun Surin.

9 King Mahachakrapat takes throne in 1549 after the usurper Worawongsa is lured out of capital by promises of his own white elephant.

stable of six other white elephants, which he had been given by elephant trappers over the years, to make Mahachakrapat the proud owner of the largest white elephant collection of any royal house in Asia.

News like that traveled fast in royal circles, and to the west King

Bayin Naung of Burma was jealous. He demanded two of the white elephants as his fair share. When the Thai king refused, the Burmese monarch retaliated by invading Thailand and sacking the capital at Ayutthaya, thereby extending Burma's boundaries to their maximum limits. The key battle in the campaign produced Thailand's most famous heroine, Queen Suriyothai. Dressed as a royal warrior, she drove her elephant in front of a Burmese general who was about to spear King Mahachakrapat, and was killed taking the blow meant for her husband. This was the first appearance of a Thai queen on the battlefield, and her bravery and sacrifice have earned her immortality in the hearts of the Thai people.

Yet while the Thais got a martyr, the Burmese got the white elephants *and* the gold to decorate Shwedagon. Over 200 years later, a white elephant was the excuse for another Burmese raid on Thailand, which changed the course of Thai history, ending a 400-year dynasty and establishing an obscure tribe of elephant catchers as the dominant rulers in northeastern Thailand for nearly 150 years.

◆ ◆ ◆

The huge fairgrounds in the provincial capital of Surin in northeastern Thailand are surrounded by food stalls with seductive aromas. Thais love good food and every celebration brings out the best recipes of the region—mud-baked chicken, barbecued baby quails, deep-fried banana slices, stir-fried noodles and vegetables, sun-dried beef, spicy pork sausages, fresh lemon-yellow mangoes eaten with sticky rice and coconut milk, fluffy sugared pancakes, and dozens of curries in shades of green, yellow, orange, and red.

But once we had stuffed ourselves sufficiently to hold us until lunchtime, we noticed another fragrance: the sweet pungency of elephants. Following our noses, we found the elephant corrals packed with dozens of pachyderms and their handlers. These were impressive men, competent and self-assured. Despite the blaring loudspeakers, milling crowds, and general confusion, their elephants were calm, confident that they were in good hands.

We followed Dr. Boonsong over to the man who was obviously in charge, a powerfully built dark-brown-skinned gentleman with specks of gray in his hair. Prasert was the *mautouw*, or master *mahout*, of the Kui tribe (called Suay by the Thai), a small ethnic group of northeast Thailand. Examining his elephant for wounds, Prasert somehow managed to look distinguished while wearing only a faded sarong. He and Dr. Boonsong were old friends from hunting trips in northern Cambodia, and he was happy to leave his elephant and chat for a while. He motioned for us to sit on bundles of sugarcane and sent one of his boys after some iced coffee laced with sweetened condensed milk.

"We Kui people originally came from Cambodia, where many elephants roamed the forests. We have always been elephant people, and our elephants helped build Angkor Wat," he told us. "But when things started to go bad in Cambodia after Angkor was abandoned over 500 years ago, some of our people moved to southern Laos and to here in northeastern Thailand."

A white elephant helped the elephant people make a name for themselves in Thailand when one escaped from the stable of King Boromoraja V (reigned 1758–67) and wandered to the northeast. The loss of a precious white elephant was a tragic omen so the monarch immediately contacted the Kui, renowned as elephant hunters, and asked them to recover the animal. Prasert explained that the royal white elephant was finally captured by a man named Surin, who was an expert at using elephant-catching magic. As a reward for his success he was given the title of "*Luang* [Lord] Surin" and awarded a district near the forests on the Cambodian border.

Nonetheless, the Burmese across Thailand's western frontier quickly heard of the white elephant's escape and sensed that this indicated a weakness in Boromoraja's defenses. They attacked the Thai capital of Ayutthaya and destroyed everything they could not carry away. Boromoraja disappeared in the confusion and was never heard of again, thereby bringing Thailand's Ayutthaya Dynasty to a close.

A mercenary general from China named Taksin replaced Boromoraja, and for the next fifteen years the Thai royal family tried to recover control of the throne. During this time the Kui maintained their loyalty to Thailand's underground royalist leaders. When the new Chakri Dynasty was finally established in Bangkok in 1782, Luang Surin was given yet more tributes to acknowledge the loyalty of his people, including the honor of having his village named after him. In the following years, the town of Surin became the capital of the province and was ruled by Kui governors until 1907, when King Chulalongkorn (the fifth Chakri king) centralized his administration and appointed governors from Bangkok.

Throughout this violent history, the Kui remained elephant men, Surin remained Thailand's capital of elephant capturing, training, and fighting, and white elephants occasionally appeared in the forests along Surin's border with Cambodia.

Prasert's young assistant came over and respectfully pointed out that it was time for the elephant rodeo to begin. We thanked Prasert for his time, and joined the throngs around the huge open parade ground. For the next two hours, Dr. Boonsong regaled us with stories of his elephant-hunting days, when vast herds still ranged across the plains; meanwhile, the Kui's real pachyderms paraded with royal regalia, reinacted famous elephant-back battles and had tugs-of-war with each other and a platoon of local Border Patrol Police. Elephants were once again showing their usefulness and versatility, this time for the edification of tourists. The brave and resourceful Kui, whose involvement with elephants has been an important force in Southeast Asian history, played elephant football with as much dignity as they could muster.

◆ ◆ ◆

Since white elephants bring prosperity to the state, Thailand's current booming economy may be due, in part, to the fact that King Bhumibol (the ninth monarch in the Chakri Dynasty) has had eleven white elephants, as many as any previous Southeast Asian king has owned; the sleepy state of Burma has just two, and devastated Kampuchea has none.

Each of the current Thai white elephants has been received with due ceremony. Of particular interest was the first female white elephant in Thai history, found in southern Thailand in early 1976. The female was therefore considered especially important and was presented to His Majesty the King with due ceremony in May 1976, on a day chosen as particularly auspicious by the court astrologers. On entering the palace grounds the elephant was showered with holy water and sand. Prime Minister Seni Pramoj made the official presentation to the King, who lit sticks of incense and paid homage to a Buddha image, while monks chanted prayers. The King climbed a platform and anointed the elephant's head with holy water. Queen Sirikit placed a garland of fragrant jasmine and colorful orchids around the animal's neck while King Bhumibol fed the white elephant two pieces of sugarcane, one inscribed with a charm inscription, the other inscribed with the holy pet's new royal name.

Eating her name carved in sugarcane, it was thought, would enable the elephant to remember it, a good test of elephant memory since one white elephant was baptized *"Phraya Sawet Sakonla Warophat Ake Udom Chate Visute Thi Mongkok Sri Sama Sakon Loma Nakanet Adisaya Sawet Iset San Komon La Phan Prom Kra Khun Paramintara Narane Soon Saima Tirat Phahana Nat Mahan Tadet Kotchera Ratana Phiset Chaloem Phop Kiet Kachon Chop Charoen Sak Phra Khak Phon Parun Vibun Sawat Akk Nakin Ratana Phra Soet Lert Faa."* (Translation: "An elephant of beautiful color; hair, nails, and eyes are white. Perfection in form, with all signs of regularity of the high family. The color of skin is that of lotus. A descendant of the angel of the Brahmins. Acquired as property by the power and glory of the King for his service. Is equal to the crystal of the highest value. Is of the highest family of elephants of all in existence. A source of power of attraction of rain. It is as rare as the purest crystal of the highest value in the world.")

◆ ◆ ◆

The western idea that a white elephant is an object which is not only valueless to its owner but is also a real burden seems to spring from an account of court life under the ancient kings of Siam. In those days of numerous concubines and a libidinous king, the story goes, there were so many offspring, nephews, and cousins vying for official state appointments that the king had to be creative to come up with sufficient titles to go around. He devised the position of Keeper of the Sacred Royal White Elephants and gave a relative a position of trust and honor by making him responsible for the care, feeding, and costuming of the pampered animals, all to be paid for out of the keeper's own purse. The keeper soon found himself penniless as a result of being forced to support huge and economically unrewarding animals which, as the sacred possessions of the king, had to have only the best of everything.

Thai historians insist that this story is apocryphal, but knowing the keen Thai sense of humor and the Asian way of getting the upper hand through a smile-clouded subterfuge, it is not unlikely that at least one Thai king had had his fun—and maintained his elephant entourage—in this way.

The British learned the cost of keeping a white elephant when they forced King Thibaw, the last Burmese king, into exile in 1885. Naturally, his white elephant (which was taken care of by thirty servants, one of whom was a minister) was exiled as well, and the

British agreed to pay for its extravagant life-style. Insensitive to its great value to the Burmese people, and unwilling to maintain what seemed an outrageous waste of Queen Victoria's treasury (after all, the animal was used to having its own palace), the British donated it to the Rangoon Zoo several months later.

◆ ◆ ◆

Although white elephants today are regarded by many sophisticated Asians with amusement tinged with condescension, they are still venerated by the common people. When a white elephant calf was born in Burma in 1958, the country's newspapers carried glorious accounts of the rare event. According to U Toke Gale, "People of all races and tribes came down from the hills—the Shans, Kachins, Karens, Chins, Kadus, and Ganans—all decked out in their colorful national dresses as if they were on their way to a religious festival. They fed the white calf with bananas, sugarcane and cooked rice, and reverently threw at her feet silver coins. . . . Some elderly people from the hills fell on their knees and gave her homage, and many were near to weeping with religious fervour." The recent ceremonies presenting Thailand's first female white elephant to His Majesty the King involved well-educated politicians (Prime Minister Seni Pramoj graduated with great distinction from Oxford) and sophisticated members of the Thai royal family, indicating that those in positions of power understand very well how important white elephants are to the common people as symbols of the monarchy and its link with Buddhism.

One insensitive Western entrepreneur attempted to capitalize on this emotional attachment of the Thai public. "Wilson's English Circus" visited Bangkok in the late nineteenth century and advertised that a real white elephant would participate in the next performance, drawing a huge crowd. According to the Norwegian traveler Carl Bock, "Two clowns came in and began jesting about the white elephant. Then in came a small Indian elephant, appearing as white as snow; not a dark spot could be seen anywhere. But the elephant left white marks on everything he touched. He was chalked all over, and when one of the clowns told the other to 'rub his nose against the elephant and he will leave his mark on you,' an ominous silence was maintained by the great mass of the people, only broken here and there by a supressed titter."

The Thais were naturally annoyed that fun was being made of an incarnated Buddha. In the usual Thai way of avoiding open criticism, they merely expressed their confident belief that Wilson would be punished for his disrespect for the Lord Buddha. Several days after the Bangkok fiasco, the elephant died at sea on a trip to Singapore. The too-clever Mr. Wilson suffered from dysentery during the voyage and died almost immediately on landing. The reputation of the true white elephant remained untarnished.

11

Mermaid Queens and Javanese Sultans

Some of the best Indonesian families claim nature spirits as ancestors.

South of Jogjakarta is the beach of Parangtritis, a sacred spot for Javanese people because *Nyai Loro Kidul*, the Goddess of the South Seas, resides thereabouts. On to this shoreline last week paraded many thousands, including representatives of the Surakarta Hadiningrat Sultanate, seated at Solo, 60 miles distant. With them came a convoy of eighteen trucks bearing 1,200 plastic bags containing the ashes of the 240-year-old palace of Solo, to be transferred to the deity's care. About 80% of the palace, a seat of high culture in Central Java, burned on the night of Jan. 31, apparently because of an electrical fault. Besides the architectural loss, priceless art and writings were destroyed. The final act, however, was considered a measure of spiritual recompense for the catastrophe. For soon after the ashes had been scattered across Indian Ocean waters—a solemn deed which had paraders on their knees in prayer—a huge wave broke on the shore. This came even as a group of dignitaries headed by Prince Hadiprabowo, representing Sri Sunan Pakubuwono XII, approached the water with offerings of food and flowers to complete the ceremony. The

breaker was taken by reverent onlookers to be a sign of the goddess's acceptance of the ashes.
(*Asiaweek*, April 19, 1985)

THE *Susuhunan* of Solo, Sri Sunan Pakubuwono XII, is the senior member of Javanese royalty, which currently consists of four rulers from two related lines. He has a Dutch education, speaks three languages (besides three different Javanese tongues), drives a Mercedes and a Toyota pickup, and traces his genealogy back 400 years to a nature goddess named Loro Kidul, the Queen of the Southern Ocean. Some close observers suggest that the burning of the Susuhunan's palace should be blamed not on the Indonesian electricity board, but on the carefree ruler's failure to properly respect the agricultural imperatives of Loro Kidul.

Loro Kidul is said to have been a beautiful, but mortal, daughter of a long-past Hindu king of Padjajaran in west Java who was transformed into a goddess of the seas. As in many such stories, Loro Kidul had a jealous, ugly stepmother. The old woman, aided by an evil wizard, cursed Loro Kidul with leprosy. The distraught and disfigured girl ran away, eventually reaching the cliffs of Java's south coast. A voice called her to come and rest among the waves. Near what is now called Nusa Kembangan she threw herself into the foaming sea and was immediately transformed back into a beautiful maiden, and became goddess of a vast and powerful underwater kingdom.

She also maintained terrestrial holdings, becoming the goddess of the active volcano Gunung Merapi ("Fire Mountain"). She divides her time between land and sea, and appears as a youthful nymph in the first half of the month and as an ugly old hag in the second half. Javanese believe that her demeanor is at times bitter and malevolent, and can only be propitiated by strict observance of complex rituals. Yet, with the fickle nature so typical of both Asian women and Asian gods, when treated properly she can also bestow great favors, such as ensuring a good catch to fishermen.

According to Soedarsono, a cousin of the Sultan of Yogyakarta and a leading authority on Javanese dance and culture, Loro Kidul "evolved from a *lelembut*, a Javanese nature spirit," that is anxious to enter people and take control of their actions. She represents both the powerful forces of the sea and the unpredictable hidden fury of volcanoes, thereby linking the underworld represented by the sea with the upper world represented by the mountains. As a goddess of the water, she is sometimes considered a mermaid queen who has clear links with the naga-kings and agricultural production. Her influence was so pervasive and her strength so awesome that she became a key player in the history of modern Java.

◆ ◆ ◆

In the late sixteenth century, shortly before the founding of the Dutch East India Company, Senopati, a historical Javanese king, is said to have gone to the southern coast of Java to meditate. He was approached by the mermaid goddess Loro Kidul, and immediately fell in love with her. They spent three romantic days and nights together during which Loro Kidul taught Senopati how to control other spirits in order to gain power over lesser men.

With this useful knowledge, Senopati conquered the other coastal principalities. According to Thomas Stamford Raffles, founder of modern Singapore and lieutenant governor of Java for a short time, Senopati was able to use Loro Kidul's guidance in a battle against the forces of the principality of Pajang. With just 800 hastily assembled, untrained troops, Senopati defeated 5,000 of Pajang's best soldiers. During the night he burned all the villages in the area and set fire to the grass to the rear of his enemy's camp, convincing them that he was retreating. Then he called on the advice of Loro Kidul, whose prophecy was so powerful, says Raffles, that Senopati fainted and fell off his elephant.

"During the succeeding night," Raffles continues, "there was a heavy thunderstorm, and on the following morning the mountain Merbabu burst with a dreadful explosion, throwing out ashes and large stones; the rivers overflowed their banks and inundated the low country, occasioning great confusion and destruction in the Pajang camp, and inducing the commander to retreat with his army forthwith to Pajang."

Coincidence or not, such a graphic demonstration of his mystical control of the elements gave Senopati, who came from an agricultural background, not from a royal line, enormous power. His "proven" liaison with Loro Kidul was awesome to both his opponents and his subjects. He subsequently made his Islamic House of Mataram supreme in Java; the royal family he founded is still the most important in Indonesia.

The mystical marriage of Senopati and Loro Kidul is essential to understanding the Javan view of nature and society. The spirit queen represents nature—the unlimited power of the ocean and sky—while the king represents the social order on earth. The union of the two elements (repeated in the legends of other Southeast Asian kingdoms) maintained the equilibrium of the cosmos and conferred great prestige on royalty well before the Mataram dynasty. Guarding the eighth-century Buddhist Kalasan temple, four miles east of Yogyakarta, are curious half-mermaid, half-elephant creatures called *makaras*. Little is known about these statues, but K. R. T. Hardjonagoro, the regent of the Susuhunan's palace in Solo, speculates that they ensure the balance of nature's elements and man's relationship to the natural powers. It is not unusual, he adds, to combine two seemingly disparate elements since "we Javanese always think in pairs of opposites—light and dark, good and evil, male and female. The makara, not surprisingly, is the opposition of land and water. We need both."

We discussed Loro Kidul with the late Lieutenant General Ali Murtopo, who fought alongside President Suharto in the revolution against the Dutch colonial government just after World War II and who was head of Indonesia's internal security force and later Minister of Information. That morning Murtopo had helped launch a major international effort to save tropical rain forests, and we watched television reports of the opening of the conference in his suite at the Hotel Bali Beach Inter-Continental. The sounds of a *gamelan* orchestra playing in the hotel's garden tinkled through the closed windows.

Murtopo explained that most Javanese believe in spirits and higher powers and, in order to make their heroes larger than life, it is not unusual to attribute to them a connection with devils, or with Loro Kidul. Just thirty years ago, President Sukarno called publicly on Loro Kidul to help him gain Irian Jaya (West New Guinea) from the Dutch. Rulers like to be associated with the mermaid queen, Murtopo told us. "Loro Kidul is legendary, a mystical creation. But everybody believes in her and always will. She is a queen who cannot die until the end of the world."

◆ ◆ ◆

One of the benefits of having Loro Kidul in one's family tree is that one can claim to be more blessed than other mortals. Senopati's grandson and successor to the Mataram throne, Sultan Agung, was able to embellish the story further, by dictating to the authors of the annals of the Mataram Regime, known as the *Babad*

Tanah Djawi. Most of the details of the story of the union between the princess/goddess Loro Kidul and Senopati, who was born a commoner, were created *after* Senopati's death in order to give Sultan Agung a royal genealogy and associate him with the ancient nature-spirit world in which most Javanese still respect. Loro Kidul gave the new royal line the legitimacy it needed to be accepted both by the people and other sultanates.

Such divine intervention has been useful to Java's rulers ever since. With the spiritual help of the Queen of the Southern Ocean, the House of Mataram prospered and produced Indonesia's most flamboyant hero, the freedom fighter Prince Diponegoro. Born in 1785, Diponegoro also was considered a direct descendant of Loro Kidul. While very much a real man, his life was clearly affected by events that have the ring of the supernatural. Witnesses claim to have seen him shot at least five times, yet on examining his body after he died in Makassar (now Ujung Pandang) in 1855, the Dutch found no scars.

The Prince, irritated by the continued presence of the Dutch (and the British under Raffles for a short while during the Napoleonic Wars), retreated to the tomb of his ancestor Sultan Agung to meditate. In a trance Diponegoro heard a woman's voice tell him that he was destined to restore Java to its original power and prestige. The woman added that he would receive a sign, a magic arrow which would protect him. When the Prince awoke there was a flash of lightning and he saw a magic arrowhead stuck in a rock, the Javanese version of Excalibur, called *Sarutana*. The voice he had heard was that of Queen Loro Kidul.

◆ ◆ ◆

Clearly, Loro Kidul is a powerful ally. Oddly enough, the Javanese sultans allowed the mermaid queen to side with the Dutch, an error of judgment which may have cost them their country. The Dutch merchants of the seventeenth century made their first landfall in west Java, the part of the island which has always been considered "the abode of the spirits." Establishing their base in what is now Jakarta, the Dutch claimed to be successors to the Hindu Padjajaran kingdom which had spawned Loro Kidul. The European annexation was not felt as a threat by the Javanese kingdoms in central Java because it occurred in westernmost Java, considered foreign territory by the Javanese because it was inhabited by Sundanese who spoke a different language and had different beliefs.

Yet the Javanese, alternatively amused and awed by the white man's presence (and appreciative of the monetary gifts the colonials offered as "homage"), had to deal with their strange new neighbors on many matters. But obviously a sultan cannot talk seriously with a commoner (and an infidel to boot). To solve the problem, Jan Pieterszoon Coen, founder of Batavia (now Jakarta), was given a royal Javanese lineage. According to the eighteenth-century Javanese historic annals, *Serat Sakondar*, the Javanese royal family declared that Coen was the son of a union between Alexander the Great's brother and a princess of Padjajaran who was considered a sister of Loro Kidul.

The Dutch were thereby given respectability and were considered kings of the spiritually important lands of West Java because they were thought to be related to Loro Kidul. "The Dutch position in West Java," says historian M. C. Ricklefs, "was thus part of a complex mythological system which assured the Sultan of Yogyakarta that the spirit forces of Java would not turn against him. By assuring other Javanese of this as well (through the medium of Loro Kidul), it contributed to the legitimisation of royal authority. And just as the Goddess had promised her aid to the House of Mataram, so it was appropriate that the Dutch, her relatives, should also be the allies of the Javanese kings." By 1677 the rulers of the House of Mataram ceded to the Dutch the entire area that comprised the ancient Padjajaran nation.

But this backfired on the innocent Javanese rulers. The Dutch soon used their west Java base, their spiritual authority (though it is not clear that they fully realized the power the Sultans had given them), and their more powerful firearms to take over all of Java and the other Indonesian islands. While the Javanese had Loro Kidul on their side, the Dutch *also* had a high-level affiliation with the goddess. The Javanese, who were stalemated and could not attack the Dutch, entered a painful 300-year colonial period, during which, according to Hardjonagoro, the Europeans tried to distance the sultans from their agricultural base by increasing the pomp and ceremony accorded the rulers, thereby encouraging the Javanese leaders to consider themselves too refined to dirty their hands by plowing the first furrow. The Dutch simultaneously took away the sultans' administrative duties, leaving the royal family with much pomp but precious little contact with their subjects.

One of the men who fought to end the colonial period in the 1940s was Sultan Hamengku Buwono IX of Yogyakarta, now the most influential of the four related Javanese rulers. He is the nineteenth monarch descended from Senopati and the thirteenth of about forty children of Hamengku Buwono VIII. In 1939, Hamengku Buwono VIII called five of his sons to his side and, without a word, named the youngest one crown prince by placing a sacred *kris* in his sash. Several days later the old Sultan died and Hamengku Buwono IX assumed the throne with the support of his brothers and uncles.

It was a tumultuous time to be sultan. War threatened in the Pacific and the power of the Dutch was waning in Indonesia since the spirit of *merdeka*—independence—was gaining force. Hamengku Buwono was a powerful leader who did not hesitate to call on Loro Kidul for help.

Like all Javanese royalty, the Sultan is Muslim, yet he pays homage to the spirit of Loro Kidul. While this might shock the more classical Muslims in other parts of the world it is all perfectly understandable to the Javanese, whose syncretic religion, although officially Islam, is actually a unique combination of mysticism and Animism with healthy doses of the flavor, if not the dogma, of Hinduism and Buddhism.

Each June 21, on the Sultan's birthday, a special ceremony takes place. The Sultan, a revered freedom-fighter and former vice president of the nation, makes the twelve-mile trek to the dangerous surf on the slate-gray southern coast of Java. At the site of Senopati's rendezvous he makes an offering to the mermaid queen that includes a full set of women's clothing and his own nail and hair clippings. Similar ceremonies are held on the slopes of Gunung Merapi, from which Loro Kidul keeps an eye on her terrestrial holdings.

◆ ◆ ◆

A visit to the southern coast will help explain the mysterious world of Loro Kidul. Frequent signs warn people not to enter the water, but every year there are bathers who do so and disappear, including, not too long ago, an eastern European ambassador. Loro Kidul clearly prefers males and is particularly anxious to acquire as servants men having the audacity to wear bathing trunks of green, her favorite color.

People disappear here with good reason. Unlike the relatively placid and shallow northern coast of the island, the coast on the south drops sharply into one of the world's deepest oceanic trenches, causing severe rip tides and carrying Loro Kidul's newly acquired male servants far from shore. It is easy to see why this natural danger impresses the local people and reinforces their reverence for **Loro Kidul**.

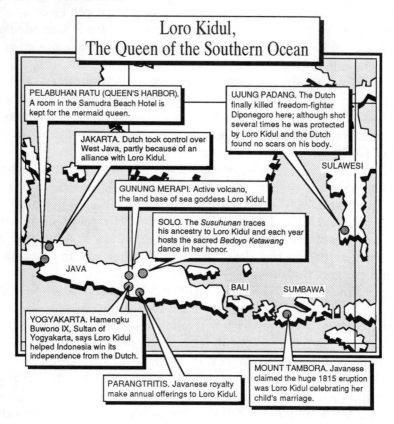

**Loro Kidul,
The Queen of the Southern Ocean**

PELABUHAN RATU (QUEEN'S HARBOR). A room in the Samudra Beach Hotel is kept for the mermaid queen.

UJUNG PADANG. The Dutch finally killed freedom-fighter Diponegoro here; although shot several times he was protected by Loro Kidul and the Dutch found no scars on his body.

JAKARTA. Dutch took control over West Java, partly because of an alliance with Loro Kidul.

SULAWESI

GUNUNG MERAPI. Active volcano, the land base of sea goddess Loro Kidul.

SOLO. The *Susuhunan* traces his ancestry to Loro Kidul and each year hosts the sacred *Bedoyo Ketawang* dance in her honor.

JAVA

BALI   SUMBAWA

YOGYAKARTA. Hamengku Buwono IX, Sultan of Yogyakarta, says Loro Kidul helped Indonesia win its independence from the Dutch.

MOUNT TAMBORA. Javanese claimed the huge 1815 eruption was Loro Kidul celebrating her child's marriage.

PARANGTRITIS. Javanese royalty make annual offerings to Loro Kidul.

Javanese believe that Loro Kidul aggressively seeks to restock her supply of men, and even today, mothers in central Java lock their sons at home during the night that the sacred dance dedicated to Loro Kidul is performed. They know that during the *Bedoyo Ketawang* dance the mermaid queen is out and about, making one of her rare terrestrial scouting trips.

We sat with Soedarsono in the family rooms of the Yogyakarta palace, filled with classical Dutch ceramic figurines, kitsch porcelain puppies, and a six-foot-tall portrait of an earlier sultan on horseback, wearing a multicolored quilt-work jacket and striking a distinctly Napoleon-like pose. We asked him what we would see when the *Bedoyo Ketawang* is performed. "The dancers in the *Bedoyo Ketawang* are dressed as brides, and undergo the same extensive preparations they would if they were getting married," Soedarsono explained as we nibbled on coconut cakes and sipped sweetened tea from German porcelain cups, part of a tea service for a hundred kept in dusty glass cabinets.

For this, the most sacred Javanese ritual performance, dancers wear dark blue, the color of protection, and the designs on their skirts, painted in gold, represent all the animals in the world—the elephant, Garuda, the naga. Their hairstyle is called "the climbing lizard."

According to one observer, "The solemnity of the moment is enhanced by the belief that Loro Kidul is invisibly present in the midst of the *Bedayo* dancers. These indeed might be the waves of Her sea at a more placid moment, with their gentle, languid undulations, floating *sampurs,* and their long trailing bridal trains." Some dancers have said they felt Loro Kidul adjusting their hands during a performance.

The *Bedoyo Ketawang* was created for Sultan Agung, who wished to immortalize the love Loro Kidul had for his ancestor, Senopati. The dance is performed every year on the date of the ascension of the Susuhunan of Solo by specially selected female relatives who recount his direct ancestral link with Loro Kidul. Nine virgins dance; the number represents the nine orifices of the body, according to Soedarsono, which relates to the "ideal goal of mankind, which is to master one's own mind, and control the human desires." The songs performed during the dance—poetically erotic with excruciatingly slow and solemn choreography—are so sacred that they have never been transcribed for fear of desecration by error. Dancers must fast before the performance and any one menstruating is not allowed even to rehearse the dance.

It is said the Sultan sometimes sees Loro Kidul quietly watching the *Bedoyo Ketawang.* At other times she makes her presence known in more dramatic fashion

"In 1966 Sultan Hamengku Buwono attended the opening of the Samudra Beach Hotel, on Java's southern coast," Hardjonagoro told us one evening during a *wayang kulit* performance.

"The night before the opening a local *lurah* (village headman) asked for an audience with the Sultan. The old man told the Prince that he had had a dream the previous night in which an old lady said she wanted her offerings. She was dressed in green.

"The Sultan thanked the stranger but explained that he would not make an offering since he was attending the hotel opening in his civilian capacity as Minister of Defence, and he wanted to separate the affairs of the state from the mystical duties of the palace. I was outside, near the pool, when the Sultan said goodnight to the well-meaning old man. Shortly after his refusal I heard the sound of a locomotive. The noise increased until it sounded like ten locomotives were coming towards the beach-front terrace where we were enjoying the hotel's hospitality. A ten-yard high tidal wave erupted from the sea, which had been calm. It washed away the hotel's buffet table and soaked all the visitors. Some trees were knocked down. Shortly thereafter the Sultan said his prayers and made the appropriate offerings, and the sea was calm once again."

The room in which Sultan Hamengku Buwono made peace with the easily irritated mermaid queen, number 319, is today kept locked and reserved only for her. Another room is kept for her near Gunung Merapi, at the leading hotel in Yogyakarta—the Ambarrukmo Palace—so she has a place to stay when she decides to visit.

◆ ◆ ◆

While Loro Kidul is a nature spirit representing the sea and volcanoes—two of nature's most powerful and frightening manifestations—her possible origin in the natural world is less glamorous. She might well be based on a dugong, the only surviving Asian species of sea cow (whose closest relative is the tropical American manatee).

Dugongs do, in fact, have some human-like attributes. For a start they look vaguely human (a bit like American President Grover Cleveland, according to one observer). Females cradle their young, which nurse at their protruding mammary glands, and the genitals of female dugongs are somewhat human-like. Dugongs communicate with each other through a series of squawks, chirps and squeals, nuzzle each other snout to snout, cough when they breathe, appear to make "kissing greetings," embrace each other with their dextrous flippers, and swim in synchronized formations.

For centuries sailors have claimed that these gentle sea mammals were women of the sea, understandable if you've been on the ocean for months without seeing anything feminine. Add to that unstable condition a bit too much *arak* at lunch and a touch of sun blindness from standing lookout during the brilliance of the day and it's easy to see how Javanese mariners might claim that they have seen Loro Kidul.

◆ ◆ ◆

Sultan Hamengku Buwono has a different perspective on his legendary ancestor. He told us that during the Indonesian fight for independence he fasted for two weeks, eating only rice and water in order to meet Loro Kidul in a vision. "I saw her, *Eyang*—I call Loro Kidul *Eyang*, grandmother—seated behind two of my nephews. She was young and pretty, as is usual in the first half of the month."

His Highness, wearing thick glasses and a long-sleeved batik shirt in his souvenir-filled Jakarta office, said that those two nephews, who were not only relatives but also close friends of his, died within the week. He then described an elaborate vision that later came true involving a search for two golden cocks and an unusual stranger. "One night during the Dutch occupation of Yogyakarta, I, and others as well who were living in the *kraton* [palace], heard soldiers moving noisily about, as if wearing armor. It is said they were the soldiers of Loro Kidul protecting the kraton. I don't know how. But we heard their drums."

This was a critical period for Indonesia, when difficult decisions were being taken about when to fight and when to negotiate. The Dutch ruled all but the 7 percent of Java which was governed, under contract, by the royal houses of Solo and Yogyakarta. Each time a sultan died, the colonial administrators would impose a new contract which successively reduced the power of the new ruler. The negotiations between Hamengku Buwono IX and the Dutch were long and difficult. According to the Sultan, the crucial moment came when Loro Kidul told him, "Give them their contract, because soon they will go home." He signed the contract, but to this day has never read it, having been reassured by Loro Kidul that the Dutch were on their way out and the contract was irrelevant. Her predictions were true: A year later, the Japanese invaded Indonesia and evicted the Dutch.

Hamengku Buwono acknowledged that while Loro Kidul may never have married Senopati, you could "spiritually, at least, trace the royal line back to her contact with Senopati." When we asked the Sultan if he really believed in Loro Kidul, he offered an oblique Javanese response: "Every year at my birthday," he responded, "people go into the sea to make offerings to her—they go in up to their necks yet nothing happens in spite of the sharks and strong currents. The genuine offerings—my fingernails and hair—are accepted by her, but the old clothes people offer her come back to shore."

Does Loro Kidul, the nature goddess who evolved into the consort of the Javanese royal family, really exist? Perhaps that question is irrelevant. She is *needed* and the Sultan of Yogyakarta accepts that need while trying to politely answer a foreigner's query about what is real and what is imagination.

"When I was four years old I was already living with a Dutch family, so my brain is in some ways a western brain," he concluded. "But many things happen which can't be explained in a logical way."

12

Messengers of the Gods

In Borneo, birds and other animals are the messengers of the gods, acting like daily horoscopes to help villagers make everyday decisions.

THE IBAN PEOPLE who dominate the lush lowland rain forests of the northern part of Borneo say that during the great flood each race fled the waters with its own writings—Europeans carried their writings in their hats, Chinese on their shoulders, and Iban slung around their waists. When they finally reached dry land, the Iban laid their writings out to dry. A flock of birds swooped down and carried away the writings, much to their horror. As a result, today the Iban have no alphabet of their own, and all the knowledge which had been collected by their ancestors is now held by the birds; this information can be recovered only by listening to the messages transmitted from the creatures of the skies who are controlled by Singalang Burong, the Iban sun-bird, their god of war and most powerful deity.

Iban live as shifting cultivators in communal longhouses. Their society is among Asia's most democratic, and women take part in most communal and family decisions. But while egalitarian, the Iban are also very competitive, and personal achievement—like the taking of enemy heads—is the prime measure of an individual's worth. The Iban realize that personal effort is necessary, but even the most diligent effort is wasted unless the gods take notice and provide guidance and advice. Omens are the prime indication that higher powers are watching.

Tuai Rumah Renang, the headman of Keranan Pinggai longhouse in Sarawak, described the importance of omens to anthropologist Clifford Sather: "When we are sent omens, it means that we are noticed by the gods. This is a thing of great importance. It is only by being noticed that we are able to excel at whatever we turn our hand to. If the gods 'see' and take an interest in us—then we are likely to become wealthy, reap large harvests year after year, and escape sickness and other misfortunes. Other people, too, will take notice and respect us. If we are not noticed by the gods, then we are 'without luck.' Nothing we do will turn out well."

Since the gods show their interest by sending omens to provide guidance, people must reciprocate by showing gratitude and respecting the omens. "This is done by acting in accordance with their indications," says Sather. "Negligence invites calamity, and in the long run gods are said to withhold their notice from those who misread or repeatedly ignore them."

Because of this belief in birds as messengers of the gods, many of the tribal peoples of Borneo today will not undertake any serious task without prior reference to the appropriate avian omens which commute between the mundane earthbound world of humans and the celestial longhouse of Singalang Burong, the bird-king. This system is both logical and helpful to the Iban, who take it even more seriously than some modern Westerners who avidly consult their daily newspaper horoscope.

The use of animal omens and oracles may have been among the first steps that early humans took toward organized religion. Animals which can communicate with humans and tell people about the future must, by definition, be blessed with supernatural powers. When people discovered that believing in supernatural messages from wildlife helped them to order their lives and gave them more confidence in an unpredictable world, people were quick to include animals in their religious beliefs.

Many of the bird beliefs in modern Borneo resemble those of classical Rome. Just as the Romans considered birds the messengers of Jupiter, so do the tribes of Borneo consider birds the intermediaries between themselves and Singalang Burong. The tribes of Borneo, like the Romans, divide their omen birds into two classes, those which give omens by singing and others which provide advice by their flight.

Singalang Burong himself, when he deigns to appear before humans, sometimes comes as a Brahminy kite, a Garuda-like bird of prey which is found along watercourses over a large range that extends throughout Borneo, east to New Guinea, and northwest to Afghanistan. As just another bird, the Brahminy kite angers villagers by stealing chickens, but when it assumes its identity as bird-god the Brahminy kite takes on much greater significance as the bringer of omens of war. Charles Hose, trying to maintain *pax Britannica* in the jungles of Sarawak before the turn of the century, once convinced a group of warlike Kenyah to make peace with an equally warlike group of Madang with the help of some lucky omens. Before departing with the Kenyah delegation, all women were sent to their dark rooms in the longhouse, and three chieftains crouched down in a rude shelter by the river to look for Brahminy kites.

"After sitting there silently for about an hour the three men suddenly became animated; one of them took in his right hand a small chick and a stick frayed by many deep cuts with a knife, and waved them repeatedly from left to right, at the same time pouring out a rapid flood of words. They had caught sight of a hawk high up and far away from them, and they were trying to persuade it to fly towards the right. Presently the hawk, a tiny speck in the sky, sailed slowly out of sight behind a hill on the right, and the men settled themselves to watch for a second hawk which must fly towards the left, and a third which must circle round and round. In the course of about half-an-hour two hawks had obligingly put in an appearance, and behaved just as it was hoped and desired that they should behave. And so this part of the business was finished."

But the group still had to slaughter pigs and chickens and anoint themselves with sacrificial blood, light special fires, and chant spells before everyone would feel satisfied that the peace mission would be successful. "For the three hawks will watch over them, and are held to have given them explicit guarantees of safety," says Hose. "And then Tama Bulen [the Kenyah chief], pretty well covered with blood, went away to wash himself. I felt as though I had just lived through a book on the Aeneid, and was about to follow Father Aeneas to the shores of Latium."

◆ ◆ ◆

Singalang Burong helps determine when you fight and when you don't. He also offers advice on other major decisions and indicates when and where you should build a new longhouse. If a Brahminy kite lands on a rooftop during construction the house will immediately be abandoned and another site must be chosen. In order to avoid this tiresome change of plans the Iban are not beyond issuing stones to small boys to ensure that such an eventuality does not arise.

As befits the chief, Singalang Burong has seven augural emissaries to handle the day-to-day affairs of terrestrial man. Like many Asians, he tries to keep things in the family—six ambassadors are his sons-in-law and one is an unmarried dependent. On entering the physical world, these seven messengers assume the outward form of a natural species, and always appear to humans in the same bird form whenever they present themselves. In recognizing this linkage, the Ibans have given each bird the same name as the deity it represents. None of them is large or particularly colorful but together they appropriately reflect the most important facets of human endeavor. The significant seven:

- White-rumped shama (Nendak, the unmarried dependent). It deals with good health, invariably providing an auspicious augury for domestic matters. In times of war it protects the life of those left behind.
- Rufous piculet (Ketupong, the most powerful of the messengers). A small woodpecker-like bird, it is the leader of the augural birds and the watchful guardian of human welfare. Like the white-rumped shama, it is commonly seen near longhouses. It is considered highly auspicious if the bird flies toward a farmer while he is sharpening his knife or resting in his field.
- Maroon woodpecker (Pangkas). It has two calls, one triumphant, the other giving an emphatic warning.
- Crested jay (Bejampong). Symbolizes swiftness and strength. The jay, together with the scarlet-rumped trogon and the woodpecker, is found along wooded trails and deals with agriculture and expeditions.

- Scarlet-rumped trogon *(Beragai)*. It foretells happiness and indicates where to find deep red earth, good for growing crops.
- Diard's trogon *(Papau* or *Kalabu)*. Its alarm call is a serious warning; it blinds enemies if its call is heard at dusk.
- Banded kingfisher *(Embuas)*. It is associated with success but a call at noon is a warning. The trogon and the banded kingfisher live in the upper levels of primary forest and are seldom seen. Their influence is subtle and sought only for important matters.

The augury provided by the birds does not indicate what a human should actually *do*, but rather encourages actions which are likely to succeed and discourages those likely to fail. To a certain extent they represent self-fulfilling prophecies. A positive augury when clearing a new field, for example, will encourage the farmer to work hard, thereby helping ensure a good crop. If, on the other hand, the augury is unfavorable, the intended activity is better abandoned until a more positive omen is seen. However, other activities are not affected—if the omen tells you to abandon setting off to war you can still go home and weed your rice field.

Most people in Borneo react to their omens with some flexibility —omens tend to be more often seen when it is convenient to see them. When an omen would be particularly inconvenient some farmers even go so far as to plug their ears with grass. "Only if the omen is conspicuous, the observer important and the occasion significant, need it be taken quite seriously," says Tom Harrisson.

In any case it is easy to understand the concept of birds as messengers. Birds have an ability people can only dream of—they can fly and are therefore close to heaven. The people of Borneo, like most of humanity, feel a need for some guidance from higher and unseen powers; they believe that the gods have chosen a natural way of revealing their wishes to people and that obeying these signs is the only way to ensure success and happiness.

Bird omens are also manipulated by purposely seeking them out, says anthropologist J. D. Freeman, "providing the Iban with the opportunity for sanctioned wishful thinking, and this, I would suggest, is a principal reason for [the omens'] popularity." In addition, the ambiguity of the message and the potential for error in interpretation provide a ready excuse when things do not turn out as predicted.

Many of the omens in daily life are neutral, but sometimes positive auguries are a matter of life and death. Before entering a battle against the Japanese invaders, an Iban warrior working with Tom Harrisson in 1944 was pleased to spot Diard's trogon (whose cry blinds the eyes of the enemy), the scarlet-rumped trogon (which ensures happiness through the taking of enemy heads and pillaging), and the crested jay (which facilitates swiftness and agility in battle). The next day the man joined in the storming of a Japanese stronghold at Song, on the Rajang River in Sarawak, attacking in the face of Japanese machine gun fire. He survived without a wound, and, as an added bonus, returned with a Japanese head and four large jars looted from the Song bazaar. This good fortune was attributed to the bird omens that made the hazardous undertaking seem auspicious. The Iban reinforce their belief in the efficacy of omens by repeating this story during longhouse parties. As the line between fact and fiction becomes hazier the importance of omens becomes stronger.

Even as the rest of the traditional culture is disintegrating through television, better river transport, and more sophisticated schools, the flying messengers continue to help people organize their lives. The seven divine messengers have been proven to carry out their tasks well. If they had not continued to serve their function they surely would not have remained such an important part of Borneo culture.

◆ ◆ ◆

The Kelabit tribe lives in a highland habitat which is different from the majestic and lush lowland rain forests of the Iban. With large areas of open grassy savannas and a more temperate climate, the upland plateau of the Kelabits receives many more migrating birds than elsewhere in Borneo, and their system of augury, which has come under severe pressure by Christian fundamentalist missionaries, has adapted to this seasonal difference.

Four avian visitors, arriving from China, Japan, and central Asia, are awaited above all, since these birds have long determined the rice-planting cycle of the Kelabits. The planting traditionally began with the arrival of the yellow wagtail, whose local name means "lots of rice," while seeding, weeding, and bundling coincide with the sighting of the brown shrike in November, the sparrow hawk in December, and the dusky thrush in January. Care must be taken not to delay planting beyond the arrival date of the yellow wagtail; otherwise the farmer will be unable to avoid another set of seed-eating immigrant birds, the munias, which arrive in hordes in March to devour any rice crops which have not yet been harvested.

These birds are more than symbols. Their arrival is determined by climatic factors that indicate, far more accurately than a fixed calendar, the change of seasons and the most appropriate time for agricultural activities. Dozens of other migratory birds also pay a visit, but the pragmatic Kelabits have found that these four are the most reliable indicators for their needs. The bountiful rice crops each year reinforce the scheduling messages carried from heaven to earth.

"In the Borneo setting," says Tom Harrisson, "it is very commonplace for wide areas to be in famine and rice crops to be very uncertain. The birds which so conspicuously fly into the Kelabit plateau from as far away as Manchuria, Alaska, Formosa, and Siberia help—or have been made to help—the [Kelabit Plateau] to be almost immune from these uncertainties."

Attempts to ignore the omen birds are made at the farmer's peril. Some young Kelabits, who had been at the top of their class at the government secondary school in Marudi, the distant district capital, were convinced by an agricultural extension worker to plant a new variety of rice which ripens long before the traditional hill-padi variety used by their fathers and grandfathers. The students convinced their skeptical parents to give it a try. The children, reasoned the elders, were far better educated than they. After all, the boys spoke English and knew mystical concepts like the periodic table of elements and the plot of *Othello.* The result? A rich crop was grown, but migrating seed-eating birds, famished after their long flight, wiped out the rice before it could be harvested. The omens clearly knew more about timing of crops than the modern young experts.

◆ ◆ ◆

While birds are the most obvious messengers in Borneo, many other species also bring messages. If gibbons are silent, this augurs the approach of a serious epidemic and precautions need to be taken. On the other hand, loud persistent gibbon cries in a drought promise rain. Gibbon calls can also be signals rather than omens— continuous calling at one spot indicates that wild pigs may be feeding on the forest floor, information that may be useful to hunters.

Other omens are downright miraculous. While on a visit to a

remote Iban village far up Sarawak's Balleh River in the troubled days just after World War II, British colonial administrator Malcolm MacDonald was told that a woman had just found a tortoise in a field which had been burned only a few days earlier. No tortoise had ever before appeared on freshly scorched ground, so the Iban regarded the event as a miracle. The tortoise was obviously a spirit and its presence was an omen of superlative good fortune for the harvest.

"The natives observed the little animal with reverence and joy," said MacDonald. "One other creature on the hillside was unprecedented. It was me. The tortoise and I were at once linked in the Ibans' minds as twin messengers from the gods, joint harbingers of glad tidings, sure pledges of agricultural fertility and prosperity for the coming year."

When MacDonald announced that it was time for him to return downstream, the Iban urged him to perform a ceremony in honor of the tortoise. He prepared a feast for the spirits, and the entire longhouse engaged in a long bout of drinking, singing, dancing, and drinking. As he staggered down to his boat, MacDonald asked the headman what he would do with the sacred tortoise. The headman replied that they would carry it up the hillside behind the farm, with dishes of food and bottles of liquor to celebrate on the exact spot where it had been found. Afterward they would cook it and eat it, to acquire in their own persons part of its divine virtue.

"Momentarily I felt shocked," says MacDonald. "Then my grief at the animal's fate was replaced by relief at my own. I remembered that a short while earlier the Ibans had regarded the tortoise and me as kindred spirits, twin messengers come to impart our special supernatural quality to the occasion. They seemed to have forgotten that I also was endowed with virtue which could presumably give strength to them. But for that lapse of memory, I reflected, I too might have ended the day's adventure in the pot."

13

The Soul
of the Tiger

In Southeast Asia, human souls sometimes transfer to animals; were-tigers help maintain order in the village.

EMIL SALIM, Indonesia's Minister of the Environment, recalls that as a child he and his friends were taught the traditional Sumatran art of self-defense, *silat minangkabau*. "Silat is based on the movements of the tiger, just as Chinese kung fu is derived from animal motions," Salim told us one evening over dinner. "We were taught that the fighting master not only had the same exquisite control over his body as the tiger did but was somehow related to the animal—the tiger was the teacher's granduncle and he couldn't harm the tiger, nor even say its name. In a sense, the man *became* the tiger."

Most urban dwellers believe that people are people and animals are animals. But the rural people of Southeast Asia, who live in daily contact with the creatures of the grassland and forest and ocean, recognize that a close spiritual tie binds wildlife with humans. While humans are different from animals in many ways, they have similar souls.

In Southeast Asia, the soul is strong, far stronger than an individual's willpower. Most living things (and, according to Animists, *everything* from lightning to waterfalls to rice to rocks) have one or more souls. "Men to whom the cries of beasts and birds seem like human language, and their actions guided as it were by human thought," wrote the nineteenth-century anthropologist E. B. Tylor, "logically enough allow the existence of souls to beasts, birds, and reptiles, as to men." This vital essence has a life force which is separate from the host body. The soul makes the difference between a living body and a dead one, and causes waking, sleep and trance, disease, and death. Souls give shape to dreams and visions.

In addition, said Tylor, "the conception of the human soul is, as to its most essential nature, continuous from the philosophy of the savage thinker to that of the modern professor of theology." The big difference is that a modern Christian theologian might attribute soulhood exclusively to humans, a spiritual elitism that most Asians find incomprehensible.

The belief in universal souls means that we are all veritable soul brothers. All creatures have ethereal and eternal souls; these souls can, and must, take refuge in a body. When one body dies, the soul can easily go to another body. It is logical therefore that people and animals can exchange souls. This interchange might occur while the human is alive and be as temporary as a bad dream, or it might happen after the human body dies and the soul chooses an animal body as its new residence.

The power of the soul is not fixed. Natural and magical processes affect it. Soul power "may be diminished by sickness, old age, and fatigue and augmented by good health and observance of one's proper station in life," according to American anthropologist Kirk Endicott. Soul power also relies on maintaining harmony with nature, by such acts as performing the appropriate agrarian rites, refusing to kill needlessly, and respecting game killed.

Belief in soul transfer (technically known as "metempsychosis") affects the behavior of people toward animals in the forest. Among the negrito pygmies of the Malay Peninsula, for example, the magnificent Rajah Brooke bird-wing butterfly (named after the swashbuckling nineteenth-century Englishman James Brooke, who became the first Raja of Sarawak) is thought to contain the soul of the great leader and must not be harmed. To laugh at any butterfly is dangerous, they believe, because some contain the quick-to-anger souls of the departed.

According to Anak Agung Gede Rai, a member of Bali's royal family of Bangli and general manager of the Hotel Bali Beach Inter-Continental, he is forbidden to eat the meat of deer, which is the family's totem. "I ate venison once, accidentally. I had to undergo a spiritual purification," he explained as we sat in his air-conditioned office overlooking the gentle waves of Sanur beach. Why the deer? we asked. "Most Balinese families have animal totems. Just look at the family temples and you're likely to see some sort of creature. In our case they say that the founder of our dynasty, back in the fourteenth century, I believe, was abandoned as a baby. An old hermit found him floating on a lotus plant. The story isn't all that different to that of Moses," he laughed. "The kindly old man fed the hungry boy the only thing he had, which was doe's milk. Perhaps the boy was actually an incarnation of the deer."

Peter Kedit, an Iban who is a curator of the Sarawak Museum, told us that his uncle's family respected a bear totem because the bear once saved an ancestor. "Even today, during special ceremonies, the shaman gets possessed by the spirit of the bear and instructs us not to eat his wild descendants."

Tigers, as dominant, fearsome, nocturnal carnivores, are the animals most commonly associated with soul transfer. In areas where man-eating is a serious problem, people commonly believe that the soul of a person eaten by a tiger becomes a soul of the tiger. Among the hill tribes of Vietnam, says Henry Baudesson (who spent years in the uplands of Indochina conducting topographical and geodetic surveys for the French colonial service), the attacks of the tiger are so frequent, ruthless, and calculated that villagers naturally ascribe them to the direct instigation and assistance of a supernatural power. In one case, a tiger which killed and ate only women was thought to be inhabited by the soul of a deceived husband. A period of marital fidelity swept through the village as a result, and all the married couples enjoyed, thanks to the tiger, a second honeymoon.

The soul of a tiger's victim is compelled to ride its back, notes Baudesson. Accordingly, hunters are careful to sprinkle a few handfuls of roasted maize around a tiger trap. When the great cat approaches, the human spirit smells the grain, is warned of the impending danger, and leaps off in time to avoid falling with the tiger into the pit.

William Baze, another French colonial, worked with a Vietnamese hunter who invariably made an offering to the spirits every time he killed a tiger which he thought might have eaten human flesh, firm in the belief that the homeless souls of the departed which had inhabited the tiger were now set free and must be appeased. "I tried hard to persuade him that he had rendered these souls a good service in liberating them and it was they who owed him a debt of gratitude," says Baze, "but he remained unconvinced. 'You never know,' he would say, with his disarming smile, 'and it is better not to risk incurring the spirits' anger.' "

Some groups are convinced that a tiger with a human soul is a friend of people and will not harm them. Among the Minangkabau, Emil Salim's ethnic group in west Sumatra, the soul of a deceased sinner transfers to a tiger. In this form, the deceased is an ally of his surviving human friends, accompanying them on trips through the forest, protecting them from danger, and helping them in difficulties.

◆ ◆ ◆

If souls leave the body and join animal bodies when the human host dies, then it makes sense that a talented individual who really worked at it could voluntarily move his or her soul into temporary residence in an animal, and thereby change his or her form (a process technically known as "transmogrification").

Shamans—individuals who use magical powers, especially trances, to communicate with the spirit world—often claim tigers as their closest associates and sometimes become tigers themselves. This man-tiger relationship stretches far back to prehistory.

Just downriver from the town of Belaga, at the longhouse of Ruman Amo, a shaman named Liwan Emang stands on a brass gong as wide as his outstretched hands and sways with the three-note melody of a *sapeh* guitar. He wears a cape of goatskin and a brightly colored Indonesian batik sarong, chants ancient Kayan poems, and puts himself into a trance in honor of the goddess Bungan, represented by the egg he holds in his hand. His voice takes on an eerie soprano pitch as he repeats the story of the religion's founding.

"I've heard that Liwan can become a leopard," explains Domian Diang, age thirty-eight, a teacher at the longhouse school. "When someone is ill he can call on the good tiger spirit [Sarawak has no tigers but the words for clouded leopard and tiger are often used interchangeably] for help." Diang explains that the shaman eats fire and blows smoke on the patient, which scares away the evil spirit. "He generally does this while alone with the sick person. I was outside the room once and heard a tiger's roar. I looked in through the cracks and thought I saw a black leopard." Diang, who comes from the Christian stronghold of the Kelabit highlands, is not only a recent convert to Bungan but also a student of Emang's in the esoteric art of communicating with the spirits. "What is the English phrase? When you go to Italy, act as the Italians."

Men wishing to become shamans must undergo an apprenticeship, just like any professionals. The shaman equivalent of a guild examination is a confrontation with a tiger which initiates the apprentice shaman into the fearful world of magical powers. The young man meditates in the forest, dances to exhaustion, and puts himself in a trance by endlessly repeating spells. When the tiger-master decides that the time is right, he appears to the shaman and bestows on him the power to communicate with the spirits.

During his trance, the shaman becomes the tiger-spirit, or were-tiger—the Asian version of the European werewolf—by casting off his rational human demeanor to enter the world of magic and receive the revelations of spirits. In the peninsular Malaysian states of Perak and Selangor, anthropologist Richard Winstedt recorded that "a magician at a séance will growl and sniff and crawl under mats and lick the naked body of a patient, his growls and movements showing that he has been transformed and so far from being possessed by his spirit helper has obtained control of it. During a séance, it is alleged, a tiger appears at least once, though experts debate whether it is the real animal or only a were-tiger."

A Malay shaman's affinity with tigers continues after his death, with his soul transferring to a tiger's body and then passing on his magical knowledge to the next apprentice shaman who seeks communion with the tiger-spirit. The corpse of a shaman was placed in a tree rather than buried, according to Winstedt, "so that he might turn into a were-tiger or so that his tiger familiar might visit him and release his soul or desert his body for that of his successor." The last shaman to be left unburied in peninsular Malaysia was placed in a tree sometime between 1870 and 1875 and was said to have become a tiger with a white patch on his shoulder. A subsequent shaman was buried, but he scratched his way out of the grave to appear as a tiger with one eye closed due to an injury caused while he was escaping his tomb.

Lieutenant Colonel A. Locke, of the colonial Malayan Civil Service, writes that the concept of were-tigers, which prey on both animals and their fellow men, is the commonest Malay superstition. According to Locke, the strength of this superstition led to the summary execution of a stranger who went to live on the outskirts of a Malayan village in tiger country in the then forested east coast. Soon after the man's arrival, a tiger began to kill both livestock and people, and suspicion fell on the newcomer, who had been noticed leaving his house at dusk to go off into the jungle, often not returning until dawn.

Some of the more enterprising men of the village built a tiger trap and baited it with a live goat. One evening the newcomer was returning to his home through the jungle when he became aware that a tiger was stalking him. There were no suitable trees he could climb, but seeing the trap he ran to it and, having entered, sprang the release so that the great door fell into place.

The man was uncomfortable but safe, since a trap that will keep a tiger in will just as effectively keep one out. At dawn the following morning the man's shouts attracted the people from the village. They gathered around the trap and gravely considered his explanation of what had happened. Instead of releasing him, however, they maintained that his presence inside the trap was proof that he was a tiger, now back in human form. They stabbed him to death with their spears, feeling no more guilt than if they had killed a man-eating tiger.

Such were-animals take numerous forms throughout the region:

• In West Java, particularly near the town of Kuningan, according to Aman Arifin, an Indonesian businessman living in cosmopolitan Jakarta, a would-be Asian Faustus might trade his soul (or the life of one of his children) in order to learn how to turn into a pig. Through the process known as *babi ngepet* or *babi jadi-jadian*, misanthropic individuals are willing to transform into the most noxious animal in the Muslim ark because they believe that a were-pig in the animal state can steal money from other villagers without being observed.

• Given the importance of elephants to the life of rural people, it is not surprising that there are tales of elephants temporarily becoming people. Anthropologist Walter Skeat tells of a villager in peninsular Malaysia who injured a crop-raiding elephant, chased it for three days, got lost, and found himself on the borders of a legendary country known to Malays as *Pak Henang*. While paying a courtesy call on the chief, the villager found that the headman's daughter was gravely injured, and the injury was exactly comparable to the injury the villager had caused the elephant. The explanation: all the inhabitants of Pak Henang are elephant-people who live there in human guise.

• In Borneo some people are said to change themselves into crocodiles. According to Charles Hose and William McDougall, who worked in Sarawak at the turn of the century, one Dayak chief was said to have been afflicted by an unpleasant skin disease. To relieve the torturous itching he bathed in the muddy river each day. But he was not alone. Villagers watching from the bank saw a large crocodile approach the old chief regularly, and, to their consternation, appear to talk with him. The number of crocodiles increased daily, and when the chief stepped from the water each afternoon villagers noticed that his skin took on the glint of crocodile skin. One day the old man simply disappeared, having, in the minds of the villagers, finally found solace for his itching skin by choosing a life in the water as a crocodile. Thus a probable case of man-eating was accepted and the kinship between man and crocodile was reinforced.

• In the Javanese *kuda lumping* dance young men go into trances and become horses, often for the edification of tourists. In a dusty clearing outside Yogyakarta, Boeyman, the cymbal player, took a break to point out that "these boys have the souls of horses in them." We watched four men in their twenties riding the Javanese version of wooden hobby horses. One was bucking, rearing, and charging off into the crowd, another was quietly being led around the courtyard by his reins, a third was galloping in circles, trying to find an exit to the paddock, the fourth was in that awkward state between reality and trance and was being administered to by the director of the dance troupe.

• Bali has many *leyaks*, people who have acquired the power to transform themselves into animals in order to cause trouble among human beings. "There is probably not a man, woman or child in Bali who could not point to several in his own village," says Walter Spies, a Dutch painter and patron of Balinese art. "He would not dare to name them for fear of incurring their anger, but he knows and can produce clear evidence of their magic practices. There is hardly anyone who has not seen a *leyak*; to us it would appear to be a domestic animal, but the abnormal speed with which a cow ran away, or something in the procedure of a white hen, would reveal it as a *leyak* to Balinese eyes."

· People in the west Sumatran region of Kerinci are widely believed by Malays to have the power of assuming at will the form of a tiger, and, according to Frank Swettenham, "in that disguise they wreak vengeance on those they wish to injure." Swettenham tells of the time that some Kerinci men sought hospitality in a Malay house; during the night a number of chickens disappeared and the chicken coop was surrounded by tiger tracks. The next day one of the visitors fell sick, and shortly after vomited chicken feathers.

Like tigers carrying a human soul, not all were-tigers are bad. If approached politely and respectfully, they can even be helpful. Ton Schilling, a Dutch colonial civil servant whose postings in rural areas of Sumatra gave him a chance to practice his pastimes of hunting and ethnography, tells of a woman who married a were-tiger and raised three sons who also had the ability to transform themselves into tigers. Schilling does not claim to have seen these men actually turn into tigers but offers interesting circumstantial evidence that the sons changed form at will and chased wild deer into his path so he could shoot them. In the most intriguing anecdote, Schilling tells of how one of the young men knew the exact location of a hunting dog, which, unknown to the hunting party, had drowned in the river and been washed ashore in a hidden hollow behind a waterfall some distance away.

Once you accept that these things happen it is not too difficult to imagine the existence of complex societies made up of were-tigers, which, according to common Sumatran belief, can be easily recognized because the human form lacks the groove in the upper lip. Walter Skeat relates that "Far away in the jungle the tiger-folk have a town of their own, where they live in houses, and act in every respect like human beings. In the town their house-posts are made of the heart of the tree-nettle, and their roofs thatched with human hair—one informant added that men's bones were their only rafters, and men's skins their house walls. There are several of these tiger-villages in the (Malay) Peninsula, the chief of them being Gunung Ledang, just as Pasummah is the chief of such localities in Sumatra."

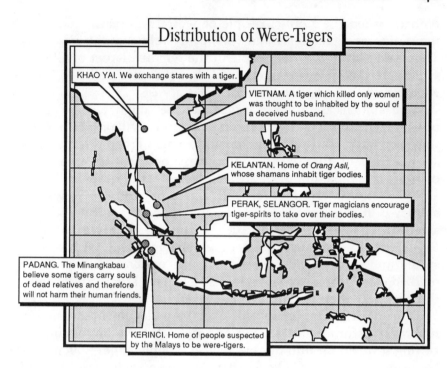

Distribution of Were-Tigers

KHAO YAI. We exchange stares with a tiger.

VIETNAM. A tiger which killed only women was thought to be inhabited by the soul of a deceived husband.

KELANTAN. Home of *Orang Asli*, whose shamans inhabit tiger bodies.

PERAK, SELANGOR. Tiger magicians encourage tiger-spirits to take over their bodies.

PADANG. The Minangkabau believe some tigers carry souls of dead relatives and therefore will not harm their human friends.

KERINCI. Home of people suspected by the Malays to be were-tigers.

Similarly, Locke tells of a settlement ruled by a tiger called Dato Paroi on Gunung Angsi in the peninsular Malaysian state of Negri Sembilan, where in human form were-tigers even study, undertake farming, and read the Koran. As elsewhere, the ancient Animist beliefs have been merged with more recent Islamic belief—were-tigers are now reading the scriptures.

◆ ◆ ◆

While most urban Indonesians, when asked, scoff at the idea that a man could turn into an animal, a certain amount of trust comes with friendship. "Yes," a friend admitted when he knew we wouldn't laugh, "I have heard about such things. When I was a boy I remember someone saying that someone in the next village could change into a pig. I myself," he stressed, offering us his pack of Dunhill cigarettes, "don't believe that kind of nonsense, of course. But there are people who do."

Where did these widespread beliefs come from, and how can they possibly survive in the face of modern science?

Trying to actually locate a were-tiger is like trying to find the end of the rainbow—it's always just over the next hill. Swettenham asked the Kerinci people of western Sumatra about their reputation as were-tigers and was firmly told that "it wasn't us." They said that it was the people in the remote district of Chenaku who were the *real* were-tigers, and that the good folks of Kerinci were afraid to visit that part of Sumatra.

Were-animals are often strangers, but they might also be dangerous and antisocial individuals in one's own village. Either way, they act like "constant watchmen," to use Freud's term, which society finds useful. T. W. Adorno explained that the individual's own unacceptable impulses are "projected" onto other individuals and groups who are then rejected. These powerful links with the spirit world provide a strong element of social control and cohesiveness: *we* would never do such a thing, though we know that *they* are capable of such threatening behavior. And, with so many spirits and souls wandering around like undercover cops in unmarked cars, people are encouraged to behave strictly according to the norms of their society.

It is unlikely that there will ever be a documented case of a human transforming into a pig or a tiger. Yet the impossibility of getting it down on film doesn't matter. People believe such things because they *want* to believe—it helps them understand unexplicable powers and events far beyond their control. And with understanding an event, or at least coining a word to describe the mystery, comes a sort of control. People can breathe easily because "if we appease the souls in the animal then the snarling tiger may leave us alone."

Religious leaders have always been particularly talented in using the tiger as a means of social control, based on the innate conservatism, xenophobic attitudes, and caution of rural villagers. *Dukuns* of Java, *halaks* among the *Orang Asli, bomohs* in Malaysia, *maw phii* in Thailand, *tadu* or *bajasa* among the Toraja of Sulawesi, *manang* among the Sea Dayak, and a host of similar shamans in other parts of Southeast Asia build on these feelings to expand their own influence, offering themselves as mediators between people and the spirit world. If every common villager had a hot-line to the spirit world, then the magicians would soon be out of business. It is clearly in the religious leaders' interest to promote strong respect for such spirits and their own ability to deal with them, a strategy not unknown among the great state religions.

Jose Furtado, who lived with the isolated Semalai tribe in Tasik Bera in peninsular Malaysia's Pahang state and who is now science adviser to the Commonwealth Secretariat and Chairman of the IUCN Commission on Ecology, told us how Nonek, a Semalai halak, consolidated his power over a large region. "He played on the susceptibility of the people," Furtado explained, "by encouraging the belief that he could transform into a tiger and was therefore in direct contact with the spirits. All the villagers, except Nonek's immediate family, were afraid to go out at night when the spirits were loose."

Anthropologists and poets have no trouble understanding why such beliefs are so strongly held. The forest contains beauty, solitude, and succor; it also is the home of deadly beasts of prey. It is not too far a step to imagine that many of the things that growl in the night could be evil or dangerous people who have assumed animal form. In the forest, under a moon, when even the smells seem to take on their own identity, things may not always be what they seem. Children, after all, have no monopoly on nightmares peopled with demons and monsters. The jungle is full of *real* nightmares which need to be personified so that they can be controlled.

To the societies that live in the forest the natural world is everything. In the forest they find plants that feed them, cure them and sometimes kill them. Daily they walk past giant trees that might contain precious honey or which might send a branch crashing down on their heads. Some animals are there to be hunted by people, provided the reverse doesn't occur. Other animals are so dangerous and unpredictable that they are best left alone; therefore, ways have been found to control them, or at least appease them.

Jose Furtado suggested that this kind of belief system provided a psychological defense against uncertainties. Reincarnation, the assumption that you might come back as a tiger or a squirrel yourself, reinforces the idea that you're part of a complex system, not something separate and apart from nature.

"These people face calamities and accidents in the forest," said Furtado. "Such hazards generate the logical response to venerate nature because nature holds so much—it provides a livelihood and a death knell. Only by making yourself an integral part of it and giving the whole a spiritual dimension can you receive satisfaction."

◆ ◆ ◆

We spent a lot of time walking through forests filled with tigers, and every time we found a tiger track, dropping, or fresh scratch mark, excitement tinged with trepidation spurred us on to try for a glimpse of the rare animal. We are certain that tigers, which stalk their prey silently, almost invisibly, saw us far more often than we saw them.

Late one afternoon in the darkening green forest of Thailand's Khao Yai National Park, we were returning to an observation tower where Dr. Boonsong was expecting us for an evening of elephant watching. As we crossed over a small ridge, we froze. A tiger was walking in our direction some fifty feet away. The tiger raised his head and looked at us for what felt like a long time. It seemed that he was deciding whether to attack the two-legged intruders. He gave a short, soft growl, calmly turned and sauntered away through the brush, leaving our path clear. We sat down to let the adrenalin in our veins take its course while we savored the memory of the tiger who meant us no harm.

14

Blood Sports

Head-hunting, once the most popular participatory sport in traditional Southeast Asia, has been replaced by spectator sports involving animal gladiators.

IT'S SURPRISING how much leisure time men have in most of the farming societies in Southeast Asia. True enough, periods of land clearing and harvesting require everybody to pitch in and work the twelve hours from dawn to dusk that never varies near the equator. But aside from these major bursts of cooperative energy that involve both sexes, most of the day-to-day chores, particularly among the hill tribes, are done by the women.

Letting the women do the work might seem like a good deal for the men, but it has a psychological price. In tropical forests, the luxuriant vegetation dominates, with mammals and birds more often heard than seen. There is no distant clean horizon to provide a feeling of space, and the tangled trunks and hidden dangers discourage solitary adventure. By contrast, as Joseph Campbell points

out, "the village compound is relatively stable, earthbound, nour-
ished on plant food gathered or cultivated mainly by women, and
the male psyche is consequently in bad case. For even the primary
psychological task for the young male of achieving separation from
dependency on the mother is hardly possible in a world where all
the essential work is being attended to, on every hand, by completely efficient females."

Although the men do the hunting, they naturally are prone to
feel inadequate in such a setting, and need to prove themselves
valuable to the women. Throughout tropical Asia, a major means
of proving one's manhood has been through something men do far
better than women: head-hunting, the ultimate blood sport.

In his major work on human sacrifice, British anthropologist
Nigel Davies found that head-hunting was almost universal in
Southeast Asia. "The cult of the head is both the most primitive
and the most enduring form of sacrifice; it was practiced in 20,000
B.C., if not before, and survived into the 1970s. However," Davies
concluded, "while heads were everywhere sought, the benefits
they bestowed differed widely from place to place. Among certain
peoples they served to keep the cosmos in being, while others desired them merely as a tonic for their warriors." A few examples:

• Among the Katu of South Vietnam there are several forms of
  socially approved homicide, when, through rather obscure signs,
  spirits have demanded fresh human blood. A raid is organized
  on a distant village and a head, preferably of a high-ranking
  individual, is taken back home. "When the raiding party return
  to their village," says American anthropologist Gerald Hickey,
  "the head is placed in a special hut that is entered only when the
  villagers need the help of the spirits associated with the heads.
  After the blood is offered on the first day, the killer and his
  raiding party retreat to the men's house where they remain for a
  month, during which it is taboo for them to communicate with
  anyone or to bathe."
• Among the Ilongot of the Philippines, who live in the rugged
  mountains just thirty miles north of Manila, head-hunting lasted
  until the early 1970s. Heads were taken in response to the various crises of life but were immediately thrown away, thereby
  symbolically jettisoning the grudge an insult had created, grief
  over a death in the family, or the increasing pressure from peers
  to take a head. According to anthropologist Renato Rosaldo, a

young Ilongot man usually hoped to take a head before marriage, thereby gaining the admiration of his fiancée and respect
from her father and brothers. Ilongot head-hunting sometimes
resulted from carefully planned ambushes and other times "from
the opportunistic deceptions of feigned friendship in which, for
example, a man can behead his companion on the trail, or his
host or guest while inside a house," says Rosaldo.

· On Indonesia's Lesser Sunda islands, particularly Sumba and
Sumbawa, ceremonial trees decorated with human skulls used to
be found in front of chief's dwellings, demonstrating the prowess of the leaders and their capacity to lead. Even today, the
skull-tree motif, *phon andung*, is common on the textiles of these
islands.

· The Marind Anim of southern Irian Jaya have a different perspective on head-hunting. According to Lee Khoon Choy, former Singapore ambassador to Indonesia, "the prime motive in
organizing a head-hunting expedition is to gather names for
their children when the supply of names has been exhausted."
Every child is named after a victim who has been beheaded, so a
victim is asked to carefully pronounce his name before having
his head lopped off. According to Lee, "Some renowned warriors
have names saved up like a name bank; sometimes they give
them away to relatives as presents."

How did such a widespread and violent custom develop? Joseph
Campbell suggests that the common sight of rotting vegetation
giving rise to new shoots in the tropical forest "seems to have
inspired a mythology of death as the giver of life, whence the
hideous idea followed that the way to increase life is to increase
death. The result has been, for millenniums, a general rage of sacrifice through the tropics; brutal human as well as animal sacrifices
. . . from whose buried parts then arose the food plants by which
the lives of the people are sustained."

In catering to both material and spiritual needs, traditional society needed to emphasize the importance of this cyclical continuity
of life. Once you accept that plants and animals have souls which
may be reincarnated, and that soul power can be transferred, the
importance of taking a head takes on a meaning totally different
from murder. As Nigel Davies puts it, "Death loses its sting when
the departed comes straight back to this earth and the end of a life
marks the beginning of another."

The Dayak of Borneo, possibly the best-known headhunters in the region, carried the practice to extremes. Any major event might disturb the cosmic order in unpredictable ways and "to restore its balance, to ward off evil, and to purify the tribe," says Davies, "human blood was essential, whether from a ritual sacrifice or a captured head. Skulls, therefore, did not merely confer physical strength as in some other lands; they were vital for the ordering of the universe, shaken by any evil done; such evil was washed away by the taking of a head. Even the use of heads as wedding gifts made sure that brides would be fertile and the race survive."

Head-hunting was sanctified by a colorful myth, recounted by Edwin Gomes. Singalang Burong, the Dayak god of war, was invited to attend a great terrestrial festival. But Singalang Burong declared that, before the feast could begin, he must call his daughters and sons-in-law from the jungle. One spoiled daughter, however, flatly refused to come unless she was given a particularly precious ornament. This ornament turned out to be nothing less than a human head. This sister of Salome got her trophy and the feast began.

The legend underlines the role of the Dayak women as prime movers in the taking of heads. "I have often been told by Dayaks," says Gomes, "that the reason why the young men are so anxious to bring home a human head is because the women have so decided a preference for a man who has been able to give proof of his bravery by killing one of the enemy."

Naturally, the Dutch colonial administrators and British rajahs who controlled what is now Indonesian Kalimantan and Malaysian Sarawak, respectively, could not permit such "barbaric" behavior in their sovereign territories—they wanted to keep the privilege of violence firmly in their own hands. After a long struggle early in this century they were finally able to stamp out head-hunting among the Dayak. But while they may have stopped the *action* of head-hunting they could not extinguish the underlying *desire*. Men need a rite of passage to make the transition from adolescent to adult. The gods need human heads to be reassured that people are sincere. "Where head-hunting has been pretty well put down by the sultan," says J. G. Frazer, "the people complain of great calamities (bad harvests, epidemics, etc.) experienced in the last few years, and trace these calamities to the discontent of the spirits at not receiving human sacrifices any more."

But the rules have changed and it is becoming more difficult to prove one's manhood or to appease the gods with blood. Head-hunting was such an important unifying force in the community that it was a Southeast Asian custom for over 20,000 years. What socially sanctioned activity could replace it?

Anthropologist V. T. King suggests that the institution of traveling in search of work and prestige has more than compensated for the cessation of head-hunting. Young would-be warriors in Sarawak travel to the cities, where they get fancy jobs and wear smart clothes to impress the ladies. Peter Kedit, a curator of the Sarawak Museum, told us how *berjalai,* a warrior's journey, has evolved. "In the old days the trophy was a head, now it might be a television set or an outboard engine. Any particularly unusual, strange-looking object could also work, provided it comes with a long story and some cash. I know a guy who returned to his longhouse with a ten-gallon hat he had exchanged with a Texan while they both worked in the Middle East. He even had a special tattoo favored by new-generation headhunters—it read 'Saudi.' "

But, while the Dayak gave up head-hunting a generation ago, most other Southeast Asian cultures hung up their swords over a century ago, usually after a few generations of Christian or Islamic dogma had been banged into their subconscious. So the men of Java, Bali, and the Philippines turned from participating in blood sports to watching them. They get their surge of masculine adrenalin when the home team wipes out the opposition in a bloody contest.

Name the blood sport and chances are that someone in Southeast Asia is setting up a match. More often than not, these contests pit animals against animals. Rams knock heads with other equally obdurate rams, horses fight other horses, wild pigs fend off dogs—even crickets, beetles, and fish are forced to become gladiators.

At first thought it might seem that the west Javan sport of *adu domba,* or ram fighting, is justified by the selection of a stronger breed of barnyard animal. But that is only part of the story, since these popular ram fights originated several generations ago as part of a renegade religious ritual. A radical sect of Muslim leaders (whose unorthodox beliefs would be severely criticized today by moderate Indonesian Moslems) in the Tasikmalaya area of West Java used the *adu domba* to celebrate *Gerebeg Maulud,* the anniversary of the birth of the Prophet Mohammed. The spirits *(onom)* which the people worshiped were unusually aggressive and demanded a sacrifice of blood and violence before coming down from their celestial resting place to join the festivities. Since human sacrifices were no longer permitted, the ram fights were a logical way of appeasing the spirits' insistence on a blood sacrifice. They also added a bit of entertainment for the mortals, since the fights, which lasted hours, were to the death.

Today it's "just for fun," asserts Mr. Hudori, a member of POR-SETDO, the Indonesian acronym for Organization for the Sporting Art of Fighting Rams. The sport is now being promoted as a pleasant way for tourists to spend a Sunday morning. Visitors can mingle in the crowd as old Sundanese men, often as hyper as the rams they own, lead their animals into the ring. The men tweak the sheep's testicles—the village equivalent of a pep talk—and step aside. Alone now, the animals slowly backstep, keeping a distrustful eye on each other. They retreat, almost into the crowd. Following an inner cue they flash toward each other on a collision course. Skulls crack, louder than you expect, sometimes with such force that one ram catapults over the other, pivoting on the front of his head. Are these beasts so insensitive they don't feel the pain? Their scrambled brains are ruled by instinct, not logic, and they scurry to their feet, slowly backpedaling once again, ready for another crash, and another, until one of them decides he's had enough or his owner throws in the towel.

During the old days the defeated ram was venerated, and when he died a (usually) natural death, was buried with great ceremony. Today, if a sheep has a cerebral hemorrhage, its body is barbecued and shared with the hungry fans who stick around for the post-game wrap-up.

◆ ◆ ◆

A couple of dozen farmers have their sticks raised while another six hold ropes restraining a pair of 650-pound bulls. Like the farmers, the nervous jockey perched on a simple plow between the two snorting farm animals is watching for the fall of the red flag and the start of a race that might make him a hero if he wins, or scrambled jockey if the bulls charge into the wooden grandstands.

They take their bull racing seriously on the Indonesian island of Madura. The sport combines elements of a circus, a rodeo, and a county fair as two pairs of cream-colored bulls race for the glory of their handlers by streaking down a grass infield.

This unique sport, called *karapan sapi*, reportedly started years ago when Madurese farmers forced their plowing teams to work faster and faster in order to barely make a living from the parched and rocky terrain. What began as agricultural necessity developed into a major sport with, in addition to the thrill of victory, huge financial rewards. A fast bull is also a strong bull, so the stud value of an animal increases with each trip to the winner's circle. A pair of champions can be worth $2,500 on a dry, rocky island where the per capita income is less than $120.

Getting a pair of big bulls ready to race is a serious investment. Doting owners often spend over $250 a season, feeding their charges medicinal herbs, raw eggs, coffee, green bananas, and Guinness Stout. It is not surprising that this is the same fodder consumed by Indonesian men in search of increased virility, for this is very much a man's sport.

Some bulls blithely wear Chinese tapestries, others sport parasols to keep the sun from weakening their spirits. Some parade with knitted skullcaps, while several display golden horn covers and wooden carvings of the Indonesian national crest. They're followed by bull fans, fervent and serious gentlemen of the village out to demonstrate their support for the home team. Wearing round black *songkok* caps and green silk jackets, these fans wave sticks and form impromptu bands with drums, congas, snake-charmer flutes, tambourines, and minicymbals.

It takes at least three strong farmers to hold the nose ropes while the nervous animals are disrobed of their elaborate decorations and the harrow and harness are strapped on. A prerace tour behind the stands reveals loyal supporters rubbing chili on the hindquarters and genitals of their favorite bulls, massaging wintergreen-like medicated oil into their eyes, and occasionally sticking a safety pin through each ear for good measure. As each race is called, the crowd of handlers moves into place, more now required to hold the jumpy, sweating animals in place. Dozens of men hold sticks high, waiting for the red flag to drop so that they can whip their favorites toward victory.

The signal falls, the beaters beat, and the bulls take off down the grass infield. Jockeys hang on for dear life, their legs wrapped around the plow, leaving their arms free. They're not racing just for the $5.00 worth of sarongs that the district government is giving away. Like the age-old head-hunting expeditions, this is a test of their manhood and the prestige of their village is at stake.

The victory is often not only to the swiftest but to the straightest. The race is a straight sprint, but many bulls run a thundering zigzag course instead, shearing off into the stands on occasion, in spite of the whipping given by the jockey jabbing their hindquarters with a short wooden stick studded with nails. If the bulls do manage to run straight, they will have covered the 130-yard course in under eleven seconds, faster than the fastest human, sending them straight into a crowd of teenagers who stand just over the finish line in their own macho game reminiscent of Pamplona, trying to figure out which way to dodge as the bulls thunder toward them.

◆ ◆ ◆

Bull stories have been mentioned in social history since the cavemen first painted toro effigies on the wall. Five centuries before the Republicans and Democrats of America took the elephant and donkey as their mascots, the Minangkabau ethnic group of west Sumatra, whose name means "victory of the buffalo," made one of the shrewdest strategic moves since Odysseus devised the Trojan horse. The Minangkabau were able to retain their independence while inflicting a painful lesson on the more powerful, but less imaginative, Javanese invaders.

"Surrender or be killed," the confident Javanese general is said to have told the Sumatrans.

"Why should we fight each other?" replied the elders of Alam, as Minangkabau was then called. "Let's find a better way."

"Very well. What do you suggest?"

"Let each of us bring a buffalo to fight our battle. If your buffalo wins we shall surrender and become your vassals. If our buffalo wins then return to Java and bother us no more."

"Agreed!" boomed the confident general, who returned to Java to get the largest, fiercest, most terrifying bull buffalo he could find.

The fight was to be held on the village square in the west Sumatran town of Padang. The Javanese proudly marched in with their prize bull, which stood almost six feet at the shoulder. The elders of Alam also entered the arena with a buffalo. But the crowd groaned with despair and would have laughed at the stupidity of their leaders had they not been terrified at the now certain outcome which surely would lead to slavery.

The Sumatran generals had walked into the arena with a suckling buffalo calf.

"Let the battle begin," the disdainful Javanese cried.

The Sumatrans were not as foolish as they might have appeared. Their tiny calf had not been fed for two days and it immediately headed straight for the giant bull, thinking the big buffalo must be its mother. The bull, of course, had no fear of the calf and stood in place. To the tips of the calf's horns the Sumatrans had attached nine sharp pieces of iron. As the calf reached the bull the youngster pressed its nose into the groin of the big buffalo, and, while it vainly attempted to suckle, the innocent calf ripped out the guts of the Javanese bull.

The Javan soldiers stopped laughing. They had lost the battle. But the people of Alam would not be quieted. Through the night they shouted their new name: "Minangkabau! Minangkabau! Our buffalo has won!"

◆ ◆ ◆

The ultimate in redirected violence may well be cockfighting, popular throughout the region but particularly important on the Indonesian island of Bali and in the Philippines, where men are men (at least when out of earshot of their women). In both the Balinese language and Tagalog, the Malay-based lingua franca of the Philippines, the word for rooster has exactly the same double meaning as it has in English, and people make similar locker room jokes about the animal/appendage.

But there is far more to cockfighting than lightly camouflaged sexual innuendo. When two roosters—who have been carefully massaged and bathed, fed specially selected grain, and had red pepper shoved down their throats—finally go at it, they are spilling blood in a centuries-old ritual. On the most basic level the sport pits one man (or village) against another in a simple test of strength —my rooster can beat yours. But in Bali cockfights are major social events that bring together, as anthropologist Clifford Geertz notes, "themes of animal savagery, male narcissism, opponent gambling, status rivalry, mass excitement, and blood sacrifice. . . . In the cockfight, man and beast, good and evil, ego and id, the creative power of aroused masculinity and the destructive power of loosened animality fuse in a bloody drama of hatred, cruelty, violence, and death. It is little wonder that when, as is the invariable rule, the owner of the winning cock takes the carcass of the loser— which is sometimes torn limb from limb by its enraged owner— home to eat, he does so with a mixture of social embarrassment, moral satisfaction, aesthetic disgust, and cannibal joy."

These fights would never be *directly* indulged in by a Balinese, since he abhors above all else the thought that a man might actually behave like an animal (for this reason infants are not allowed to crawl on the floor lest they develop animal ways). The blood from a wounded cock helps purify the earth and pacify the spirits, yet the temple guardians can rightly say that *they* had no part in such a base exercise as an animal sacrifice.

This is ritualized violence, with many of the behavior patterns and colorful characters one might find at a prizefight. For a start, one of the rigors of cock "training" is that the birds lead celibate lives. They are carefully matched against opponents of roughly equal size and ferocity. Their 2.5-inch-long spurs, which can be sharpened only during eclipses and when the moon is dark, are affixed to the birds' ankles by experts, whose fee is the spur-legs of the defeated rooster. An experienced trainer is in the corner to tend to between-round injuries. There is an official timekeeper and an umpire whose decisions are never questioned. More-or-less official odds are set, the betting is heavy, and the crowd is out for blood. In the Catholic Philippines, where cockfighting is the unofficial national sport, a central bookmaker called *kristo* takes center stage before each event. With arms outstretched he may take as many as 100 bets for each fight and not write down a single one, while hundreds of agitated spectators make their own side bets, screaming across the special government-built arenas, "*Sa Pula*," the red, or "*Sa Puti*," the white. Cockfighting is such a distinctly male activity that women generally remain on the sidelines, selling food and ruefully accepting the likelihood that their husbands may come home without a peso in their pockets.

Although cockfighting has been banned by government decree in many parts of Southeast Asia, it is hard to close a gambling den. The men want and need to participate in the rituals of the fight, which remind them, at least symbolically, of the times when a real man came home with blood on his hands, not motor oil or suntan lotion.

This is particularly the case with young men who have been well educated but who are unemployed, living between two societies. Prize fighting cocks may be their badges of success. Jimmy Garing Usit, age twenty, from the Iban longhouse of Rumah Engkang just outside the town of Kapit, proudly showed us Manok, his prized red fighting cock. "A good *biring* [fighting cock] can win $500 in a few weeks," Jimmy explained. "This one? Not bad, lah," he continued in excellent Malaysian English. "I've won $100 with him. I could sell him for twice that amount. The best fighting cocks are imported from Texas, you know. This one is one-quarter American."

Journalist Brian Stoddart suggests that the cockfight is one of the most significant means of protecting Balinese social institutions against the ravages of an international tourist economy. "Even if the tourist network widens across the island and creates even more dependents," he says, "the cock-fight, and similar cultural weapons, will ensure the continuance of what are essentially two cultures: the real and the superficial. Even while the tourist relaxes on Sanur Beach, buying a sea turtle shell or a postcard, the real Bali is still just a few hundred yards and years away, crushed in around a small square watching two fighting cocks restate an ageless tradition."

◆ ◆ ◆

In Borneo, where many young men have fathers who helped make this island the decapitation capital of the world, one aspect of the head-hunting ritual lives on.

We had been sitting in an open boat all day, paddling slowly up a tributary of Sarawak's mighty Rajang River on the way to an isolated longhouse school we had long promised to visit. After several hours the unending spectacle of dense riverine forest became repetitious. We had headaches and longed for some shade and a cold drink. We arrived at the Iban longhouse just before sunset. Before we could bathe or change clothes we were led up to the longhouse along the slippery notched log that the Iban sardonically call a ladder.

We were unexpectedly honored guests at a wedding, and while waiting for the ceremony to begin we were offered refreshment. Warm Gold Harp beer. *Tuak* rice wine. Dog's Head stout. Martell brandy. Distilled *arak* rice liquor. Then seconds, and thirds. The bride was sixteen, covered with jewelry made from silver dollars issued during the British colonial period. She was dressed in her finest red sarong and her best bra, a no-nonsense super-sturdy model built for years of dependable service.

After a dinner that was heavy on roast pork fat and tinned cuttlefish, with fourths, fifths, and sixths on liquid refreshment, the dancing started. We were reluctant stars. The girls wrapped capes of clouded leopard skin and hornbill feathers around our shoulders (the next morning we saw that the capes were carefully placed on wooden suit-hangers and kept free from dust by a plastic bag from the Federal Hotel, one of the most luxurious in distant Kuala Lumpur), tied on headdresses of woven rattan and hornbill feathers, handed us razor-sharp *parangs,* and let us loose to imitate the graceful movements of the Iban men who had previously performed the ritual dance of the headhunters. The music was at times a live guitar-like *sapeh,* at other moments tape recordings of the Beatles and Skeeter Davis. The split-bamboo porch swayed and cracked underfoot. Pigs squealed below as we stalked the enemy, crept up behind him, and in a flash of masculine courage lopped off his head to bring back as a souvenir to the impressed young ladies. They giggled. They howled.

We felt good to be involved in what British colonial administrator Malcolm MacDonald called "the noblest artistic achievement of the Bornean tribes. [Dancing] is a proper pastime for red-blooded he-men, true warriors," he wrote. "Good dancers are held in esteem, and they win the admiration of fans just as Hollywood film stars do in wider and often less discriminating circles." We cried our final war cry, swooped our final swoop and sat back, exhausted. We didn't give the girls a real hunted head, so they didn't really sleep with us as custom dictates. Instead they gave us more arak, served with what we were confident were admiring glances.

15

Monkeys in the Rafters

On the isolated Indonesian island of Siberut, modern civilization plays havoc with hunting practices that always left something for a rainy day.

JUST GETTING TO SIBERUT was an act of faith. Lying sixty miles off the west coast of Sumatra, the Bali-sized island is so far off the beaten track that the only transport is by the occasional trading boat from the busy mainland port of Padang. It took us several hours to find a captain who was going that way to pick up a cargo of rattan and copra, and to convince him that a few passengers sitting on the deck wouldn't sink his thirty-foot diesel tub.

Siberut just may be the world's most zoologically interesting island of its size—smaller than Florida's Everglades National Park or the Caribbean island of Trinidad. Separated by a deep oceanic trench from the Sumatran mainland for half a million years, Siberut's isolation from the mainstream of evolution has allowed no fewer than four species of primates to develop independently of their mainland brethren. No other island of its size has *any* endemic primates, and Borneo—100 times the size of Siberut—only equals Siberut's four endemic species. Siberut's primates are:

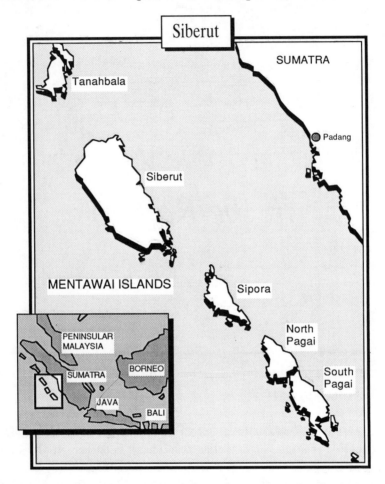

- The *bilou* or Kloss gibbon. Of the nine species of gibbons, this is the only one that lives on small islands. Its particularly melodious call seems to have been ancestral to all other gibbon calls. Like other gibbons, it lives in permanently mated family groups which defend a territory.
- The *joja* or Mentawai langur. The only monkey in the eastern hemisphere which lives in permanent pairs, the joja has a social life quite different from the other fifteen species of leaf monkey, all of which live in harems of one male and several females.

- The *simakobu* or pig-tailed langur. So strange that it is usually placed in a genus all its own, the pig-tailed langur differs considerably from its closest relative, the long-nosed proboscis monkey found on Borneo 600 miles away. The simakobu has a short snub nose, a pig-like tail, and two forms of color (some are dark gray, some are golden); it lives in two different social structures (some form pairs, some form harems).
- The *bokkoi* or Mentawai macaque. A member of the very widespread macaque genus, which ranges from Gibraltar to Bali, the bokkoi is most closely related to the larger pig-tailed macaque of the mountains of Sumatra. This is a strange relationship because the macaque usually found on small islands is the long-tailed macaque which is widely used in the medical research trade. The bokkoi is the most colorful of the macaques and is often thought to represent the first macaque to arrive in Indonesia.

The Siberut fauna includes far more than just monkeys—there are also four species of squirrel, a small owl and a snake which are found nowhere else. And many of the birds found on Sumatra haven't made it to Siberut; with pheasants, woodpeckers, barbets, and babblers missing, other birds have filled the gaps.

But perhaps even more interesting than the primates are the indigenous people, who represent an archaic tradition which was common to much of the archipelago 10,000 years ago when agriculture was just developing. When first contacted by Europeans less than 200 years ago, the people had no tobacco, alcohol, betel nut (the favorite chew of many Asians), villages, pottery, chiefs, crafts specialists, metal, rice or other food grains, or woven cloth, and only recently have they taken on some of these trappings of modern society. The protein they need still comes from fishing, pig-raising and hunting the primates and other animals of the forest, while most of the calories are still provided by sago and taro—bland high-carbohydrate staples that grow in swamps and are considered food for savages by city dwellers, yet yield more calories per unit of farmer effort than rice. Their simple dibble-stick shifting agriculture requires that only small patches of forest of less than an acre be cleared, but not burned—quite a different approach from most other tropical shifting agriculture systems in which fire plays a vital part. On Siberut, the fields merge with the forest, causing much less disruption than most other agricultural systems.

In spite of considerable pressures, this traditional economy provides a comfortable living for the people. It is also ecologically sound because spirits helped restrain the people from taking too much out of the forest. Modern conservationists call this "sustainable utilization." The people of Siberut, if they ever thought to put a name to it, probably call it "making sure you've got something to eat tomorrow by not being greedy today."

◆ ◆ ◆

As the sun goes down, the passengers lose sight of Sumatra and try to sleep on the rolling deck, waking with each rain squall and then, exhausted, slipping into an uneasy sleep filled with dreams of the sharks lurking alongside hoping for another ship to go down. Every time the "put-put-put" of the motor skips one of its "puts," hearts skip a beat—if you drift past Siberut there is only open sea between you and the rocky shores of Madagascar, a trip deliberately made six hundred years ago by the hardy Austronesian sailors who first settled that subcontinent off the coast of Africa.

The captain is descended from many generations of seafarers, including more than a few pirates, and he knows the west Sumatran waters well. His compass holds true, and dawn breaks on a low, green island on the horizon. The mate pulls in the fishing line which he threw among a flock of squawking terns, quickly fillets the twenty-inch mackerel that went for the aluminium foil bait, and fries up breakfast. Some of the passengers even keep it down.

After what felt like a hazardous trip, landfall on Siberut is disappointing. The island is mostly mud, with few rocks and only some low hills sticking their heads above the swamps.

One thing Siberut does have is an abundance of navigable streams, which means that most local transportation is by small dugout canoe, quite a relief from the noise and fumes of the diesel trading boat. But while internal-island transport is relatively easy, people do not casually drop in on their neighbors for a monkey barbecue. Each of the fifteen river basins of Siberut has its own group of people, each with a local dialect and a distinct suspicion of its neighbors. Head-hunting was a common pastime until the Dutch colonial government, reflecting the same moral principles as British colonials in Sarawak, put an end to the custom.

Siberut's neighboring islands have already lost most of their forests and their traditional culture. But Siberut still has enough forests to justify an international conservation program to save its wildlife, and some of Siberut's remote valleys still harbor people living the sort of Neolithic life that once was common on other Indonesian islands.

We poled our way upstream for most of the day, hopping out to drag the canoe over sandbars, and finally arrived at a large longhouse far upriver. As we threw our rucksacks on the floor, we noticed the long string of human-like skulls, decorated with flowers, hanging from the ceiling. We asked Ama'n Djenga Kerei, a local hunter we had hired because of his ability to speak Indonesian—a rare talent among the rural people of Siberut—what they were. "Monkey skulls, *tuan*," he answered. "The spirits of the monkeys live in them, so we try to keep the skulls with their friends so that the spirits of wild monkeys will want to live here too. It makes them easier to hunt."

Hunting is a major social activity for the men of Siberut. While they hunt almost everything except snakes and crocodiles (which are taboo), the primates, pigs, and deer are particularly sought.

A hunter stalks his game with a bow and arrows tipped with sharpened palm leaf stems; the arrows are painted just below the tip with a nerve poison made from a mixture of ground root from *Derris elliptica* (commonly put in rivers to poison fish and adapted by western agriculturalists as a natural pesticide) and bark from *Antiaris toxicaria*, two of the standard plant-based poisons used throughout Southeast Asia. But the Siberut hunter adds another ingredient: the tiny green chili pepper. Spicy enough to bring tears to even the hardened curry-eater's eyes, the chili increases local circulation and accelerates the action of the poison.

Hunting is not undertaken lightly. Preparation involves intense rituals in which the hunter makes offerings to the spirits of the animals he hopes to kill. We asked Reimar Schefold, a Swiss anthropologist who has spent many years among the Sakkudei clan in one of the most pristine areas of Siberut, about the spirits in the monkey skulls.

"It's not only monkeys that have spirits," Reimar explained. "Everything from people to pigs, rocks to weather, has its own spirit which is quite separate from its 'host' and is free to wander as it wishes. That's why you see that everybody has a different pattern of tattoos—they want to make sure that their spirit can recognize the right body when it comes back from its nightly travels.

"These spirits are in constant harmonious contact with each other, bringing an internal harmony to the environment. But man's activities constantly threaten to disturb this harmony, particularly by hunting. In order to reduce the disturbance and to restore the balance of the creation, the people accompany all their activities with various religious ceremonies, broadly referred to as *puliaijat*. During these ceremonies the people pray and make offerings to the spirits which constitute 'the beyond,' and they make beautiful decorations and carvings to please the souls or spirits."

This explanation helped us to understand how a relatively small island that is well stocked with hunters could still manage to have forests filled with primates. The respect for the harmony of nature seemed to be a key element of living in balance with the limited available resources, helping both forest and monkey survive an effective predator. From a human point of view, respect for nature's harmony means that there are always monkeys to hunt.

Souls are everywhere on Siberut, so felling a tree—which would certainly destroy a soul's house—involves complex ceremonies to propitiate the spirits. The expense and difficulty of these ceremonies help limit the number of trees that are cut down. Similarly, a set of rituals must be followed before hunting the primates. The monkey skulls in the longhouse—called *uma* on Siberut—harbor souls, and the hunters ask those monkey skull-souls to call on their relatives, the living monkey-souls in the forest. The message from skull-soul to living-soul is simple: "Let your body be shot so you can be reunited with us in the warm, dry, and comfortable uma."

Ama'n Djenga Kerei, who now prefers his Christian name of Potiphar, introduced us to a *sikerei*, or ritual specialist, and translated for us as he explained his ritual to help the hunters. "I sacrifice a chicken," the old man told us, "and by looking at the patterns in the chicken's entrails I can tell whether the spirits agree that the time is right for hunting. If they are ready for a hunt, they also reveal in the chicken intestine what direction the hunters should go to find monkeys. It is taboo for me to hunt, but if the hunters are successful, then I get a share of the meat. I work with the spirits to make the hunters successful."

If the hunters return with monkeys, they clean the skulls, hang them in the longhouse, and decorate them with colorful leaves and flowers thought to possess magical properties. This care persuades the souls of the dead animals to stay in the uma rather than wander into the forest.

All monkeys are fair game except the golden form of the pig-tailed langur, our guide explained. People consider that monkey to be so mystical that they do not allow the skulls to be hung in the uma. When the first sikerei ate this monkey, the story goes, all the animals disappeared; today the animal is left alone to make sure that such a calamity does not happen again. Gibbons, too, are seldom hunted; they are considered magical creatures which bring illness to the hunter and his family if they are killed.

Of course, in times of extreme need both the gibbons (which are the easiest to hunt of all the primates because of their territorial calls and their restricted territories) and the simakobu in its golden phase can be hunted. They are the emergency larder to which the community may turn when threatened with starvation.

The rituals of Siberut hunters, the cultural restraints, and the accompanying taboos have prevented overexploitation of the primates. The result: a rare example of equilibrium between people and monkeys.

This delicate balance is being upset by new pressures from the outside. Although well over three quarters of the Indonesian people are Muslim, freedom of religion is guaranteed as long as people believe in one of the approved religions—Buddhism, Christianity, Confucianism, Hinduism, and Islam. The intricate religions of Siberut and dozens of other island cultures are not recognized because they lack dominant gods, a religious bureaucracy, holy books, and well-established and documented doctrine. More important, they lack people to stand up and fight effectively on their behalf. As a result, many individuals who thought they had a perfectly good set of beliefs are being coerced to join the mainstream and forget about the spirits in the wind and the souls in the monkey skulls hanging in the rafters.

During the past sixty years, Christian missions of two denominations have established about fifty villages on Siberut with government encouragement and support, each bringing 50 to 100 people from many longhouses and several clans together in one place to live in small, nuclear family houses. This process has been accelerating since about 1960 when the government instituted its own programs, bringing in better medical care, food subsidies and public health programs. This has resulted in a dramatic increase in population, from less than 13,000 in 1961 to over 18,000 in 1977 (a growth rate of about 3 percent per year, nearly twice as high as the Indonesian average).

On Siberut, the replacement of the traditional religion by modern influences, as represented in this case by Christianity, has led to a basic change in the economy of the island, with considerably greater emphasis on producing a surplus for sale, clearing more land, gathering more rattan, wearing store-bought cloth, growing rice, and settling down close to the church. Increasing contact with the mainland has generated the need for cash, greatly weakening the whole barter-subsistence pattern which enabled people to live independently on the island.

Sometimes the local government takes particularly harsh measures to speed up the deterioration of the traditional culture. In mid-1980 the mayor of the southern half of Siberut decided that the traditional ceremonies must be stopped, so he required the 319 sikereis within his jurisdiction to hand over all their ceremonial paraphernalia. He also demanded that all monkey skulls kept in some of the southernmost villages should be burned. According to reputable accounts, he seemed to be attempting a single-handed destruction of Siberut's "primitive" culture.

This holier-than-thou attitude is particularly ironic because ceremonies analogous to those on Siberut continue under the "approved" Islamic religion. At the time the sanctimonious mayor was issuing his edicts, a trading vessel carrying pigs from a Chinese pig farmer in Padang on mainland Sumatra unloaded in the tiny harbor of Muara Siberut. The boat's crew, devout Muslims, demanded that the vessel be ritually cleansed before the return voyage, involving the services of a *dukun*, the west Sumatra Islamic equivalent of a pagan Siberut *sikerei*.

The dukun said his Arabic prayers and slaughtered two chickens, one of them particularly highly prized because of its black feathers and black legs. This made a bit of a mess on the deck of the boat but it was considered worthwhile in order to get rid of the evil pig spirits. Tony Whitten, who was on the island at the time studying gibbons, was saddened by the irony. "The sailors and dukun would defend what they were doing as absolutely necessary," Tony said, "but defend equally vehemently their convictions, learned at school, that the beliefs of the Siberut people were primitive and had to be changed."

Throughout Indonesia's outer islands one sees a new colonial, the Indonesian bureaucrat, who imposes Indonesian clothes, language, values, and beliefs on what he considers to be societies made up of simple, child-like, illiterate savages. Most of these men undoubtedly mean well, but the doctrine smacks of *in loco parentis*.

And the ecology of the traditional cultures is seldom given a moment's thought.

The Indonesianization of Siberut gave people incentives to move out of the forest into the coastal villages where they could be more easily "helped." This also gave the government the chance to sell timber concessions which now cover almost the entire island. Some cynics even suggest that the financial gain from concessionaires is the real reason for the government's missionary zeal on Siberut. But whatever the motivation, the Malaysian and Filipino timber concessionaires brought with them new pressures on the environment and the social fabric, ranging from increased hunting to silting of rivers resulting from deforestation to prostitution and venereal disease.

The collapse of the sustainable age-old hunting system has meant increased pressure on all the animals of Siberut. Traditional hunting and associated ceremonies are now performed by few people, and skulls of primates are frequently discarded or, at best, relegated to a small shelter outside the house. The times and places of hunting expeditions are no longer determined by ritual occasion, but are now largely a matter of whim or opportunity. Release from age-old taboos has meant that the relatively easily hunted gibbons are more intensively sought.

On the other hand, the hunting that does continue is still with traditional bows and arrows, a frequently frustrating activity that requires considerable effort and practice, as well as the assistance of spirits. As long as the villagers do not have easy access to shotguns, the overall hunting pressure on the primates could well be reduced since the new generation spends less and less time in the forest acquiring the traditional hunting skills their fathers took for granted.

But guns are certain to become more common, and the chain saw is certain to continue its relentless buzzing course. Most observers wouldn't put money on much of Siberut's forests lasting into the next century.

◆ ◆ ◆

Conservationists tend to be optimists. Every day news reports cross our desks that might incline the cynical to throw up their hands and take up a profession with fewer devilish variables nipping at their best-laid plans. Most conservationists know the odds against saving Siberut's primates but choose to try to overcome these odds. Siberut is moving out of its innocence, regardless of whether everyone thinks it's a good idea. How can conservation make this dramatic cultural transition as positive as possible for both people and wildlife?

Some individuals in the Indonesian government are seriously concerned about maintaining the dignity of rural people. At their request we helped prepare in 1980 a conservation master plan for Siberut. It was unusual in that the future of humans and animals was looked at together, recognizing that people relied on wildlife and vice versa. It suggested a rather ambitious new approach to conservation that was to:

- develop Siberut's economy by using a maximum of locally available materials and expertise, and by building on existing cultural elements.
- establish a system of zones to control land use, including a nature reserve which would cover 10 percent of the land.
- renegotiate existing timber concession agreements and ensure that further logging would strictly follow sound ecological guidelines.
- manage the wildlife so that the survival of all species would be assured, yet allow traditional hunting to continue under a new system of controls.
- enlist the support of the local people for the conservation program, educate the people of Indonesia about the value of Siberut, and bring the world's attention to the importance of the island.

A modern trend in conservation is to calculate the benefits people get from nature. The planners who manage a country's development have to weigh elusive benefits like the watershed protection offered by forested hillsides against the hard cash that can be had by cutting the forest and selling the timber. While many of Siberut's natural values are intangible, we did a rudimentary cost-benefit analysis which suggested that the proposed conservation plan was economically feasible. The proposed system could be economically sustainable, an important consideration to a government that is rightly concerned about spending its limited development funds wisely. Yet there is another, underlying argument that Indonesians, with their innate sense for the eternal, incalculable values, equally appreciate. The Siberut conservation master plan would save irreplaceable natural values held in trust by the country for its people and those of the world. This is in stark contrast to the ephemeral economic gains to be obtained from "mining the green gold" of Siberut's forests, earning a quick profit for the loggers but destroying the ecological integrity of the island and leaving the people much worse off than before.

Emil Salim, then Minister of State for Development Supervision and the Environment, warmly welcomed the plan, calling it "an important new step in Indonesia's efforts to link conservation of the environment with socio-economic development. This plan," Salim continued, "shows how the values of the Siberut culture can be maintained, and how the natural environment can be saved, while the people are gracefully brought into the mainstream of Indonesian society."

Salim discussed the plan with the governor of West Sumatra, who agreed with its major provisions. A detailed management plan was prepared for the proposed nature reserve, which was formally approved in 1982. But these positive steps were countered by continued logging, strong efforts by local officials to destroy the local culture, and power plays among local administrators in which the villagers were the main victims.

"You're not going to win this one," an Indonesian acquaintance in the Ministry of Finance told us one night over a beer and pizza. "You've got right on your side, and all that, but the tide of change is too powerful for you guys."

"What if we really publicize the issue and embarrass the government into doing something?" we suggested.

"Sure, you've done that in the past and it usually works. But it's like the anticorruption drives that the government propounds every few years. There is lots of noise and excitement, but after a few months, when the publicity dies down, it's business as usual."

It is too early to tell what will be the long-term impact of the plan, but like conservationists everywhere we take solace in Sir Peter Scott's conviction that "We shan't save all we should like to, but we shall save a great deal more than if we'd never tried."

16

Boar and Peace

Where wild pork is a dietary staple, Islam and its prohibition of pig-eating have difficulty catching on. And in New Guinea, pigs determine when you go to war.

WE SPENT MUCH OF OUR TIME in Sarawak traveling to isolated schools where we tried to help primary school teachers implement a new English syllabus. While we were not trained teachers, the syllabus relied as much on showmanship and classroom games as it did on pedagogic theory, so we were able to offer at least a few suggestions to the teachers who taught in difficult conditions, usually with little outside encouragement, often without proper supplies, and sometimes without support of the local longhouse community. Many of the teachers were well trained and capable of teaching two classes at once; some were untrained and got their jobs by being related to a government official. While the work was rewarding, the real fun began in the afternoon when school let out and we could join the teachers and older students in fishing and basketball. On a really good afternoon we might take the hand-made wooden school desks out to the river and, using them as boats, have a regatta.

Our appreciation of rural ways was not shared by our Malay superior in the Education Department's divisional headquarters in Miri. He was a city boy from Kuching and considered Miri a rural backwater. This contrasted with our perception of the town—we spent most of our time upriver and, like country bumpkins, viewed Miri as a miniature metropolis when we visited it after months in remote longhouses. Our boss was a reasonably competent bureau-crat who took care of no more and no less than he had to. Above all, he was a Muslim, which caused him all sorts of discomfort when he had to travel to visit the Animists and Christians upriver.

The people of Sarawak are generous to visitors. The Kayans of Long Terawan, far up the Apoh River, jump at any excuse to have a party, which generally consists of dancing, drinking (often forced on you by the prettiest girls in the longhouse, but that's another story), and a banquet of roast pork.

While we were able to join the festivities, our Malay colleague sat cross-legged on the floor on a longhouse porch quietly eating an alternative dinner. He nibbled on tinned corned beef that had been prepared for him in a *halal* manner (in accordance with Islamic dietary laws) by the Education Department's Malay boatman. The rest of us had great fun digging into a hyper-cholesterol meal of fried pork fat, grilled pork ribs, and french-fried python (which tastes like chicken). While we quaffed warm beer and rice wine, he sipped warm orange soda.

The pig separates people in Borneo far more effectively than any artificial boundary. While Muslims are forbidden to eat the ani-mal's flesh, most Buddhists, Hindus (who don't eat beef), Chris-tians, Confucians, and Animists adore pork and recognize that the best way to survive in the rain forest or wilderness areas is by eating the most common large mammal: wild pig. The result is that the Islamic Malays and Melanaus have stuck to the urban centers, river valleys, and coastal areas where meat comes from fish and domestic ruminants like cows and sheep, while the pig-eaters pop-ulate the hills where wild game is plentiful. This fundamental eco-logical difference between the coastal Muslims and the inland Christians and Animists has underlined the "we vs them" tensions in Sarawak, the only state in Malaysia where the Malays, who control the central government, are in the minority. One third of the state's population is indigenous, one third is Chinese, and just 20 percent are Malay.

In rural Asia, wherever forests cover the land, large herds of pigs are there for the taking. And where the forests have gone, domestic pigs are ready to take their place at the dinner table. Pigs are remarkably effective at converting table scraps, offal, and agricultural wastes to edible protein, so it is not surprising that they were one of the first meat animals to be domesticated. Archeological evidence suggests that pigs were first domesticated in Thailand over 10,000 years ago, as part of the system of shifting cultivation. Even today, in villages near forests, wild piglets are often captured for raising or eating; most of the domestic pigs in these areas have considerable wild genes in them since they often forage in the forests where they crossbreed with wild boars.

Pigs were taken along by the early Austronesian explorers when they settled Polynesia several thousand years ago (though it appears that the sailors got so hungry on their long trip to New Zealand that they ate their pigs, and Maoris had no pork until the Europeans arrived). In more recent times, Asia's wild pigs have colonized Australia, South America, and some of the moist forested regions of the United States (late in 1986 feral hogs in California searching for food rooted up a baseball field and a manicured lawn around an IBM plant).

◆ ◆ ◆

As we sat munching our Borneo barbecue on the common porch used by the three dozen families who lived in the longhouse, scraps of food fell between the cracks in the floorboards and were gobbled up by the mangy, skinny dogs below. We took eleven of the loud dogs hunting with us the next night.

A good place to hunt wild pigs is under a durian tree. Wild durian trees grew not too far from the longhouse and we headed there shortly after dusk. The pigs approached too, eager for a meal of the favorite fruit of most creatures, human and otherwise, in Southeast Asia.

Alfred Russel Wallace, in his classic *The Malay Archipelago,* noted that natives and Europeans in the Malay archipelago reckoned the durian "superior to all other fruits." It reminded Wallace of "a rich butter-like custard highly flavoured with almonds, but intermingled with wafts of flavour that call to mind cream-cheese, onion sauce, brown sherry and other incongruities." The American traveler Caspar Whitney suggested that "If the meat of a banana were squashed and mixed with an equal quantity of rich cream, a smaller quantity of chocolate, and enough garlic to stamp strongly the whole, the result would be, it seems to me, about the nearest approach to the consistency and combination of tastes afforded by the durian." Another observer compared the sensation to eating strawberries and cream in a poorly kept public toilet.

This high-protein taste treat is the size of a large coconut, surprisingly heavy, greenish brown, and covered with dozens of nail-hard short spikes that are so sharp it can be painful to pick up the fruit if the stem has broken off. The durian tree grows to a hundred feet, so falling durians can be a hazard to unwary passersby.

The height of the durian season is a great time to hunt. "All animal kind," says Whitney, "is animated by an insatiable lust for the fruit itself, and quick to fill with savage anger against whatever stands in the way of satisfying its appetite; for not the least remarkable quality of this remarkable fruit is the amatory effect it has upon those who consume it. All durian-eating Malays—man and beast—are aflame with erotic fire. The jungle resounds with the fighting of love-lorn brutes, and the towns awaken to courtship and indulgence." A favorite saying in Borneo longhouses is, "When the durians are down the sarongs are up." And bringing back a fat pig along with a durian is a sure way to a maiden's heart.

The Kayans with whom we were hunting used both shotguns and blowpipes—the latter six feet long with a perfectly straight bore carved out of unblemished hardwood and a dart made from a thin palm leaf frond and tipped with strychnine. This weapon gives the pig a sporting chance. The usual scenario is to shoot the grunting animal while it tears into a durian. The dogs then run it down while the poison takes effect. Sometimes, though, the pig turns on the hunters. The dogs, cowards all, quickly scatter, and the hunters, at least the brave ones, try to save their skins with the bayonet-like steel blade attached to the end of their hardwood blowpipes.

Pig hunting provided good stories to tell around the campfire, with a few scars as evidence. One does not play games with an angry wild pig.

Carveth Wells, an engineer who helped build the railroad in colonial Malaya, recounted an incident that showed how dangerous an angry pig can be. "A planter in Kedah named Parker was walking through his rubber estate one morning and saw a large pig on the other side of a ravine tearing the bark off one of the young rubber trees. Thinking he would frighten the animal away, he shouted and struck his cane against a tree, making a loud crack like a rifle shot. The boar looked up and then to the dismay of Parker rushed down the side of the hill, crossed the ravine, climbed up to where he stood, and savagely attacked him. The animal rushed between Parker's legs and, as it passed, deeply gashed both legs with its tusks. The boar then did it again and was about to do it for the third time when Parker, with his trousers torn to pieces and very seriously injured, lay down and rolled himself to the bottom of the ravine—an undignified performance which undoubtedly saved his life. As it was, he spent weeks in the hospital, and when he came out there were five or six long deep scars on the inside of his legs, in between his knees and his thighs."

◆ ◆ ◆

One of the reasons pigs are so important for the residents of Borneo longhouses is because there are so many of them. One of the world's largest animal migrations occurred in 1983 when perhaps a million bearded pigs wandered through the interior of Borneo. Yet this pig migration, comparable to the famed wildebeest migration which annually sweeps across the Serengeti in Tanzania, is virtually unknown to the outside world because it takes place in the privacy of the jungle.

It's also a migration which is difficult to predict, because it depends on a massive population explosion of the bearded pigs, which in turn depends on consecutive years of prolific fruiting of the dipterocarp trees which provide the animals with their richest source of food. Since the trees in different parts of Borneo produce their fruits, locally known as *illepe* nuts, at slightly different times, the pigs can exploit the seeds over a long period by migrating up and down mountainsides, across rivers, and through swamps. A good fruiting year allows the migrating pigs to build up a large population, since a well-fed female can produce as many as ten piglets in a single birth. When a second good fruiting year follows and enables the previous year's piglets to survive and breed, the pig population explodes. The human population does well too, since illepe nuts, which are used to manufacture chicle, an ingredient in chewing gum, are an important, but irregular, source of secondary income.

When heavy crops of illepe nuts were produced in 1980 and

again in 1981, tribesmen in longhouses throughout central Borneo began buying shotgun shells and making poison darts for their blowpipes. The expected pig eruption came in 1983, and the hunters were in pig heaven—hunters in the Sarawak's Baram and Silat region alone slaughtered some 20,000 bearded pigs, an average of 33 per family. This massacre did not greatly affect the pig population; Julian and Serena Caldecott, who were studying the economics of wild pig hunting in Sarawak at the time, estimated that this hunt took only 8 percent of the total estimated 250,000 bearded pigs in that part of Borneo.

The shotgun has begun to replace the spear and blowpipe. The Caldecotts estimated that two thirds of hunted animals die by gunfire, mostly on land, rather than in the water. This was not the case during a similar massacre in 1954 when tribal hunters used their spears to ambush so many bearded pigs as they swam across a river that the water was fouled for miles by gore. Downstream, angry Muslims threatened war.

While the coastal Muslims enjoy their chickens, fish, goats and beef, for most of the diverse peoples living in Borneo's interior the bearded pig is still the prime culinary delicacy. The Caldecotts estimate that 22,000 tons of pork are eaten each year in Sarawak alone. The fat is stored in oil barrels or biscuit tins, the lean meat is pickled, fermented, or stacked over smoky fires, the mandibles are lovingly cleaned and displayed, and exceptional canines are traded up and down the rivers, they explain.

The 1983 bearded pig migration has already begun to enter local folklore and admiring young boys listen to the hunting stories of their elders and prepare for the next pork windfall. Sadly for the hunters in the upper Baram, that migration may never come. Loggers are planning to take all the commercial timber from the region in the next ten years. The commercially valuable dipterocarp trees which produce the illepe nuts will be devasted, and other fruiting trees that feed the pigs will have been disturbed. Scientists in other parts of Borneo have found that bearded pigs virtually disappear after extensive logging, so the people of the Baram may have seen the last of the mass pig migrations, at least for a while.

In Sarawak alone, to replace the wild pork with meat from domestic animals will cost at least 100 million U.S. dollars per year far into the future. While the income from timber may last for a few years, the forests of Sarawak are expected to be exhausted of timber within a decade or two. "Surely," the Caldecotts conclude, "it would be more cost effective to manage wildlife properly in the first place." And conserving forested habitat is the best way to help both pigs and hunters.

◆ ◆ ◆

People in New Guinea are even more dependent on pigs. When we were in the Vogelkop (Bird's-head) area of Irian Jaya helping a construction company with its public relations problems, we paused at a small village whose people had had a fair amount of contact with outsiders, both western and Indonesian. Some of the village men worked for oil companies as laborers and the oil companies had helped build a school and clinic. We were startled to see a woman sitting in front of her small wooden house listening to the radio, cleaning yams, and suckling a baby pig at her breast. When the piglet had finished, the woman's year-old daughter took her turn.

We should not have been surprised at such maternal devotion, for the island of New Guinea is the pig center of the world. Men value their wealth in pigs first and wives second, and the four-legged possession can be worth more than the two-legged one.

The Maring people, who live in the Bismarck Mountains of Papua New Guinea, have evolved elaborate pig-oriented rituals which border on pig love. "In the ambience of pig love one cannot truly be human except in the company of pigs," reports anthropologist Marvin Harris in *Cows, Pigs, War and Witches*. "Pig love includes raising pigs to be a member of the family, sleeping next to them, talking to them, stroking and fondling them, calling them by name, leading them on a leash to the fields, weeping when they fall sick." Pig love goes even further, and includes sacrificial feasts where the pig's flesh is absorbed into the flesh of the human host. And as with headhunters who "capture" a spirit by taking a head, the respected spirit of the pig joins the spirits of the humans when the pig is sacrificed and eaten.

For a people who depend on a rather boring carbohydrate diet, the great pig feast held once or twice a generation is something to look forward to, and to tell stories about. It provides an opportunity for the wealthy to buy loyalty from neighbors, and to ensure a plentiful supply of allies for battles with neighbors.

Fieldwork carried out among the Maring by University of Michigan anthropologist Roy Rappaport has demonstrated the importance of the pig ritual in the ecology of these highland farmers. The pig cycle, described in great detail by Rappaport, works something like this:

About every twelve years each Maring clan holds a year-long pig festival known as *kaiko*, which includes a massive slaughter of pigs followed by several months of fighting with neighboring tribes. After a number of battles, both victors and vanquished find themselves entirely bereft of adult pigs with which to curry favor from their respective ancestors and to support the fighters. Fighting ceases abruptly when pig-bankruptcy is declared and the belligerent tribes slink off to plant small, sacred trees called *rumbin*.

A war magician explains to the dead ancestors that the people have run out of pigs. He promises that all the energy will be devoted to raising more pigs and only when a new herd of pigs has been raised, enough for a kaiko big enough to thank ancestors properly, will the warriors uproot the rumbin trees and return to the battlefield.

This cycle of sacrificing all your pigs, fighting, and then rearing more pigs is part of a complex ecosystem that effectively adjusts the size and distribution of the Maring's human and animal population to conform to available natural resources. As in most of Southeast Asia, the women in this society do the hard work. They nurse the baby pigs, and when weaned the piglets trot after the women like puppies while the women tend the vegetable gardens. The cute little piglets grow into pests that have to be kept out of the vegetable gardens, no easy task.

Although the domestic pigs regularly forage in the wild, the women are nevertheless required to feed them. Pigs are omnivorous and like the same things people do, so pigs and warriors are fed the same boring diet of sweet potatoes and yams. Since an adult pig weighs more than an adult man, a woman has to work harder to feed an adult pig than to feed her husband.

The domestic pig population grows quickly. Families soon need more garden space, which means gardens must be cut out of virgin forest. While this is onerous for the men, who find they actually have to do some physical labor, it is even a greater inconvenience for the women, who have to work much harder and travel farther to get to their fields. Eventually the village disperses and households move closer to the gardens. Security breaks down (there is a constant fear of being ambushed by neighbors who steal wives) and tension increases. Women become irritable and nag at their husbands and yell at their kids. At this point agricultural productivity is down, the social system is strained, the pigs threaten to destroy the women and the gardens, the ancestors are getting restless, and a new generation of would-be warriors is itching to throw some spears at their cousins.

The men ask themselves, "Are there enough pigs for a kaiko?" When the answer is yes, the cycle is ready to repeat itself. Rappaport concludes, "The regulatory function of ritual among the . . . Maring helps to maintain an undegraded environment, limits fighting to frequencies that do not endanger the existence of the regional population, adjusts man-land ratios, facilitates trade, distributes local surpluses of pig in the form of pork throughout the regional population, and assures people of high-quality protein when they most need it."

This system is beginning to break down. In the early 1960s, when Rappaport was carrying out his study, the government of Papua New Guinea was already beginning to introduce a number of cultural changes aimed at stopping tribal warfare. Some simple societies, such as the Maring, are governed by sacred conventions that overshadow human authority, while more sophisticated societies have authorities with little sanctity but great power. As a society develops, says Rappaport, "technological sophistication is likely to place highly effective weaponries in the hands of authorities, weaponries not generally available to their subjects. An authority with great power can dispense with sanctity—as Napoleon said, 'God is on the side of the heavy artillery.' "

◆ ◆ ◆

When the United Nations allowed the peoples of what was then West New Guinea to decide whether to join the Republic of Indonesia, the Indonesian government sent troops to ensure a fair vote. Muslim President Suharto, eager to win the hearts and minds of the mountain people known as Ekari, instructed the soldiers to bring a gift of pigs from Hindu-dominated Bali.

Whatever the political and social advantages of the gift, the unseen medical results were tragic. The gift pigs carried tapeworm, a parasite with a complex life cycle: tapeworm is passed through the human gut in feces, the human waste is eaten by pigs, and the pig meat is eaten by the human. The egg hatches in the human and the embryo flows to the brain where it continues to develop. The brain becomes inflamed, and the patient suffers epileptic-like convulsions and bizarre personality changes.

Robert Desowitz, a specialist in tropical medicine at the University of Hawaii, found during fieldwork in the region that the pig tapeworm had been endemic in Bali for at least sixty years, and that a favorite Balinese dish is an undercooked pork preparation in which the tapeworm larvae "are cleverly disguised by the legendary spices of the Indies." But tapeworm is under control in Bali, partly because the pig meat is at least somewhat heated, which kills some tapeworm eggs, and also because the Balinese are fastidiously clean in their personal habits, and pigs have less chance to root in human wastes and complete the tapeworm cycle.

But once the Balinese pigs reached highland Irian Jaya, where pork is barely cooked and toilet habits are the most basic, the people quickly became infected. The outbreak of pig tapeworm disease (cysticercosis) became known when, in 1971, a bewildering epidemic of severe burn cases was reported among the Ekari. "Some of the twenty-five to thirty cases each month were so bad that limbs had to be amputated," reports Desowitz. "All patients gave similar accounts. While sleeping, they had been overcome by an epileptic seizure and had fallen unconscious into the household fire."

Tapeworm is relatively easy to kill but neither of the solutions—refrigeration and cooking—were applicable to the Ekari. In contrast to the ritual communal slaughter of pigs by the Maring, the Ekari don't like to share. They kill their pigs secretly in the middle of the night and throw them on the fire just long enough to warm up the meat but not long enough to wake up the neighbors. Improved cooking would obviously stop the spread of the dangerous disease, so a health educator was sent out from Jakarta to explain to the Ekari how important it was to roast their pigs thoroughly before devouring them.

The Ekari chief was bitter that the disease introduced by foreigners had corrupted the tribe's pigs and religion. "We are not blind," he told Desowitz. "We can see the seeds that give us the illness in the pig flesh. But no one lives forever and if we must die, then we must die. Life is no longer of pleasure. We are only half men. The Indonesians will not let us make the warfare that gave us manhood. I no longer care if I eat the corrupt pig flesh."

The pig culture of the Australoid tribesmen deep in the hills of western New Guinea is being undermined, ironically because the predominantly Muslim officials of Indonesia's central government offered them the gift of pork.

"When the missionaries brought us the coughing sickness many years ago [a pertussis epidemic in 1956], we rose in anger," the chief added. "This time we have no heart to do so."

17

Jungle Tractors

The elephant is one of Southeast Asia's most valuable animals, but large areas of forest are needed to keep the wild breeding stock from devastating plantations and farms.

Many people are bound to be surprised if told that there is available in Burma an extremely versatile, multi-purpose, self-regenerating heavy duty machine of great strength and the delicate sensitiveness of a ballet dancer, which is readily adaptable to all kinds of terrain and work conditions, including the capability of working in four feet of water, requires a minimum of maintenance, is able to work efficiently on all grades of a limitless fuel that grows on trees, and has a phenomenal built-in memory. And the beauty of it is that it does not cost us any foreign exchange. (Burma *Daily News*, July 24, 1963)

THE WORLD BANK, which uses funds from rich countries to promote development in poor ones, has mixed feelings about elephants. On the one hand, the Bank is frustrated by elephant herds that sabotage their expensive development projects. Elephants have devoured bank-financed rice plantations in Sri Lanka, stopped (with the help of environmentalists) a proposed dam in Thailand which would have flooded their most important remaining habitat, and flattened vast palm oil plantations in Malaysia.

On the other hand, some World Bank officials appreciate that elephants are often the appropriate technology for extracting commercial timber, and have stipulated as part of their loan agreements with Burma that elephants must be used to move teak logs from the forest to the roadhead. The Burmese government was happy to agree. In an official statement, the Ministry of Agriculture and Forests stated, "In spite of the efficiency of heavy machineries, elephants are irreplaceable for short distance skidding. Moreover, they are most versatile in difficult terrain and in view of the less damage they do to the forest soils and natural regeneration during the course of timber extraction they are still to be preferred to machines. Due to the world-wide escalation of prices and the high initial costs of heavy machines, elephants will continue to be very useful in the timber industry."

Although the elephant, as the real-life version of Ganesh, the elephant-headed son of Siva, is revered throughout Burma, Thailand, Laos, and Kampuchea, pragmatic Southeast Asians also appreciate the animal's unique abilities as tank, tractor, and executioner.

The first recorded use of domestic elephants was in combat as early as 326 B.C., when King Porus of the Punjab in northern India mustered an elephant army against Alexander the Great at the Battle of the Hydaspes. Alexander was duly impressed, and was reported as saying, with his customary modesty, "At last I have met with a danger suitable to the greatness of my soul."

Alexander's battlefield skills rose to the test, however. He ordered his men to fire arrows (from a safe distance) to harass the animals while brave light horse calvary cut the elephants to ribbons with razor-sharp spears, thereby turning the crazed animals against their own foot soldiers and sowing panic among the Punjabis. Alexander captured a number of elephants in victory but used them only as baggage animals, knowing from experience how unreliable they could be in battle.

Asian generals continued to use elephants until the advent of firearms, which made the nervous animals too prone to panic. Elephants served the same role as tanks on modern battlefields.

Indochina was a hotbed of intrigue, revolution, conquest, and bloodshed long before French and American advisers came onto the scene. During the Angkor period a thousand years ago, the Cambodian army reportedly had 200,000 war elephants, which are commemorated on the famous stone carvings on Angkor Wat's thousand-foot-long "Elephant Terrace."

Cambodia maintained its elephant troops for several centuries. Undeterred by this fact, the Kingdom of Champa (in the area that is now southern Vietnam) nevertheless invaded Cambodia in 1170 A.D., after first convincing the Annamese of northern Vietnam to remain neutral. The invading Chams were winning until Cambodian King Tribuvandityavarman ordered the Royal Elephant Regiment into action. "The Chams," according to British scholar John Audric, "had been promised the rich prize of Angkor, with loot and women in abundance, and they fought with reckless courage to storm the earth defenses and risk a fearful death in the crocodile-infested moats to gain the golden city. The attempt at invasion failed, and the elephants thundered after the fleeing Chams, trampling the dead and dying in the bloody carnage of the battlefield."

But even with great numbers of elephants on the battlefield and endless reserves of expendable foot soldiers, sometimes the kings met face-to-face on elephant-back to settle matters, thereby avoiding excessive bloodshed and reestablishing their claims to semidivinity. During the "White Elephant Wars" with the Burmese, for example, Siam's King Naresuan (reigned 1590 to 1605 A.D.) fought and killed the Burmese Crown Prince on elephant-back, bringing a pause of several decades to the hostilities between the two countries. Such a test of bravery and fighting skills between leaders seems an ideal way of settling differences. (Imagine how different modern history might have been had Lyndon Johnson and Ho Chi Minh challenged each other across a muddy field before charging their elephants into a man-to-man spear duel, while the troops cheered them on from the sidelines and demonstrators waved their placards accompanied by TV announcers calling the play-by-play.)

These elephant-back tests of bravery resulted in some of the most outstanding monarchs the world has ever seen, including Rama Khamhaeng (reigned c. 1275–1317), often considered Thailand's greatest king. A stone engraving composed by Rama in 1292 gave a firsthand version of Thailand's earliest recorded elephant battle, and also illustrated the importance of elephants at that time:

When I had grown and reached the age of nineteen, Khun Sam Chon came to attack. . . . My father's people fled and dispersed in complete disorder. I did not flee, I climbed on the elephant Anekaphon and drove it in front of my father. I began a duel of elephants with Khun Sam Chon. I smote his elephant . . . and put it out of the battle. Khun Sam Chon fled. Then my father gave me the name Phra Rama Khamhaeng [Rama the Strong] because I had smitten the elephant of Khun Sam Chon.

Using elephants as a major weapon, Rama Khamhaeng expanded his kingdom west to Pegu in Burma, south to the tip of the Malay Peninsula, north to the Mekong River, and east into Cambodia. His extensive realm was even larger than the contemporary Majapahit Empire that stretched across the Indonesian archipelago.

A scholar and a patron of the arts, Rama Khamhaeng invented the Thai alphabet and brought the art of ceramics from China to the pottery kilns of Sukhothai and Suwankhalok. His reign, during Europe's Middle Ages, was probably the most enlightened in the world at that time, and Southeast Asia has never seen its equal.

Few other kings were as capable or civilized. When not using elephants to fight their neighbors, many Southeast Asian rulers used the animals to keep order in their own houses. With their awesome power, elephants made excellent executioners, particularly for the heinous crime of *lèse majesté*. In cases of attempted coups, the guilty party was staked out on the ground and the elephant stepped first on each of the victim's limbs, crushing the bones. After giving the plotter time to confess his crime publicly and swear allegiance to the king, the elephant put one forefoot on the condemned man's head and the other on the stomach, neatly shifting his weight to put the wretch out of his misery.

The Thais had another way of dealing with thieves. Out of rattan they wove a large ball, about three feet in diameter, similar to the grapefruit-sized version used throughout Thailand for the volleyball-like game called *takraw*. However, the elephant's takraw was riddled with sharp iron spikes pointing inward, rather like an inside-out cactus. Into this sadistic piece of athletic equipment was placed the thief. The ball was carried gently out to a large open playing field, where two elephants would amuse themselves, and the crowd, by kicking the ball back and forth, urged on by the cheering public. The poor pilferer spent a rugged thirty minutes and by half-time was usually reduced to a pulp; his remains were then fed to pariah dogs.

Foreigners were not exempt from execution by elephant. In the eighteenth century, the King of Burma hired a thousand Portuguese mercenaries because of their familiarity with modern firearms. Like mercenaries throughout history, their rough behavior irritated the conservative local community. According to British sea captain Alexander Hamilton, the Portuguese general in command of the regiment spotted a pretty virgin about to be married and ordered his sergeants to carry her back to his quarters for his own amusement.

The shamed, disconsolate bridegroom killed himself, and the parents of the young couple stormed through the streets of Martaban, calling upon all honorable Burmese to avenge the virgin bride and her martyred groom. The people were sympathetic and the noise of the tumultuous crowd reached the ears of the king. The monarch, a good politician, sensed the mood of his subjects and became so incensed that he ordered the city to take arms and massacre the Portuguese.

According to Hamilton, "The King's Orders were put in Execution so speedily, that in a few Hours all the Portuguese were slaughtered, and the guilty Criminal was taken alive, and made fast by the Heels to an Elephant's Foot, who dragged him through the Streets till there was no Skin nor Flesh left to cover his Bones, which Spectacle appeased the enraged Populace."

In modern times, elephants have been most useful in war as baggage animals. During World War II, the Japanese offensive to break into India from Burma depended largely on the transport provided by 350 baggage elephants. The Japanese were ultimately unsuccessful, having been stymied by the long line of supply and a sturdy guerrilla defense.

During the Vietnam War, elephants were so widely used by the Viet Cong as baggage animals that American helicopter gunship crews were ordered to shoot any elephants they saw. Even wild elephants were considered potential baggage animals by U.S. and South Vietnamese pilots. One crew member in a helicopter gunship told us that he was still bothered by the screams he had heard several months before, as bullets from his .50-caliber machine gun tore into a herd of wild elephants in Cambodia.

◆ ◆ ◆

Today elephants are put to more productive use in the teak forests of Thailand and Burma, where they are far better suited for their work than any machine. About 5,400 elephants still work in the teak forests of Burma, while Thailand, with less rugged hills and more foreign exchange, has about 4,800 domestic working elephants, and Kampuchea, Laos, and Vietnam together have about 1,800.

Elephants are also highly prized as pack animals, though they can only carry about 10 percent of their body weight (human backpackers often carry 30 to 40 percent of their body weight, and some Nepalese professional porters carry loads as heavy as they are). The value of elephants lies in where they can go, not just how much they can carry. Visiting northeast Thailand in the rainy season, Henri Mouhot—rediscoverer of Angkor Wat—came to admire his pack elephants:

The elephant ought to be seen on these roads, which I can only call devil's pathways, and are nothing but ravines. . . . It is necessary, I repeat, to see him at work like this in his own country, to form any idea of his intelligence, docility, and strength, or how all those wonderful joints of his are adapted to their work—fully to understand that this colossus is no rough specimen of nature's handiwork, but a creature of special amiability and sagacity, designed for the service of man.

Well-trained elephants are one of nature's marvels. It is common for trained elephants to respond to thirty commands, including such useful tricks as "Push the object with your feet," "Pick up that peacock feather," and "Squirt water under your belly." J. H. Williams, who worked and lived with elephants in the forests of Burma for twenty-five years, says that domesticated elephants have even been known to stuff mud into the bells round their necks to muffle them before going forth to steal bananas at night. Mike Woodford, a British veterinarian who worked with the Burmese in elephant management, told us that elephants working in sawmills will reposition the huge logs so they can be cut in the most efficient manner, sometimes gently scolding their human overseers for not noticing the problem themselves. U Toke Gale reported that an excited domestic bull elephant destroyed the harness rack and all the gear belonging to other elephants in his camp —but left his own equipment untouched.

Elephants are so intelligent that they do not always require a human overseer. Four well-trained riderless pachyderms spent years transporting contraband between Cambodia and Thailand. The human smugglers would innocently pass by the customs post empty-handed, while the elephants followed far behind and listened for the signals which the leader of the gang gave them from time to time by blowing into a shell. According to the number and pitch of the notes they heard, the elephants would know whether to advance, look out, halt, or take cover. If the customs officers were patrolling the forest, the elephants would separate and make their way across the frontier by rough forest tracks, and if the officials happened to hear them they concluded that they were wild and naturally kept out of their way. But the scheme was given away by the frequent appearance of the same men blowing more or less the same notes just at the times when "wild" elephants were known to be in the neighborhood. With the help of local informers, the customs officers learned of the plot. Together with armed police they set out to arrest the elephants, but the four-legged smugglers put up a heroic struggle in which one of the elephants was killed before the others surrendered. Their human masters escaped in the confusion.

◆ ◆ ◆

While the elephants which are put in man's service are extremely useful, wild elephants can be serious pests when humans invade their forests with development projects. In Vietnam, the colonial French administration often felt that elephant herds realized the danger of encroaching civilization because the animals seemed to demolish all the telegraph poles, bridges, and isolated forestry stations they could find. They pulled down miles of wire, twisting it so thoroughly that repair gangs spent days untangling it and putting the telegraph back into action. "As fast as they repaired the system it was damaged again," says William Baze, who had the unenviable task of making development work in the Vietnamese forests, "and as the months went by the unbroken rhythm of damage-repairs-damage-repairs became intolerable. Bridge-rails were twisted or pulled out, milestones over-turned and shifted, forestry huts robbed of their roofs and doors, barrels of cement or coal-tar belonging to the Public Works Department were rolled along the roads and hidden all over the place—until it had gone beyond a joke and everybody had had just about enough of it." Baze ambushed and shot a few of the biggest males among the elephant guerrillas, which seemed to sufficiently discourage the others that the projects could proceed.

The World Bank has been particularly disturbed by the depredations of wild elephants in their projects to convert forests to plantations. "We found recently that there have been major cost over-runs because of elephant damage," Robert Goodland, an environmental expert at the World Bank, told us. For example, a $90 million oil palm plantation in Malaysia cost 94 percent more than planners expected, in large part because of elephants. Goodland said that the elephants not only ate the palms, but clearly showed their irritation over the project by walking along the rows and methodically stepping on each plant, causing a loss of 2 million palm tree saplings.

The World Bank and conservation officials have tried various ways of minimizing the man-elephant conflict, without much success. "You've got to remember that this is the largest terrestrial mammal, and its major strategy is to search for food by going from place to place," said wildlife biologist John Seidensticker. "Nothing ever holds them back for very long."

Sumatra, where domestic elephants have not been used since the sixteenth century, is suffering from serious elephant-people conflicts. Villagers have been killed—one 1985 victim was a seventeen-year old girl who was "kidnapped and killed by a herd of marauding wild elephants which ran amok in a village in southern Sumatra," according to the official Antara news agency. Entire hamlets have been flattened by herds of charging elephants in areas where historic elephant habitat was being taken over by migrants from overcrowded Java. Commendably, and rather surprisingly, the Indonesian government has refused to take the easy way out and massacre any elephants that set foot onto agricultural land. Instead, it has sponsored elaborate and costly roundups. But moving large herds is risky business, and even if the elephants are translocated they may decide after a few months to return.

The 2,000 to 4,000 wild elephants in Sumatra cause so much damage that an elephant reform school was set up in the early 1980s in the Sumatran province of Lampung. Two elephant tamers from Thailand have been hired as disciplinarians and tutors. The school's first class has six students. "The oldest is 3-year old Siti Nurabaya, who used to belong to a wild gang of elephants," a news story in the Indonesia *Times* announced.

Willing to try anything, Indonesia's Ministry of Forestry ruled that elephants can be kept as pets as part of a new program designed to encourage man and beast to live together peacefully, the Jakarta *Post* reported. Director General of Forest Protection and Nature Conservation Rubini Atmawidjaja explained that the elephant

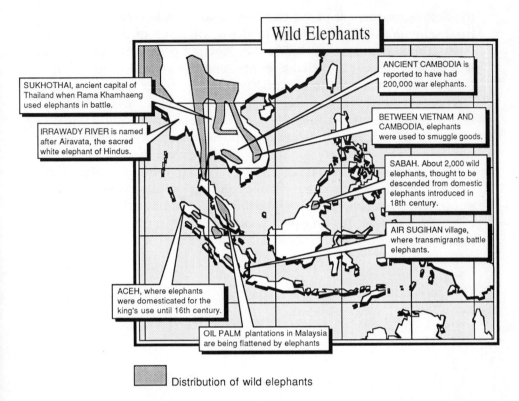

Wild Elephants

SUKHOTHAI, ancient capital of Thailand when Rama Khamhaeng used elephants in battle.

IRRAWADY RIVER is named after Airavata, the sacred white elephant of Hindus.

ANCIENT CAMBODIA is reported to have had 200,000 war elephants.

BETWEEN VIETNAM AND CAMBODIA, elephants were used to smuggle goods.

SABAH. About 2,000 wild elephants, thought to be descended from domestic elephants introduced in 18th century.

AIR SUGIHAN village, where transmigrants battle elephants.

ACEH, where elephants were domesticated for the king's use until 16th century.

OIL PALM plantations in Malaysia are being flattened by elephants

Distribution of wild elephants

population in Sumatra was continuing to increase despite limited habitats being available (in fact, the elephant population was declining, but the habitat was being destroyed at an even faster rate). He said that "anyone wanting an elephant for a pet could catch it by himself and raise it in his house." No one has yet come to his office requesting an elephant permit, Rubini complained.

◆ ◆ ◆

Traditional hunters seem to have had relatively little impact on elephant populations, and traditional shifting cultivators probably even improved the habitat for elephants. When people took over the elephant's favorite habitat in the seasonally flooded lowlands to plant irrigated rice, the elephants were able to hold their own by retreating to the hills and uncultivated grasslands. These habitats easily supported sufficient elephants to provide the captive animals which made important contributions to the cultures of the wet rice civilizations.

The advent of the colonial era brought plantation agriculture, the first serious threat to the elephant's survival. Each new agricultural scheme raises the volume of the death knell of Asia's largest land animal. It seems inevitable that isolated pockets of elephants will soon disappear and that the total population will drop further from its current estimate of 25,000.

The best hope for the elephant is that governments will soon realize that most of the hilly parts of Southeast Asia should remain as forest, so that lowland water supplies are protected and timber can be harvested to meet both local and export needs. Then, as long as substantial areas of land are devoted to limited, sustainable forestry, conflicts between elephants and agricultural land could be minimized and Asia's most important wild animal might have a chance to survive. It's an open question whether the international marketplace will permit such a rational course.

18

Avengers in the Forest

Man-eating tigers help maintain village discipline, but these powerful symbols are losing out to the forces of modern development.

People in Nantulu, Sumatra, feel anxiety about the rage of tigers in their village, threatening their lives. The beasts came from nearby forests and roamed at night in the villages. Last week two villagers were attacked to death. A folktale said the killing of a young tiger by the villagers had raged the beasts against them. (Indonesia *Times*, December 18, 1979)

"THE STRIPED ONE" evokes terror in many rural Asians, and there are places where nobody will even mention its name for fear of attracting its attention. The bloodthirstiness of man-eating tigers has entered the consciousness of millions. This sanguine reputation is not undeserved. Consider:

- Richard Perry, in his book *The World of the Tiger*, estimated that tigers have killed at least 1 million Asians in the past 400 years, an average of 2,500 per year.

- In 1979, police in Riau Province, Sumatra, claimed that more people were killed by tigers than by their fellow humans; thirty people were killed by the animals compared with twenty-five murder victims.
- Major A. D. Ackels, a Vietnam veteran, reported that tigers regularly scavenged bodies on Indochinese battlefields. Some, he said, even grew bold enough to attack live soldiers.
- From April 5 to 8, 1974, one tiger killed twenty-four people of the Lisu tribe in a remote village in the Hpanma Bum region of northern Burma.

Historically, tigers have infested grasslands and forests from Siberia and the Caspian Sea south through India and Southeast Asia to Sumatra, Java, and Bali. Despite the tiger's dangerous reputation throughout this large area, the village people, who might be expected to have the greatest vested interest in seeing the tiger exterminated, often have great respect (admittedly tinged with fear) for the big predator. Many villagers welcome tigers to help them control the deer, pigs and monkeys which come to forage on their hard-earned crops—just as they keep house cats to try to control rats. The occasional loss of cattle to the tiger is considered a part of life.

As biologist John Seidensticker put it, "Far back into history, man has lived with tigers, sometimes competing with them directly for food. Men killed tigers; tigers killed men. But both were bound together in a fragile web, molded and bound by the nature of their relationship with each other and their environment."

Traces of the ancient relationship between tiger and villagers survive today. The negrito pygmies who live in the forests of southern Thailand and peninsular Malaysia gather forest produce and hunt with blowguns and poison darts much like their australoid ancestors of 20,000 years ago. They consider tigers to be the avenger of the Supreme Being (Karei) who will punish only those who break the tribal taboos.

A similar belief has survived among many of the former Animists in Sumatra who adopted Islam some 500 years ago. Because the tiger is considered to be entrusted by Allah to carry out deserved punishment, logic insists that anyone killed must have been a sinner. When 100 people were killed by tigers near Bengkulu on the southwest coast of Sumatra in 1951, this was seen as the re-

venge of Allah and not something to blame on the tiger executioners.

Islam also brought in a powerful means of protection. Lieutenant
Colonel Locke said that if you asked your Malay guide why a tiger
attacked his human victims from behind, "he will tell you that this
is inevitable, because on the forehead of every person is inscribed a
verse from the Koran proclaiming man's superiority over all other
creatures. It is this inscription that the tiger cannot face."

The uneasy cohabitation between people and tigers changes as
people move into the forests that once were the tigers' domain.
Tigers may harvest too many villagers or an excessive number of
cattle and must pay the penalty. But even when a tiger exceeds his
bag limit, hunters take great pains to ensure that only the guilty
tiger is taken, and that innocent tigers are left alone.

Captain Henry Baudesson describes a case in the Annamite
Mountains of Vietnam where a tiger had fallen into a pit which
had been dug to trap deer. The tiger was not injured, but "the
natives were terrified lest it should die," says Baudesson, "in which
case its spirit would never cease to molest them. So they decided to
set it free . . . offering it their humble apologies for having already detained it so long."

When the tiger killed twenty-four Lisu villagers in Burma, the
army was called in to kill the tiger, which it did with little difficulty since the tiger had lost its fear of people and could be approached easily. The late U Tun Yin, Burma's grand old naturalist,
told us in 1979 that shortly afterward the Lisu gathered around its
head and said prayers for two minutes: "We have not been ruthless
in killing the tiger. The tiger had killed a number of persons for no
reason. May the tiger rest in peace."

Villagers realize that certain precautions can help prevent tiger
attacks. One of the most widespread beliefs is that naming the
tiger, or speaking disrespectfully of it, will inevitably attract unwanted attention. As a result, people avoid calling the tiger by
name. Among the Moi of Vietnam, says William Baze, the tiger is
called "the gentleman" because it would be upset and angry to be
called an unkind name. In Sumatra, Dutch civil servant Ton Schilling noticed that tigers which were causing villagers problems were
called *nenek*, ancestor, to appease them.

The man-tiger relationship probably reaches its most sophisticated state among the Minangkabau, the dominant cultural group
of western Sumatra. While now mostly Islamic, they have retained,

in various forms, a number of Animistic beliefs. A tigress is considered the legendary ancestor of the people of Agam, one of the three original areas of the Minangkabau and a region well populated by tigers. Certain powerful Minangkabau men are "tiger magicians" (*pawang manangkok harimau*), figures of spiritual strength, bravery, fortitude, and extraordinary abilities.

Just as we call a plumber when the sink clogs, a Minangkabau village that is plagued by a tiger calls in a *pawang harimau*, for a fee which may be as much as $250. Once the specialist is satisfied that nobody has been overtly sinning, he first tries to convince the tiger that it really should return to the forest and stop making life difficult for his friends the Minangkabau. If diplomacy fails, the pawang requests permission from the forest spirits to trap the tiger, and then builds a tiger trap which is placed in a likely spot in the forest. At the trap he recites a long series of Arabic prayers, in order to show that the whole process is linked with the modern Muslim beliefs of the people. The prayers are followed by special tiger-capturing songs in the Minangkabau language, accompanied by a bamboo flute.

Different songs attract different sorts of tigers. A female tiger is enticed by telling her that her lover has already entered the cage and is eagerly awaiting her arrival. She is called "rich widow," a term of respect in matriarchal west Sumatra, and invited to join her lover on a heavenly tiger island, a metaphor for the tiger cage.

"The beautiful vocal melodies, set to elegant poetic meters containing delicate allusions, metaphors and polite points of etiquette, are in keeping with the animist Minangkabau belief that the character of the tiger family is one of diplomacy and elegant cunning," says Margaret Kartomi, an Australian anthropologist. "The anthropomorphic attribution to the tiger of morals, sexual love, and even artistic feelings is certainly pre-Islamic and probably goes back to the ancient Animist beliefs of the Minangkabau. The practice of singing Muslim prayers is probably an addition to the originally purely animistic tradition, in order to make it more acceptable to the devout Muslims in the community. The resulting artistic synthesis is very much in keeping with the whole Minangkabau way of life."

Pawangs are even used by the Indonesian government. Wartono Kadri, then head of the Department of Nature Conservation, told us in 1982 that his department keeps three pawangs on permanent retainer so that they can be called upon to try to capture problem tigers without killing them.

Sometimes the pawang harimau fails to capture the tiger. This is taken as evidence that the tiger was innocent of the sin of eating a human being or domestic animal. If a tiger is accidentally killed in a trap set for another animal, the pawang harimau is called in to placate the forest spirits and convince them that revenge against humans is not necessary.

But as time goes by, the old tiger magicians are dying out and the young men of the villages are spending their time in school, not in the forest. They learn a different way of viewing the world and forget their people's age-old respect for the tiger. Instead, some of them go for the easy money to be made by selling tiger skins to the Chinese middlemen who in turn earn large profits from tourists eager to have a magnificent souvenir of tropical Asia.

When we visited high-ranking military officials in Jakarta we were sometimes startled to be greeted by a snarling stuffed tiger guarding the sitting room. One cabinet minister, who was sympathetic to conservation issues, told us that he wanted to get rid of his tiger, but could not do so since that would embarrass other senior officials who had no intention of giving up their purchased trophies.

Indirect pressures affect the tiger as well. As modern forms of development spread into Minangkabau country, more of the forest is cleared and the tigers are pushed into areas of remaining wilderness which are far smaller than the thousand square miles of good habitat which are required to maintain a healthy population.

◆ ◆ ◆

Dr. Boonsong was excited. He had just received a telegram from an old friend in southern Thailand's Nakhon Si Thammarat Province who needed help in dealing with a tiger who was stealing goats from villagers. "We must go at once," he said. "We don't want the villagers to trap the wrong tiger. And we must convince them not to take out their anger on all the tigers in the forest."

Dr. Boonsong quickly made train reservations while we packed our bags. Within an hour, we were on the train with a gaggle of students going home for vacation in "Second-Class Sitting." As we settled down for the fourteen-hour ride south, Dr. Boonsong bought us some Singha beer and started telling us stories of tigers he had hunted in his youth. While his commitment to conservation was unquestioned, several of the students sitting nearby grilled Dr. Boonsong politely but earnestly. Why had he killed such magnificent animals? Didn't he follow the Buddha's teachings? How could he preach conservation when he had been a killer?

Dr. Boonsong was in his element. It was obvious that he enjoyed the give and take with bright and inquisitive students, and they in turn clearly respected Dr. Boonsong for his lifelong battle to save Thai wildlife. He did not apologize for having been a hunter. "Hunting is only wrong," he suggested to the students, "when it might destroy the population of the animal being hunted. When I hunted tigers, I respected them, in a way even worshiped them. I knew that they could kill me if I made a mistake, and the deadly danger represented by the tiger made me feel more alive. But," he continued, "I would never hunt a tiger now unless it was a man-eater. Tigers are now so rare that they are a national treasure."

A stunning fifteen-year-old girl with frank eyes wondered if the tiger's rarity might not be at least partly because Dr. Boonsong had hunted them. "I don't think so," he responded. "I have killed only seven tigers, and four of them were man-eaters that I was asked to kill by villagers. And when I stopped hunting tigers in the late 1950s, there were still plenty. But in recent years, poachers have become well organized and you can find hundreds of tiger skins for sale to rich tourists in Bangkok. And what may be even worse, the tiger's habitat and the animals he hunts for food are also being destroyed to make way for new farms. We must all respect the tiger," he concluded, "because he is the Lord of the Forest and stands for all that is magnificent in nature."

Dr. Boonsong repeated this message to the villagers in Nakhon Si Thammarat, adding the practical point that if they killed the tigers, then pigs, deer, and monkeys would multiply and eat their crops. "And if a tiger is really threatening your village," Dr. Boonsong advised as the villagers listened politely, "you should try to trap it where it is causing trouble, so you know you have the right one. Tigers that mind their own business in the forest should be left alone." We left the next morning with the thanks of the local people for coming. No doubt they had their own spirited discussions after our departure.

◆ ◆ ◆

The tiger's character has made it an admired adversary of hunters, the national animal of India, a valued component of traditional medicine, an important advertising symbol, and a central theme in the mythology of the region. These values have earned the tiger enough public support to generate a major effort to keep it alive despite foreign demand for its skin and for the crops which could be grown in its habitat.

Known as Project Tiger, the campaign has been one of conservation's most dramatic success stories. According to Guy Mountfort, a founder of WWF and one of the originators of this conservation effort, the tiger, "a dominant animal species which in the 1930s had a probable total population of about 100,000, had dwindled in only 40 years to a mere 5,000 or so." With increased support from all governments in the region, the big cat's world population has recovered to some 7,000 today and the animal's future is reasonably secure in at least some places.

Peter Jackson, chairman of the IUCN Cat Specialist Group and former project manager of Project Tiger, notes that the programs, which involved setting up large nature reserves, "have shielded the animals from direct persecution, protected their prey and improved habitats. In the process, degraded land has been rehabilitated, forest productivity increased and water supplies improved—to the benefit of people as well as animals."

But tiger habitat is going fast, and people are pushing deeper into what was once tiger country. Tigers are forced into increasing conflicts with people, leading to deadly results for both man and tiger. The end game of this process was seen several years ago on Java, where the tiger had led a precarious existence for several decades.

"We might have no more than three, or at most five, tigers left in Java, all in Meru Betiri," explained John Seidensticker in 1978. "We have waited so long to do anything about the Javan critter that it may not be possible to save him. Remember that just ten years ago there were a dozen or so tigers in Ujung Kulon [in west Java], but they didn't make it there even with virtually no hunting pressure or conflicts with people. Even so, we have the responsibility to see that every possible effort is made to take the management actions that will give the tiger his best chance for survival."

Confined to a tiny corner of an island the size of Greece or New York State occupied by 100 million people, the Javan tiger had found itself in the middle of a political storm at the highest level of the Indonesian government. Shortly after President Suharto repeated his call for the need to protect the Javan tigers in Meru

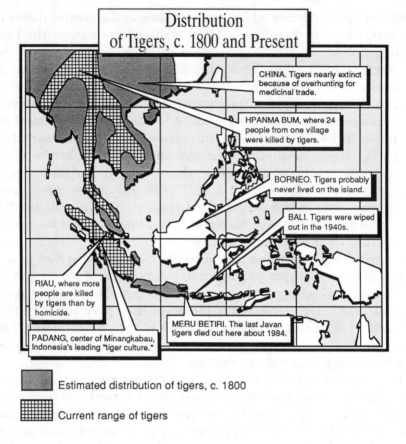

Distribution of Tigers, c. 1800 and Present

CHINA. Tigers nearly extinct because of overhunting for medicinal trade.

HPANMA BUM, where 24 people from one village were killed by tigers.

BORNEO. Tigers probably never lived on the island.

BALI. Tigers were wiped out in the 1940s.

RIAU, where more people are killed by tigers than by homicide.

PADANG, center of Minangkabau, Indonesia's leading "tiger culture."

MERU BETIRI. The last Javan tigers died out here about 1984.

Estimated distribution of tigers, c. 1800

Current range of tigers

Betiri, which would have involved moving 5,000 people from two rubber plantations in the reserve, a delegation to Parliament criticized the government's plan as contrary to the humanitarian principles of the state philosophy. "The government should avoid sacrificing thousands of people only for protecting four tigers," said the representative from East Java. Since the Indonesian Parliament is officially based on *musjawarat* and *mupakat*, the principles of universal consultation and compromise in which debaters bore each other into agreement, the anti-tiger lobby stymied the conservation effort.

But the Javan tiger also had some powerful supporters. Julius Tahija, a war hero who fought the Japanese in World War II, a member of the WWF International Council, Chairman of the Board of Caltex Pacific (which produces more than half of Indonesia's oil), and a leader of Indonesia's economic recovery following the Sukarno years, argued the tiger's case strongly with President Suharto. "Meru Betiri and the Javan tiger," Tahija said, "are a part of Indonesia's national heritage in the same way that the temples of Borobudur and Prambanan represent our cultural heritage. These monuments are unique and once destroyed cannot be replaced, so nobody is likely to propose their removal to make way for a cement factory, a housing complex, or some other form of development. Yet living natural monuments such as the tiger are similarly both unique and an irreplaceable part not only of our national heritage but that of mankind as a whole."

The President agreed, and issued the necessary orders. But it was too little, too late and the local villagers, in the age-old Asian way, were able to effectively ignore the commands from the capital. In 1984 IUCN determined that, since no tiger spoor had been seen for several years, the Javan subspecies had become extinct, following in the footsteps of its Balinese cousin several decades earlier. Meru Betiri is still an important protected area, but Java's tigers have faded into legend.

◆ ◆ ◆

People have a strong emotional need for the "essence" of the tiger. In Java, the tiger is an ancient cultural symbol of mercurial and violent power, representing the baser human impulses (in Freudian terms, the id). The tiger is the emotional antithesis of the Javan ideal of steadfastness and restraint. This Javanese calm is often symbolized by the wild cattle, called banteng, which represent the peaceful intelligent man in control of himself (the superego). These two opposite forces are considered vital parts of the human world, elements which must be kept in proper balance in order for an individual to maintain internal harmony (a healthy ego).

This symbolic balance has long been represented in the *kekayon* or *gunungan*, the large, triangular shadow puppet that represents the universe in all its complexity. The gunungan (mountain) is put on the screen at the beginning and end of each *wayang kulit* shadow puppet play, the most popular form of entertainment in Javan villages, and appears on the country's coins. The triangular shape represents Mount Meru, the holy mountain of the Hindus, where the "tree of heaven" grows. On the gunungan, this tree is filled with monkeys and birds, symbolizing the world of nature created by the Supreme Being. Underneath the tree, at the center and widest part of the gunungan, are a tiger on the left and a wild ox on the right, standing in balanced opposition above a small house with ornate doors. But the doors are closed, representing the difficulty humans have in attaining peace of mind. Only by balancing the opposing emotional forces can the doors open and peace be achieved.

In the colonial period the Javanese staged popular tiger-banteng battles in order to see a real-life bloody battle between the id and the superego. When the Dutch started threatening the sovereignty of the Javanese sultans during the late eighteenth century, public tiger-banteng battles were often held for the entertainment of visiting Dutch dignitaries. The Dutch were ignorant of the symbolic content of these battles. The local sultans, however, viewed the fights as allegories of the Javan-Dutch confrontation, with the Dutch (whose national symbol is the lion) being represented by the tiger: quick and deadly, but lacking staying power. The Javans were symbolized by the banteng: powerful yet restrained and placid until aroused, at which time they went to battle with a singular strength of purpose.

The Dutch were surprised when the seemingly placid banteng was almost always victorious. Thomas Stamford Raffles, founder of modern Singapore and lieutenant governor of Java during a short British rule while Napoleon Bonaparte ruled Holland, was well aware of the symbolism of the battles. "It may be readily imagined," he said, "with what eagerness the Javans look to the success of the banteng."

In 1788, Jan Greeve, the Dutch governor of Surakarta in central Java, visited the great Sultan of Yogyakarta, Mangkubumi, who is the ancestor of a direct line leading to the present Sultan Hamengku Buwono IX. Greeve was shown the usual battle, but suggested that a second tiger be thrown into the battle, as the first tiger was tiring quickly. The second tiger immediately attacked the banteng, but was also driven back and soon joined the first tiger, which was resting in a quiet corner of the arena. The Javans used the gentle tactic of poking burning torches at the tigers to spur them into action, but this only made the animals so furious that they attacked each other. Both tigers died a bloody death. Mangkubumi found this vastly entertaining, since the "Dutch" tiger had even had reinforcements (the British?) and the two tigers had turned against each other while the "Javan" banteng stood calmly by, doing nothing more than chewing its cud to attain vic-

tory. This fit very well the Javan strategy for overcoming its powerful Dutch adversary by patiently wearing it down, a tactic still
effectively used by Javanese businessmen and bureaucrats when
they feel threatened by aggressive foreigners.

◆ ◆ ◆

Now, less than 200 years after Jan Greeve's visit to Yogyakarta,
the tiger's real battle on Java has been lost. Tigers in Sumatra and
mainland Southeast Asia are doing somewhat better, but inexora-
ble human pressure on the land to harvest timber for export, or to
grow market crops, means that tigers everywhere are now fighting
for their survival. While the banteng has won on Java, the balance
of the ideal world of nature has been lost and the quality of life for
all people on this overcrowded island is suffering from the environmental abuses of its limited resources. Formerly a symbol of
nature's power, the Javan tiger is now a symbol of paradise lost.

19

Here Be Dragons

People traditionally learned to live with dangerous crocodiles through common sense, myth, and ceremony. Crocodiles have their good points and may be more valuable in the swamps than as leather.

UNTIL 700 YEARS AGO, Southeast Asia was *terra incognita* to Europeans. Alexander the Great had bullied his way to the Indian subcontinent; but in general the world the early European cartographers knew stretched north to Norseland, south to the Mediterranean, and east to Egypt. Within these confines, empires-of-the-moment were colorfully defined. But what of the lands beyond the known borders? In that era before Marco Polo the early mapmakers could agree only that the netherworld must be a fearsome place indeed, filled with such horror and mystery that no one would ever return from a visit. So to fill in the blank spaces to the east the early European geographers conscientiously inscribed a warning: "Here be dragons."

They had no idea how right they were.

For in the tropics of the East, dragons are alive and well, embodied as the crocodiles which are still the dominant predators in rivers, lakes, and swamps. Like many things Asian, the dragons of the east are complex and surprising. The eastern dragons are not the fearsome, humorless monsters of biblical allegory and medieval European imagination. Just the opposite.

"The Eastern dragon," writes the Japanese philosopher Okakura Kakuzo, "is the spirit of change, therefore of life itself. Hidden in the caverns of inaccessible mountains, or coiled in the unfathomed depth of the sea, he awaits the time when he slowly rouses himself into activity. He unfolds himself in the storm clouds; he washes his mane in the blackness of the seething whirlpools. His claws are in the fork of the lightning, his scales begin to glisten in the bark of wind-swept pine trees. His voice is heard in the hurricane, which, scattering the withered leaves of the forest, quickens a new spring."

The idea of the dragon, found through much of tropical Asia, was always strongest in China. The stylized creature may have been based on the Chinese alligator, an animal found only in China whose closest relative lives in Florida. This dragon ancestor spends the winter in its cold, muddy den and emerges in the spring, bringing with it the return of nature's energies; it is thus the symbol of the reproductive force of spring, and a protector of Chinese culture. Adding golden wings and a hot breath produced a symbol which understandably came to personify the emperor.

Tropical Asia is a paradise for crocodilians (crocodiles can show a toothy smile even when their mouths are closed while alligators just smirk—their teeth fit neatly together when their jaws are shut), with the beasts infesting rivers, estuaries, and coastlines from Pakistan to Australia. The saltwater crocodile covers the whole region, and four freshwater species live in India, Thailand and Indochina, the Philippines, and New Guinea. The two most fearsome forms are harmless to people; the gavials which live in India and Nepal and false gavials inhabiting freshwater swamps from Burma to Indonesia are both fish-eaters armed with a long narrow snout packed with dagger-like teeth.

Just as tigers dominate the land from India to Sumatra, so crocodiles rule the waters of tropical Asia. From Borneo and Java eastward, they are the dominant carnivore, and the animal most feared by people. A creature which is known to attack and eat people is given considerable respect, at least partly in the belief that the animal's power comes from close links with the spirits. Although crocodiles frighten, like tigers they are venerated and respected, and at times given anthropomorphic qualities and treated like people. It has been live and let live, since most people were cautious about tempting the crocodiles and also because the crocodiles were protected by taboos and generally inefficient hunting methods.

The Tempasak Dusun of Sabah, for example, don't kill crocodiles because one of the beasts once married a Dusun girl. This crocodile, the myth goes, had five toes on each foot, instead of four like most crocodiles. According to British anthropologist Owen Rutter, "The people of Tempasak say that if they could be certain a crocodile had the regulation four toes, they would not hesitate to kill it, but since crocodiles seldom proffer their feet for inspection, they prefer to run no risks in slaughtering a possible relative by marriage."

The feelings of veneration and awe toward crocodiles have been expressed in some unusual ways in the past, particularly in the eastern Indonesian islands where crocodile attacks have always been made more frequent by human overpopulation.

• On the island of Ceram in the Indonesian Moluccas, women were thought sometimes to mate with crocodiles. The offspring were always twins, one human, one reptilian. The baby croc born of this union was released into the river and fed by its mother until the crocodile's human brother was old enough to take over the responsibility. In return, the crocodile's magic protected the family. On ceremonial occasions large boating parties took food out to the river, singing to their crocodile brothers and inviting them to join the feast. Drawn by the music, the crocodiles soon appeared and devoured rice, tobacco, and betel nut.

• According to German anthropologist W. F. A. Zimmerman, some groups even practiced what might be considered preventive maintenance. In the 1700s the Rajah of Kupang, on the east Indonesian island of Timor, annually sacrificed a royal virgin to the estuarine crocodile, logical enough since the royal family considered themselves descendants of crocodiles. The girl, beautifully dressed in her finest sarong, doused with perfume and garlanded with flowers, was placed on a sacred stone at the water's edge where she patiently waited for her suitor to carry her off to his riverine lair. She accepted this rather cavalier treatment because she had been taught that the crocodile would marry her and treat her like a princess.

· On the east Indonesian island of Buru, priests determined that a sudden increase in crocodile attacks was due to the passion a crocodile prince felt for a certain girl. The priests forced the unfortunate girl's father to dress her as a bride and deliver her to the crocodiles.

In all these cases people made a deal with the crocodile. "We'll look after you," the humans seemed to say, "if you leave us alone." Muslims in some parts of Indonesia believe crocodiles, like tigers, are forbidden by the natural law laid down by Nabi Sleman (King Solomon) to kill humans. If any crocodile breaks Sleman's law, it will be driven out of its group and forced to live alone.

Sometimes the crocodile finds it hard to stick to a fish and game diet, and must be captured. As with tigers, this requires a *pawang*, who uses both magic to deal with the spiritual side of hunting and long practical experience to deal with the animal side of the beast.

Throughout the coastal region of Southeast Asia, wherever the fierce saltwater crocodile still survives, certain gifted men have become crocodile bounty hunters. According to Edwin Gomes, a missionary who spent seventeen years living among the Dayak of Borneo, "whenever a human being has fallen a victim to one of these brutes, a professional crocodile catcher is asked to help to destroy the murderer. The majority of natives will not interfere with the reptiles, or take any part in their capture, probably fearing that if they did anything of the kind, they themselves may some time or other suffer for it by being attacked by a crocodile."

◆ ◆ ◆

Some crocodile hunters make the wayward animals an offer they can't refuse:

> Ye crocodiles who are upstream, come down.
> And ye crocodiles who are downstream, come up.
> For I will give you all good food.
> As sweet as sugar and as fat as coconut.
> I will give you a beautiful necklace.

As the chant continues the caller's voice reaches the moaning intensity of a man deep in prayer—or wracked with pain. His piercing voice carries far over the water and the crocodile, perhaps imagining that it belongs to a man in distress and therefore an easy meal, approaches and takes the bait of rotten meat.

◆ ◆ ◆

Malaysian officials called in local and Indonesian crocodile pawangs to capture an animal that attacked at least seventeen people living near Sarawak's Batang Lupar River in the early 1980s. One victim was a prawn fisherman who was said to have been held aloft in the reptile's jaws and paraded back and forth in a grisly show of defiance. Stories circulated that the crocodile, named *Bujang Senang,* (a play on words that literally means "happy bachelor" but also refers to "a young man from the nearby Senang River") was the invincible ghost of a murdered Iban warrior which could be captured only through supernatural means. When the police hunters failed to kill the offending croc, the pawangs were called in to capture the beast through magic.

After several years of effort, Malaysian authorities proudly exhibited the carcass of a fifteen-foot-long crocodile. For the moment, it was once again safe to bathe in the Batang Lupar.

◆ ◆ ◆

People who are faced daily with the possibility of being attacked and eaten by a predator far more powerful than themselves have developed psychological and religious defenses against fear: crocodiles are our spiritual brothers and won't hurt us; they only take sinners, and I'm good; I haven't done them any harm, so they won't hurt me; I won't take unnecessary risks by calling their attention to me; and if I *really* have a problem I can call in a pawang who will use his magic to deflect any danger from me.

Still, it never hurts to have insurance. An old man who ran the ferry across the Barito River at Banjarmasin in southern Kalimantan in the 1920s set himself up in business. "He has capitalized his skill and cunning by organizing himself into a sort of crocodile liability company," noted the American traveler E. Alexander Powell. "Anyone may secure a policy in this company by paying him a weekly premium of 2.5 Dutch cents. When one of his policy holders is overtaken by death in the form of a pair of four-foot jaws the old man turns the ferry over to one of his children and sets out to fulfill the terms of his contract by capturing the offending saurian, recovering from its stomach the weighty bracelets, anklets and earrings worn by the deceased, and restoring them to the next of kin."

◆ ◆ ◆

While the man-crocodile relationship may be a bit fragile at times, societies that include crocodiles in their belief systems actually live in better harmony with their environment and enjoy increased productivity from the rivers, lakes, and estuaries which provide sustenance to both man and crocodile.

Modern cultures generally share with simpler societies an emotional feeling that conservation is necessary and good, a feeling that is possibly part of the collective subconscious which was earlier represented by mythology. But modern societies often have a need to rationalize things, so scientists, as high priests of technology, have studied the reasons for conserving crocodiles. Their investigations have shown what the tribal people have always known and expressed in their mythology—crocodiles provide a definite benefit for humans. Consider:

- In areas with a long dry season, crocodile wallows and other diggings become important drinking ponds for wildlife (though not without risk to the drinker).
- Young crocodiles eat large quantities of snails and have been credited with helping to control snail-spread diseases such as schistosomiasis.
- Studies have shown that the presence of crocodiles in a river actually *increases the yield of fish,* which by itself justifies the veneration village societies have for the beasts. Crocodiles eat ailing fish in a significantly higher proportion than healthy fish, thus improving the common health of the fish stock. By preying on the most common fish, they balance the fish population; any species which suddenly becomes dominant is put back in its proper proportion. Crocodile droppings are nutritious for the fish and contain critically important chemicals.
- Crocodiles have a tremendous effect on the flow of nutrients in the river. The river bed is a rich mud saturated with algae and small animals. When the crocodile swims, the broad sweeps of its tail and serpentine twisting of his body stir up the river bottom, releasing nutrients on which fish can feed. Crocodiles are supreme scavengers, a point recognized in India where officials announced, in September 1987, that 150 crocodiles were to be released in the Ganges River to clean up the remains of the approximately 100,000 corpses cremated on the river banks at the Hindu holy city of Varanasi.

By serving both a conservation function and a deeply felt mythological need, beliefs promoting coexistence with crocodiles became integrated in human cultures.

◆ ◆ ◆

Geneva's new Confederation Centre is the most exclusive shopping mall in a city that relishes its designer boutiques. Nina Ricci, Gucci, Giorgio Armani, and other *haute couture* houses give the neighborhood an expensive style.

We went there one blustery January day, looking for a new camera we had heard about. Geneva in the winter is often misty, gray, and damp, and we reminisced that in Jakarta on a January Saturday morning we would be heading out to the Thousand Islands for some scuba diving and a lobster lunch. In Geneva we settled for reasonably fresh oysters at an unreasonable price, but not until after our companions dragged us into a shop with a discreet notice that *créations mode* were to be found within.

We shuffled in wearing our jeans and ski parkas while the elegant saleslady, much to her credit, was pleasant even when we said we were just looking. While the ladies tried on boots that neither they nor we could afford, we roamed around the carpeted showroom and saw stylish pangolin cowboy boots and python pumps. We asked the price of an attractive pair of blue crocodile evening shoes. "One thousand francs, just over six hundred dollars at today's exchange rate, messieurs," the saleslady said without a smile. "They're very beautiful, *n'est-ce pas?*" While one of us agreed, the other whispered to our ladies that the time on our parking meter was running out, and we should do the same.

◆ ◆ ◆

The dictates of style have changed people's perception of crocodiles. Crocodiles had lived comfortably for 200 million years before anybody noticed that their skins make good wallets, but now that hunters have been stimulated by a strong seller's market, crocodiles everywhere are being slaughtered for their hides. And people get greedy. A Papuan hunter told us that a few years ago a drought forced the crocodiles into a small area of the swamp where hunters could easily shoot as many as they wanted. Such an opportunity attracted villagers from miles around; the men from the village, who had traditionally hunted at a sustainable level, were forced to shoot as many crocs as possible so the outside hunters would not take all the skins.

The result? The glut on the market drove prices of crocodile skins so low that hunters could barely meet their expenses. And even worse, the crocodile population was so reduced that the traditional hunters had great difficulty finding any wild crocodiles. Overexploitation had destroyed a sustainable source of income, largely because nobody had the responsibility to protect the reptiles.

Concerned governments, of both importing and exporting nations, have taken legal steps to ensure that the world can have both its crocodiles and its handbags. Traditional controls on exploitation are being replaced by sanctions that modern governments understand—fines and jail sentences. Most Asian countries now give crocodiles some legal protection, though enforcement under isolated conditions is always difficult.

A more effective way of controlling trade is at the receiving end, so all trade in crocodiles is now regulated under the Convention on International Trade in Endangered Species of Wild Fauna and Flora (CITES). This agreement controls dealings in wildlife and wildlife products by requiring that every animal and animal product carry a certificate of origin to prove that it did not come from a country where it is protected as an endangered or threatened species. International commercial trade in crocodiles is prohibited among the more than ninety countries which are party to the treaty unless the animals derive from captive-bred or certain wild populations which are known to be able to sustain some harvesting. Even then, strict quotas attempt to limit the impact of commercial trading on wild crocodiles.

Trade regulations, however, only work when there is something to buy and sell. Where will the supply of "legal" crocodiles come from?

Some people hope that the answer can be found in crocodile "ranching," which involves leaving the large adults in the swamps while their eggs and young are collected for rearing under some sort of controlled environment for the three or four years it takes for them to grow large enough to become billfold material. This approach is based on sound biological sense. Female crocodiles can lay up to seventy eggs per year, and most of them hatch. But it's a tough new world for the baby croc because in the wild it is the breakfast of choice for all sorts of predators, including storks, herons, fish, turtles, giant frogs, and even adult crocodiles, which together ensure that over 80 percent of the young that are hatched never celebrate their first birthday.

But baby crocodiles saved from predators and brought into captivity grow quickly, gaining one pound of weight for each two pounds of food consumed (cattle, pigs, and sheep require three to five times as much food to gain the same weight). According to a study by the U.S. National Academy of Sciences, this "makes crocodiles probably the most nutritionally efficient land animal for commercial husbandry. Only the growth of some fish is comparable."

Ranching seems a sensible approach to managing crocodiles in Papua New Guinea, where the human population is sparse and extensive areas of swampy crocodile habitat cannot really be used for anything else. With 30,000 crocodiles on ranches in Papua New Guinea, villagers have sufficient stock to earn a reasonable living by supplying skins that keep European boutique owners happy. The availability of ranched crocodiles also takes pressure off wild populations so that crocodiles can continue their life in the rivers and estuaries.

In theory, the same system could be widely applied in remote areas of the lowland tropics, where crocodile skins may provide the only readily marketable resource. Jayapura is a bustling town on the northern coast of Irian Jaya, the Indonesian part of New Guinea. Among other things, it contains most of the country's crocodile ranches, but Indonesia does things differently from Papua New Guinea and many of the ranches seem to be little more than fronts for the sale of skins taken from the wild. They are supposed to rear juveniles up to thirty inches long caught in the wild, but in fact animals of all sizes are being taken. To make matters worse, Indonesia's regulations only allow the export of crocodile skins which have been tanned, and Ron Petocz, who spent six years in Irian Jaya helping the Indonesian government develop a network of protected areas, told us that the only tanning factory is partially owned by nature conservation officials. It seems highly unlikely that the Irian Jaya crocodile trade is going to be carried out in the sustainable manner which seems to be working in Papua New Guinea.

◆ ◆ ◆

In crowded Thailand, the New Guinea "ranching" model can't work because few crocodiles survive in the wild and most of the

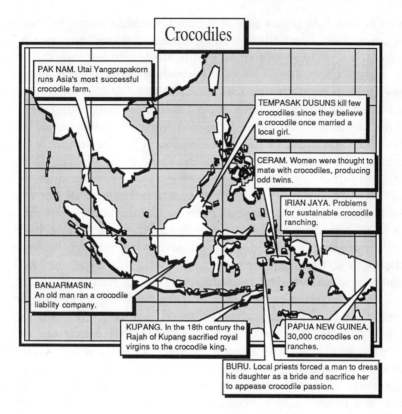

Crocodiles

PAK NAM. Utai Yangprapakorn runs Asia's most successful crocodile farm.

TEMPASAK DUSUNS kill few crocodiles since they believe a crocodile once married a local girl.

CERAM. Women were thought to mate with crocodiles, producing odd twins.

IRIAN JAYA. Problems for sustainable crocodile ranching.

BANJARMASIN. An old man ran a crocodile liability company.

KUPANG. In the 18th century the Rajah of Kupang sacrified royal virgins to the crocodile king.

PAPUA NEW GUINEA. 30,000 crocodiles on ranches.

BURU. Local priests forced a man to dress his daughter as a bride and sacrifice her to appease crocodile passion.

crocodile habitat has been taken over by man. The innovative Thais have found another way to provide crocodile skins for the market: farming crocodiles bred in captivity.

The most successful crocodile farm in Southeast Asia is in Pak Nam, thirty miles south of Bangkok in the mangrove swamps near the delta of Thailand's Chao Phya River. Owned by a Chinese immigrant, Utai Yangprapakorn, the farm is so successful that Utai is able to send each of his twelve children overseas for an education he never had.

Dr. Boonsong took us down to help Utai prepare some papers for IUCN's Crocodile Specialist Group, which gave him the chance to tell the outside world how his system worked. Utai explained how he got started. "I began the crocodile farm in 1950 with $500 and just 20 little crocodiles I caught in the swamp. I tried to learn all I could about crocodiles and their breeding habits, and I attempted to duplicate their wild conditions here on my farm. By 1960 we hatched 150 crocodiles and now we're hatching between 3,000 and

5,000 a year." At Utai's Samutprakan Crocodile Farm and Zoo Co., Ltd., two vast crocodile breeding tanks took up two and a half acres each and dozens of small peninsulas extended into the brackish water. Crocodiles basked everywhere, like singles around a Beverly Hills pool. In the trees toward the back of the pen the wall was lined with little sliding doors leading to the nesting pens.

Utai described to us the long and intricate courtship of crocodiles, the unlikeliest of lovers. Submission by the female is an important part of the process, and the male must always be bigger than the female in order to overcome her initial reluctance, which she often expresses by loud hissing and puffing up of her cheeks. The male never bites her, but butts her with his head or thrashes her with his tail. Once she has submitted, his behavior becomes much more suave. He sidles up alongside his consort, rubbing his nose against hers, stroking her belly with his nose, and sinking quietly underneath and blowing bubbles to gently stimulate her underparts. After a long sojourn of gentle courtship, mating finally takes place in the water after sunset. The male roars, warning all other males to stay away and once again impressing the female with his grandeur. The female answers by raising her head high out of the water, her jaws wide open and pointed to the sky. The male rubs his body alongside the female, grasps her around the neck in a tender caress, hooks his tail under hers to lever himself into position and bends his body under hers, in a reptilian Kama Sutra. The female sometimes lies on her side so that her vent is turned to receive the male. Sometimes they copulate for only a few minutes, sometimes for nearly an hour.

A few weeks later the female enters her nesting box where she lays her eggs. She is then chased out of the nesting box and the staff of the crocodile farm take over her maternal chores. They ensure that the temperature of the nest is optimal, keep a watchful eye on the eggs, and, after ten weeks, open the nest to release the young.

The crocodile farm, which by 1974 was supplying 80 percent of the Thai crocodile skin trade and has now virtually cornered the market, is one of the major diurnal tourist attractions around Bangkok. Each year 1 million visitors come to gape, and Utai not only earns money from admission ($3.00 for foreign tourists) but from refreshment stands, elephant rides, photographers who take a picture of you with a tame python wrapped around your shoulders, stands selling fish to feed the crocodiles, and gift shops that sell stuffed baby crocs. Lacquered crocodile heads go for about $15 while tiny feet are a bargain at $3.00 each.

Skins earn Utai between $90 and $250 each, depending on size, species, and the strength of the international market. Not only the skins are valuable, however. The meat is sold to local restaurants ($2.00 per pound) and as a treatment for asthma, and teeth are used in Thai medicine. Utai's total take from an average crocodile (skin plus meat) in 1986 was about $350.

Utai strolled along the elevated walkway built to give visitors a closer look. "Each pond has over 200 breeding crocodiles," he explained, "with one male to every three females. We want to make sure each male finds the lover he likes," he added with a smile as tolerant as a Bangkok massage parlor mama-san.

Utai's papers were well received, even though the chairman of the Crocodile Specialist Group was still suspicious—with some justification—that Utai was buying wild crocodiles brought to him by rural villagers. Utai was made a member of the group, but was later expelled when he started using similar captive-breeding methods for tigers, which he fed with surplus crocodile meat. Apparently it's all right to make a profit out of raising cold-blooded reptiles for their skins, but quite another matter for a private individual to commercialize the king of cats.

◆ ◆ ◆

Conservation laws were not needed in the days when people and crocodiles lived in a sort of balance, killing each other with reasonable discretion. But in past times, the benefits of a healthy crocodile population far outweighed the possible advantage of indiscriminantly killing crocodiles. Today, the seductive market of the industrialized countries lures rural people to overhunt, thereby upsetting the balance. Most ranches are not conservation-friendly because they regularly take young crocodiles from the wild to replenish stocks. Even crocodile farming operations top up their animal populations with wild animals—it seems that wild crocodiles will be free of abuse only when there are no more left to be captured.

On the other hand, ranching operations which are run well, such as the ones on Papua New Guinea, can stop the harvesting of adults and are therefore a step forward. Ranching needs the wild crocs, and, in the words of Ron Petocz, "If the resource can't be used, especially such an ugly and 'dangerous' animal, there will never be enough lobby power to maintain crocs in the wild."

The crocodile skin trade may indeed be necessary to ensure the survival of the wild animals at a time in history which requires an economic value be applied to every resource, but the abuses of the trade in Indonesia are making the ideal of "sustainable use" a mockery. Animals which were so well adapted that they flourished for eons may be unable to meet the challenge of fashion. "The time may have come," Dr. Boonsong told us, "when we must choose between a few more fancy handbags and dancing shoes and the survival of the last remaining ruling reptiles."

20

Drugstores on the Hoof

Apothecaries in Southeast Asia prescribe animal products as the medicine of choice for a surprising array of ailments, but the drug supply is running out.

A SHIPYARD FIRE in Singapore several years ago killed more than seventy people. One of the survivors, a fifty-year-old laborer, was critically burned over most of his body. Western medicine failed to alleviate his suffering, so his family turned to a traditional Chinese doctor. The doctor prescribed powdered cyst from a porcupine brain, one of the rarest animal medicines. The man's concerned employer went to medicine shop owner Choong Chor Fong to purchase the substance. Mr. Choong, president of Singapore's Ming Tai Co., Ltd., explained to us that the patient showed immediate improvement upon downing the cyst, which cost about U.S.$ 250 for 1/100 of an ounce. After two additional treatments, the worker recovered fully.

It's not news to many westerners that medicine men all over the world use plants to treat burns, injuries, and common maladies ranging from colds to warts. Less well known is the fact that animal parts too are widely employed as traditional remedies throughout Southeast Asia. The international trade in creature cures from Asian forests and swamps is booming. The inventiveness of these concoctions, not to mention their impact on certain animal populations, is astonishing. Some examples:

- In 1984 and 1985 Thailand exported about 2.7 million dried and smoked gecko lizards, which are taken by Chinese to cure respiratory illness. In 1984 more than 150,000 pounds of turtle shells, used in various Chinese medicines and valued at $1 million, were exported.
- Crocodile scales cooked in butter are a cure for toothaches and boils in some parts of Indonesia.
- In northern Sulawesi, lice from human hair are stuffed into a banana and gulped down as a cure for asthma and hepatitis.
- In Vietnam, bones of monkey arms are boiled for ten days to make a tonic intended to improve circulation and cure severe rheumatism.
- Scales of the pangolin, a curious-looking scaled anteater, are claimed by the Chinese to be useful for a wide variety of skin ailments.
- Powdered deer antlers are ingested in many parts of Asia for enhancing virility, treating kidney ailments, and rejuvenating aging tissues.
- The official Chinese *Barefoot Doctor's Manual,* which is the basis for the primary medical care received by the majority of that vast country's population, prescribes rhino horn for a wide variety of illnesses including encephalitis B and typhoid.
- A Siamese prescription in the nineteenth century for "morbific fever" was an exotic cocktail: "One portion of rhinoceros horn, one of elephant's tusk, one of tiger's, and the same of crocodile's teeth; one of bear's tooth; one portion composed of three parts bones of vulture, raven, and goose; one portion of bison and another of stag's horn, one portion of sandalwood. These ingredients to be mixed together on a stone with pure water; one half of the mixture to be swallowed, the rest to be rubbed into the body; after which the morbific fever will depart."

Do these treatments actually work?

Many people scoff at such "unscientific" uses of animal parts, but the truth is that many animal substances do have genuine medicinal value. Drugs made from the venom of Russell's viper may control hemophilia. And, had it been available at the time, a drug made from the venom of the Malaysian pit viper might have sufficiently relieved Richard Nixon's phlebitis that he could have testified at the Watergate trials.

The venom of the many-banded krait is being used to duplicate the symptoms of myasthenia gravis, the nerve disease that killed Aristotle Onassis. The 500 components of the venom of a Southeast Asian snail that has killed at least twenty bathers offers "great potential" for understanding the same ailment and other neurological disorders such as muscular dystrophy, according to Dr. Baldomero Olivera, a Filipino molecular biologist quoted by Bob Mims.

Experiments in India have shown that musk from the musk deer stimulates the heart and central nervous system, and acts as an anti-inflammatory agent for the treatment of snake bites. A recent study at the Worker's Hospital in China's Hunan Province determined that powdered elephant skin is effective against inflammation, gastric ulcers, chilblains, external hemorrhoids, and chronic rheumatoid arthritis.

According to Noel Vietmeyer of the U.S. National Academy of Sciences, deer velvet is used in hospitals and in prescription drugs in China, Korea, and the Soviet Union; it purportedly dilates blood vessels and stimulates production of red blood cells and is therefore widely used in treatment of heart disorders and anemia. Research in the Soviet Union has shown that the velvet of deer antlers contains a substance called pantocrin which has been proven in clinical trials to be useful as a tonic and for accelerating the healing of wounds and ulcers.

However, the majority of the traditional creature-cures used throughout Southeast Asia are unlikely to appear on the shelves of your corner drugstore. They are taken mostly on faith, and the fact that few objective studies have been done to test scientifically their effectiveness hardly seems to matter. The doctor and patient believe that popping a porcupine pill will cause the illness to disappear. And, often enough, the patient will feel better, even though many animal medicines are inactive chemically.

Clearly, the patient *wants* the medicine to work and the body follows the mind's instructions. Author Norman Cousins, who claims to have cured himself of ankylosing spondylitis, a debilitating back ailment, through self-imposed laugh therapy, says, "Investigators have found substantial evidence showing that the placebo [generally a sugar pill that the patient believes is a medicine] can actually act like an authentic therapeutic agent. The placebo is powerful not because it 'fools' the body but because it translates the will to live into a physical reality by triggering specific biochemical changes in the body."

Dr. Jon Levine of the University of California at San Francisco has found that a placebo will stimulate the body to produce quantities of natural pain-killing substances that are chemically similar to opiates; a placebo given for pain may be as effective as eight milligrams of morphine, a modest dose.

Less scientifically minded observers might call this the "chicken soup factor," the widely held belief that many of life's ills can be cured by tender care and mother's cooking. We discovered the universality of this method of treatment in the Sarawak town of Binatang when our "foster mother," a rotund Malay woman with gold teeth who spoke no English, surprised us with chicken soup when we suffered a mild case of jungle fever. "Drink this and you'll feel better," she said. And we did.

German folklorist Alexander Krappe attributes the medical success of mind over matter to a belief in magic, especially homeopathic or imitative magic, which suggests that a desired result can be brought about by mimicking the result—if a particular animal has good night vision then by eating its eyeballs you too will be able to see in the dark.

Monitors, the large iguana-like lizards found along watercourses throughout tropical Asia, illustrate how medical magic works. The monitor has a powerful digestive system that can convert any organic matter—even bones—into food for its body, so its viscera are believed to give the same gastrointestinal advantages to anyone eating them. "Similarly," says Florida State University herpetologist Walter Auffenberg, "since it is prolific and produces many eggs, its flesh is widely appreciated as an aphrodisiac. And since a monitor tends to get few infections, is powerful for its size and clings to life, even when badly wounded, it is thought to have healing powers."

Medical magic is sometimes helped along by wishful thinking. Bertrand Smythies, who wrote the standard reference book on the birds of Borneo, told how the people of Sabah would break the legs of newborn common coucal chicks, believing that the parent birds, in order to cure the injured young, would forage for healing herbs which they would half-digest and then regurgitate to use as a dressing on the chicks' limbs. The legs quickly healed and the goodness of the medicine, the people believed, was retained in the blood of the chicks. Sometimes the procedure was repeated several times before the chicks were collected and bottled whole in brandy; this was considered a cure-all, especially for rheumatic complaints.

◆ ◆ ◆

Feeling a bit dreary? Coming down with tuberculosis, fever, dropsy, or skin lesions? Just bitten by a snake? Having trouble responding with sufficient vigor to the romantic overtures of your partner? Troubled by evil spirits sent your way by a local practitioner of the black arts?

There's a medicine chest on the hoof for all these maladies—the rhinoceros, the mainstay of the Asian medicine trade. There are three rhino species in Asia: the Javan, confined to the small Ujung Kulon National Park on the western tip of Java; the Great Asian One-horned or Indian, found in the riverine swamplands of Nepal, Bhutan, Assam, and a few other parts of India; and the aberrant Asian Two-horned or Sumatran, which is actually found in Indochina, Sumatra, peninsular Malaysia, and Borneo and is the smallest, hairiest, and most primitive rhino. All are so rare—fewer than 70 Javan, 1,800 Indian, and 800 Sumatran rhinos survive today—that medicinal products from the Asian species seldom reach the market and demand is now being met by the less desirable African rhinos.

Whatever the species, nothing is more versatile than a rhino. Almost all parts of the beast are believed to have superb medicinal value. Best of all is the horn, which really isn't horn at all but agglutinated hair—rather like a fat fingernail growing out of the top of the rhino's nose. The mythology which has arisen about the protuberance has caused rhinos no end of trouble.

In a few parts of Asia, notably western India, rhino horn is believed to be among the most powerful of aphrodisiacs, even more effective than steamed python or ginseng, a theory first proposed in the West by Marco Polo who misidentified a Javan rhino as a unicorn. Observation of rhinos in the wild lends credence to this belief, since sex is one thing the otherwise unimaginative rhino does well. The late professor Dr. Bernard Grzimek, the German scientist best known for his book and film, *Serengeti Shall Not Die,* but also the author of a major encyclopedia of animal life, noted that "great Indian rhinos copulate for about one hour during which the bull ejaculates approximately every three minutes. To become capable of such sexual prowess seems to be desirable to many Asiatic people."

The peculiar shape of the Sumatran rhino's penis supports the perception of the animal as a powerful lover (homeopathic magic). The appendage has a natural crossbar about four inches from the tip which projects two inches on each side. This is thought to be such a stimulus to domestic harmony that the men of the Sarawak Kenyah and some other Borneo tribes imitate the rhino and undergo the painful surgical procedure of having implanted in their penises a rhino-like *palang,* a bamboo, bone, or horn crosspiece to which may be attached knobs and other conjugal accessories. The animal and human palangs are the most popular exhibits in the Sarawak Museum and the subject of much conjecture. When we were in the Peace Corps in Sarawak, a colleague wrote to the Peace Corps doctor in Kuching asking whether it was a good idea to have a palang implanted and thereby become better integrated into the community. The American-educated physician, Dr. Daniel Kok, advised against it.

In the dwindling number of drugstores where you can find rhino horn, some druggists still insist that it reduces fever—probably the most common use—or improves sexual ability. Roche Products, Ltd., in England, an associate of the giant Hoffmann-La Roche pharmaceutical concern, tested rhino horn, at the request of WWF, for its antipyretic, anti-inflammatory, analgesic, spasmolytic, diuretic, and bacteriacidal properties. The results were all negative.

The findings of an English laboratory have not deterred many Asians from using the horn for an incredible variety of ailments. Coupled with the Asian rhino's great rarity, this has driven up the price of the horn until it is worth almost its weight in gold. There are indications the trade is coming under control, however, partly due to a decade of lobbying effort by conservationists and partly because there aren't many of the animals left—IUCN estimates the world rhino population has decreased 89 percent since 1970, a more dramatic decrease than any other large mammal.

High prices have put the more valuable rhino parts far beyond the reach of the common Asian—the average wholesale price of Asian rhino horn is $4,000 a pound and raw Asian rhino hide, used to treat human skin diseases, costs $290 per pound in Singapore. There are, however, various "renewable rhino resources" which are not nearly so dear and are widely appreciated. Probably the most common is rhino urine.

At the Rangoon Zoo, a visitor has a discreet word with the keeper of the two Indian rhinos and hands over a plastic bucket. One of the keepers feeds bananas to "Bhunte," one of two rhinos given to the Burmese people by the King of Nepal in 1980, while another keeper stands behind the animal with the bucket to collect its urine. The urine, belonging as it does to all the people of the socialist republic, is free, but the visitor gives the zookeepers a small tip for their help.

And in Ujung Kulon, home of the only remaining Javan rhinos, we often saw the guards collect rhino droppings, which are thought to make an excellent poultice to heal leech bites. The guards also soak up rhino urine in their handkerchiefs and use the valuable fluid to cure their children's earaches.

◆ ◆ ◆

Although the rhinoceros is by far the most widely prescribed pharmaceutical animal of Asia, the tiger is certainly second. Many rural Asians cling to the belief that most illnesses are caused by evil spirits which can be warded off if the proper defensive steps are taken. What could be a better ally than the potent and fearsome tiger? Tigers are painted on Buddhist temple walls to scare away malignant spirits, tiger scrolls are hung in Chinese houses to keep disease devils out, Chinese mothers paint tigers on their children's mumps-swollen cheeks, and the shoes of small Chinese children are embroidered with tiger heads to prevent fevers.

If mere pictures are so powerful, consider the benefits you can obtain by consuming or wearing actual parts of a tiger. Uses we have identified include:

- *External organs.* The tail is ground and mixed with soap and applied as ointment for skin diseases. The hair is burned to drive away centipedes. Sitting on a tiger skin rug cures fevers caused by ghosts. The whiskers are used as a charm to give courage and immunize against bullets. Claws are carried in the pocket or worn as amulets to give the wearer courage.
- *Internal organs.* The brain is mixed with oil and rubbed on the body to cure laziness and acne. The heart is eaten to acquire strength, courage, and cunning. Gallstones, when added to

honey, cure abcesses on hands and feet, and when applied to the eyes, will stop persistent watering. The eyeballs are rolled into pills, a sure cure for convulsions. Eating the meat will make a person impervious to snakebite.

• *Bone.* When added to wine, this makes a traditional Taiwanese general tonic. Floating ribs are carried as a good-luck talisman. The small bones of the feet are tied to a child's wrist to prevent convulsions, while the bone from the tip of the tail wards off evil. In Indochina, the small bones of the tiger's shoulder prevent tiger attacks and give their owner physical superiority over his foes.

The person who wears a tiger talisman for protection places the same faith in a symbol as the truck driver who keeps a St. Christopher's medallion. Some people, however, seek more than preventive medicine, and the tiger's prodigious sex life convinces numerous aging Chinese gentlemen that they can achieve similar prowess by eating the animal. When a female tiger is in breeding condition the male stays with her for up to a week doing little else but copulating; one pair in a zoo had 106 matings in just four days. It is hardly surprising, then, to discover that tiger penis is considered to be the most powerful aphrodisiac in the Chinese pharmacopoeia.

Esmond Bradley Martin suggests that so many tiger penises are offered for sale in Asia that few of them can be the genuine article because there simply aren't that many tigers. Wong Seng Huei, age forty-two, a prominent Chinese physician in Sibu, Sarawak, showed us expertly counterfeited tigers penises, thin, curved, and convoluted like the real thing. "These are from Hong Kong," he explained. "They're made from ox and deer tendons. Not too expensive, only about $15. And anyway, you can't get the real ones anymore at any price." Does the customer know these are fake? "I never claim these are from tigers," Mr. Wong says. "If they ask me, I tell them. It doesn't make a big difference. People buy them anyway."

◆ ◆ ◆

As long as rural societies hunt animals for their own food and medicine, there is generally little danger of depleting the supply. But when outside market demands and the promise of quick profits encourage hunters to concentrate on rare or slowly reproducing animals, trouble starts. Today, the worldwide demand for medicinal animal parts is unprecedented, and the implications for many Southeast Asian wildlife populations are not good.

All the medicinal uses mentioned above, coupled with habitat losses and the high price of tiger skins in the fur trade, have had a devastating effect on the cat's populations, from Bali to the Caspian Sea to Siberia. Musk deer throughout their Himalayan and Chinese ranges are being severely depleted, solely for their musk pods, which produce an odorous substance valued as a heart stimulant and aphrodisiac; even worse, the snares set for musk deer in China often catch endangered giant pandas instead.

Other animal populations suffer as well. In one recent seven-year period, sixty tons of pangolin scales were exported from Sarawak, representing over 50,000 animals. In a nine-month period in 1978–79, Hong Kong officially imported a thousand pounds of rhino horn, taken from approximately 160 of these endangered animals. Vietnamese scientist Dao Van Tien fears that the demand for monkey bone marrow used to treat arthritis is threatening some macaque populations in his country.

Pisit na Patalung, secretary-general of Wildlife Fund Thailand, said populations of Thailand's two bear species—the Asian black bear and the sun bear—are dropping so quickly that they could disappear from the country in the next few years. The main problem: visiting businessmen, primarily from South Korea, purchase bear gall bladders hoping to be cured of a wide range of illnesses, including chronic fatigue, digestive problems, inflammation, blood impurities, hemorrhoids, and various liver, stomach, and intestinal ailments. The price of such a useful drug is high: roughly 200 U.S. dollars for a medium-sized, three-ounce gall bladder from a sun bear. With such high prices as a stimulus, fake bear gall bladders are beginning to hit the market.

The rest of the bear is good food, too, and some Bangkok animal dealers and restaurants charge between $600 and $1,000 for a live bear, which is sometimes tied to a post outside the shop for inspection by customers and then, according to Khun Pisit, beaten to death when purchased. Since one bear brings in more than the average Thai earns in a year, Thai poachers are not deterred by the risk of fines if they are caught.

While nobody condones cruelty to animals, it is difficult to deny the value to people of the medicinal animal trade. Dr. Boonsong, who was instrumental in introducing antibiotics to Thailand just before World War II, also understands how medicinal animal remedies are ingrained in many Asian cultures, particularly in remote areas. He told us that when he visited an isolated Lisu village in northern Thailand's Chiengrai Province, he found a woman suffering from a high fever and delirium. Her family asked Dr. Boonsong for medicine. He had none. Then they called in a different kind of medical specialist, an old hunter known to all as an effective healer. Giving her a potion of monkey blood, he sat up all night with the woman, calling in her relatives to provide support. By the next morning, the woman's fever broke and she seemed well on her way to recovery.

The healer and his medicine, of course, received the credit, but Dr. Boonsong explained that the cure may well have been bed rest, the herbs put in the blood drink, and the psychological support of her family. Naturally, folk healers maintain that traditional medicines still have their uses. As a Chinese apothecary in Bangkok told us: "Modern drugs are certainly much stronger and can cure some things my medicines can't touch. But, for many illnesses, western medicines are too strong and do as much harm as good. My treatments are aimed at controlling symptoms, keeping the patient alive, if not comfortable, until the disease runs its natural course."

◆ ◆ ◆

The continued use of animal medicines faces two serious obstacles. The first is a negative one: The rhinos, tigers, and musk deer which cure, regardless of whether empirical data prove the point, are being wiped out, partly because those animals are so successful as walking drugstores. The second might balance the first: Urban people are turning away from old-fashioned remedies. Choong Chor Fong, the druggist we met in Singapore, told us, "Many of my customers, like my sons, have university educations and think differently than the older generation. We have to adapt. If a customer doesn't want an animal medicine there are many other effective treatments we can offer." Pharmacists in many Asian capitals stock vitamins and antibiotics next to the elephant skin (for boils) and monkey bones (circulation); Vicks cough syrup and Alka-Seltzer within grasp of dried crocodile meat (asthma) and bear gall bladder (digestive system). It is a simple matter for the druggist to reach for the aspirin instead of the rhino horn to treat fever, although his profit margins may suffer.

Clearly, not all Asians accept the widespread use of animal medicines. In 1986 Malaysia's Deputy Health Minister, Datuk K.

Pathmanaban, warned the public of the dangers of patronizing street-side medicine men who claim they have miraculous cures for serious diseases. The health ministry promised to step up its program to eliminate roadside doctors, who sell treatments such as the fetus of a white deer.

Yet animal medicines are continually being used by rural people. Increasingly, the folk cures are being studied and appreciated by Western pharmacologists. Western pharmacists know well the value of wild plants in medicines—more than 40 percent of all the pharmaceuticals sold in the United States, an industry worth $3 billion annually, have a natural plant base. But the vast medical potential of animals is just beginning to be tapped.

The stage is set for a new conservation juggling act: keeping the healer's medicine shelves stocked with animal products while minimizing the impact on wildlife populations. If the supply and demand are balanced, it would be another case where animals have been saved because they are useful.

21

Animal Bazaar

The call of the wild often is drowned out by the cry of the highest bidder.

In an unusual action begun quietly last week, the U.S. Fish and Wildlife Service has banned all wildlife imports from Singapore—worth an estimated $17 million each year—because of that country's refusal to abide by international protections for rare animals. . . . the ban has ended Singapore's alleged $3 million to $5 million traffic to the United States in illicitly obtained animal products. (Los Angeles *Times,* October 3, 1986)

IN THE TWELFTH CENTURY, an Indian-Indonesian prince from Sumatra, who traced his ancestry back to Alexander the Great, visited a swampy outpost of his realm and encountered a large cat, probably a tiger. In the retelling the animal became a lion, and the insignificant outpost of the Srivijaya empire became "Singapura," Malay-Sanskrit for "Lion City."

Today the relentlessly mercantile island nation of Singapore is still involved with animals. Singapore, a country smaller than New

York City with virtually no wildlife of its own, had, until late 1986, steadfastly avoided joining the Convention on International Trade in Endangered Species of Wild Fauna and Flora (CITES). Although its Southeast Asian neighbors had joined the convention to help save their wildlife, Singapore went its own way and profited as a major entrepôt for rhino horn, reptiles, elephant ivory, sea turtles, and pangolin skins from the surrounding nations.

Then came the news in 1986 that Japan had imported some 52,000 pounds of "Malaysian" crocodile skins (representing perhaps as many as 60,000 animals) through Singapore in the seventeen months following the imposition of Japanese regulations in 1985 restricting such trade. According to Tom Milliken, director of TRAFFIC (Japan), a group set up by WWF and IUCN to monitor the wildlife trade, Malaysian records show the export of only 3,700 pounds of skins during the same period. The remaining 48,300 pounds of skins could not have come from Malaysia because there are not that many crocodiles left in the country, and because they included skins of species found only in South America.

This led to a U.S. ban on all Singapore animal products, which included important trade in propagated ornamental tropical fish. The *Straits Times* of Singapore called the action sudden, unilateral, and arbitrary. "It would appear . . . that the US is not prepared to take Singapore's word [that it would join CITES] at face value. . . . It is offensive to try to press-gang sovereign states to sign legally-binding international conventions through threats aimed at targets [tropical fish] completely unrelated to those conventions."

"We have always stood by the spirit of CITES," a Singapore National Development Ministry spokesman argued.

Not everyone agreed. "The ban is necessary because there's too much money being made in trading in endangered species and the only way you can get governments to act is by hitting hard," countered Dr. Ginette Hemley, head of the TRAFFIC (U.S.) office.

Singapore has since become a party to CITES and the trade ban has been lifted.

◆ ◆ ◆

Singapore achieved prominence relatively recently. After a five-year term as lieutenant-governor of Java during a short period of British control of what is now Indonesia, Thomas Stamford Raffles stopped at sleepy Singapura in 1819 and bought the island from the Sultan of Johore for the British East India Company. The British needed their own port since they did not have access to the harbor at Batavia (now Jakarta), which was once again under Dutch control. Raffles started Singapore on its commercial track by declaring it free of customs duty, and today it is one of the world's leading ports, a city created to service the marketing of goods to and from Southeast Asia.

Southeast Asians are good at marketing. They give people what they want. This results in a lucrative business for some, but many animals wind up losing their freedom, or their skins, in the process. Throughout the region, foreign consumer demand is putting excessive pressure on animals, both the well known and the obscure.

- The total annual world trade of live animals, ivory, skins, and finished items such as shoes and handbags currently is between $2 billion and $5 billion; up to a third of the trade is illegal.
- Of birds imported into the United States 3 of every 4, including rare parrots from Southeast Asia, have been taken from the wild; 1 million birds were imported in 1984 and mortality in many shipments exceeded 50 percent. Agents of the U.S. Fish and Wildlife Service seized 103 illegally imported palm cockatoos which are fully protected in their native Papua New Guinea, Indonesia, and Australia. The birds were estimated to have a street value of over $1 million.
- Rhino horn is so sought after that thieves broke into the Kuala Lumpur zoo and sawed off the horn of an African black rhino. In the Bogor Zoological Museum in Indonesia, not only were the horns stolen from mounted specimens on display but plaster replacement horns were stolen three times within a single year.
- Don Carr, a U.S. government official, suggests that "the interface between drugs and wildlife is more common than we know," since wildlife smugglers are often also drug smugglers. Obdulio Menghi, an official of the CITES Secretariat in Switzerland, said that snakeskins in a legal shipment were once liberally dusted with a "preservative" that turned out to be heroin. Other smugglers place drugs in the same canvas sacks as poisonous snakes, hoping the customs inspectors will be dissuaded from closely examining the shipment.
- TRAFFIC (Japan) continuously observed several major pet stores in Tokyo and uncovered a persistent trade in gibbons from Thailand. In September 1983, eleven primates were found hidden in the carry-on luggage of a Japanese tourist returning from Thai-

land, where the maximum penalty for illegally exporting protected gibbons is six months' imprisonment and a $200 fine. Al-
though five animals were dead, the smuggler claimed that they
were all his pets. Gibbons bring prices as high as $2,000 in Japa-
nese pet shops.

· In a celebrated case, the director of one of Japan's leading zoos
wrote to the Jakarta Zoo asking for birds of paradise, which are
not allowed to be exported from Indonesia. He suggested: "But
considering strict regulation on import of the said birds, it is
suggested that the name of item is to be specified just 'magpie'
instead of 'bird of paradise' on all necessary documents and
when shipped, the tail of birds is to be pulled out and birds to be
painted watercolour so that our sincere desire to get the birds
can realize by any means."

Animals and animal products have been traded for centuries in
Southeast Asia. Historian Wilfred T. Neill notes: "While the spice
trade was particularly important in luring Chinese, Indians, Arabs
and finally Europeans to Indonesia, much earlier exploration of
that country, and the spread thereto of cultural traits from mainland Asia, can be credited to Chinese or Indian demand for marine
products, hornbill beaks, edible birds' nests, plumes, sharks' fins,
rhinoceros horns, and materia medica derived from the animal
kingdom."

Some of these animal products were used as medicine, some as
expensive decorations and trophies. This trade has long taken its
toll on animal populations throughout Southeast Asia, but the improved international transportation and economic prosperity
which followed World War II increased the rate of exploitation so
rapidly that strong steps needed to be taken to prevent numerous
species from being threatened by the expanded trade.

What is being done to help the world's tigers, musk deer, dugongs, rhinos, and birds of paradise? While all Southeast Asian
countries have new laws and new protected areas, enforcement in
the forest of regulations made in a distant parliament is very difficult, particularly when economic incentives and new western-oriented education programs are breaking down the customary controls on consumption. It is likely there will always be a buyer
somewhere. Any villager able to produce a fresh pair of Sumatran
rhino horns can earn himself a new automobile.

One approach is to change consumer behavior. One of the conservation success stories of the seventies was convincing thousands of wealthy women that they would be unfashionable (and possibly the subject of attack by conservation-minded vandals) if they wore coats made out of leopard and tiger skins. Only a few women of a certain age in the fashion centers of Europe continue to wear their somewhat *outré* catskin jackets, agreeing, no doubt, with the argument put forward by Gina Lollobrigida some years ago that "by the time I bought the coat the tiger was already dead."

Esmond Bradley Martin has tried a similar approach to stem the trade in rhino horn, suggesting that people be given an alternative. He has convinced a growing number of traditional Asian medical practioners to substitute the relatively common and easily available saiga antelope horn for the scarce, and generally illegally procured, rhino horn when prescribing treatments to relieve high fever. Ironically, the stout saiga antelope from Siberia was itself almost extinct fifty years ago. "Then the Russians stopped the hunting until the 1950s and the saiga built up from a very small population to well over a million in the 1960s and now the Russians have gone back to hunting it," Martin explains.

Legal restraints, public education, and substitute products seem to be stemming the rhino trade. Martin notes that in spite of the scarcity of rhino horn, Asian prices for the commodity have increased by only some 8.5 percent a year since 1979, barely keeping up with inflation, and the retail price for raw Asian rhino hide, used to treat human skin diseases, has actually gone down.

◆　◆　◆

Deep in the vast main cavern of the Niah Caves in Sarawak, a torch reveals bamboo poles bound together with strips of rattan to reach the ceiling, in some places over thirty stories above the pungent floor of packed guano, where men sweat over their shovels. In the near-total darkness and amid the incessant chatter of bats and swifts, men harvest the great cave's riches from top and bottom.

At dusk, several million bats darken the cave's entrance on their way out to harvest some of the forest's nocturnal insects, meeting a smaller number of swifts returning to roost in the caves after an active day of catching flying diurnal insects. Sixty Malay guano collectors, members of the Niah Bat Guano Cooperative Workers Society, begin their last trip of the day, carrying on their shoulders burlap sacks filled with some 120 pounds of smelly, oozy guano, which will be sold as first-class fertilizer. Eager to go home and have a bath, they trot along the slippery raised wooden walkways that traverse the swampy four miles from the cave to the nearest tiny harbor.

The roof of the cave offers considerably greater profit and danger. Shirtless, barefoot men with the courage of a Flying Wallenda hold on with one sweaty hand to a perch and with the other use a long pole to scrape the nests of black swifts off the ceiling. These saucer-shaped nests are made primarily out of bird saliva, appropriately termed "nest cement" because it alone affixes the nest to the cave roof or walls. Although the substance is a glycoprotein of negligible nutritive value, Chinese traders centuries ago exchanged porcelain, iron, gold, and textiles for the delicacy. Today Chinese restaurants throughout Southeast Asia serve the hardened bird saliva as bird's nest soup, usually cooked with barley sugar or shark's fin but sometimes stuffed into pigeons. It tastes like nothing in particular but is said to be soothing for the lungs and, naturally, to be an aphrodisiac.

The nests of white swifts are even more valuable. In 1978 the Gomantong Caves in Sandakan, Sabah, produced some $100,000 worth of white swift nests, which are worth as much as $450 for a pound of the best quality, while black swift nests sell for a paltry $15 per pound.

The bird nest business may not last. In Niah only five professional collectors, all old men, are licensed by the Sarawak Museum (the cave is an important archeological site) to risk their necks to feed gourmet Chinese. And even if new collectors could be found there may be few nests for them to collect. Insecticides commonly used throughout the neighborhood alter the swifts' metabolism, causing them to lay eggs with thinner shells, which results in fewer successful births. Dr. Y. C. Kong of the Chinese University of Hong Kong, noting that every year 1,000 tons of edible nests of swifts are imported to Hong Kong, speculates that an ecological hazard may result from the elimination of swifts since they are valuable insect predators. While the trade lasts, the swift-rich caves of the Baram River are valuable property for the owners, mostly Kayan and Kenyah aristocrats.

After each thrice-yearly auction of bird nests, substantial sums of money come into the longhouse economy. The effect is shown by the recent history of Long Laput, the longest longhouse in the country, which stretches more than 250 yards along the Baram River and houses 600 people. Malcolm MacDonald observed that the people of Long Laput "were ruined by money. Since the labour of birds building nests, they reflected, provided them with a comfortable income, they need not themselves labour hard in their fields. If they ran short of home-grown padi, did they not possess the wherewithal to buy more rice? Yet they did not, in fact, save their spare cash for that purpose. They had so much money, they argued, that it did not matter if a little were devoted to the pleasures of living—and in the end they squandered almost all of it on carousals, transforming much of the rice which they did produce from invigorating food into intoxicating liquor."

◆ ◆ ◆

Regardless of what they do with the profits, people throughout Southeast Asia are making money selling their wildlife. The centuries-old trade in wildlife from Southeast Asia has grown remarkably with increased demand from the industrial nations and improved transportation.

Many animals once protected by traditional controls—taboos, lack of markets, inadequate technology—find their survival is now in the hands of marketing experts who pay little attention to the source of their business. We met one of the most successful dealers in Bangkok when Dr. Boonsong wanted to photograph some of Thailand's rarer mammals to illustrate our book describing the country's 264 species. When an animal-model was needed, Dr. Boonsong turned to the animal dealers.

We loaded the car with his Nikon cameras, tripods, electronic flashes, and the large glass-fronted box he had designed for allowing animals to pose in a natural position while he photographed them. After fighting Bangkok's traffic for an hour, we turned up an inconspicuous lane on the outskirts of the city and stopped in front of an imposing wrought-iron gate. Dr. Boonsong beeped his horn and the gates swung open, leading us into the compound of Khun Suphin, one of Thailand's largest animal traders.

Suphin greeted us warmly, for he and Dr. Boonsong had long shared an interest in wildlife. But while Dr. Boonsong had turned to altruistic conservation aimed at convincing Thais of the value of their wildlife, Suphin demonstrated the value of Thai wildlife by selling it abroad. Dr. Boonsong's friendship with Suphin would cause us no end of complications with well-meaning animal-welfare lobbyists.

Suphin's stockade was large and clean, but densely packed with cages filled with animals from all parts of the country, as well as from Burma, Laos, and Cambodia. It had the heady smell of a zoo at close range and sounded like the set of a Tarzan movie. Shrieks, whistles, barks, and animal songs blocked out the street noise. Birds were by far the most numerous of the animals, and we picked our way among the coops watching the numerous young girls on Suphin's staff feeding papaya and bananas to the fruit-eating birds, unshelled rice and peanuts to the seed-eaters, and chunks of raw meat to the owls, hawks, and eagles. We saw several species that were so rare we had never seen them in the wild, including a white-eyed river martin (which had been discovered in 1968 at Boraphet Lake in central Thailand by one of Dr. Boonsong's protégés) and a statuesque sarus crane, which Suphin said came from Cambodia. The girls giggled as we asked them questions, but they obviously took their work seriously, and, like good Thai mothers, tried to make sure that all their charges got enough to eat. We were impressed at how healthy the birds looked, and began to wonder whether we had been wrong in condemning all animal dealers.

Suphin showed us more of his compound. "Here is something very special," he said as he led us to a shady corner with two thick-barred cages. "Orangutans. I have four of them, from Indonesia. But I also have a big problem because they eat a lot and I can't sell them. The Forestry Department has banned the sale of orangutans, even though they don't come from Thailand. I tried to give them to a foreign zoo, but I can't get an export permit even if I won't make any profit. I'm really stuck." We nodded in sympathy, both for Suphin and for the orangutans sitting quietly in the corner, gazing up at us with blank eyes.

Suphin took us into his office, where his young and charming wife was doing the accounts. She stood up and gave us the traditional, graceful Thai greeting of holding hands together in front of the nose and giving a slight bow. We returned the *wai.* She called for a servant to bring cold drinks, then invited us to sit down. As we came closer, a low but insistent growl stopped us short. Crouching next to Mrs. Suphin was an adult male leopard, with his ears erect in the attacking position. Mrs. Suphin murmured reassurance, and the leopard relaxed. We did too, but just a little, not entirely comfortable with a deadly and unpredictable cat within springing distance.

While we helped Dr. Boonsong set up his equipment, Suphin and a number of his workers brought in the models which were to pose for portraits: an otter civet, two banded palm civets, a moon-rat, a banded linsang, and a Burmese ferret-badger with two young.

The novelty of having foreigners on the premises began to wear off and the compound staff returned to their tasks. While Dr. Boonsong took pictures, we unobtrusively wandered outside to satisfy our curiosity about the rest of the compound. We saw the monkey section, packed with macaques waiting to be sent to medical laboratories. A relatively spacious closet-sized cage was devoted to the juvenile monkeys who were old enough to be separated from their mothers. Individual adult males of four different species were incarcerated individually in cages that were hardly big enough for the monkey to turn around in, though an irate newspaper report that monkeys were "kept in cages half their size" was clearly an exaggeration. We passed quickly through the monkey section, seeking fresh air, but found just the opposite: the morgue. Dozens of corpses—small birds, monkeys, civets, a hawk-eagle—were awaiting disposal. The tropical sun beat down on the rotting animals, and the smell of death hung heavily in the air. We quickly rejoined Dr. Boonsong and Suphin, anxious to retreat to the relative calm of the Bangkok traffic and unable to forget the price that animals pay for being part of the international marketplace.

◆ ◆ ◆

Leaders of modern Singapore encourage others to describe the nation as an efficient Swiss-like financial hub positioned, Israel-like, amid Muslim neighbors. It is a country that has worked for what it has; it is not a country for the faint of spirit. Not surprisingly, Singapore has wiped out most of its natural wilderness in the process of modernization. The fact that 300 people were killed by tigers in Singapore in 1857 seems otherworldly today. Singapore's nature is there, but it is either in transit or in two excellent zoos.

The Jurong Bird Park lies in the middle of a vast, booming industrial park constructed on land reclaimed from the sea. Six hundred businesses, factories, and shipyards are within screeching distance of Spanish flamingos and Australian emus, South American rheas and New Guinea cassowaries, Antarctic penguins and Arctic geese. We found it an excellent place to see some of the world's most spectacular birds, many of which bathed in the pool at the foot of the bird park's man-made waterfall, the highest in the world.

We usually do our bird-watching by awakening at dawn and walking quietly through the forest or sitting in damp, uncomfortable hides; at the vast Jurong Bird Park we sat in a canopied tram which played recorded bird calls as we passed each exhibit. The honking of the Tasmanian black swan still echoed as we read in the park's official guidebook:

Co-existence of nature and industrial man will have to be maintained as the world of nature is an integral part of the cosmos. Man must realize that he is responsible for his fellow creatures and their survival rests in his hands.

22

Brown Ivory

Monkeys can be troublesome for farmers, but selling them into slavery stirs another kind of conflict.

THE PLACE is a dank, steamy mangrove swamp along the southern coast of Sumatra. A young long-tailed macaque monkey we will call Kra has only recently ventured away from the security of his mother. He plays with other juveniles while his mother crouches down on the exposed swamp mud, eating crabs and insects.

People approach in boats. Kra's mother hears the alien noise and gives an alarm bark. Kra leaps onto her back and they scamper away, along with the other thirty-two macaques in their group. A few desperate monkeys take to the sea and try to swim to safety. They are easily scooped up by the hunters and stuffed into a small cage. Others are quickly entangled in a large net. Most of the group head for the tallest tree, their usual line of defense. Axes make short work of it and as the monkeys tumble the men club the big male monkeys and stuff the screaming females with clinging young into sacks. For each monkey the capturer earns $2.00.

At the animal trapper's compound Kra is put into a small cage with nine other juveniles. They are brought water and chunks of cassava, a fleshy, high-carbohydrate tuber which Kra is going to have to learn to like, as it will be the only food he gets for some time. About 15 percent of the other monkeys have died of injury or stress. As a survivor, Kra is treated reasonably well, considering he is a prisoner, being fed regularly, given clean water, and even examined by a veterinarian.

Kra greets each new group of monkeys with the dispassionate gaze of a prisoner of war who has seen it all. After several weeks Kra and fourteen others are put into a shipping crate and sent to Jakarta, first on a hot, dusty truck journey during which he almost suffocates from the exhaust fumes, then aboard the air-conditioned atmosphere of an aircraft cargo hold. The Sumatran middleman has earned $50 for him.

The ninety-five-minute flight from Palembang arrives at Jakarta's domestic airport in the late morning. Kra is then carted across the sprawling, traffic-congested city to the international airport where he sits, drinking some warm water, until the early evening departure of the flight to Amsterdam. The monkeys arrive in Holland six hours later than planned, by which time the impatient animal dealer has already left to go to a football match. The busy warehouseman puts the monkeys in the back of the storage area, and then piles several other cages on top.

What happened next was reported by Dutch journalist Dick van Hoorn: "There was a very strange smell around the monkeys' wooden cages, so the wildlife officer stationed at the airport opened two cages. What he saw was ghastly. In one cage were 15 monkeys, nearly all wounded, and in the other cage there were 11 monkeys, seven of them dead. They had obviously died from suffocation. Their eyes were hanging out of their sockets and they had bitten off their own tongues."

Kra was one of the four "lucky" survivors from his crate, and he was sent to a reputable medical research institute, which bought him from an animal trader for $175. He was well looked after, with nourishing, though boring, food, good medical care, and a clean cage. He could even see some other monkeys, though they were out of reach.

Soon the laboratory technician gave him an injection that was to prove fatal. He was being used to test the effects of a new drug which, if all went well, would be used to treat cancer in humans.

Kra had deliberately been given a massive overdose to show what might happen to human patients in similar circumstances. After six days all his hair fell out, his eyes turned glassy, and he suffered from endless diarrhea. The next day he died, but his service to humanity was not yet over—his internal organs were carefully dissected and examined and the results were meticulously analyzed together with forty-nine other macaque postmortems. A year later the research report was finally filed, the new drug was approved for human clinical trials. One hopes human suffering will be lessened.

◆ ◆ ◆

With the exception of the Amsterdam airport details and the Dutch journalist's quote, the above scenario is fictional. It accurately represents, however, the current state of the monkey-trading business. The high mortality in capture and transport, coupled with the more visible suffering of the animals in the predominantly Western laboratories, has created a surge of public approbation against the monkey trade and animal experiments.

◆ ◆ ◆

At midnight during the 1984 Memorial Day weekend, two women and three men broke into the University of Pennsylvania's Experimental Head Injury Laboratory in Philadelphia. Their mission: get evidence that would stop cruel laboratory experiments on monkeys.

"There was a dirty old stairway that led into the subbasement," recalled Mary [not her real name], one of several dozen members of the highly secretive Animal Liberation Front (ALF). "They definitely didn't want anybody to enter the lab. The door was made of metal and had a strip painted on it with a big, red lightning bolt and a warning that read, ELECTRICAL HAZARD. DO NOT ENTER. So we knew we were in the right place."

The group stole thirty-two videotapes that revealed, among other things, "pictures of pistons being thrust through the heads of baboons, animal brains attached to twisted wires encased by metal helmets, and unanesthetized primates crawling away in pain from operating tables," according to journalist Robert Weil. The tapes, which were widely circulated to television editors and legislators, also presented "a highly unflattering portrait of the researchers themselves . . . among other research infractions the technicians wore no masks during surgical procedures and smoked cigarettes during primate operations," Weil wrote in *Omni.*

Throughout much of the Western world, a small but very vocal and visible minority protests experiments on primates and other laboratory animals. Few concerned people though go to the extremes of the guerrilla squad that broke into the Head Injury Laboratory, one of whom compared cruelties inflicted on animals with the crimes waged against humans at Dachau and Bergen-Belsen. "If you could only look into their eyes, then you'd see the validity of the comparison," she argued, equating her group with the French Resistance.

Meanwhile, ignored by most of the vocal westerners, the people of Southeast Asia have their own monkey problems. Villagers throughout Southeast Asia fight a different kind of guerrilla war against annoying, voracious primates which do not have the good manners to realize that they are supposed to behave in the spirit of lofty idealism and good fellowship exemplified by Hanuman, the monkey-general hero of the *Ramayana.* Some primates in their natural habitat in the forests of Southeast Asia are troublesome to farmers. Being clever animals, they know when and where the best food can be found.

At the end of the rainy season in 1975 we were spending the night in a small village in the Phu Phan Range in northeastern Thailand, nestled far up a valley and surrounded by a deep forest. We ate a meal of mud-baked chicken and glutinous rice, garnished by the tasty curry known as *kaeng kheo wan kai,* which contained several handfuls of cannabis flowers, and then rolled our sleeping mats out on the hut's bamboo floor, prepared to dream the night away.

After making sure we were comfortable, our host, a farmer named Goragote, who used to be a guide for Dr. Boonsong, excused himself, took a flashlight, a blanket, and a shotgun and went out to his ripening rice fields to spend the night in an elevated watchtower. Early the next morning we heard a fusillade and wondered if terrorists had infiltrated across the Mekong River from Laos and were coming to collect their "taxes" from the village. After a quick discussion about whether to hide in the hut or retreat to the forest, we heard the shots being replaced by shouts so we courageously rushed out to see if there was anything useful we could do.

Invaders had indeed come from the forest, but rather than terrorists they were a horde of about fifty stump-tailed macaque monkeys attracted by Goragote's rice. While he drove away one monkey patrol, another group sneaked into the other side of the field and stuffed as much rice as they could into their voluminous cheek pouches. We yelled and waved our arms as we ran toward the monkeys, hoping to scare them into retreat. Our combined forces were successful, though it seemed that most of the monkeys were able to pack away a full breakfast.

Leaving his son to guard against a counterattack, Goragote took us back to his house where his wife was serving a rice gruel and papaya breakfast on the veranda. Dr. Boonsong told us how dangerous the stump-tailed macaques are to farmers in remote areas. "These monkeys seem to think they are still Hanuman," he explained. "They are bold and fearless and unless they know that a villager has a gun, they are very difficult to drive away until their bellies are full. Sometimes they even invade isolated huts and attack people trying to defend their crops. Harvest season is hard work in many ways, and many villagers make sure that they grow enough rice to allow the monkeys to take their share."

Monkeys can also be mean, vindictive creatures in their dealings with each other. Most species of the largely tree-dwelling leaf monkeys, for example, live in "harem" groups in which one male dominates three or four females and has exclusive sexual rights to his consorts. But such a "harem king" usually reigns for only a few years, after which he is ousted by a younger and more powerful male. And once a new harem king takes over a group he will immediately kill the youngest babies fathered by his predecessor. Without her nursing baby, the mother soon comes into estrous and, several months later, has *his* baby.

This monkey against monkey aggression would all be of little more than academic interest were it not that monkeys often treat humans with the same rough-and-ready attitude with which they treat their closer relatives. The expansion of people into primate habitats makes conflict inevitable.

In early 1980, "Hundreds of monkeys bit and scratched a boy of nine to death in South Kalimantan," according to a Reuters news report. In Sumatra eight months later, the Indonesia *Times* reported, "A big herd of monkeys [are not only] roaming around the village making the villagers afraid, but like to chase the villagers, especially the country women."

Country women, especially the young ones, seem to be a favorite target. Peter Kum, a former executive at Radio/Television Malaysia, told us that many years ago, the women of Kuang, about fifteen miles from Kuala Lumpur, were so terrorized by a huge pig-tailed macaque monkey that they refused to go tap rubber in their smallholdings. "It would hide up a low tree and when a woman walked underneath, it would drop suddenly and grab the woman's sarong and pull it off," Kum related. "This happened to several women. The men were left alone. The villagers tried unsuccessfully to trap the monkey but it seemed to know all about traps. The *ketua kampong* [headman] went after the monkey with his shotgun. But the monkey, instead of fleeing, kept just outside the effective range of the shotgun. The villagers asked me to help, knowing I was a keen hunter. I managed to ambush it after trying for three consecutive Sundays."

These antics are sometimes treated with surprising equanimity. A widely circulated Indonesian news story reported in 1980:

A fat monkey of still undetermined species twice raped a 23 year old woman who was tending her field in Dawuan Village, West Java, the national news agency, KNI, reported here today.

The agency said that Madam On Madrai fell asleep in the shade after working in her field when the male monkey came along.

The monkey tore off her panties and calmly had intercourse with her. Waking up soon afterwards, Madam Madrai was shocked to see what was happening and ran away.

KNI said the monkey chased her until she was exhausted then raped her again in the bush. The woman's husband said he was not going to report the case to the police. "After all, it was only a monkey," he was quoted by KNI as saying.

The noble demeanor of Hanuman is obviously quite different from the complex reality of primate behavior. Instead of acting like a paragon of classic literature, our closest relatives often behave like the hoodlums of pulp fiction.

At least part of this divergence between the ideal and the real is due to proximity. Primates who stay away from people retain their good reputations. Gibbons, for example, live high in the trees and seldom have anything at all to do with people. As a result, these small apes often serve as symbols of the distant and remote forest. Since gibbons don't raid crops and are indicators of a healthy forest ecosystem, several of Thailand's hill tribes believe that gibbon calls have a beneficial effect on the growth of crops, and they like to have a large number of gibbons in the forests.

When monkeys invite themselves to feast on a farmer's harvest, attack his children, and rape his wife, admiration of Hanuman the monkey-general quite understandably gives way to fury at the macaque monkey-thugs. Since farmers are expanding into what was formerly the abode of the wild primates, the macaques are forced to come into closer contact with *Homo sapiens.* The conflict between people and the other primates is a long way from being resolved.

◆ ◆ ◆

There seem to be enough monkeys to export some, at least of the more common varieties which are the ones of greatest interest to the medical trade and causing greatest trouble for villagers. A 1975 survey by Carolyn Crockett and Wendell L. Wilson, funded by the U.S. National Institutes of Health (one of the largest users of monkeys for medical research), estimated that there were 14 million long-tailed macaques in Sumatra and suggested that the total population of this species for all of Indonesia might be 35 million.

In 1980, Indonesian wildlife officials, deciding that the forests had enough monkeys to support a trade in brown ivory, authorized the export of 15,000 monkeys of three species, including 10,000 long-tailed macaques.

This particular bit of monkey business did not present a conservation problem, particularly since Indonesian officials put quotas on trapping in the regions where monkey populations were lowest. Further, all animal traders were licensed, no export was allowed directly from the point of capture (in order to control the number of animals sold), and all exporters were required to have adequate holding and veterinary facilities.

This seemed an example of "sustainable utilization," a conservation term that encourages people to use, and make money from, wild natural resources as long as such trade does not endanger the resource.

This pragmatic approach sometimes puts the people-oriented conservationists in conflict with the animal-oriented conservationists. Can both groups achieve their objectives?

Chuck Darsono, one of Indonesia's most capable suppliers of laboratory animals, claims that it is feasible, and profitable, to be engaged in selling monkeys in a humane way. Yet the sad fact is that up to two thirds of all long-tailed macaques that are trapped die before they reach their destination, according to a recent Indonesian government estimate.

Concerned by these high mortality rates, Malaysia, which exported 18,000 macaques in 1978, banned the export of monkeys in 1982, largely at the urging of animal welfare groups, and Indonesia out of humanitarian concern temporarily suspended exports of macaques in 1980 immediately after the Amsterdam airport incident in which a third of the animals died in transit.

Such cutoffs are of considerable concern to the pharmaceutical firms which require primates for testing vaccines. Karl-Goeran Hedstroem, a veterinarian at the Swedish State Bacteriological Laboratory, speculated that if the temporary Indonesian ban had continued (it didn't), his country could have found itself with a shortage of polio vaccine.

Shirley McGreal, founder of the International Primate Protection League, has led an effective campaign to stop the trade in monkeys, apparently feeling that it is better for the farmers to shoot and eat the monkeys which are raiding their crops than it is to send them to biomedical research institutions in industrialized countries.

Groups like hers have had mixed results. In a national referendum held in December 1985, 70 percent of Swiss voters defeated a bid proposed by an animal rights group to ban use of animals in medical research. A U.S. federal appeals court ruled in 1986 that an animal rights group does not have legal standing to contest animal use in research. On the other hand, in November 1986 public pressure forced environment ministers of the twelve European Economic Community countries to agree to reduce the number of laboratory experiments on live animals by about a third (about 30 million animals a year are used in experiments in European Community countries) and to avoid inflicting unnecessary pain and suffering on animals.

However, moral outrage over animal cruelty is irrelevant to the villager in northern Sumatra who has just earned the equivalent of three months' farm earnings for helping to catch a large group of monkeys which had been raiding his crops. Further, his children have been inoculated against polio with vaccines which have been tested on long-tailed macaques, and a new vaccine against malaria—the scourge of rural Asia—may well become available in the foreseeable future, following intensive tests on monkeys.

While Ms. McGreal (who keeps her own pet gibbons) hasn't succeeded in stopping the trade, her scare tactics have certainly been successful in limiting its extent and in improving export and shipping conditions. But sometimes she goes too far.

When we visited the headquarters of Khun Suphin, one of Thailand's largest animal dealers, we noted the plight of several orangutans that had been imported from Indonesia but which Khun Suphin could not re-export because of restrictive legislation. Dr. Boonsong was concerned that Suphin's orangutans would be stuck in their small indoor cages for the rest of their lives, so he supported Suphin's request to send the orangs to a foreign zoo at no profit. Ms. McGreal was outraged at Dr. Boonsong's suggestion that the animals would be better off in a modern zoo than in Suphin's animal compound and launched a long and vituperative attack on Dr. Boonsong, and on us as well, since we were working with him and shared his views.

One of our colleagues, John Blower, who had been instrumental in establishing national parks in Ethiopia, Uganda, and Nepal before going to Indonesia to run an FAO (Food and Agriculture Organization of the United Nations) project on developing national parks, was concerned at this attack. He wrote to McGreal: "I admire the work you are doing and your almost fanatical dedication to your chosen cause. But I do think that being too fanatical in this conservation business, and attacking with tooth and claw anyone who doesn't see exactly eye to eye with you, can do more harm than good—not only to you personally, but more important, to the cause which you seek to promote. One of the saddest things about working in conservation is the bitter rivalry which one so frequently encounters between both individuals and organizations working in the same field, and presumably motivated by broadly similar ideals and objectives. This not only causes a great deal of unnecessary unpleasantness, but does little to convince others of the rightness of the cause concerned."

◆ ◆ ◆

The spread of the global marketplace has encouraged people to move into monkey habitat to grow crops, and has given monkeys a market value. Some of the displaced monkeys fight back, some are shot, some are shipped to zoos, and others are sacrificed to help people develop new drugs, test the crash-worthiness of automobiles, and ensure the safety of lipsticks.

On the practical side, monkeys which raid farmers' crops must be controlled, either by keeping them away or by removing them.

The moral question comes if the monkeys must be removed. Is it better to destroy the crop-raiding monkeys immediately, or to capture them for a slower death in a zoo or in the service of medical research? The greater human benefit might come from the latter fate, but concerned people like Shirley McGreal remind us that animals can be considered to have rights too. And in the arena of international public debate, the animal rights groups often have a louder voice than the farmers whose livelihoods are threatened.

23

Equals Among Equals

Colonial traders were accompanied by Western scientists who found the orangutan a suitable creature to study; the modern trade in timber threatens the "man of the forest."

WE DIDN'T REALLY BELIEVE that the fat little Skyvan, which looked like a giant white bumblebee, would actually be able to fly. But the pilot of the squat Forestry Department plane convinced us otherwise. We lifted off from the short Samarinda airstrip in East Kalimantan and headed west for Kutai Nature Reserve, among the best areas to find one of Southeast Asia's most interesting animals, the orangutan.

Soedjarwo, the Indonesian Director General of Forestry (now the Minister of Forestry—his portfolio continues to include nature conservation), had kindly made one of his forest survey planes available to us so we could show some of Indonesia's protected areas to Dr. Fritz Vollmar, then director general of World Wildlife Fund. We were accompanied by our colleague John Blower, who acted as guide. "What you are going to see is somewhat startling," John said with the understatement typical of long-time British expatriates. "The government granted a timber concession for a magnificent forest just to the west of the Kutai reserve. Somehow the concessionaire convinced the Forestry Department that the only way he could get the logs out would be by building a road *through* the reserve. Of course roads are expensive, so to pay construction costs the concessionaire negotiated a special permit that allowed him to cut 'just a few' hardwood trees that grew within a half a mile of the road."

By this time, we had left behind the inhabited coastal strip, with its oil platforms, gas storage tanks, and plantations. We were headed toward one of the richest forests in Borneo for primates and hundreds of species of birds. The Skyvan was designed especially for aerial survey, so we all had excellent views out of the large plexiglas portholes.

"That river we're now crossing is the reserve boundary," John pointed out. "The logging road is just to the north." Clearly, John had mixed feelings about looking down, in much the same way drivers feel like voyeurs when they rubber-neck as they pass an accident on the highway. Peering down, we saw a road that appeared to have been designed by an artist working in spaghetti. The road meandered pointlessly, then doubled back on itself every few miles to form huge U-shapes. No straightaway seemed longer than a few hundred yards. We could hardly imagine a less efficient road, so we asked John for an explanation.

With a look of profound disgust, John told us that before surveying the route for the road the concessionaire surveyed the location of the most valuable trees in the reserve, which might be worth $1,000 each. It was then a simple matter to build the road so that it gyrated within a half mile of each precious forest giant, which meant that the tree could be legally felled. No wonder the road was still far from completion even after several years of labor.

When Fritz Vollmar had a meeting with Soedjarwo and asked him about Kutai, the Forestry chief understandably responded that Indonesia needed the income from forestry to pay for the nation's development, and that the trees would regrow soon enough. Taiwan, South Korea, and Japan were all clamoring for Indonesia's valuable tropical timber, the country's second largest source of foreign exchange after oil. "And once the most valuable trees are gone," Soedjarwo logically pointed out, "the reserve will have little commercial value and it will therefore be easier to defend against exploitation threats."

The conflict with logging interests was a constant irritant in our work in support of Indonesia's conservation efforts. Whenever we found an area appropriate for a reserve, we usually learned that a timber concession had been given; sometimes two or three concessionaires had overlapping claims. Many of the concessionaires were foreign businessmen with Indonesian partners who were amassing considerable wealth. However, some of the lucrative concessions were held by the military or by universities, who used the income to help meet their basic running costs.

We were not the only ones frustrated by the Indonesian approach. Weyerhaeuser, the giant American timber and paper products company, was alone among the more than 400 foreign and domestic timber concessionaires in Kalimantan in actively replanting cut areas and using ecologically appropriate methods to fell the trees and bring out the logs. Identified as "the best of the S.O.B.s" by *Audubon* magazine, they obtained considerable press coverage in the late 1970s as environmental "good guys" when they vocally pulled out of Indonesia, claiming it was impossible to make a profit because of the high cost of operating in an environmentally sensitive manner. Weyerhaeuser felt that the government's demand for excessively high concessionaire fees and short-term profits did not support their replanting efforts, even though reforestation had been a condition to granting the concession.

Late in 1979, more than two years after our flyover, John Blower came into our office trying to decide whether to let his disgust give way to cynicism or just to scream in frustration. "They finally finished the road through Kutai," John fumed. "And guess what? The concessionaire discovered that it was cheaper to float the logs down the Mahakam River than to take them out by his expensive forest highway. The buggers are going to abandon the road, after having built it because it was the only way to get the logs out. It's outrageous."

Although setbacks like this occurred all too frequently, we persevered in Kalimantan. We were encouraged that others in the government supported nature conservation efforts in the region, particularly efforts to save one of the world's most fascinating animals: the orangutan.

◆ ◆ ◆

The Western fascination with orangutans goes back to the early merchants and adventurers, who returned to Europe telling of creatures so strange that skeptical sponsors might well have thought that the explorers had been overexposed to the tropical sun.

Though Marco Polo on his visit to northern Sumatra in the thirteenth century vaguely described what might have been either a gibbon or an orangutan, Dutchman Jacob de Bondt (Bontius) is credited with being the first Westerner to describe the orangutan. He presented a drawing of a female who hid "her secret parts with no great modesty from unknown men, and also her face with her hands (if one may speak thus), weeping copiously, uttering groans, and expressing other human acts so that you would say nothing human was lacking in her but speech. The Javanese say, in truth, that they can talk, but do not wish to, lest they should be compelled to labor. The name they give to it is Ourang Outang, which means a man of the woods, and they affirm that they are born from the lust of the Indian women, who mix with apes and monkeys with detestable sensuality."

Was this really an orangutan? De Bondt was working in the early seventeenth century, at a time of amazing revelations from the newly discovered worlds of the Americas, Africa, and Asia. "One uneasily feels that in those early days sharp Malays passed off cretinous step-sisters on credulous scientists, in this thirst for sensation and data," says Barbara Harrisson, who founded the first orangutan rehabilitation center at Bako in Sarawak in the 1960s.

Whatever the source of his drawing, de Bondt's name for the creature has stuck even though the term "orangutan," based on the Malay *orang hutan* or "man of the forest," is not used locally to describe the ape—the most common local name is a variation of *maias,* as the animal is called in most of Borneo.

The early foreigners were adventurers first and zoologists a distant second. They wanted to prove that there really were such things as giant red apes, so they eagerly collected specimens, no doubt to avoid having to face the amused skepticism that today greets those who claim to have seen the abominable snowman.

They were followed by gentlemen with more serious credentials who were interested in documenting the fabulous diversity of the tropical Asian rain forests and providing specimens to the great American and European museums. Natural history from the early nineteenth century to World War II was studied more by assassination than observation. By shooting the mysterious animal, you document nature and make scientific history.

Alfred Russel Wallace was perhaps the most illustrious scientist who worked in Asia's forests in this "golden age" of discovery in tropical Asia. Developing the theory of evolution years before Charles Darwin, the great naturalist was also a great humanitarian, conservationist, radical socialist, money reformer, spiritualist, and vegetarian. The gentle and liberal Wallace also wielded his rifle like some modern scientists click their Nikons, bagging at least seventeen orangutans between 1854 to 1856 in the territories which are now parts of Malaysia and Indonesia. He found that the big red apes didn't die easily.

On one occasion, ". . . one of the Dyaks called me and pointed upwards, and on looking I saw a great red hairy body and a huge black face gazing down from a great height, as if wanting to know what was making such a disturbance below. I instantly fired, and he made off at once, so that I could not then tell whether I had hit him.

"He now moved very rapidly and very noiselessly for so large an animal. [Wallace followed him and poured bullets into him, finally cutting down the tree in which the animal had taken refuge]. . . . On examination we found he had been dreadfully wounded. Both legs were broken. One hip-joint and the root of the spine were completely shattered, and two bullets were found flattened in his neck and jaws. Yet he was still alive when he fell."

Other naturalists followed Wallace until the museum specimen cases were filled to the brim with hairy red rugs and long rows of orangutan skulls. William Hornaday, who later helped found the New York Zoological Society, was perhaps the last great orangutan bounty hunter, killing at least forty animals in 1878.

◆ ◆ ◆

The natives no doubt understood the motives of the scientist-collectors very well, because they had been slaughtering the big red apes for millennia before the Europeans came on the scene, and for a similar reason: to earn glory.

Dayaks use the same word for people-hunting and orangutan-hunting, and a completely different word for the hunting of monkeys and gibbons. Some Dayak tribes, thinking orangutans possess a human soul, are said to have eaten the red apes in order to gain soul power, although Lord Medway (now the Earl of Cranbrook), who spent many years in Malaysia studying wildlife and is perhaps the world's leading authority on the mammals of Borneo, says that in historic times the Iban have not hunted the animals for food.

According to G. S. de Silva, chief game warden of Sabah, Malaysia, the Kadazans of remote parts of the state killed orangutans for both food and trophies, collecting the ape heads as they would those of humans. They also decapitated their own deceased relatives and hung the skulls inside their longhouses where both human and orangutan skulls were venerated.

The antagonistic relationship between orangutans and men can be traced to the beginning of human history in Southeast Asia. Near the small Javan village of Trinil, paleontologists have found the bones of prehistoric orangutans in such close proximity to remains of early man that they have concluded that people were eating the apes. Other orangutan fossils have been discovered in limestone caves in Vietnam, southern China, Borneo, and Sumatra, and some experts are convinced that these remains are the result of people going after orangutan heads and then eating the victims.

Many of these fossils are found where orangutans no longer occur, even though the habitat is still suitable. Early humans collected fruits and vegetables and hunted animals in the same habitats preferred by orangutans—river valleys, hill country, and swamp edges—so clashes of interest have probably enlivened the relationship for eons. Some early hunters may well have driven the apes to local extinction, and the lack of orangutans in Java and Indochina today may be due at least partly to the efficiency of human hunters.

◆ ◆ ◆

During the late 1960s, the timber concessionaires began to accelerate their efforts in Indonesia, as the commerce-oriented government of Suharto replaced the protectionist decade under the radically nationalistic Sukarno. As Indonesia began to open up, the loggers were joined by a new generation of field scientists who used binoculars instead of guns. Achievement was no longer based on specimens collected, but on data collected from free-living animals. The modern field scientists wanted to study *everything* about the creatures of the forest—where they lived, what they ate, the content of their feces, and where, with whom, and how frequently they bred.

George Schaller, who became renowned for his studies of the mountain gorillas in Zaire, Uganda, and Rwanda-Burundi, tigers in India, lions in Serengeti, mountain sheep in the Himalayas, and pandas in China, was the first field biologist of the modern era to study orangutans in the wild, spending two months in 1960 in the forests of Sarawak.

Schaller showed the way, and he was followed in the late 1960s and 1970s by a succession of field biologists who braved the isolation, miserable climate, and threats to their health to write their versions of the orang's biography. Long-term studies were carried out by Peter Rodman in East Kalimantan; R. K. Davenport, David Horr, and John MacKinnon in Sabah; Herman Rijksen, John MacKinnon, and Chris Schurmann at Gunung Leuser in Sumatra; and Biruté Galdikas in South Kalimantan. Numerous other scientists have carried out shorter studies.

It's not easy investigating a secretive and solitary animal which has made a point of staying out of our way. "Watching orangutans must surely be one of the most bizarre activities, even among naturalists who are wont to go to great lengths and put up with fair discomfort in order to catch rare glimpses of Life's more obscure mysteries," wrote John MacKinnon, who spent 1968–71 in Borneo and Sumatra. "The orangutan is rare, quiet and shy and to track him down in his jungle haunts is like trying to find the proverbial needle in a haystack. All the while that the intrepid primatologist is wandering through this shady and hostile world his strength and patience are constantly being drained by biting flies, ticks and blood-sucking leeches, clinging mud and tearing thorns, oppressive heat and humidity, the growing weight of his pack, regular drenching by tropical downpours, loneliness, hunger, thirst, and despondency. More often than not he fails to find his elusive quarry and must try again on the morrow."

It takes a special sort of person to keep at it. Biruté M. F. Galdikas is perhaps the best known of the orangutan researchers for her over fifteen years spent in Kalimantan's Tanjung Puting Nature Reserve. As one of the protégés of Louis Leakey, the discoverer of evidence of early man in east Africa (others were the late Dian Fossey, who studied gorillas in Zaire and Rwanda, and Jane Goodall, who specializes in the chimpanzees of Tanzania), Galdikas went to the swamp forest of southern Borneo in 1971 with her husband Rod Brindamour to study "the person of the forest." When not mothering infant orphan orangutans, she was in the forest learning some of the secrets of the life of the great ape. She encouraged Indonesian students to help her collect data, and sent willing Dayaks up the trees to collect botanical specimens to determine what the apes were eating. While her impact on other scientists has been relatively slight, her research efforts have been made famous among the general public by two cover stories in *National Geographic,* in 1975 and 1980.

Biruté Galdikas has made a real commitment to orangutans, and her presence in Tanjung Puting has kept the loggers out. Soedjarwo is fascinated by her. Whenever we met with him, he would always make a point of asking how she was doing. "It's wonderful how somebody could leave behind all the advantages of Western civilization to live in the remote jungles of Kalimantan to study orangutans for so long," he mused one day in his luxurious office in Jakarta. She was also respected by local government, and more than any single factor has been responsible for keeping the reserve intact, at least in her study area. Nobody would try to "pull a Kutai" in Tanjung Puting as long as she was around.

Studying orangutans for long periods in a remote area has meant considerable personal costs for this scientist. Five years into her study, Galdikas' life was complicated by the birth of a son, Binti Paul, named for a provincial official who was a close family friend. As a dedicated scientist, Galdikas turned a potential ticket home to UCLA to the advantage of her research.

"Bin's development during the first year helped clear up my own thinking," says Galdikas. "Up to that point most of my adult life in the forest had been orangutans and more orangutans . . . I had reached the point where the line between human and ape was getting somewhat blurred . . . I was actually beginning to doubt whether orangutans were all that different from human beings. But Bin's behavior in his first year highlighted the differences very clearly, and offered me a new perspective."

◆ ◆ ◆

While riding in a pram at Biruté's spartan but functional base camp in Tanjung Puting, Princess, a five-year-old orangutan, molded her hands into signs that meant: "You-Out-Up," indicating that she wanted to get out of that contraption and back on Papa's shoulder where she belonged. Swinging on one of her long arms she hoisted herself on to Gary Shapiro's neck, her russet hair a perfect match for the American scientist's scraggly red beard.

While Princess tugged at his little remaining hair, Gary calmly explained what he was doing in the forest.

"I'm trying to teach Princess to speak Ameslan," Gary said. "That's American Sign Language, but I don't call it that since the Indonesian authorities might get uptight about their orangutans learning a foreign language."

Biruté considered Gary an important part of her research program. "My hope was that perhaps we could actually get into the orangutan's head," Galdikas explained, "and find out what he thinks about life in the forest, how he patterns his world."

School for Princess began at six forty-five in the morning. Gary sat her down squarely in front of a small table on which he placed a hand mirror. "Princess, *apa ini?*" he asked in spoken Indonesian, pointing to the mirror. What is this?

With all the excitement of a ten-year-old boy forced to practice the piano when he'd rather be out playing football, Princess flicked her thumbnail against her teeth—the sign for "nut," which meant she thought she deserved a reward.

"Princess!" Gary yelled. *"NO!"*

Patiently Gary gave her a peanut for her incorrect response, molded the correct response in which the signer shakes the flat hand repeatedly in front of the body, and took careful notes that later would be analyzed with the help of his university's computer.

He replaced the mirror with a watch. Princess decided that Gary's pipe looked more interesting and she grabbed it from the side table and started chewing. Gary was not amused since this was his last pipe—his student had already mangled two other briars.

"Apa ini?"

By this time Princess was standing on her head. She softly rolled over, scratched her belly, and started investigating our backpacks, which were sitting in a corner of the wooden cabin.

"PRINCESS! You're gonna get it!"

This time she got it right, touching her ear with her index finger. After her reward of two peanuts she grabbed a woven bag and placed it over her head. She sat quietly, munching on an empty plastic film container.

The attempt to communicate was exasperating work, and as much as Gary and Princess obviously enjoyed being together— Biruté claimed Gary was "an equal among equals"—the difficulty

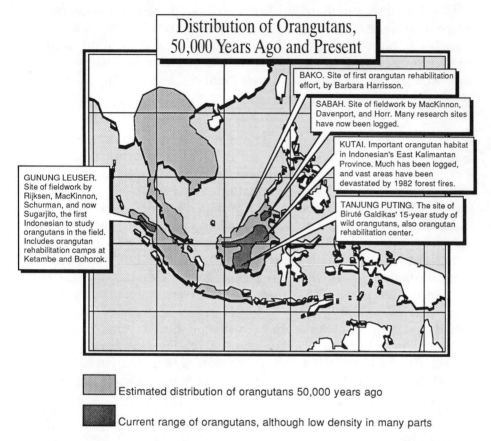

Distribution of Orangutans, 50,000 Years Ago and Present

BAKO. Site of first orangutan rehabilitation effort, by Barbara Harrisson.

SABAH. Site of fieldwork by MacKinnon, Davenport, and Horr. Many research sites have now been logged.

KUTAI. Important orangutan habitat in Indonesian's East Kalimantan Province. Much has been logged, and vast areas have been devastated by 1982 forest fires.

GUNUNG LEUSER. Site of fieldwork by Rijksen, MacKinnon, Schurman, and now Sugarjito, the first Indonesian to study orangutans in the field. Includes orangutan rehabilitation camps at Ketambe and Bohorok.

TANJUNG PUTING. The site of Biruté Galdikas' 15-year study of wild orangutans, also orangutan rehabilitation center.

Estimated distribution of orangutans 50,000 years ago

Current range of orangutans, although low density in many parts

of teaching an ape who didn't want to be taught could have driven a lesser man to distraction.

With no other human infants in the remote jungle camp, Princess became Bin's favorite playmate. "I was extremely concerned when Bin, after outgrowing his gibbon stage (where he called and leaped around like the ex-captive gibbons near camp), began mimicking Princess," Biruté explains. "Their facial expressions, sounds and posture became very similar. Bin always had to be watched, for he would try to follow Princess and play with her in the trees. At the age of three he could do a perfect orangutan imitation. It would not have been any cause for concern except that, with no other children in camp, orangutans were becoming his role models.

"And Bin was picking up sign language, although we rarely taught him. He didn't talk to Princess; he signed to her as he also did with other nonsigning orangutans."

Concerned that perhaps the jungles of Borneo were not the best place to bring up his son, Rod Brindamour took Bin back to start a new life in North America. Biruté Galdikas' total dedication to the orangutan kept her in the forest, where she was recently wooed and wed by one of her Dayak tree-climbers. Her research continues.

◆ ◆ ◆

As the pace of forest exploitation picked up in Indonesia and Sabah, scientists increasingly began to hear the buzz of chain saws in their study areas. Concerned about the impact of logging on the orangutans, they used the information they had collected to help save the apes and the forest. Data provided by these ecologists on population size, feeding habits, breeding behavior, and annual range of wild orangutans have enabled park planners to design protected areas large enough to ensure the survival of the species. And the publicity which often accompanies field studies helps to convince governments that their wildlife has a worth far beyond the value of animals for trade. Cover stories in *National Geographic* are a clear indication to leaders in distant capitals that they are expected to hold these animals in trust for their citizens and the world. But local politics is often far more powerful than international opinion when governments are deciding how to use their resources.

24

A Snowman
in the Jungle

A little-known tropical version of the Himalayan abominable snowman represents man's wild alter-ego. Destroying his forested habitat may also threaten the human spirit.

MORE THAN 100,000 native laborers and 16,000 American, British, Canadian, and Dutch prisoners of war died from starvation, cholera, malaria, and beatings while building the World War II "death railway" along the River Kwai. The Japanese hoped the 250-mile railroad line would help them transport war materials from Thailand into Burma, but Allied bombers destroyed the line's main bridge, the famous "Bridge on the River Kwai," shortly before the end of the war.

Thirty years later, we were in Kanchanaburi Province with Dr. Boonsong, to do some research for our book on the mammals of Thailand. We climbed into a wooden railroad car, which pulled out of the station and soon crossed the iron bridge which had been reconstructed by the Japanese (and bears a plaque reading "Made

in Japan") as part of their war reparations to Thailand. Because the
railroad was abandoned after the war, most of the railbed had been
reclaimed by the forest and we were able to take the train only a
short distance upstream. Reaching the end of the line, we left the
train and climbed into a long, skinny skiff with a noisy outboard
engine whose long shaft allowed the skipper to steer the craft up
crooked creeks, raise the propeller out of the water to avoid obstacles, and splash pretty girls on the riverbanks. During the entire
six-hour trip our ears rang from the muffler-less roar. Speeding up
the river, we passed limestone cliffs where early man had made his
home in caves along the water's edge. Our mission was to learn
more about one of modern Thailand's most fascinating cave-dwelling animals: Kitti's hog-nosed bat.

The hog-nosed bat is the smallest mammal known. One of Dr.
Boonsong's protégés, Kitti Thonglongya, discovered it in 1973
when a dozen or so became tangled in a net he had erected just a
hundred yards from the death railway. Kitti's discovery astonished
the scientific world. The lightweight bat (.06 ounces) had a face
only a mother could love and was so unusual that an entirely new
family had to be created for it, the first newly discovered family of
mammals in nearly a hundred years.

While the diminutive bat was an incredible discovery, finding
novel animals isn't all that surprising in Thailand. It was the third
new bat Kitti had discovered in two years, and in 1968 he had
discovered a new bird, the white-eyed river martin, just 120 miles
north of Bangkok, in the reed beds of the country's largest lake.
When our book on the mammals of Thailand was finally published
in 1977, 38 out of the book's 264 species had been discovered after
1900, including five described only since 1970 and two, identified
by our colleague Joe Marshall, which had never been described
before.

Our skiff passed through some of the most scenic country in
Thailand. Dark green forests cloaked the massive limestone peaks,
riddled with caves that offered ideal roosting sites for bats. Many
of these caves had also yielded stone tools and fossils, revealing the
sorts of animals hunted in the preagricultural days.

Reaching Sai Yoke waterfalls, where a small stream joins the
Kwai down a set of limestone stairs, we checked in at the forestry
station where we would stay and introduced ourselves to the overseer of an experimental teak plantation. Refreshed from a swim in

the river, we joined our host at the campfire as evening fell. He invited us to join him to scan the darkening sky for bats.

While we waited, Dr. Boonsong told us about other recent discoveries of Asian mammals. "My friend from India, E. P. Gee, found a new species of monkey, the golden langur, in 1956 at the Manas Sanctuary in Assam, a wonderful place for wildlife," he told us. "And the first new cat of this century, the Iriomote Island cat, was described from a small island between Japan and Taiwan in 1967. But the most interesting is the kouprey, a kind of wild ox I used to hunt in Cambodia in the early 1950s. They weigh as much as gaur but they're taller and slimmer. It's lovely to see how gracefully they run. They were totally unknown to western science until 1937 when an animal dealer sent one to the Paris Zoo with some other animals from Saigon. Everybody thought it was a banteng until somebody who really knew Asia's animals recognized it as something new and very special."

We got up to throw another log on the fire and give a turn to the spit on which a barking deer was browning. "But what is really interesting," Dr. Boonsong added with a smile, "is that there may well be another unknown animal living not far from here. The Karen hill tribe people know it very well, though they are afraid to shoot one. It's called *tua yeua* in Thai, and it seems to be something very much like an orangutan. But of course orangutans now live only in Borneo and Sumatra. Wouldn't it be wonderful if we could find one?"

Suddenly Dr. Boonsong reached for the binoculars that always hung from his neck like an amulet. "Look!" he whispered. "See those tiny creatures flying around the bamboo? They look like big moths, but those are Kitti's bats!"

It soon got too dark to see and we moved closer to the fire and our dinner of venison, baked eels, fish curry, and vegetables. We asked Dr. Boonsong more about the tua yeua. Had he ever seen one? "No, but they must be both rare and shy," he responded. "The interesting thing is that two respected Westerners *have* seen them, and reported it to W. T. Blanford at the British Museum. A man named Davison was out collecting specimens in the 1880s near Mount Muleyit in southern Burma when he saw a tua yeua ten feet away, standing erect. He said it was dark red and too big for a gibbon but he couldn't shoot it because his shotgun was loaded with bird shot." We nodded, having heard this kind of thing often—the classic "you should have seen the one that got away" story.

"But an army captain named Bingham did even better around the same time," Dr. Boonsong continued, ignoring our grins. "Somebody actually gave him a dead one, a big female covered in grizzled red hair. But it was already decomposing by the time he had received it so he could only save the skeleton. Naturally, the skeleton has been lost, so we still don't have any hard evidence that the tua yeua really exists."

We awoke early the next morning, anxious to be off at first light to search the limestone caves to see if we could be the first to find where Kitti's bat roosted during the day. But while our business was bats, we also spent a lot of time looking for bones and stone tools, as well as suspicious footprints.

◆ ◆ ◆

The tua yeua is just one of many such creatures which may live in forested regions throughout Southeast Asia. Most people know that many of the big animals—orangutans, tigers, rhinos—are being threatened by humans converting the animals' habitats for the benefit of international trade. But few people realize that we are losing animals before scientists have an opportunity to discover them.

The Himalayan abominable snowman or *yeti* is by far the most famous of these yet-to-be classified creatures, leaving footprints to startle expeditions each climbing season. The latest yeti discovery was "confirmed" by a fuzzy photograph of an alleged yeti that appeared in the September 1986 issue of a British magazine, *BBC Wildlife.*

The yeti may grab the headlines, but he is only a small part of the story; tropical Asia has almost as many types of unknown yeti-relatives as it has countries. Reported by many rural people living near the great wildernesses, they all seem to be hominoids, a word that means "man-like" and which includes monkeys, apes, ape-men, cavemen, and humans. Instead of arbitrarily picking one of the many local names for these creatures, we'll call them "unidentified tropical Asian hominoids," or *untrahom* for short.

Untrahoms are not taken very seriously by the stern gatekeepers of western science, who insist that every species must be represented in a museum by a standard "type specimen" before its existence can be officially acknowledged. And it must be written up in a respected journal. Kitti Thonglongya died playing badminton in February 1974 before he could finish the technical paper that would have introduced his hog-nosed bat. The animal officially existed only after it had been described in the *Bulletin of the British Museum of Natural History* by one of our colleagues, John Edwards Hill. It seemed a fitting memorial to Kitti, who had devoted his life to helping Dr. Boonsong discover Thailand's fauna.

Although the scientific community scoffs at untrahom sightings, the local people are well acquainted with them—that's why they give them names. And enough respected authorities have collected evidence of these strange creatures to at least give pause to the skeptics.

- Chinese researchers interviewed a hundred eyewitnesses and gathered hard evidence such as hair, footprints, and droppings to "prove" the existence of the *ye ren*, a Bigfoot-type animal living in the mountainous jungle area of Sichuan, the home of the rare and reclusive giant panda.
- Noted biologist the Earl of Cranbrook collected descriptions of a large unidentified primate called *beruang rambai* on the Sarawak/Kalimantan border in central Borneo. "The people of the area are familiar with the orangutan," Cranbrook noted, and he speculated that this "hairy bear" was neither bear nor orangutan but probably a relict species of *something*. The earl would not speculate further.
- American soldiers in Vietnam had encounters with what was described as "an orangutan-like creature," although there has been no evidence of orangutans in Indochina for 50,000 years. A veteran of the war, now a special investigator for the U.S. Customs Service, who was in Bangkok to investigate the illegal reptile trade, told us that two men in his platoon had had their heads torn off by the powerful beast.
- Professor Vo Quy, a slight Vietnamese ornithologist who has managed to maintain his scientific stature as well as his devotion to wildlife in incredibly difficult conditions, has taken photos and plaster casts of large (fifteen inches long) human-like footprints found in the jungles of North Vietnam. He told us that the hill tribes carefully avoid the forests where these huge creatures are said to roam.
- John MacKinnon, studying orangutan ecology in the Malaysian state of Sabah, found footprints of the *batutut*, a print "so like a

man's yet so definitely not a man's that my skin crept and I felt a strange desire to return home. The prints were roughly triangular in shape, about six inches long by four across. The toes looked quite human, as did the shapely heel, but the sole was both too short and too broad to be that of a man and the big toe was on the opposite side to what seemed to be the arch of the foot." Natives told MacKinnon that the batutut feeds on river snails that it breaks open with rocks, and MacKinnon did find snail shells that seemed to have been shattered by rock hammers. The batutut, which natives have never seen and consider a nocturnal ghost, walks upright like a man, is shy of fire, and kills people before ripping out their livers.

Assuming that untrahoms would survive best in isolated, untouched forests, the most productive place to look for them may well be the Kerinci-Seblat area in the mountains that form the spine of Sumatra. Centered around Sumatra's highest peak, the active 12,500-foot Mount Kerinci volcano, this 4,000-square-mile area has been called "the attic of Southeast Asia" by British naturalist Ivan Sanderson because it holds so many strange plants and animals. Rare plants of the area include the Rafflesia, the world's broadest flower which is appropriately named the stinking corpse lily—a parasitic plant with neither stem nor leaves whose three-foot-wide blossom exudes a most disagreeable scent; and the five-foot-tall phallus lily, a plant whose name reflects its structure but which, unlike its namesake, blossoms only every third year. The short-eared Sumatran hare, which makes its home near Mount Kerinci, is the only rabbit known to live exclusively in deep forest.

In addition to these oddities, the area has no fewer than eight species of primates, one of the highest densities anywhere in the world; the world's best population of the extremely rare and elusive Sumatran rhinoceros; and a healthy population of Asian tapirs, large, long-snouted throwbacks to the prehistoric age, whose nearest relatives live in Brazil.

The central Sumatran highland is also the prime habitat for the untrahom *sedapa,* and numerous sightings were reported there in the 1920s. A Dutch hunter named Oostingh came across a strange human-like animal sitting on a log. At first he thought it was just a medium-sized native with thick square shoulders. "Then I saw that it was not a man," Oostingh reported. "The creature calmly took several paces, and then, with his ludicrously long arm, grasped a sapling, which threatened to break under its weight, and quietly sprang into a tree, swinging in great leaps alternately to right and to left. It was not an orangutan."

Not far away, and around the same time, Dutch physician Dr. Edward Jacobson found very small, broad, and short human-like footprints similar to the batutut tracks MacKinnon found 1,600 miles away fifty years later.

Perhaps the best description of that era was provided by a Dutch settler named van Herwaarden, who found a sedapa in the deep forest of Sumatra's Bukit Barisan range. He is quoted by the Belgian naturalist Bernard Heuvelmans:

The very dark hair on its head fell almost to the waist . . . [its] brown face was almost hairless. The eyes were very lively, and like human eyes. The nose was broad with fairly large nostrils, but in no way clumsy. Its lips were quite ordinary. Its canines showed clearly from time to time, they were more developed than a man's. I was able to see its right ear which was exactly like a little human ear. Its hands were slightly hairy on the back. Had it been standing, its arms would have reached to a little above its knees; but its legs seemed to me rather short. This specimen was of the female sex and about 5 feet high.

More recently, David Labang, with Sarawak's National Parks and Wildlife Department, told us of an encounter he had in the peninsular Malaysian state of Pahang, just 24 miles to the east of Kuala Lumpur, and about four miles off the main road. Out collecting specimens for the University of Malaya, he accidentally caught a wild dog in a trap. The *Orang Asli* who were serving as guides were horrified and insisted that the animal be released immediately. "It belongs to the tiny *Uyan* people who live in the forest, and they will harm us if we hurt their dog," David was told.

This intrigued David, who awoke early the next morning to hide near a spot by the river where the little people had often been sighted. "I saw some movement in the wild ginger leaves. I focused my binoculars on what I thought might be a wild animal. Instead I saw true to form a tiny naked man about three feet high with short, thick, seemingly curly hair, thin limbs, brownish skin, rather hairy body, and looking exactly like a human being (except for his odd size), coming confidently down the hill towards a fallen tree trunk lying across the Cimperoh River. I wavered between shooting and capturing the creature, but decided on the latter. I rushed out from my hiding place to chase after him and did so for about a hundred yards but he was quick and agile and I soon lost him in the undergrowth."

◆ ◆ ◆

We spent several days crawling in and out of grayish-white limestone caves, and collected numerous species of bats. But we discovered no further sign of Kitti's bat, nor of the tua yeua.

We paused for an early lunch on our last day, peeling back the thin young bamboo in which our rice had been steamed that morning and eating it with small chunks of tasty barbecued fruit-bat meat from specimens we had collected and skinned the previous day. Leaning back against a cool slab of limestone with a full stomach, we were happy to have had the meat, fantasizing about how the old hunters used to live. But we also chatted about the morality of collecting animals for the cause of science; after all, most species did better before they were discovered, since discovery all too often is followed by exploitation. We asked Dr. Boonsong whether he saw any conflict between the collection of animals and his live-and-let-live Buddhist faith. He thought about the question for a few minutes before replying: "Kitti died at a young age, but I won't die so easily. I will linger on, and pay for my sins. I try to compensate by making merit through good works in conservation, and I could do even more if I had more funds. But I'm afraid that my fate is already sealed. I will have to suffer for the lives of animals I have taken." He offered his fatalistic prophecy with a shrug, realizing that he could do nothing about it. The prophecy proved uncannily accurate.

Quickly finishing off our cold lunch with several bananas the size of a thumb, we returned to the caves. Toward the end of the day, we began to feel claustrophobic as we crawled on our bellies through a tiny opening. The flashlight batteries were beginning to dim, and so were we. The only thing that kept us going was Dr. Boonsong, sixty-seven years old and hardly winded despite a heart condition that required regular treatment. And, as usually happens, we found Kitti's bat in the last place we looked.

We dropped down an unpromising sinkhole to find ourselves in an exquisite limestone cavern, filled with floor-to-ceiling columns sparkling with minerals dripped from the ceiling, small pools of water floating on limestone platforms, and a roof studded with stalactites. We would have liked to excavate for fossils, but Dr. Boonsong sent us slithering through a small crevice which seemed to provide a passageway deep into the earth. Finally coming to the end of the cave, we found a tall chimney and at the top about a dozen Kitti's bats were dangling like limestone fruits, their tiny clawed feet firmly holding on to the rough stone ceiling. Shining his light upward, Dr. Boonsong whispered exultantly, "Kitti's bats!" They took flight as soon as the light hit them, an appropriate response for an animal that had eluded human attention for so long.

But Dr. Boonsong was ready with his butterfly net and he caught several. We photographed them for our book, then carefully pickled several voucher specimens for the natural history museum's reference collection. Our viewpoint was that we were contributing to the body of scientific knowledge. Dr. Boonsong was adding more black marks to his *karma,* his Buddhist destiny.

We felt good that evening, having accomplished our major objective. But at the same time, we were thoughtful about Dr. Boonsong's prophecy. We were also disappointed that we had not found any sign of the tua yeua, even though we knew firsthand how hard it is to find evidence of these creatures—we had just returned to Thailand from spending two years in the eastern Himalayas actually looking for evidence of the yeti and had found its spoor only three times (though that's another story).

While walking around the Himalayas we had had lots of time to think about what a yeti might be. Now, back in Thailand, we shared our ideas with Dr. Boonsong. "The first possibility," we argued, "must be the orangutan." We speculated that some might have survived from the ancient population which once lived in southern China and Vietnam but was thought to have died out over 50,000 years ago. Their fossils are found in limestone fissures just like the ones we had been crawling through, so they might have lived in country such as this in prehistoric times. Recent field studies of the orangutan have shown that massive orangutan males spend much of their time on the ground, occasionally walking upright, so this could account for tales of the yeti or tua yeua walking man-like on two legs. The fossils of the orangutans which lived in southern China thousands of years ago are nearly 40 percent larger than their modern Indonesian descendants, so they surely spent even more time on the ground than the modern forms.

In the field our table manners took a tumble. We shoveled in huge mouthfuls of rice and chicken rolled in rice flour and noticed that Dr. Boonsong was still listening to our theories about unknown primates. His silence spurred us on to explore the *Gigantopithecus* option. Fossils of *Gigantopithecus,* the largest primate that ever lived, were found in the same areas as the old orangutans. We don't know too much about him, we lectured, since most of his remains have been found only in the form of "dragon's teeth" sold as a powder by Chinese apothecaries. A number of scientists think he's the best candidate for an ancestor of the large "Bigfoot"-type untrahoms—the Himalayan yeti or the Chinese ye ren. *Gigantopithecus* is known to have survived up to about half a million years ago, so he was around at the same time as our ancestor *Homo erectus*. Their fossils have been found together in China, and paleontologists speculate that tool-using *Homo* may have been hunting the much larger but less clever *Gigantopithecus.*

The night was turning chilly and Dr. Boonsong reached his hand out and pushed a log deeper into the campfire. We sat around the comforting blaze as our ancestors must have done. Like them, we stared into the dancing shapes in the flames and speculated on the inexplicable: "Another possibility is *Homo erectus* himself, the last 'man-ape' before our own species evolved. He's been found in both Java and China, so he must have at least passed through Thailand. Intermediate in size between modern man and the east African *Australopithecus*, he was only five feet tall and weighed about ninety pounds, roughly sedapa-sized.

"The last 'fossil' to consider is Neanderthal man, which has been found in several places in tropical Asia, including Borneo's Niah Caves, where he apparently killed orangutans for food. Anthropologist Myra Shackley has collected information which convinces her that a number of isolated populations of Neanderthals still survive in various parts of Asia, from Mongolia to China. Some Russian and Chinese scientists agree with her."

Dr. Boonsong, aware of the firm belief in untrahoms among rural people, but ever the logical scientist, asked, "But how could any of these ancient forms have survived?"

"We know that many predecessors of humans were contemporaries and might have fought for similar ecological niches," we responded. "The victors were our distant ancestors who came down from the trees and, using tools, took over the plains, eventually learning to manage fire and, ultimately, invent agriculture and send rockets to the moon."

Starting to get carried away with our hypothesis, we continued, "Now let us suppose that one or more of the prehistoric primates

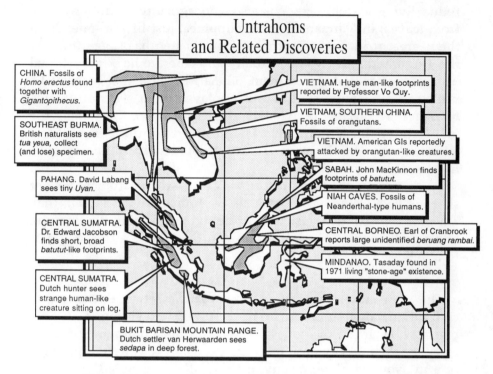

Untrahoms and Related Discoveries

CHINA. Fossils of *Homo erectus* found together with *Gigantopithecus*.

SOUTHEAST BURMA. British naturalists see *tua yeua*, collect (and lose) specimen.

PAHANG. David Labang sees tiny *Uyan*.

CENTRAL SUMATRA. Dr. Edward Jacobson finds short, broad *batutut*-like footprints.

CENTRAL SUMATRA. Dutch hunter sees strange human-like creature sitting on log.

BUKIT BARISAN MOUNTAIN RANGE. Dutch settler van Herwaarden sees *sedapa* in deep forest.

VIETNAM. Huge man-like footprints reported by Professor Vo Quy.

VIETNAM, SOUTHERN CHINA. Fossils of orangutans.

VIETNAM. American GIs reportedly attacked by orangutan-like creatures.

SABAH. John MacKinnon finds footprints of *batutut*.

NIAH CAVES. Fossils of Neanderthal-type humans.

CENTRAL BORNEO. Earl of Cranbrook reports large unidentified *beruang rambai*.

MINDANAO. Tasaday found in 1971 living "stone-age" existence.

The distribution of unidentified tropical Asian hominoids, or "untrahoms," as reported in the text.

Remaining original forest

did not become extinct at that time but fled into the deep recesses of the forest and managed to survive in that remote habitat. Such an animal would have needed considerable intelligence to stay out of the way of its weapon-wielding human cousins. We all know how the people of Borneo practice their head-hunting on the orangutans who share their forests."

"You may be right," Dr. Boonsong conceded, though it was clear he was not entirely convinced. "But there is another possibility. These creatures may actually be forest people who just make a very serious effort to stay away from civilized people."

Dr. Boonsong had a point. Tropical Asia is ethnically one of the richest parts of the globe. Among these are people like Malaysia's Orang Asli, who, while notoriously shy, are known to science. But the possibility that some groups remain undiscovered was brought home dramatically in 1971, when the now-famous Tasaday were found living a stone-age existence (no agriculture, clothes made from leaves) in Mindanao, the Philippines, just fifteen miles from the nearest road. Swiss journalist Oswald Iten has suggested that the Tasaday discovery was actually an elaborate hoax perpetrated by a glory-seeking government official, because the Tasaday he visited in 1981 wore clothes and displayed other signs of outside influence. Regardless of whether the Tasaday are "genuine," the interesting point is that many of the world's anthropologists and journalists were quite prepared to accept that an unknown tribe had been discovered.

We agreed on one thing before we crept into our tropical-weight sleeping bags. Whether untrahoms are human or subhuman, they are probably content just where they are, reflecting Sir Edmund Hillary's thought: "There is precious little in civilization to appeal to a Yeti."

◆ ◆ ◆

The next morning, as we packed for the return downriver to civilization, another point occurred to Dr. Boonsong. Carefully placing our jars of pickled Kitti's bats in his aluminum specimen case, he asked, "Why hasn't anyone been able to collect a specimen of a tua yeua or a yeti or any of these other creatures?"

In the first place, it would be hard to see such a shy and seemingly rare animal. John MacKinnon notes that it is almost impossible to see the Sumatran rhinoceros, which inhabits the same inaccessible tropical rain forest as the sedapa, tua yeua, and batutut. "Sumatran rhinos are big, rare, and stupid, and I've never been able to see one despite spending years roaming around forests where they live," MacKinnon explained to us over a beer one evening at his house on the shoulder of Gunung Gede volcano, south of Jakarta. "It would be a lot more difficult to see a sedapa, which is smaller, smarter, and just as rare. It's probably nocturnal, but without reflecting eyes, so your chances of seeing one would be miniscule."

One of the most interesting parts of the whole untrahom controversy is how those who have had a chance to collect one have somehow been restrained from actually pulling the trigger, almost as if they were afraid of what they would find. David Labang chose to try to capture one alive rather than shoot it, and Davison came up with a good excuse for why he did not fire. The Dutch planter van Herwaarden, who had an excellent opportunity to shoot one and thereby end the controversy, refused to pull the trigger: "When I raised my gun to the little female I heard a plaintive 'hu-hu,' which was at once answered by similar echoes in the forest nearby. I laid down my gun and . . . the sedapa dropped a good ten feet to the ground . . . before I could reach my gun again, the beast was almost 30 yards away. It went on running and gave a sort of whistle. Many people may think me childish if I say that when I saw its flying hair in the sight I did not pull the trigger. I suddenly felt that I was going to commit murder."

An important psychological factor may be at play, one that we experienced in the Himalayas: We somehow didn't really *want* to find the yeti. John MacKinnon had the same feeling with his batutut tracks. "I was uneasy when I found them," MacKinnon recalls, "and I didn't want to follow them and find out what was at the end of the trail. I knew that no animal we know about could make those tracks. Without deliberately avoiding the area I realize I never went back to that place in the following months of my studies."

Untrahoms clearly evoke visceral reactions in many people. For rural villagers, they may symbolize man's rejection of his animal nature, an age-old internal conflict of a species whose culture sets it apart from its closest relatives. Yet this separation is always somewhat ambivalent, as people both deny their jungle essence and secretly savor it. Untrahoms are the Mr. Hyde to our Dr. Jekyll.

People are fascinated by discoveries of fossil hominids and reports of the field studies of gorillas, chimpanzees, and orangutans. The great apes are among the most popular zoo exhibits. Scientists studying the orangutan often feel a strong kinship with the animals, and when field biologists in Borneo and Sumatra gaze into the placid eyes of the orangutan, they are looking at a kindred soul, a fellow being with feelings, intelligence, and emotions. Malcolm MacDonald, former governor-general of colonial Malaya and Borneo, thought that "these members of the order Primates contemplate you, when you meet them, with melancholy eyes, as if they had just read Darwin's *Origin of Species* and were painfully aware of being your poor relations who have not done so well in life."

But most people are uncomfortable when they get too close to their animal selves. The Balinese, who consider themselves among the earth's most culturally advanced people, routinely file their children's teeth straight across in order to ensure that their "animal-like" canines do not extend beyond the other teeth.

Animal-like behavior is also frowned upon. Throughout Southeast Asia, special emphasis is placed on making sure that people act like humans, not like wild beasts. Careful upbringing and age-old traditions ensure that fundamentally human characteristics are drummed into children from a tender age. It is best to stick close to Mom, and learn that human children do not gulp down their food, that people do not speak in loud, vulgar voices, that adults do not fight in public, that even a beggar is treated with courtesy. Each human being is part of the human family, and virtually all of the region's cultures use familial terms—grandmother, father, uncle, younger sister—to greet and address both friends and strangers.

Among the rural people who are in daily contact with "wild nature," the various forms of untrahoms are an ever-present reminder of what it means to be man-like, yet not human. Mothers emphasize the gap that separates *Homo sapiens* from the other hominoids when they tell children that an untrahom will get them if they are naughty. Untrahoms live in the forest, away from people, but people fear and respect both them and their forest home.

But times are changing. The great forest areas which shelter untrahoms—be they batutut, sedapa, beruang rambai, uyan, ye ren, or tua yeua—are fast being sold to concessionaires, chopped into smaller fragments, or cleared by shifting cultivators. Rural people, who define their humanity both by what they are and what they are not, are moving to the cities or large villages and the concept of humanity is being redefined. Instead of being the home of the human spirit, the rain forest is often considered by the educated urban people as unproductive wilderness that can best serve humanity by being sold for timber and cleared to grow rubber and oil palm. They are too sophisticated to worry that the destruction of the untrahom's rain forest habitat takes away the home of a relative we will probably never meet in person.

◆ ◆ ◆

On the one hand we are thinking, rational, moral humans. On the other hand we share the same ancestors with the apes, as well as 99 percent of our DNA. But while many people can accept intellectually an ape in the family tree, they do not necessarily want to look in the mirror and be confronted by a hairy alter-ego.

We shudder when we read newspaper stories like the tale of Xu

Yunbao, who was photographed before he died in 1962 and whose corpse was exhumed and examined in 1980. "Born to a peasant woman in central Sichuan province [China] in 1939, his body was covered with hair and he was bent at the waist," the UPI report in the *Straits Times* read. "He grew to a height of only 3 feet and used all four limbs when walking. Xu refused clothing even during winter and lived on a diet of raw corn, vehemently rejecting cooked food. His brain capacity never grew over 350 ml [an average man has a brain capacity of 1,200 to 1,500 ml] and his spinal column and limbs were even more backward in construction than those of the Peking Man who lived more than 400,000 years ago. His skull, which shows the primitive characteristics of man's ancestors hundreds of thousands of years ago, was only eight cm in diameter on birth."

Xu resembles the prehistoric ancestors we are trying to disinherit from our consciousness. The description of him isolated in a tiny village causes the same emotional reaction we might have to capturing an untrahom and putting it on display, or shooting one and filing it away in a specimen drawer at a museum. This might be a remarkable achievement for science, but it might also be a low point for humanity. Perhaps it is better that the untrahom not be discovered.

Myths and legends of giants and ape-men have survival value for mankind—we need to be reminded of what our life might be like if we did not have culture, that uniquely human attribute. As the distinguished British primatologist Dr. John Napier suggests, humans need to experience feelings of awe. "Husbands, fathers, elders, statesmen, dictators, presidents, chairmen, and grand masters are all very well as god-figures, but they are inadequate because they lack the essential ingredient of remoteness. Man needs his gods—and his monsters—and the more remote and unapproachable they are, the better."

The jungle snowman may or may not exist in reality. But there is no question that it has an eternal home in the human spirit.

25

Return to the Wild

The illegal fad of keeping orangutans as pets is disappearing, but trying to put the animals back in the forest often proves difficult.

"DEBBIE, GET OFF THE GROUND!" As a worried mother might scold her child for playing in the traffic, biologist and orangutan rehabilitator Rosalind Aveling was teaching her pupil one of the facts of orangutan life. Unlike the forest floor in Borneo, which is relatively safe, the jungles of Sumatra are stalked by hungry tigers, so special care is required by orangutans wanting to take a stroll.

Rosalind and her husband Conrad (now in eastern Zaire acclimatizing mountain gorillas to the presence of tourists) were physicians, teachers, nannies, playmates, and adopted parents in the 1970s to twenty orphaned orangutans at the Bohorok Orangutan Rehabilitation Centre west of Medan in Sumatra.

Their job was created by a bizarre aspect of the global marketplace. Orangutans were being captured to meet the demand for unusual pets. The governments of Malaysia and Indonesia had enacted laws which not only ordered the confiscation of the household orangutans but instructed that they should be rehabilitated for a life in the wild.

The orangutan trader first had to separate a baby from its mother. Nobody discovered a more efficient technique than Alfred Russel Wallace's. "We found it to be a rather large one, very high up on a tall tree," the great naturalist wrote. "At the second shot it fell rolling over, but almost immediately got up again and began to climb. At the third shot it fell dead. This was also a full-grown female, and while preparing to carry it home, we found a young one face downwards in the bog. This little creature was only about a foot long, and had evidently been hanging to its mother when she first fell. Luckily it did not appear to have been wounded, and after we had cleaned the mud out of its mouth it began to cry out, and seemed quite strong and active."

It is difficult to resist the young apes. We have felt paternal as we held infant orangutans in our arms and scolded mischievous apes that stole (and ate) our soap as we went to the river to bathe.

These are wonderful pets, the closest you will ever get to an infant without having to worry about college tuition eighteen years later. It is not surprising that the fad caught on. Soon many Indonesians and Malaysians had these status symbols, each captured at the expense of its mother's life. By the 1960s, hundreds of orangutans were in captivity in both countries, and hundreds more had been shipped off to foreign zoos to entertain visitors anxious to see the antics of their closest relatives. In 1985, the population of orangutans in zoos was at least 850, and most had left martyred mothers behind in Borneo or Sumatra. But the real cost was much higher. Often both mother and infant were killed in the "collection." Barbara Harrisson estimated that perhaps as many as five orangutans were killed for each healthy baby successfully collected.

Concerned authorities, such as Tom Harrisson, became alarmed at the increased hunting of orangutans and the associated large-scale selling of baby orangs into bondage. Although no census of the orangutan population had yet been conducted, Harrisson was certain that the ape was endangered. "It is safe to put the world population of orangs in 1961 as under 5,000," he wrote. "It may well be half this." This estimate stuck, and even as late as 1966, the authoritative *Red Data Book* of IUCN continued to quote the figure of 5,000 orangutans left in the wild.

Tom Harrisson sounded the alarm based on a gut feeling, not data. At that time, only George Schaller had studied orangutans in the forest, but he was working in Sarawak, which is not the best place to find them.

Nevertheless, the public outcry led by the Harrissons caused the orangutan to be recognized as an endangered species. The governments of Malaysia and Indonesia, the two countries where the orangutan now occurs, banned the trade and prohibited the keeping of orangutans as pets. Zoos furiously bought up baby orangutans before the ban took place and one of us worked his way through graduate school in the late 1960s as a zookeeper taking care of seven baby orangutans which had been spirited out of Indonesia in the last days before reputable zoos adhered to the trading ban.

Enforcing the new conservation laws was an important step, but a new problem arose: What do you do with any young pet orangutans which are confiscated or voluntarily surrendered?

Easy. Turn them in to the proper authorities. In his position as curator of the Sarawak Museum, Tom Harrisson became the reluctant recipient of baby orangutans confiscated by the government of Sarawak, eventually having twelve of the red-haired bundles of joy placed in his care. Fortunately, his wife Barbara was willing to become a foster mother.

But babies become bigger babies, then children, then adolescents who get totally out of control. The Harrissons' patience wore thin and, with the mixed feelings of parents sending their children off to boarding school, they shipped six of their young charges off to European and American zoos. Barbara was so attached to them that she accompanied them most of the way on the ship, and visited them frequently once they had been ensconced in their respective menageries.

The Harrissons went through this whole experience with considerable misgivings. "Is it right to pay this price for keeping the Orang alive? Should they be in zoos at all?" Barbara asked. "We like good zoos and have kept many Borneo animals as pets ourselves, but we feel that the Orang is a special case and needs human re-thinking. Is it too much to hope that our own private, simple, small-scale and inexpensive experiments may not at least imply a way which could be followed up by the great, rich, public institutions of the world? A way to keep Orangs free, yet for view. . . .

"And if the worst comes to the worst, perhaps man can presently repay his load of evolutionary guilt by acquiring enough knowledge to *put back* a new generation of 'western-born Orangs,' to re-enter their Asian homeland afresh."

Thus concern for a species which appeared extremely rare, mixed with a heavy dose of guilt, yielded a result which seemed only logical: Put the captive orangutans back in the forest. The concern of the 1960s became the activism of the 1970s. The rehabilitation movement which the Harrissons started at Bako in Sarawak, where orangutans were extremely rare, took off in Indonesia, where orangs were far more common. Rehabilitation centers were established to help the young animals learn how to adapt to life in the jungle in Ketambe (1971) and Bohorok (1973) in Gunung Leuser National Park in Sumatra and in Tanjung Puting Nature Reserve in southern Kalimantan (1971).

Putting orangutans back in the forest was not as simple as it sounded, nor as successful as might have been hoped. And while rehabilitation ultimately proved misguided, it was successful in ways the original proponents never expected.

The term "rehabilitation" is perhaps unfortunate, generating visions of juvenile delinquents at reform school. The orangutans we visited at Bohorok were cute characters, especially Lucu (Indonesian for "droll, funny"), a two-year-old who got carried up the hill each morning to the feeding site on the shoulders of a warden. Lucu, Rosalind explained, was still too young to spend the night out by herself, but she visited the other rehabilitating orangutans during the day, learning how to build nests and forage for fruit.

Sitting forlornly on the feeding platform when we arrived was Matilda, looking like a jilted lover. Her expression improved only marginally when she spotted Warden Jemas carrying a backpack full of bananas and a bucket of milk. Her friends soon joined her, coming out of the trees from all directions, lining up for a cup of milk and some fruit. Like human children, some of the apes were playful and gregarious, others somber and solitary. They dribbled milk down their protruding lips and picked banana crumbs off their red potbellies. They hung upside down and pounded Jemas on the head until he gave them yet another cup of milk, which they drank upside down, defying the laws of physics. We were in a behavioral twilight zone, watching one of our closest relatives go through the process of learning from human teachers how to be orangutans. Obviously much of the orangutan personality is ape personality, based on millions of years of genetic inheritance. Yet an equally important influence on the behavior of the rehabilitants is human, since most of these animals were raised during their formative years by Indonesians who treated them like their own children.

Rosalind pointed out that Bohorok's goal was not simply to save a few orangutans from a life of domesticity, but to use the orangutans as an appealing symbol for the need to conserve the habitat that is home to Indonesia's wildlife. Over half of the orangutan habitat has already been destroyed by logging, and half of the remainder is due to be cleared in the next ten to fifteen years. Converting forests to boards or plantations continues to reduce rapidly the total number of orangutans which can earn their living from the jungle.

Using rehabilitation to increase public concern has worked up to a point. Each year up to 5,000 domestic visitors and 1,000 foreign visitors come to Bohorok, making it one of Sumatra's major tourist attractions and a source of local pride and revenue. In spite of the high visibility, in early January 1981 farmers began illegally felling large dipterocarp trees in the state forest opposite the rehabilitation center. A parade of government officials, beginning with local district officers and extending to federal ministers, visited the site over several years and promised action. So the idea of conservation had clearly taken hold. Yet in spite of official concern, the logging "not only continued but increased its pace," according to Tony Whitten and Johanne Ranger, "since it was clear to those working on the slopes that the series of visits by teams from various organs of local government might one day result in a ban on felling. It was only logical to get as much marketable timber out as possible, and to clear and burn land and to plant crops before any such ban came into effect."

At the Bohorok rehabilitation center we saw several recently confiscated animals in quarantine. "Please don't play with that one," Rosalind scolded as we went to visit a caged orangutan who appeared greatly in need of company. "He's had polio," Rosalind explained as we quickly withdrew our hands. "How about this one?" we asked, reaching into a different cage and patting another friendly ape on the head. "Not him either. He's got dysentery." Because of their biological similarity to humans, orangutans in captivity often pick up human diseases and could spread them to wild animals if they were not first quarantined, tested, and treated.

John MacKinnon has reported that several Dayak longhouses in central Kalimantan keep female orangutans in the longhouse for use as primate equivalents of inflatable dolls. In an article in the prestigious British journal *New Scientist*, he called the world's attention to the danger that Dayak men, tempted by a long evening's revelry, might spread venereal disease through at least part of the wild orangutan population by infecting captive female orangutans which are later released in the wild.

When baby orangutans are raised with humans the problems can be psychological as well as medical. At the rehabilitation camp in Tanjung Puting, Biruté Galdikas was extremely concerned about one of her charges. "I had raised Sugito from infancy," Biruté reported in *National Geographic* in 1980. "I had cuddled him, called him endearing names, and handed him tidbits of food. Taking my cue from the wild orangutan mothers I was observing, I had let him cling to me night and day. . . .

"Now Sugito was 7, and I faced the dreadful consequences of inadvertently raising an orangutan as a human being—an adolescent who was not only incredibly curious, active, and tool using, but one who killed." For despite Biruté's best mothering efforts, Sugito had picked up a bad habit—he held baby orangutans under the water until they drowned. Perhaps even worse, he had tried the same trick with a human visitor to the research camp.

Biruté, like any mother with a child turned criminal, was puzzled and distraught, since wild orangutans are normally not killers. "Sugito was something different," Biruté rationalized. "Perhaps the biblical analogy was apt: Raised by a human mother and exposed to human culture, he had eaten of the 'tree of knowledge' and lost his orangutan innocence. Now, in a very non-orangutan way, he was acting out his jealousy of the infants who had seemingly replaced him in my affection."

It appears that in at least some cases, the orangutan may think that he *is* human. A baby orangutan named Gondul was confiscated from his owner and given to Biruté to raise until he was old enough to return to the forest. Gondul lived with Biruté and her first husband, Rod Brindamour, for several years, sleeping in their bed for warmth and companionship until he became too big to manage. Biruté moved him across the river (orangutans can't swim) to a sort of "half-way house," where he could live in the forest but still come to a feeding station if he couldn't find enough figs or durians in the forest. Gondul slowly weaned himself from human companionship and stayed away from the feeding station for longer periods until he finally disappeared altogether, a graduate of a seemingly totally successful course of rehabilitation to wild living.

Several years passed and in the swamp forest Gondul matured into orangutan adolescence. One day, one of Galdikas' Dayak assistants came running back to her research station. "Dr. Biruté," he exclaimed, "Gondul has come back! But he is behaving strangely and seems fierce. I am frightened to go across the river to feed the other *maias* who need their bananas."

But Biruté, who considered Gondul almost a son, was confident that the orangutan would not forget his foster mother. When the next feeding time came, she hopped into the canoe with her Indonesian cook and a visiting colleague from the Montreal Zoo, and paddled over to the feeding platform. Gondul, who was high in a tree, spotted the procession and swung through the branches, dropping lightly onto the feeding platform.

He casually walked over to the cook, Biruté told us, grabbed her sarong, and ripped it off. He threw the servant down and mounted her. After a rapid series of thrusts accompanied by grunts, he gave a low moan and ejaculated, then leaped off the feeding platform and swung hand-over-hand through the trees.

Biruté was so shocked by this that she could only stand by, helpless, as the powerful beast pleased himself with her servant. But perhaps she should not have been so surprised, for in her research in the wild Biruté had found just what field biologists John MacKinnon, Herman Rijksen, and Chris Schurmann had found in their orangutan studies: Young male orangutans just entering adulthood are often rapists. The females normally enjoy voluntary sex only with the large dominant males. These mighty animals, whose huge throat sacs, long hair, and wide cheek flanges are badges of their fully mature masculinity, are capable of defending a territory against other males seeking mates or a durian lunch. But the young males, who are fully mature sexually yet are not powerful enough to establish a territory of their own, skulk around the forest quietly by themselves trying to avoid the dominant males and sneaking a quick meal when they can.

Even a barely mature male orangutan is much larger than a fully adult female, so when he comes across a female, rape often ensues. Perhaps Gondul had experienced an identity crisis from his long years in captivity and was not quite clear on the distinction between people and orangutans. And if rape was normal for him, why not rape a female human?

This can happen to the best of folks. During the filming of *Tarzan the Ape Man,* actress Bo Derek came dangerously close to being sexually assaulted by the orangutan C.J. after her leading man, Miles O'Keeffe, was tossed aside by the enamored, seemingly tame, ape. *Playboy* magazine, in a graphic picture spread showing the incident, noted that during a love scene "C.J., the jealous orangutan, didn't much like the idea of Tarzan and Jane having fun without him. In a totally impromptu move, he pulled 195-pound Miles O'Keeffe off Bo, interrupting one of the movie's steamier scenes. . . . 'We wrestled with him for an hour and a half,' recalls Bo. 'Orangutans are several times stronger than people and have four things to grab you with.' "

Lest anyone think this is the equivalent of romping with a puppy, take a look at the film's final credit scene. As Tarzan and Jane roll in the sand the orangutan obviously wants the action for himself. The actors' faces become concerned and frightened; what started out as a cute episode almost had an unexpected climax.

◆ ◆ ◆

Scientists began to have reservations about the wisdom of putting orangs back in the forest. Alongside the orangutan rehabilitation effort, fieldwork revealed considerable amounts of new information about the range and population of wild orangutans, indicating that they were not nearly as rare as had been feared by Tom and Barbara Harrisson.

John MacKinnon even thinks that orangutans are frequently overcrowded because their forest habitat has been destroyed faster than their numbers have been depleted. One result: homeless orangutans become bad-tempered nomads and seriously disrupt the social harmony and breeding success of surviving populations. There may well be too many orangutans for the remaining forests, not too few. Well-publicized rehabilitation efforts remain a useful tactic for raising public awareness about the problem, provide tourists with a chance to see orangutans, control trade, and stimulate research and education. But it is useless, and in some cases detrimental, to try to reestablish orangutans in the rain forest. Because the forests are being cleared so rapidly by loggers and shifting cultivators, the habitat available for orangs may be insufficient to hold even the present population.

Looking after orphan orangutans is as irrelevant to orangutan conservation as sending food is to the task of ending famine, MacKinnon suggests. "Indeed it could well serve conservation better," he continues, "if, through the eyes of a documentary television camera, the orphan orangutan were seen being coldly butchered, if that is what it takes to win wider public sympathy for the orangutan's plight and save the rainforest."

Nevertheless, the well-meaning orangutan rehabilitation programs have had considerable impact in demonstrating to the public that keeping baby orangutans is illegal. Since the rehabilitation centers were highly visible and had international participation, the governments were forced to get serious about confiscating captive orangutans and reducing commerce in an endangered species of particular interest to people.

The word that keeping baby orangutans is illegal is getting out to the villages, where the threat of fines and confiscation is helping to keep hunters off the orangutans' backs. We saw this change of attitude firsthand on a Sumatran bus. Bus journeys in Sumatra are exercises in discomfort, taken in ancient converted trucks with pads on the ceiling to prevent fractured skulls when passengers are thrown out of their seats by the shock of hitting a particularly rough spot in the road. The bus trip from Medan to Kotacane, on the way to the orangutan rehabilitation center at Ketambe in Gunung Leuser, took nine bouncing hours. We hadn't felt sensation in our legs for a long time. We could see they were still safely scrunched up into our chests, elbowed into place by two ancient sarong-clad Batak ladies with the marvelous ability to simultaneously chew betel (theirs) and munch coconut rolls (ours).

Batak ladies are not like mild-mannered Javanese. One aggressive old crone sitting between us fought for territory and jabbed her elbow into the kidneys of one of us and then went to sleep on the other's shoulders. The bus's suspension was history and we tasted the fiery lunch of brain curry and chili-fried chicken we had had three hours earlier at the Romeo and Juliet *nasi padang* restaurant during the bus's only rest stop. We shifted as much as we could into a vaguely more comfortable position and struck up a conversation with the old lady's buddies.

"Yes, one of the men in our village has a baby orangutan for sale, a baby whose mother was shot." As we inquired further another passenger murmured a warning to the loquacious old lady and, following a quick conference held in the Batak language, she changed her story. "The mother wasn't shot, somebody found the baby in the forest. And anyway it has now died. I would be very happy if you would visit my village anyway, but it is far out of your way and it might not be very convenient for you." The rest of the trip passed in companionable silence.

26

A Question of Breeding

*People have big plans for the rare and elusive Sumatran rhino.
Will the politicians or the conservationists determine its future?*

IN APRIL 1985, workers on an oil palm plantation in peninsular
Malaysia were astonished to see a strange beast casually walking
through their plantation. About the size of a small cow, it was
covered with long red hair and had two small horns on its nose.
They immediately recognized it as a Sumatran rhinoceros, one of
Asia's rarest and shyest creatures. This one was a young female,
and the workers had little difficulty in capturing it. When notified
of the capture, the conservation authorities in Kuala Lumpur were
ecstatic. They hoped that this, the first Sumatran rhino to be captured in thirty years, could form the basis of a captive rhino breeding program the government had been hoping to establish at the
Melaka (Malacca) Zoo.

A few months later, the King of Malaysia (a ceremonial post
taken in turns by the sultans of the various states of peninsular

Malaysia) visited the King of Thailand on a state visit. Royal protocol experts decided that the most appropriate gift from one monarch to another was an animal so rare that a trained field biologist got a good look at it only once during the course of a six-year study; an animal which probably had been exterminated from Thailand's forests: the Sumatran rhinoceros.

Swallowing their disappointment, but bowing to royal command, the Malaysian conservation authorities packed up the rhino and sent it off to Thailand. The King had no convenient place to keep such an animal on his palace grounds, so he entrusted it to Bangkok's Dusit Zoo, where it joined a stable of white elephants as part of the King's menagerie.

◆ ◆ ◆

Sumatran rhinos are wanderers, migrating freely up and down mountain chains and seldom staying very long in any one area. According to British naturalist Theodore Hubback, who was chief game ranger in colonial Malaya in the 1930s, they "invariably go through the thickest undergrowth they can find and deliberately leave a gamepath to go through, or under, or over some fallen tree, which appeals to their sense of humor, I suppose."

It seems to greatly favor the steepest, wettest, most inconvenient country, and is therefore a difficult beast to study. During a three-year study in Sumatra, Marcus Borner, a young Swiss scientist whose wife was helping to rehabilitate orangutans, stayed night and day in camouflage tree-hides in hopes of seeing a rhino, once for three weeks, twice for two weeks, but never saw even one. Clearly, extraordinary methods are required to discover the secrets of this hairy little rhino.

Dutch scientist Nico van Strien decided to use indirect methods. He concentrated on just one small part of Sumatra's Gunung Leuser National Park, at 3,474 square miles Indonesia's largest reserve (as big as Yellowstone) and considered to be one of the most important conservation areas in Southeast Asia. Each year, he would take several trips into the remotest part of the reserve, the Mamas Valley, usually by helicopter. There he searched for half-chewed branches, collected rhino spoor, and studied the ground for footprints. And make no mistake, it's difficult to get a clear footprint. First the terrain has to be just right—damp mud is best. In addition the rhino has the annoying habit of placing its rear foot in the same place it put its forefoot, producing a mess instead of a clear print. But through amazing persistence, Nico amassed the world's best collection of plaster casts of Sumatran rhino footprints, totaling over 750 footprints, weighing a ton, and occupying 250 cubic feet when packed.

"There are only about 150 rhinos left in Sumatra," he explained to us one day at his base camp in Ketambe. "And I have casts of perhaps thirty of them. This is Mini, this is Tiba, and this is . . ."

"Hang on, Nico," we protested. "How can you tell the difference between these casts. They all look the same to us."

"Look closely," he instructed. "This one has a longer forehoof. In this one the side hooves are more widely separated, in this one they take a sharper angle, and in this one the two side hooves are extraordinarily large. I used to think all of these belonged to Umar, but now that I have a more complete collection I think they belong to two or three others."

The Sumatran rhino is in serious trouble, largely because it has been avidly sought for the medicinal trade. Only about 100 of the 150 surviving in Sumatra live in habitats which are likely to be viable in the long run. The others are in very small groups, isolated in small forest patches that are quickly shrinking as the loggers and agricultural developers move in.

In spite of the Sumatran rhino's retiring behavior, poachers still enter the poorly guarded reserve in search of the animal, which can be worth a farmer's fortune on the black market. Nico showed us one of the traps used by the illegal hunters. "They build a runway of bamboo on a rhino path and place a trip wire near the ground. When the wire is broken, a heavy spear, embedded in a log, drops through the shoulder blades of the rhino, which eventually bleeds to death." Nico once found sixteen such traps in his study area.

In addition to poaching, the Gunung Leuser area has another problem. People. While Sumatra's population is much lower than Java's, eight distinct dialect groups live in Sumatra's fertile Alas River valley, which penetrates like a spear deep into the Gunung Leuser National Park. The original residents like the Alas and Gayo have been joined by immigrant Bataks from the Lake Toba region and now over 160 villages crowd the area, with the population growing at almost 15 percent a year. Roads, technology, and the marketplace stimulate such growth.

We followed Nico out to the porch of his comfortable Ketambe Research Station. He pointed across the river which marks the

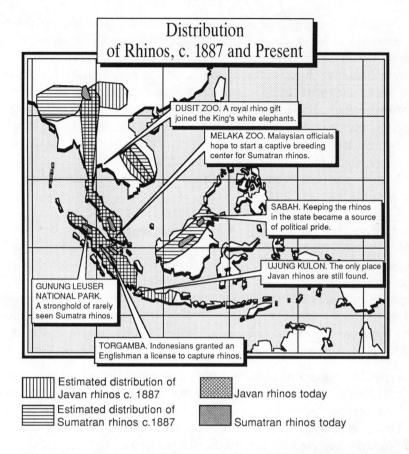

Distribution of Rhinos, c. 1887 and Present

DUSIT ZOO. A royal rhino gift joined the King's white elephants.

MELAKA ZOO. Malaysian officials hope to start a captive breeding center for Sumatran rhinos.

SABAH. Keeping the rhinos in the state became a source of political pride.

UJUNG KULON. The only place Javan rhinos are still found.

GUNUNG LEUSER NATIONAL PARK. A stronghold of rarely seen Sumatra rhinos.

TORGAMBA. Indonesians granted an Englishman a license to capture rhinos.

Estimated distribution of Javan rhinos c. 1887

Estimated distribution of Sumatran rhinos c.1887

Javan rhinos today

Sumatran rhinos today

boundary of the reserve and we saw hills which shifting cultivators had cleared to plant corn. We were reminded of the comment of Gerson Sinaga, then the regional conservation chief, who wryly noted that the farmers' philosophy is "to make a *ladang*, a clearing, for their grandchildren, even if those grandchildren are not yet born." Nico added, "These farmers practice their slash and burn agriculture but don't realize that by destroying the forest to build *ladangs* they contribute to landslides, floods, droughts, and, ultimately, to an unstoppable destruction of the environment."

But while Nico is a conservationist, he is also a humanist. He raised a critical point: "While you must save the forest it is also vital to limit population increase and improve agricultural methods. People must have an opportunity to earn a reasonable income and lead lives of self-respect."

◆ ◆ ◆

By 1984, a number of reserves had been established for the Sumatran rhino but there was still concern about their ultimate survival. Estimates of the total population of the species were in the low hundreds; they had apparently disappeared from Thailand in the past few years, and no more than thirty remained in Sabah and Sarawak. Illegal hunting was still rampant in Sumatra and Sabah, and poachers were known to have taken three rhinos in Sabah in 1984 and two more in 1985. None had been in captivity since the last one died in Copenhagen in 1972, so there was little hope of releasing captive-bred individuals to reinforce declining wild populations.

Clearly, this species needed all the help it could get. Action on Sumatran rhinos was considered the highest priority by IUCN's Asian Rhino Specialist Group, so they convened a meeting between interested scientists and government conservation officials from Indonesia and Malaysia. They quietly met in Singapore (an ironic venue since Singapore at that time was the major entrepôt of illegal rhino horn) in October 1984 to work out a plan for saving the remaining Sumatran rhinos. The resulting plan, agreed to by all parties, had three main elements:

- Provide support to conserve viable populations of wild rhinos in sufficiently large areas of protected habitat in Sumatra, Sabah, and peninsular Malaysia.
- Develop a public education program aimed at earning the support of local people for the Sumatran rhino.
- Establish a captive propagation program for the Sumatran rhino in the countries of origin and in North America and Europe, using animals which have no hope of surviving in the wild.

The last point was the trickiest. For one thing, how do you decide when an animal has no future in the wild? According to Nico van Strien: "If it is concluded that preservation in the wild is not feasible or does not contribute to the survival of the species, because the remaining habitat or rhino population is insufficient for survival or cannot be protected against destruction, the population is 'doomed' and capturing some or all of the animals is the best option for conservation. Some will argue that all Sumatran rhinos, and in fact all large mammals, are doomed, others will hesitate to call any population doomed, because saying so seals the fate of the population. A realistic and balanced decision should be pursued."

Another difficulty was how to capture the rhinos, and where to send them once they were captured. A consortium of American and European zoos participating in the Singapore meeting pledged an impressive amount of financial support for rhino protection measures in their natural habitat, expertise for capturing the rhinos, equipment, training of conservation experts and zoo officers, and technical assistance in captive breeding. In return, the American and European zoos would receive several pairs of rhinos on loan for breeding. The animals would be owned by the country of origin (Malaysia or Indonesia) and any offspring would be shared between the owner and the zoo.

Everyone considered this an ideal solution, which had been calmly and carefully discussed among all interested parties. A foreign market for rhino horn had led to the rhinos being ruthlessly pursued throughout their range, they reasoned. A foreign market for timber and agricultural products had led to the destruction of the rhino's habitat. Now foreign interest in conservation was trying to turn the tide and ensure that rhinos continued to be part of local forest ecosystems. Who could possibly disagree?

The Malaysian state of Sabah, for one. Sabah, whose remnant population of rhinos was facing imminent eternity from poachers, immediately turned a conservation problem into a political *cause célèbre*. Sabah's wildlife authorities operate independently from those in peninsular Malaysia and they resented any implication that they were incapable of protecting their own rhinos. And if rhinos had to be captured, they could surely breed them as well in Kota Kinabalu as in Los Angeles.

Sabah accused the western zoos of exploiting the country's rhinos. "Taking away the rhino to be bred far overseas is a great loss to national pride while foreign countries gain kudos for breeding endangered species and [this] will further endanger the survival of the species," noted an official of the Malayan Nature Society. "The optimistic promises of successfully breeding rhinos overseas will seriously undermine the long-term safety of the rhino habitat as it may lead to the rounding up of rhinos for captive breeding from areas that would then become 'available' to log or clear-fell rather than conserving these areas as national parks. As a result all the plants and animals in that area will be lost as well."

The Sabah argument asked what dignity a species has once it is taken out of the wild. "What does such 'survival'—as a virtual museum display—really mean?" asked a local conservationist.

"What possible benefit can survival for its own sake have, except as a curiosity for future generations of goggling schoolchildren?"

Everyone agreed that rhinos in captivity are no substitute for rhinos in the wild. But wild rhinos face a bleak future everywhere, while captive rhinos at least stand a chance and can draw public attention to the predicament of the wild animals. At about the same time as the Singapore conference, a similar meeting of experts in Africa determined that two subspecies of black rhino in Africa appeared to have become extinct in the past few years while being "protected in their natural habitat." In contrast, the southern white rhino of Africa, through captive breeding of the last few surviving animals some years ago, now is thriving because of many successful reintroductions to natural habitats throughout its former range.

According to IUCN Director General Kenton R. Miller, "Whenever it is practicable, every major threatened species should be undergoing captive breeding in more than one location, taking advantage of both the most modern techniques of reproduction and the most advanced techniques of genetic management. This is not to say that a species such as the Sumatran rhino has a better chance of survival in artificial conditions. Rather, the prudent course is to insist upon having an adequate breeding population in captivity as an additional safeguard while the fight to preserve the species in nature goes on. It would be irresponsible to do otherwise."

Many Malaysians welcomed this view. An editorial in Kuala Lumpur's *New Straits Times* on September 11, 1985, stated: "In matters of conservation, there is little room for parochial attitudes and for meaningless slogans about national heritage. Malaysia holds in trust for the whole world some of the rarest and most interesting wildlife. It's not a responsibility to be taken lightly. Malaysia cannot take the risk of unwittingly allowing it to have the dubious distinction of being known as the last place on earth where the Sumatran rhino roamed."

Mohamad Khan, Director General of the Department of Wildlife and National Parks (which has no jurisdiction over Sabah or Sarawak) and chairman of IUCN's Asian Rhino Specialist Group, said the captive breeding project "has my full support because I see it as the only alternative to saving the rhino population in Sabah. It is clear that this project is designed as a long-term plan for the survival of this species and therefore should enjoy the full support of all Malaysians."

The advice of peninsular Malaysia's top conservation officer came at an unfortunate time. Joseph Pairin Kitingan, a Christian and an ethnic Kadazan, had just been elected chief minister of Sabah in an upset victory over the candidates of Islamic parties which had the support of the central government in Kuala Lumpur. Sensitive to the desires of his largely non-Islamic electorate to maintain the maximum possible independence from peninsular Malaysia, Kitingan announced that the Sabah government would develop its own conservation program for the Sumatran rhinos by mobilizing local resources and expertise.

Indicating Sabah's seriousness, the chief minister said that the equivalent of 1.5 million U.S. dollars would be devoted to saving the Sumatran rhino, including captive breeding and the establishment of a new wildlife reserve. While the foreign zoos and the central government were disappointed, Sabah had lived up to its responsibility to conserve its wildlife. Interest in conservation had been aroused in a large segment of Sabah's population, a critical factor in a part of Malaysia where the forests have been heavily exploited for export of timber or palm oil to the industrialized countries which were now seeking to assist in conserving the rhino. The rest of the Sumatran rhino world could carry on with its plan; the state of Sabah had its own.

◆ ◆ ◆

The Indonesians took quite a different approach. While they participated in the Singapore meeting and gave their support to the group's plans, they immediately cut their own separate deal with John Aspinall, who had used the fortune he earned from running a series of gambling casinos in England to establish the Howletts and Port Lymphe (U.K.) zoos. The agreement signed between Aspinall and the Indonesian Department of Forest Protection and Nature Conservation carefully avoided any mention of the Singapore agreement, the conservation masterplan for the rhinos, and the oversight role which was to have been played by IUCN to ensure that the whole operation was on the up-and-up. Perhaps worse, it added a clause stating that 50,000 U.S. dollars was to be "donated" to the government-run Indonesian Wildlife Fund for each rhino, making the arrangement appear to be a straightforward animal-trading transaction rather than the more idealistic conservation program that was designed in Singapore. The Indonesian authorities claimed that the funds would be used to promote conservation of the rhino in the wild, but no detailed plans on how the money would actually be spent have been made available.

Aspinall's pragmatic approach in Indonesia appears to have worked. An area of forest in Sumatra known as Torgamba was due to be either cleared and replanted in oil palm or given to transmigrants from Java for small-scale agriculture. Any rhinos, along with elephants, tigers, and other wildlife living in the forest, would surely have been doomed. "The rate of forest destruction is frightening," Aspinall told us. "In the Torgamba district we visited a logging camp which 5 years ago was 5 miles *inside* the forest. Now it is 5 miles *outside* the forest."

Elaborate pit traps with sloping sides were dug, and many more tapirs than rhinos slid into them. The frightened animals (of the seven rhinos captured, three had infected leg wounds caused by poachers' snares) were placed in crates and hauled by hand over three miles of forest path. One animal committed suicide by banging her head against the stockade wall. Two animals remained at base camp. The others were loaded aboard a chartered white and yellow Airfast DC-3, and were sent to zoos in the U.K. (where one has died of unknown causes), Indonesia, and Malaysia.

◆ ◆ ◆

The intention at the Singapore meeting was that all captive rhinos would be managed as a single herd, with the most modern captive breeding techniques used to ensure that the herd increased at the fastest possible rate. These techniques were to include transferring embryos from Sumatran rhinos to foster mothers of other rhino species; exchanging frozen rhino sperm among the zoos; trading animals between zoos to ensure appropriate breeding groups; and conducting sophisticated research on how to further promote the captive breeding of the last Sumatran rhinos.

As part of the overall effort, WWF president, the Duke of Edinburgh, wrote to the King of Thailand requesting that the Malaysian/Thai rhino be considered part of the world breeding herd. When the King of Malaysia presented a lone female Sumatran rhino to the King of Thailand, it appeared that half the available breeding stock had just been sent off to solitary confinement and a life of involuntary celibacy. King Bhumibol agreed in principle to the request, and to help facilitate breeding, he offered Phu Kheo Game Sanctuary as a field site—an area where we had found footprints of the Sumatran rhino ten years before but which is now devoid of rhinos. He directed the commanding general of the Second Army Area, which has jurisdiction over security matters in the province, including the safety of the animals in the sanctuary, to pay particular attention to conserving the rhino's habitat.

◆ ◆ ◆

In December 1986, we returned to Bangkok for meetings on coastal and marine conservation. Since the closest we had ever come to a Sumatran rhino was the examination of tracks and droppings in the forests of Thailand and Sumatra, we headed for the Dusit Zoo immediately after checking into the hotel. The taxi drove past Chitralada Palace, the residence of the Thai royal family, and raced through the expansive parade ground in front of the House of Parliament, the site of numerous coups and coup attempts. Jumping out of the taxi at the entrance to the Dusit Zoo, we quickly paid our 10 *baht* (40 cents) entrance fee, plus an extra baht for our cameras, and entered the lush green zoo to be welcomed by the howling of gibbons. At last we would see one of Asia's rarest animals, one we had done our bit to conserve through surveys and field projects.

We approached the first zookeeper we saw and asked him where the new *krasoo* was kept. "*Dai pai laew,*" he responded with a fatalistic shrug. The rhino had died already. The zookeeper explained that the rhino had been put in a pen designed for an African black rhino so the bars were too far apart—the smaller Sumatran rhino had caught her head between the bars and had panicked when several keepers started pushing her nose in an effort to disentangle it. Struggling wildly, the rhino broke her neck.

We were crestfallen at *still* never having seen a Sumatran rhino, disgusted at the poor management, and heartsick that the world had lost one of its few fleeting opportunities to save the littlest rhino. A royal gesture had turned into an unnecessary tragedy.

27

Gnawing
Persistence

The only wild animals to really benefit from human progress in Southeast Asia are the rats, which eat people out of house and home. Are rats the wave of the future?

THE STREETS OF GENEVA are generally deserted at 10 P.M. This came as a surprise to us when we moved here from Indonesia, where things slowed down at night, but not much. In Jakarta our second favorite nocturnal pursuit was eating, and if you ate the right things your favorite pursuit would also benefit. We also found that the tastiness of the food was in an inverse relation to the cleanliness of the surroundings. Many a night we shared wooden benches with truck drivers, students, and lovers and munched on *sate torpedo*, a variation on traditional grilled brochettes made from the action part of the ram's anatomy; *sop kambing*, a rich goat soup; *gado gado*, slightly cooked vegetables with peanut sauce, all washed down with Guinness Stout. More often than not, other creatures came to dine, and the scurry of street rats was a constant, and not-too-pleasant, sideshow.

The rats ate as well as we did, and considerably better than many Jakarta residents. They are prospering everywhere, and in terms of economic impact, the rats are easily the stars among Asia's wild animals. Despite the rat's economic clout, tigers, rhinos, and elephants get most of the wildlife press, because they are big, attractive, fierce, and threatened with premature extinction at the hands of humans. But the meek, sneaky, and subtle may inherit the earth. If people continue to overexploit the larger wild animals and their habitats, rats could well be harbingers of the wild animals that will survive to share earth with humanity.

"The rat" is really lots of species—at least 250 in Southeast Asia alone. And there are lots more of them than there are people. While it's hard to get an accurate census of the whole region, studies of small areas are revealing:

- Rangoon may be Asia's rattiest city, according to a United Nations rat eradication project, with 25 to 40 million.
- The Philippines is thought to be Asia's rattiest country, with 12 rats per person. India is not far behind, with a rat-io of 10 animals per person and a total rat population far exceeding the human population of the world. China's 3 to 4 billion rats eat an estimated 15 million tons of grain a year.
- Several years ago, farmers in one province in Thailand poisoned 680,000 rats, about 2.5 per acre, and found to their dismay that this did not significantly reduce rat damage to the next rice crop.

Rats do so well in Southeast Asia for some obvious reasons. They are small and secretive, living where they can't be seen and coming out mostly at night. Often taking shelter under a farmer's roof or in an urban slum, they are protected from predators such as owls, which ironically are persecuted by people. They eat almost everything—garbage, chickens, coconuts, fruit, and fish. Worse, they seem to especially appreciate the same foods the villagers prefer, and their persistent gnawing makes it very difficult to keep them away from the rice.

Rats are great travelers, and joined the early Austronesians on their explorations. Taking sea voyages in the bilge class, rats have jumped ship and become established on all the islands of Thailand, the Philippines, Indonesia, and the Pacific, being the only species of terrestrial mammal found on some of the smallest or most isolated islands.

They also reproduce prodigiously. Theoretically, a pair of the most prolific species can produce 20 million baby rats in just three years. While they haven't quite taken over the world, their reproductive potential enables them to snap back from any temporary human attack, no matter how determined.

As a result, rats have prospered as people continue to alter habitats to the rat's liking. The largest genus of mammals is *Rattus*, with about 570 species, accounting for well over 10 percent of all the species of mammals. Since they first appeared some 10 million years ago in Asia, rats have been one of the region's most successful exports. They have spread to cover virtually all parts of the globe, except for the polar regions and the most inhospitable deserts. This proliferation has resulted in many species but minimal divergence in form—all rats closely resemble their original Asian ancestor.

Most of this great multitude of rats are innocuous, going about their own business in forests and grasslands eating insects, nuts, and fruit and in turn being eaten by snakes, owls, and civets. Like the orangutans, elephants, and tigers with which they share a dependence on tropical forests and wild grasslands, they suffer from habitat loss. The country rats generally leave people alone, and most hunters look upon them as a source of food, not as a pest.

"The rat" that makes Asians cringe is just four species: the brown, or Norway rat, the fat, mean city rat, which has migrated from northern and central Asia to cities in America, Europe, and tropical Asia; the native roof rat, carrier of "the black death" in medieval Europe; the rice field rat, scourge of the paddies; and the lesser bandicoot rat, denizen of the barns and godowns where rice is stored.

These four are "commensal" with mankind—literally "sharing our table." They scurry around buildings, help harvest crops, enjoy the grain stored by rice farmers, and take their share of the surplus food sent to market. Interestingly, the two that Asia has exported to the rest of the world—the brown and roof rats—apparently learned their free-loading ways relatively recently, once trade between Asia and Europe began to thrive.

While common in Southeast Asia, these animals were unknown in Europe until the Crusades, when roof rats, recognizing a good thing when they saw it, accompanied the bedraggled heroes in their ships returning home from a tough campaign against the Saracens. By the end of the thirteenth century the roof rat had become such a successful Asian immigrant that it provided employment for the Pied Piper of Hamelin, and by Shakespeare's time it was such a nuisance that days of prayer were set aside for protection against its ravages, and rat catchers were important officials (see *Romeo and Juliet*, Act II, Scene 2).

But the dominance of the roof rat was short-lived, for in the eighteenth century a newer, improved, more ferocious invader arrived from east of Russia's Lake Baikal: the misnamed "Norway rat." Replacing the smaller, more agile roof rat in most areas, the Norway rat reached England in 1728, the east coast of America in 1775, and California in the 1850s. The roof rat continues to thrive today throughout Southeast Asia, but the temperate zone is now dominated by its "Norwegian" big brother. As the cities of tropical Asia have grown and become ports of call for freighters from far away, the Norway rat has invaded the wharfs and is moving into the urban slums.

◆ ◆ ◆

Rats have voracious appetites, in some places gobbling up nearly a third of the food produced—more than enough to eliminate hunger everywhere, if people got what the rats get. Indian authorities claim that rats eat enough grain to supply four *chapati* pancakes per day to each of the country's 650 million people. Each bandicoot rat in a Bangkok rice warehouse eats about twenty pounds a year, enough to feed a human family for a week.

In Bali, rats are often a scourge during the harvest period. Anna Mathews, who was studying religious ceremonies in the village of Iseh, was concerned that the rats were going unchallenged. "The villagers sat idle and watched the rats take the food from their mouths and the mouths of their children. Village children grew thin while rat-babies waxed fat and lusty. Our house squeaked and groaned with rats. They ran around the rafters at night, ate shoes, clothes, paper, rice and fruit in untrammelled latitude. Not one of our boys would take a stick to them.

" 'What's the good,' one of the boys replied when questioned. 'If I kill one rat, Chief Holy Mouse will send more—four rats will spring up where the one rat died.' "

When she asked him why Holy Mouse doesn't stop his rats from tormenting human beings, the boy looked at Mathews condescendingly. "It's our fault, of course. We have made him angry. Perhaps he feels neglected because not enough sacrifices have been made in his name. The rats are to remind us to honor him. He'll call them back when he's ready."

Too late the authorities acted. A fund of roughly $25 was allocated for offerings to Holy Mouse. A high priest dedicated them, high on the slopes of Mount Agung, and an edict was issued: since Holy Mouse had received his dues it would be quite in order to kill his henchmen. Free poison was offered by the government and many rats were killed, but it was too little too late to save the harvest.

Many rice farmers throughout the region have been convinced by development agents to use chemical fertilizers, improved varieties of rice, tractors, mechanical pumps, and newly available irrigation water to grow a second crop of rice for the market—this is the essence of the "green revolution," which uses the goods provided by the international marketplace to stimulate higher production. But in some villages, rats have destroyed virtually the entire second crop, a disincentive to human industriousness and a demonstration of how quickly rats are able to respond to a new opportunity.

Rats do have some characteristics which humans admire. Due to their ability for locating, acquiring, and hoarding abundant supplies of food even during famine conditions, rats are regarded by Chinese as the symbol of industry and prosperity. Because rats are said to have been the first animals to heed the Buddha's call, they are immortalized as the first of the twelve animals for which years are named (1984 was the most recent Year of the Rat).

Hindus worship rats as the vehicle of Ganesh, the giant potbellied and elephant-headed god who helps in overcoming difficulties. It might seem a bit ridiculous to have an elephant riding around heaven and earth on a rat, but there is a certain logic to it. According to Heinrich Zimmer, "Ganesh forges ahead through obstacles as an elephant through the jungle. . . . treading shrubs, bending and uprooting trees, fording rivers and lakes easily; the rat can gain access to the bolted granary. The two represent the power of this god to vanquish every obstacle of the Way."

◆ ◆ ◆

Khao Yai National Park has some of Thailand's best remaining forests. But before Dr. Boonsong was able to have the area declared a national park, farmers had invaded some of the valley bottoms and cleared parts of the forest for growing crops. The land was not particularly good and the climate was wet, so weeds soon took over. What was left behind were large areas of grassland, now grazed by deer, pigs, and elephants. And rats.

At least some of these fields must be crossed when you undertake any long trek through the park. We made camp one night at the edge of one of these clearings, weary after a long day's hike. As usual, we inspected our bodies for ticks, leeches, and mites which we might have picked up. One little chigger was an ankle biter and particularly difficult to remove, but a burning ember from the fire finally convinced him to fall off.

The next morning we broke camp and headed back to Bangkok. A week later, we could barely climb out of bed. We had a high fever, hallucinations, a splitting headache, and painful joints. We dragged ourselves to the doctor, who took samples of our various essences and gave us the bad news: *"Rickettsia tsugtsugamushi*. You've picked up scrub typhus, which chiggers carry from grassland-dwelling rats to people. Tell me, have you been in any grassy savannas lately?"

We passed the next few days downing antibiotics and painkillers, and were soon back on our feet. But many people are not so lucky, and rat-carried diseases were a scourge in the time before antibiotics. Some experts maintain that the thirty or so human diseases carried by rats have taken more lives than all the wars and revolutions ever fought. And Hans Zinsser, the American physician who developed the vaccine against typhus, claims that rat-borne typhus has altered human destiny more than any person whose name appears in the history books.

The battery of debilitating rat-carried diseases includes trichinosis, rabies, leptospirosis, murine typhus, scrub typhus, Lassa fever, tularemia, and salmonellosis. Many of these are most dangerous in the urban setting, where dense populations of both people and rats provide a potentially explosive situation. By far the most dreaded and still potentially most dangerous threat is bubonic plague, "the black death." Carried by a flea which infests the fur of roof rats, the bubonic plague is estimated to have killed one out of every three Europeans in the fourteenth century. In subsequent centuries the disease swept through India, West Asia, and China, arriving in Hong Kong in 1894 and forcing over 100,000 people to flee. In the late 1960s, plague came home to roost in war-torn Vietnam, which recorded over 90 percent of the world's cases of black death at that time.

Small wonder people on farms and in the cities throughout Southeast Asia make valiant efforts to control rats, using numerous and ingenious weapons. They have devised intricate traps, cages, and a multitude of poisons; employed dogs, cats, snakes, and mongooses to chase them; and tried to gas, sterilize, drown, and electrocute them. Yet no matter what is done, rats flourish everywhere in the region.

Poison is perhaps the most popular modern approach, but rats have a highly developed sense of taste and are so innately cautious that the poisons need to be slow-acting, killing long after they have been eaten. As a result, some campaigns have had tragic side effects. In Indonesia, eighteen people died in early 1983 after eating rice treated with a rat poison. The villagers in Lampung, Sumatra, knew the rice was poisoned but since their harvest had failed (partly due to rats) and they were hungry, they felt compelled to eat it. They washed the rice thoroughly and one man volunteered to act as a human guinea pig; but the poison did not take immediate effect and the man lived long enough for other villagers to convince themselves that it was safe to eat the tainted grain.

Obviously the standard solutions—poisoning, rat traps, cats— haven't had much of an impact on rat populations. So communities in Southeast Asia have attacked the problem in a number of imaginative ways:

- Bridegrooms in Central Java have been ordered to produce a dowry of at least twenty-five dead rats before being allowed to marry. The town council of Pekalongan went one step further, declaring that not only must twenty-five dead rats be presented before marriage, but the same number was required to process a divorce.
- Mayor Aurelio Freires of Salamanca in the southern Philippines organized a beauty contest in 1980 for local maidens. Each vote cast in the contest had to be accompanied by a rat tail. Local newspapers reported that "after a hotly contested battle, the winner was Miss Carmelita Caraso who rode to victory on the strength of 17,834 rat tails. The runners-up were Miss Lolita Carayfan, 17,595 tails, and Miss Helda Antondocan, 15,155."
- Another solution used by Asian exterminators is poisoning by hardening of the arteries. The Sabah (Malaysia) State Rice Board told farmers that the "simplest, safest, and cheapest" method of

killing rats in rice fields was to put food mixed with cement at strategic points.

- Some traditional methods balance violence with respect. In Bali, according to Sir James George Frazer, the distinguished Scottish anthropologist, the rice harvest is accompanied by an all-out effort to catch rats, which are then cremated in the same way that human corpses are burned. But two lucky individuals are given a reprieve, as a means of seeking forgiveness from the spirits of the other rats. They receive a little packet of white linen and the villagers bow down before them, as before gods or spirits, before releasing them to tell their friends how nice humans are.

- Traditional villagers in eastern Indonesia's Kangean Archipelago go even further, hoping to get off easy by lavish symbolic bribery. The Dutch anthropologist J. L. van Gennep found that just after weekly prayers at the mosque are completed, four pairs of rats are solemnly united in marriage by a priest. Each pair is put in a miniature canoe, which is filled with wedding gifts of rice and other fruits of the earth. The wedding procession then escorts the rodent couples down to the shore, accompanied by the same singing and beating of drums that are used to announce a human wedding. With due respect and somewhat hypocritical wishes for a productive future, the honeymooners are launched on a one-way love-boat cruise out to the deep blue sea.

- Some realistic villagers have realized that they will never be able to do away with rats, so they have figured out a different way to bite back. Literally. They eat them. Rat meat is highly nutritious: it contains 17 percent fat, 3 percent carbohydrate, and 62 percent protein—three times the protein content by weight of a fast-food hamburger. Farmers in Thailand's Pathum Thani Province, fed up with a rat plague which cost them more than half a million dollars' worth of rice a year, spent a weekend catching 70,000 rats and barbecuing the "rice field rabbits," for a party attended by 2,000 villagers.

- Jakarta-based businessman Hennoch Tampi told us that in his hometown of Menado in north Sulawesi, the market is sold out of forest rats by nine each morning, with housewives paying up to $2.00 each. "No wedding party is complete without a rat dish," he explained while stirring up a batch of *kawok* curry: skin, clean, and cut the rat in small pieces. Throw away the tail, leave the head intact. Chop plenty of chili, red onions, leeks, ginger, lemon grass, and basil and fry in coconut oil. Add the meat and fry for five minutes. Add water and stew for half an hour. Serve at weddings and other special occasions.

- A Filipino entrepreneur tried, unsuccessfully, to market canned rat meat under the catchy brand name STAR, "RATS" spelled backward. His investors are now putting their hopes on a rat sausage. Bangladesh is trying to make the best of their rat problem by exporting rats to rodent-eating countries like Thailand and China.
- On the reasonable theory that rats only prosper where people are sloppy enough to make them feel at home, Singapore added a legal element to its rat eradication program. Under that immaculate island-nation's Environmental Public Health Department Act any person harboring a rat can be arraigned in court.

If all else fails, how about using the ultimate western solution for dealing with national security problems: vaporize the rats with nuclear bombs. This may seem a rather extreme measure with several unpleasant side effects. Anyway, it won't work. A population of rats has thrived on the tiny Pacific atoll of Eniwetok, site of forty-three atomic bomb tests in the late 1940s and 1950s. Although the island will be unsafe for human habitation for another 25,000 years, the rats show no mutations or abnormalities, although they are thoroughly contaminated with radioactivity.

◆ ◆ ◆

Human beings have been remarkably successful as a species, and the major ecocultural revolutions of agriculture, irrigation, and the world marketplace have led to a steady increase in the human population. Southeast Asia now has almost 400 million people, and despite widespread family planning efforts, the population is still growing at over 2 percent per year. Cities are expanding, the countryside is becoming more densely populated, and forests are being cleared at a rapid rate. Most of the large animals are suffering in this process, but the rats that have adapted to human presence are doing better than ever. Even the most modern technology has not been able to keep rats away from our dinner table. The best that people can do is to grudgingly accept the freeloaders and hope they don't invite too many of their relatives to join the feast.

28

---

*Monuments
to Folly*

*When conservation is neglected for the sake of building dams,
local people suffer, sometimes noisily.*

"SITUATED IN THE VERY MIDST of an Archipelago, and closely hemmed
in on every side by islands teeming with varied forms of life, its
productions have yet a surprising amount of individuality. While it
is poor in the actual number of species, it is yet wonderfully rich in
peculiar forms, many of which are singular or beautiful, and are in
some cases absolutely unique upon the globe." Alfred Russel Wallace was writing in 1859 about the Indonesian island of Celebes,
now called Sulawesi.

This island's fascination has lasted until the present, and we paid
particular attention to our field projects in North Sulawesi when
we managed the Indonesia Program of WWF and IUCN. The large
island east of Borneo, shaped like a malnourished orchid, was isolated from the other Indonesian islands even at the periods of lowest sea level, and evolved on its own. Borneo is just eighty miles

away, but the only one of its twenty-four carnivores to reach Sulawesi—the Malay civet—was introduced by humans. Instead, Sulawesi, the world's eleventh largest island—a bit smaller than England, Scotland, and Wales—has marsupials from Australia,
numerous rodents found nowhere else, the strange babirusa "pig-
deer," and the anoa, a pygmy water buffalo. About 90 percent of
its mammals are found nowhere else.

We went to visit John MacKinnon on one of our first field trips.
John had earlier done some of the best work on orangutans, and
had studied all the other apes in Asia and Africa. Eager to try his
hand on a new fauna, he had begun a two-year assignment in the
Minahasa region in North Sulawesi. Walking through the scrubby
coastal forest of Tangkoko Batuangus Reserve near Menado, we
saw clouds boiling overhead and jamming up against the peak of
the Tangkoko volcano, making it look almost as if the cone were
once again springing to life after a silence of 150 years. We turned
inland and headed uphill. The sky turned threatening, then
dumped buckets of water on us as we entered a lush, verdant forest. The last Tangkoko eruption, in the early nineteenth century,
had wiped out most of the vegetation, so the new trees were all
relatively young and fast-growing species which produce a lot of
fruit.

"It's an amazing forest," John told us. "With so many trees in
fruit, we have lots of fruit-eating mammals and birds. Hornbills,
maleo fowl, and fruit pigeons are all common and there are about
two macaque monkeys per hectare, more than I've seen anywhere.
It's even a greater density than found in the mature lowland forest
of peninsular Malaysia, which has six or seven species of monkeys
and apes."

Something else was special about these monkeys. "I've found
groups comprised of only females with babies, the only known
example of such nursery groups anywhere in the world," John
pointed out. "It might be because the great amount of available
food frees them from the male's oligarchy. But it's perhaps even
more likely due to a lack of predators. With no carnivores around,
maybe the maternity ward doesn't need male protection."

After several days in Tangkoko, we headed down the highway
to the Dumoga Valley, probably the best place in Sulawesi for
babirusa, the hairless pig whose upper incisors grow through the
roof of its mouth, curl up over its nose, and curve back toward the
eyes. Twenty years ago, the Dumoga Valley—located midway

along the northern arm of the island—was almost completely covered in forest. Then the construction of the Dumoga highway opened up the area to a wave of new settlement; more recently, Balinese and Javanese farmers have moved into the valley under government-sponsored transmigration schemes.

The dominant crop in the valley is rice, and a major irrigation system was being developed with World Bank money to ensure that the land would be as productive as possible for the immigrants. But as new migrants moved into the area and "first-generation" settlers sold their fields to the newcomers and in turn cleared new lands, more and more forest was cut. These frontier farmers denuded the forested hillsides that provided the water for the lowland rice farmers.

In addition, timber concessionaires were greasing up their chain saws and building maintenance roads along the irrigation canals which would make it easier for people to move into the area. A Canadian mining company rushed to the frontier, eager to exploit the nickel deposits found in the Dumoga region. All this meant a reduction in the potential water flow from feeder rivers and increased the likelihood that the vital irrigation canals would become clogged with silt.

It sounded like one of those situations where both development project and forests were headed for disaster. But a chain of circumstances that should happen more frequently turned a potential ecological tragedy into a modest success story. We hatched a strategy on that trip to Dumoga that included politics, golf, local self-interest, the World Bank, and a long string of government officials.

John was the key factor. He is not only a highly respected ecologist, but a good golfer as well. And since many serious decisions are discussed first on the golf course, he often played with the Governor of North Sulawesi, the Minister of Forestry, and local development officials. He explained to his sporting colleagues the ecological arguments for protecting the forests and the need for very strong measures to maintain the forest and thereby have enough water to operate the irrigation works.

But science seldom wins development arguments by itself. While tactfully ignoring his partner's slice, John suggested that the Indonesians would come out heroes if they insisted that the World Bank, which was funding the entire irrigation scheme, also protect the watershed. They could do this relatively easily by supporting the establishment of the Dumoga-Bone National Park, which would include some 700,000 acres of primary tropical rain forest. John four-putted and explained that for little more than 1 percent of the total cost of the project, this conservation investment in a valuable irrigation scheme would help to minimize siltation and ensure a steady year-round flow of water. John did not say, hooking his ball into a pond, that this is what the World Bank, WWF, and IUCN had advised all along.

The local residents, who had the power to make decisions affecting Dumoga, were happy to support measures that would keep shifting cultivators and loggers out of the forests. Back in Jakarta, we argued the case with the World Bank, the Irrigation Department, and the Forestry Department. We also enlisted the aid of environmentalist colleagues in Washington, D.C., who put pressure on the World Bank from that side. All of these efforts, coupled with John MacKinnon's logic and sporting graces, led to the first case in Indonesia where a major development agency had fully and effectively recognized protected area conservation as an integral part of rural development.

A management plan has now been prepared and reasonable progress has been made in its implementation. While it is still too early to determine the success of the effort, indications are that Dumoga is one of Indonesia's best-managed protected areas. It is being held up by the World Bank as the model of how to promote links between conservation, the interests of local people, and development.

◆   ◆   ◆

Sadly, the Dumoga model is rare. Too few of the big development projects incorporate conservation and appeal to the self-interest of the local people. Too many of them are both destructive of the environment and of little lasting benefit to anyone but the foreign consultants, construction firms, and the country's elite.

In Sarawak, for example, the people living at the headwaters of the Rajang River are furious. In 1981, the central Malaysian government, based on the other side of the South China Sea, decided to build a huge hydroelectric dam at the Bakun Rapids, twenty miles upstream from the tiny town of Belaga. At 687 feet high, it would be taller than the Aswan High Dam, and on a similar scale to the Hoover Dam. By March 1986 nine feasibility studies—costing 4.6 million U.S. dollars—had been completed and five more were planned for a project that was estimated to cost at least $3.9

billion and which would have produced 2,400 megawatts of electricity, almost as much as the whole of Malaysia needed in 1985.

Local people argued that 4,300 indigenous people would be displaced by the 180-square-mile lake—roughly the area of Singapore—and questioned whether they should suffer in order to provide electricity to the industrial sector in peninsular Malaysia.

Leo Moggie, a Sarawakian who is the federal Minister of Energy, Telecommunications, and Posts and who was formerly a district officer in the division encompassing the site of the proposed dam, argues that Bakun would reduce Malaysia's reliance on gas-fired and coal-fired power plants. Bakun is also "part and parcel of our ordinary development program for rural communities," he says. "Sooner or later, they have to give up their mobile, isolated lifestyle of shifting cultivation and become a central community. They will be given full compensation for the loss of private property. Their social structure and institutions will be maintained as far as possible. The local population will be given preference for jobs, and afterwards the reservoir fisheries, new agricultural activities and the exploitation of forest resources will continue to improve their income."

Not convinced, Kayan and Kenyah leaders representing the fifteen longhouses that would be submerged by the reservoir recently presented to the government a petition to which 2,000 signatures and thumbprints were affixed: "We don't want to lose the heritage of land given by our ancestors. Our land is our survival and to flood it would mean the extermination of our peoples." Several angry Kayans declared they would fight to the death. Fortunately, the government may not be calling their bluff, having recently decided to indefinitely postpone the dam project because it is too expensive. Even if the dam is not built, however, local people may still be forced to translocate. Most are reluctant to leave their homeland.

◆ ◆ ◆

In the Philippines, the government planned to dam the Chico River (one of an estimated 861 dams under consideration) in northern Luzon, the country's principal island. This plan led to an armed, bloody struggle between Igorots, or "people of the mountains," and the Manila-based armed forces. "Unlike their lowland neighbors, the Igorots of the Chico area remained fiercely independent during the centuries of Spanish colonial rule in the Philip-

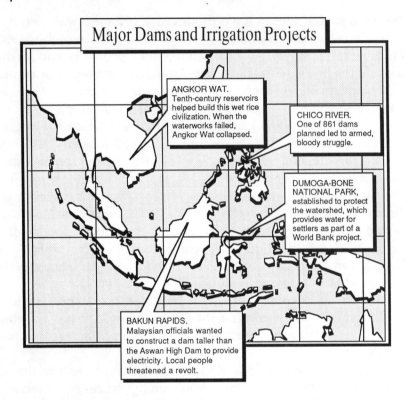

Major Dams and Irrigation Projects

ANGKOR WAT.
Tenth-century reservoirs helped build this wet rice civilization. When the waterworks failed, Angkor Wat collapsed.

CHICO RIVER.
One of 861 dams planned led to armed, bloody struggle.

DUMOGA-BONE NATIONAL PARK, established to protect the watershed, which provides water for settlers as part of a World Bank project.

BAKUN RAPIDS.
Malaysian officials wanted to construct a dam taller than the Aswan High Dam to provide electricity. Local people threatened a revolt.

pines, and the eight decades of American administration and economic domination that followed," notes anthropologist Charles Drucker. Bishop Francisco Claver, himself an Igorot, says that the culture of his people "is linked inextricably with the land: with their fields, their burial grounds, their sacred groves, hence with the particular piece of land their villages are built on." In the fight, the Igorots found themselves allied, perhaps unintentionally, with the nationwide revolutionary movement opposing President Ferdinand Marcos, and journalist Sheilah Ocampo saw the antidam guerrilla activity as "the most important conflict yet between the Marcos administration and the communist insurgents." In 1986 President Aquino recognized a *fait accompli* and canceled the dam plans.

◆ ◆ ◆

Today most big dam projects are designed to produce electricity because "power—and in particular cheap power—is considered the *sine qua non* of development," according to Edward Goldsmith and

Nicholas Hildyard, who have made a major study of the social and environmental effects of large dams. Developing countries find it hard to resist the temptation to be relatively free of the oil stranglehold and thereby have a clean, long-term source of energy they can control themselves. The disadvantage is that the energy is often used to exploit the country's resources. At the very least, it requires that those resources be used at a far more rapid rate than they were when most energy came from animals, crops, and wood.

Dams are also built to supply water to farmers and to control floods, as they have for millennia. Yet history shows repeatedly, according to Brent Blackwelder, Director of Water Resources at the Environmental Policy Institute, that "big dams and water projects have not only failed to achieve their basic objectives but are also leaving a legacy of unsurpassed cultural destruction, disease and environmental damage. [There is] a dramatic difference between the rhetoric of project promoters and the grim reality."

Massive water resources development programs have been the source of political power for ages. One of Southeast Asia's first major irrigation schemes has a message relevant to us today.

Most people think of Angkor Wat in terms of fabulous temples, with statues in the form of huge faces watching over intricately carved stone reliefs. These temples were models of heaven, and the leaders of the ancient Khmer Empire were megalomaniacs of the first order. But building these monuments to Siva, Brahma, and Vishnu, and their servants—Naga the serpent king, and Garuda, the lord of the skies—required much more than power. Productivity was needed; swamps had to be drained and dry land needed to be irrigated to produce sufficient food to feed the priests and construction workers.

Using foreign technology from India, the god-kings directed a massive rural development program which included some of the largest water management projects in the world at that time; the Yasodharatataka Reservoir, built in the tenth century A.D., for example, had a surface area of 4 square miles and required that 50 million cubic yards of soil be removed. "The great canals reached out over the plains, the water of the immense dams glittered in the sunlight, rice paddy upon rice paddy stretching away to the horizon," says Swedish sociologists Jan Myrdal and Gun Kessle. "The new [means] of production had released the productive forces, people fell into ever greater misery, and the temples rose ever more vast and beautiful. The surplus grew. The population increased. Labor was in demand and could be exploited."

Angkor grew up as a strongly centralized state, with a god-king surrounded by loyal priests who used new irrigation techniques to create incredible wealth for themselves. The god-kings needed to demonstrate their divinity and maintain internal order through constant military adventures. And surrounding nations were always ready to claim a share of these vast riches. As a result, Angkor was in a chronic state of war.

The great wealth and the military machine of the Khmers were built on increased development, but this had a cost. "Trees had been cut down in vast numbers and the wood used for building," says historian John Audric. "This uprooting of the 'plugs of the soil,' as they are called, caused disastrous floods in the rainy season." The canals became clogged and epidemics of malaria swept through the city, caused by the mosquitoes which bred profusely in the now stagnant swamps. The farmer saw the deterioration of the once-magnificent reservoirs which his forefathers had died building, listened with skepticism to government promises that the reservoirs would be restored, and voted with his feet by melting into the countryside. The ruinous policy of deforestation which had been followed by King Jayavarman led to the soil losing its tightening, drainage, and absorbent qualities, thereby setting the stage for tragedy.

Word of Angkor's problems leaked back to its enemies the Thais, who were growing in strength through more enlightened and smaller-scale development policies. In 1428, after centuries of skirmishes, the Thais attacked in force.

The troops were spurred on by tales of Angkor's delights awaiting the conquering heroes. "It was said—and with truth—that even the hundreds of concubines were adorned with collars of rubies," reports Audric. The numerous dancing girls wore transparent dresses secured with clasps of gold, with strings of plump pearls encircling their necks and plunging between their bare breasts. In the royal palace, the dancing floor was made of silver, and the most beautiful, graceful, and talented girls were trained to play the role of *apsaras*, the seductive celestial nymphs who dwell in Indra's paradise. They danced steps of abandon, twisting their half-clad bodies in sensuous movements, and broke their hymens on golden *lingas*, reports Audric. Of course, only the king and his close associates were able to participate in these activities; they argued that this sexual excess was an essential element in worshiping the cult of Siva and could not be entrusted to lesser men.

But stories of the orgies leaked out, and with this kind of pep talk the Thais attacked enthusiastically and successfully, entertaining the captured dancers, looting all valuables, and burning everything that was flammable. Weighed down with booty and more or less satiated, the Thais withdrew, leaving Angkor in chaos. The population of Angkor, at that time over 1 million, was left with no means of producing food. Just as in the horrific days in 1975 following the conquest of Phnom Penh by the Khmer Rouge, the people of Angkor fled to the countryside, and reverted to shifting cultivation. But since the forests had been cleared and the soils exhausted, the land had lost its heart and could no longer support people. Anarchy reigned. The human population plummeted, and wildlife returned to claim the abandoned fields.

◆ ◆ ◆

Governments are rightly concerned about the long-term impact of large dams and irrigation projects. Too many dams, starting from the time of Angkor, have brought only short-term benefits and have inadvertently led to the destruction of forests and wildlife. Once the complex irrigation systems start to break down through lack of maintenance, siltation, or civil disturbance, they deteriorate quickly. And in the following breakdown of public order, famine, disease, and even war may well result, if Angkor Wat in 1428 and Phnom Penh in 1975 can be taken as evidence.

People need to manage their water well if they are to prosper in the monsoons of Southeast Asia. Some irrigation systems are ancient, and have been in continuous production for hundreds of years. The terraces of Banaue in the Philippines or Bali in Indonesia are excellent examples. The construction of these systems required a strong authority, but the systems are more attuned to the needs of the local farmers than to the government in a distant capital. The *subaks* (water management cooperatives) of Bali operate independently of government, and have survived because they adapt to local needs. While Bali has no temples to rival the grandeur of Angkor Wat, it has thousands of local temples which meet the needs of the local people.

Yet the central governments, encouraged by development aid agencies, continue to think big, to nobody's long-term benefit. A 1986 World Bank survey of 200 major dams built in the past forty-five years revealed that sedimentation, caused by wash off of soil in the wake of deforestation, leads to an average 2 percent loss of storage capacity every year.

Foreign experts have long been a major factor in the man-nature relationship in Southeast Asia, bringing first irrigation and the accompanying state religions, and later massive civil engineering projects aimed ultimately at stimulating foreign trade. In some ways, large dams are the modern equivalent of grandiose temple complexes built centuries ago.

The great ceremonial centers of Java—fabulous temples such as Borobudur and Prambanan—were all constructed in a burst of creative energy that lasted less than 100 years. This outburst of energy has been called by anthropologist Jan Wisseman Christie "one of the greatest concentrated acts of conspicuous consumption in the region." During the period of rapid construction of religious monuments, foreign experts from India played a prominent role, and most royal inscriptions were written in Sanskrit.

The fashion for large state temple complexes dedicated to Hindu and Buddhist deities did not last long. The Indian architects and engineers, their consultancy contracts expired, soon returned home and the use of Sanskrit as the language of inscriptions died out. "While there is no reason to believe that available rice surpluses were inadequate to support such major building efforts," Christie says, "it is possible that these complexes may have been abandoned in part because of their relative expense—that not enough people saw them to justify their cost. The smaller ancestor shrines which replaced them were both culturally and geographically more accessible to the village populace."

Just as the rustic gods derived from animals of the forest needed to be adopted by the state religions, so did the structure of the religious edifices need to become accessible to the villagers. While the state religions still prosper throughout Southeast Asia, their period of concentrated power as illustrated by the breathtaking monuments of Borobudur and Angkor Wat was short-lived because it served too narrow a spectrum of interest and concentrated too much power in too few hands.

The parallels between then and now become clear if you substitute foreign development experts from industrialized countries for Indian experts, English for Sanskrit, and major dams for huge temples. Smaller irrigation projects which serve the needs of the local people can be seen as equivalent to the smaller village temples.

Small waterworks have proven to be more likely to continue to function long after the contractors have left. Future generations may acclaim the architectural courage of twentieth-century presidents who built monumental dams, just as our generation acclaims the architectural excess of the god-kings of Angkor Wat. But it is also likely that our descendants will see, perhaps more clearly than we can, that these massive projects often come with a monumental price tag—the degradation of the environment and the impoverishment of the people who depend on nature's long-term productivity.

29

*The Cycle
of Progress*

*People and nature in Southeast Asia are part of the cosmic cycle
of eternal change. How does modern economic development fit
into the vision of fiery chaos and the flowering lotus?*

Assisi, a small medieval Italian village on the sunny southern
slopes of Mount Subasio, was selected by WWF as the site for a
1986 conference aimed at involving the world's religions in the
conservation movement. In a tea shop on the ground floor of a
stone building, which was already weathered when St. Francis
preached to the animals in the thirteenth century, we asked Dr.
Karan Singh for advice about our inquiry into the relationship between people and animals.

Karan Singh had been appointed regent of Jammu and Kashmir
at the age of eighteen by his maharaja father, and when the old
order of maharajas passed in India, he became the first elected
governor of the state. At thirty-six, he was appointed Minister of
Tourism and Civil Engineering in Indira Gandhi's cabinet. He over-

saw the modernization of the Indian civil air fleet and the creation of a major tourist industry, then became Minister of Health and Family Planning when India first developed its national population policy. He served as chairman of the Indian Board of Wildlife and oversaw the design and implementation of Project Tiger, one of the world's most successful conservation programs. During all of this, Dr. Singh was chancellor of the University of Jammu and Kashmir.

In 1981, deciding to emphasize the spiritual side of life, he started a new religious movement known as the Virta Hindu Samaj, which sought to strengthen Hindu society in the face of modern challenges.

He was interested but somewhat bemused by our efforts to understand the relationship between people and wildlife in tropical Asia. "You are working too hard to find a scientific explanation for everything," he pointed out. "That's a failing of modern industrial society. In our eastern view, people and animals are part of the same thing, created by the same Almighty Force, governed by the same laws of nature, and subject to the inevitability of life's cycles. It's very simple."

"We know that," we protested. "But the unity of all life doesn't seem to prevent people from destroying both animals and forests in the name of profit. The traditional beliefs don't really seem to be serving nature's needs very well in the modern age."

Singh, dressed in a well-tailored gray Nehru suit and matching cap, sipped thoughtfully on his steaming mint tea, his dark, intelligent face smiling slightly as he tasted the delicate flavor of the finest Darjeeling leaves. "Look back at Hindu mythology," he suggested. "You know about the churning of the Sea of Milk, the event from which everything was derived. If you wish, you can consider the Sea of Milk as the equivalent of the primordial ooze from which modern scientists say life on earth evolved. But remember that the churning was just one event in a long and inevitable cycle. The ancient Hindu texts say that each of the world cycles is 4.3 billion years long. If you insist on scientific confirmation, you might note that 4.3 billion years is roughly the age of the earth, according to modern geological discoveries."

Each world cycle, we understood, is subdivided into four ages, and the later in the cycle the worse things get. We are now well into the fourth and last age, one which has been described in a thousand-year-old Hindu classic, the *Vishnu Purana*, as occurring "when society reaches a stage where property confers rank, wealth becomes the only source of virtue, passion the sole bond of union between husband and wife, falsehood the source of success in life, sex the only means of enjoyment, and outer trappings are confused with inner religion."

That morning Dr. Singh had spoken to 600 people at the conference, a small audience for him since his religious speeches back home draw over a million of the faithful. But he is a natural teacher and a born showman and loves playing to an audience, even if it is only two curious conservationists.

"Since we are now reaching the end of the cycle, when the commitment to *dharma* [duty] is at its weakest, we have no choice but to accept that egoistic, devouring, blind, and reckless elements have the upper hand. But remember the parable of the maharaja who commanded his wise men to invent a sentence which would be appropriate in all times and situations. After working on the problem for a year, they presented him the words: 'And this, too, shall pass away.' This final age will presently disintegrate into fiery chaos, according to the myth, and will subsequently burst forth again, fresh as a flowering lotus, ready to resume the inevitable cycle."

Although tempered by a long exposure to Asian approaches to life, we were trained as members of a pragmatic, industrialized society and were only partially convinced by such fatalism. After all, hasn't history shown a steady growth of economic prosperity? If anything is inevitable, surely it is progress. Or is it?

Helpless to resist our compulsion to rationalize things, we considered the four ecocultural revolutions that have shaped Southeast Asia. Was it fatuous to think that human efforts might alter the inevitability of the cosmic cycle?

The first revolution was the harnessing of fire by hunters, which enabled people to have a major influence on the distribution of forest and grasslands. Only a few of the descendants of these early people still survive as hunters; people like the *Orang Asli* in Malaysia are the people who live in closest contact with nature and have the richest store of traditional knowledge.

The second revolution was the domestication of plants and animals, which brought shifting cultivation to the region and led to perhaps a hundredfold increase in human population. Almost all hill areas are still occupied by shifting cultivators, many of them from minority tribes. "Slash and burners" represent the largest segment of Asian society which has retained an intimate relationship with the natural world. These forest farmers dominated the region for over 5,000 years, but didn't have the political acumen or surplus wealth to develop great kingdoms.

That was the role of the irrigators, who were swept into power as part of the third ecocultural revolution. Using new techniques taught by foreign advisers, they produced sufficient surpluses of rice to support kings, cities, monumental architecture, state religions, and a twenty- to thirtyfold increase in human population. Royalty cleverly did not discard old beliefs; rather they built upon the mythology and folklore of the hunters and shifting cultivators and consolidated their power by claiming kinship to animals such as white elephants, miraculous birds, mermaid queens, giant poisonous snakes, and fierce crocodiles.

The fourth ecocultural revolution—the spread of the world marketplace—has been more significant in its impact on nature than the earlier three revolutions combined, as populations have increased yet another twenty to thirty times. The expanding world marketplace has been accompanied by the technological arrogance that leads governments to believe that ever-greater applications of technology and money can overcome any natural obstacle. World trade and industrial growth have resulted in massive changes in the landscape, spurred on by hungry foreign markets. Rivers are dammed to provide electricity for factories and people living in the cities, rain forests are converted to plantations, and poor soils are made productive by means of expensive chemical fertilizers, pesticides, oil-driven tractors and pumps. All Southeast Asian countries, and the vast majority of their citizens, have been drawn into the global economy and encouraged to purchase goods and services previously unavailable or unnecessary. All Southeast Asian countries (except oil-rich Brunei) have had to borrow to pay for this progress, and the international banks expect governments to repay development loans with foreign exchange. Since trade is dominated by agriculture and natural resources, governments are forced to sacrifice the products of forest, field, and ocean, often selling off their capital assets to pay the interest on the nation's loans.

Schomburgk's deer disappeared when the Thai swamps where it lived were converted to rice fields to feed people in Saudi Arabia and Brazil. The Javan tigers fell victim to plantation agriculture which brought more wealth to power brokers and financiers in Amsterdam and Jakarta than to villagers in east Java. Many other species—rhinos, elephants, wild buffalo, and Eld's deer, to name a few—are about to disappear, directly or indirectly, at the hand of humans.

Traditional human societies are also deteriorating, and much of the complex and productive traditional knowledge which had steadily accumulated over the centuries is being lost along with the animals. Because of the changes that have come with the world marketplace, pigs are no longer effective in maintaining the ecosystem balance of the Maring people of New Guinea; the logging of east Malaysian forests is destroying the bearded pig migration which is part of an important natural and cultural cycle; the intricate Animistic hunting culture of Siberut is being destroyed by a combination of missionaries and government officials; and populations of elephants have been reduced to such a low level that brave elephant hunters such as the Kui are unable to practice their age-old skills and have been reduced to performing in circus-like exhibitions.

Many of the farmers who are selling their crops to distant markets are now wealthy enough to have television, and, if central government culture ministries permit it, prefer to watch "Dallas" rather than listen to their elders ramble on about headhunting trips and encounters with were-tigers and nature gods. Modern means of transportation, usually fueled by oil in one form or another, enable them to go to the nearest town for a chocolate bar from Switzerland, a bottle of beer from England, a can of powdered milk from the United States, an injection of penicillin from Germany, or a motorcycle from Japan.

But not everybody is fully convinced that modern ways are the best. Like most of the 2.5 million Balinese, the men of a village water committee we met grow "miracle" rice varieties, the new, more productive strains developed as part of the green revolution. But we were surprised to see that in a small corner of their *sawah* they were growing the taller traditional rice varieties that have fed Balinese for generations. The old rice, we were told by our Balinese friends, is the only form of grain that will placate the backyard nature gods.

Six hundred miles to the east, the land is too arid to grow rice, so fearless oceangoing hunters from the island of Lembata jump from the bows of fragile sailboats to drive harpoons deep into the broad backs of whales. They have been offered "progress" and have politely declined.

Once the thirty-foot-long handmade wooden boat is at sea, the oars are shipped and the rectangular palm leaf sail is run up, while the crew of fifteen begins scanning the sea for signs of suitable large game: false killer whales, sharks, marlin, and several species of dolphins. Just about anything that swims is fair game, except for baleen whales, which are taboo. Suddenly a lone bull sperm whale about as long as the boat is sighted in the distance, recognized by the forty-five-degree angle of his blow (baleen whales normally blow straight up).

As the boat approaches the whale the crew hurriedly recites the Lord's Prayer and a Hail Mary while Alouisius Sanga, the harpooner, takes command from his bowsprit, guiding the helmsman with arm signals. Sanga, a dark, short, wiry man of thirty-two, gets set, tenses, then springs from the platform with his arm cocked. In midair he slams the harpoon home, and appears to hang momentarily suspended before landing on the back of the astonished whale. With blood gushing from its back, the whale dives, leaving Sanga treading water until he is picked up by his boat. The harpoon cable runs out quickly and, after a few tense moments, the boat is suddenly jerked under and Sanga finds himself back in the water, this time with the rest of the crew to keep him company.

After ten minutes or so the boat suddenly pops up like a cork. The whale is surfacing and it is a dangerous time—several of the village men have been killed by the whales' thrashing tails, either by direct blows or from gaping wounds caused by shrapnel-like splinters sent flying from timbers shattered by the whales' blows.

The crewmen clamber aboard their boat and start bailing out while the whale takes them on what New England whalers used to call a "Nantucket sleighride." As the whale weakens, the men pull in the rope and bring the mortally wounded giant alongside. Some of the crew jump into the water, ignoring the sharks which are attracted by the blood, and repeatedly stab the animal. Within twenty minutes the whale is dead and the hard work begins. Now the men must put their backs into towing the colossus five miles back to Lembata.

As evening approaches, the boat pulls on to the beach. Excited villagers pitch in to butcher the whale, leaving nothing to waste. Some of the meat is eaten fresh, some is dried in the sun and later traded for vegetables with other villages in the mountainous interior of the bleak island. Since sperm whale meat contains twice as much crude protein per weight as beef (60 percent vs 30 percent) and three times as much protein as pork, it is a critical source of nourishment for the islanders.

Concerned about the hazards to fishermen, and the cruelty to whales that are injured but not landed, the Indonesian government requested the assistance of the UN's Food and Agriculture Organization to try to improve the whaling techniques of Lembata with a modern diesel ship, nylon ropes, and new methods. The FAO project had little impact, despite the best efforts of a master fisherman from Norway. The hunters of Lembata were happy to have nylon ropes and used them in their rigging. But they steadfastly held on to their traditional softer fiber ropes for the harpoons, maintaining that they needed the suppleness of fiber to control such large animals. A diesel fishing boat sounded like a nice gift. But the hunters were concerned about maintenance and the need to purchase fuel. These would require them to formally enter the cash economy by selling meat to people in large towns who pay in cash rather than bartering with their mountain neighbors for vegetables and forest products. They also worried about the social impact such a dominant ship would have on the system of collectively owned handmade sailing boats whose success depended on the skills of the sailors and the luck of the draw. A system which was in balance with the resource, which brought benefits to the entire island and bred hunters of supreme courage, was stronger than well-meaning "progress."

"If we became dependent on this motorboat," Sanga asked, "what would happen to us when it broke down, or we had no money?" He might have inquired as well what would have happened to the people if it became too easy to kill whales or if the great sea mammals disappeared. Today their whaling is within manageable limits, and the fishermen of Lembata intend to maintain the delicate balance epitomized by a contemporary Ahab.

◆ ◆ ◆

Modern governments often act as if the way to take care of nature is to treat it as a government sector. This view was brought home to us the evening after our talk with Karan Singh. We sat at a dinner table in an elegant Italian restaurant with Dr. Sumitro Djojohadikusumo, whose former Indonesian cabinet posts included Minister of Trade and Industry, Minister of Finance, and Minister of State for Research, as well as ambassador to the United States. Over a flinty Torre di Giano 1982 that accompanied a delicate *pennette spigadoro* Franciscan style, Sumitro, a graduate of the Sorbonne and the Netherlands School of Economics, who had earlier attended his first WWF event as an international councillor, politely tried to redirect the conversation away from mermaid queens who speak with Javanese sultans and brave men who sing to seduce man-eating tigers into traps.

"Why are you so interested in such things?" he finally asked, slightly exasperated and realizing that we weren't going to give up.

"Because it seems to us that they have survival value for people," we said, pouring now the Rubesco Riserva 1978.

"They used to, perhaps, but not today. Loro Kidul is a myth. She's not real and has no relevance for our people. The future is in science," asserted the immaculately tailored professor. "We certainly need a healthy natural environment, and saving nature should be a priority for every right-thinking government, but not necessarily for the reasons you give. If we are to make further progress we need the natural resources, we need the income, we need the timber, we need the water, we need the fish. We can apply science to manage nature so that everyone benefits, even the animals."

This is an attractive idea, maybe even a necessary one in a period of powerful pressures to consume forests, wildlife, and soil. Contemporary governments are concerned primarily with increasing productivity and economic growth through expanding foreign trade. They no longer view the relationship with nature as a foundation of society, but they do take it seriously enough to have established bureaucratic government conservation agencies, wildlife protection laws, systems of protected areas with wildlife police forces, captive breeding programs, and rehabilitation schemes for animals like orangutans. Conservation agencies document on paper information that is either already well known by rural people or completely irrelevant to the villagers' traditional life-styles, often calling on foreign expertise and international assistance to implement this new way of dealing with nature by throwing paper at it. Such efforts are usually based on a perception of reality which is consistent with the whole philosophy of the world marketplace: people have control and power over nature so they have the responsibility to put things right.

But despite determined efforts and major expenditures, results from this approach have been generally disappointing, possibly because government conservation departments ironically tend to pit people *against* nature. The village hunter becomes a poacher when he crosses a national park boundary; responsibility to manage living resources is given to a government department with a staff of urban bureaucrats; the forest which provided a sustainable supply of goods and services to the people living around it is given to an outside timber concessionaire whose objective is to earn maximum profit in the shortest time; and traditional beliefs which related people to nature are challenged by new materialistic belief systems which come from distant and alien cultures.

The approach of the international marketplace to conservation ignores the centuries-old Asian beliefs that people are *part* of nature, and overlooks the role that wildlife has played in molding and refining everyday human behavior. Conservation, if it is to work, must integrate social, cultural, and economic considerations. A government-led, but chronically underfunded, conservation department by itself can do little more than slightly slow down the pace of exploitation of nature which is demanded by the global market, and perhaps save a few of the most outstanding areas as living museums.

For virtually all wild animals except the rat, the "progress" of the fourth revolution has spelled disaster. From nature's point of view, the passing of modern industrialized society and its world-wide trade would be a great boon.

From the point of view of Asian philosophy, the demise of materialism is not a question of if, but rather of when. People have seen how suddenly things can change. They know about the failed megalithic development projects at Angkor Wat, abandoned in part because deforestation led to erosion that ruined the kingdom's irrigation system. They understand that relatively small volcanoes kill people every year in Indonesia, and that another monumental eruption like Toba, Tambora, or Krakatau is sure to come at some time and throw Indonesia into chaos. All countries in the region have suffered recent wars, revolutions, or insurrections, and civil unrest can come at any moment. Southeast Asia is no stranger to upheaval, and despite the best efforts of development planners, little evidence suggests that the future will be any less tumultuous than the past.

The town of Balikpapan, near Kutai Nature Reserve in East Kalimantan, offers a glimpse of what can happen from uncontrolled exploitation. "In the 1970s, Balikpapan, as an Indonesian center of oil and gas production second only to Sumatra, became worldly overnight," wrote American journalist Barbara Crosette. "Its airport became the country's second busiest after Jakarta's. It boasted one of the country's most expensive hotels, cinema complexes and a cosmopolitan society. Its population nearly tripled." Then, as international oil prices started to slide, the city's public services disintegrated and people moved to the nearby hills. "Outside of town, people trying to grow food for themselves or crops to sell for cash are deforesting hills, causing landslides and floods." The government turned to the area's timber, the country's economic safety valve when oil prices slump. This produced cash, and an unexpected side effect. When vast amounts of kindling produced by timber operations became tinder dry because of a drought and burst into flames, the result was the world's worst forest fire in decades. An area the size of the Netherlands, or twice the size of New Jersey, was turned into cinders. The yellow-brown haze forced the cancellation of airline flights in Singapore, 900 miles to the northwest.

Had the flaming part of the cosmic cycle come again?

◆ ◆ ◆

Scientists have long known about climatic cycles—sunspots, seasons, ice ages, and so on. The period between ice ages has been found to vary from 10,000 to 30,000 years, and we have been in the present one for about 15,000 years. But people may be hastening the onset of the next ice age; many experts say that the clearing of the tropical forests combined with the burning of wood, coal, and oil is causing fundamental changes in the global heat balance. The climate is getting warmer, and warming has always been followed by cooling which leads to an ice age.

Even more immediately, the world market system is based on oil, a resource that will eventually run out and bring fundamental change with its demise, regardless of what energy source replaces it. In short, the recent decades of economic growth are merely an instant in the cosmic cycle, bringing the real but ephemeral joys of wealth to many people.

We asked Karan Singh about what will happen at the end of the current world cycle. "It is certain to continue to its inevitable conclusion: fierce heat and drought, followed by flood," Dr. Singh told us. The present cycle, according to Hindu mythology, will end when Vishnu himself becomes the energy of the sun, the whole world dries up, the earth splits open, and a deadly blaze of heat evaporates the waters of the world. When the life force has been totally dehydrated, Vishnu becomes the wind, the cosmic life-breath, and then turns into a gigantic conflagration which consumes everything. Finally, Vishnu will shed a torrential rain, sweet and pure as milk, to quench the fires. The suffering earth will at last reach *nirvana*, the ultimate nothingness. Vishnu will again recline on the Universal Serpent floating on the milky sea and dream about the next cycle.

We finished our tea, then walked up the hill toward the Cathedral of St. Francis, where the Franciscan friars were sharing their quarters with the distinguished visitor from a distant philosophical shore. Standing in front of the gate to the monastery as a light rain began to fall, we asked Singh if he really believed in the apocalyptic view of the inevitable cosmic cycles of Hindu mythology.

"Similar visions can be found in all the great religions, including Islam's Ghiama and Christianity's Apocalypse, and in myths from the Incas, Mayas, Egyptians, and other early civilizations," he replied in a calm voice. "And if you insist on seeking a scientific explanation, you might look at descriptions of the environmental impact of nuclear warfare. Some of my *saddhu* colleagues, who spend their lives in contemplation, have told me that their visions of the coming end of the world cycle include mushroom-shaped clouds of fire.

"Surely there can be no question that life on earth will ultimately cease to exist—even the sun is not immortal," Dr. Singh concluded. "It's just a matter of time. According to the Hindu scriptures, this last age in the world cycle will last exactly 432,000 years."

As we turned to walk up the hill to our hotel, he flashed us a melancholy smile and asked: "I wonder what year this age began?"

30

The Fifth Revolution

The global marketplace cannot continue to be environmentally destructive. What role will wildlife have in man's next ecocultural revolution?

SOME OF OUR FRIENDS in Jakarta, Bangkok, Singapore, and Manila were dubious of our work with wildlife, a subject they did not find very relevant to their modern lives. Why does a computer salesman need to worry about tigers? Like many urban people, particularly those who have the most sophisticated educations, they had turned their backs on nature and instead placed their faith in supermarkets. They conveniently ignored their dependency on the forests and fields as they instead became reliant on a continuous flow of goods from far away.

Their rural relatives, in contrast, continued to rely on intricate means of survival based on a close affinity with nature. We have seen basic wildlife-oriented beliefs reinterpreted and made relevant to widely different societies. We have seen people deal with man-eating crocodiles, crop-raiding monkeys, and psychotic orangutans. We have talked with tiger magicians, elephant cowboys, and apothecaries selling rhino-horn medicine. We have visited longhouses in Siberut draped with monkey skulls which help people hunt, and longhouses in Sarawak where farmers use bird omens to help them with their planting. We have met sultans and kings who derive at least part of their power from association with ancient mermaid, snake, and hornbill deities. We have been caught up in the excitement of cockfights and bull races, and been moved by religious ceremonies denying that a man is a snake.

The hunter seeking grazing prey recognizes a spirit of the grass; this becomes the rice goddess of the wet rice farmer. The Animist links a snake spirit with regeneration; this develops into the *naga* of the Hindu and Buddhist, which also flourishes as the *kris* of the Muslim. Omen-carrying birds linking the sky and earth are eagerly sought by Animist and Christian alike; in another form, the respect for birds evolves into the Garuda of Hindu mythology, which is also the national bird of predominantly Islamic Indonesia, the symbol of the Buddhist king of Thailand, and part of the national coat of arms of predominantly Christian Philippines. All forest dwellers know well the mischievous monkey; in the form of Hanuman he becomes a hero of the Hindu epic, the *Ramayana*, and a major character in public entertainments among Christians, Muslims, Confucians, and Buddhists alike. Animals are part of human life in Southeast Asia.

But both animals and human cultures are threatened by the global marketplace. International trade, and all that goes with it, has enabled the human population in the region to increase from less than 100 million when Dr. Boonsong was born to nearly four times that today, and the per capita income has increased fiftyfold as well. Nature's suffering has been an inevitable side effect of this unprecedented increase in the number, wealth, and productivity of people supported by the land's natural resources.

◆ ◆ ◆

Since change is inevitable, what might be the basis of the fifth ecocultural revolution?

Some 50 years ago the Dutch administrators of what is now Indonesia banned a set of predictions made 800 years earlier. During World War II the Japanese invaders did the same, fearful that the "Joyoboyo prophesies" would inspire the people to revolt.

King Joyoboyo—also known as Jayabhaya—reigned in east Java from 1135 to 1160, during one of Java's golden ages. Joyoboyo was not only a successful warrior but also a gifted poet and astrologer. He drew on the Indian *Mahabharata* epic to create the *Bharatajudha*, a masterpiece of Javan literature which has been turned into a popular *wayang* play which illuminates the conflict between good and evil.

But he is remembered most of all for his disturbingly accurate predictions. He forecast that the Majapahit Empire would rise a century after his death (it began in 1294) and would last some 200 years (its last outposts fell around 1518). In the longer term, he predicted the course of Indonesia's colonial history. A "white buffalo with blue eyes" (the Dutch) would occupy Indonesian soil, but would be driven off by a "yellow peacock" from the northeast (the Japanese). In a desperate struggle to retain Indonesia, the "white buffalo" would commit adultery with a crocodile. The Javanese interpreted this to mean that the Dutch would conspire with the British to regain their colonial possessions, which is what happened just after World War II. But ultimately, predicted Joyoboyo, the "black ants will lay eggs on fine ashes," which the Dutch interpreted as the seditious idea that the Indonesian people would achieve their independence by revolution, and prosper. Joyoboyo's final prophecy might instead be interpreted to mean that the fifth ecocultural revolution will be built on the collapse of the international marketplace. The rural folk who are closest to nature will abide.

What can be done today to ensure that sufficient wildlife, and human knowledge to manage it, can survive the fourth revolution to support the fifth one? Modern governments will need to do a delicate balancing act: They need to make the best of today while preparing for the unknown conditions of tomorrow. Priests and power brokers, politicians and educators, are trying to make the best of it in an exceptionally dynamic moment in the history of the human species. They would be well advised to bear in mind the popular Minangkabau proverb, "*Alam terkembang menjadi guru,*" which loosely translated means "you will never go wrong if you take nature as your teacher," when preparing a future that will almost certainly include:

Self-sufficiency. While some level of long-distance trade will certainly continue, societies will become increasingly self-contained, and draw mainly on locally and regionally available resources for the necessities of life. Water buffalo will remain the most common tractor for the rice fields, and the pigs, cattle, and chickens—all of which have wild relatives in the forests—will remain the stars of the barnyard as they adapt to new conditions and develop numerous local varieties. Elephants will be the main heavy-duty machines in the rural settings, with wild herds providing the best source of replenishing the stock.

Once oil-based chemical fertilizers and pesticides recede in significance, farmers will adapt today's crops to create new varieties adapted to local conditions. Throughout the region, villagers will harvest animals, medicine, fruit, and building materials from their adjacent forests, often using the forests as an emergency reserve to deal with exceptionally bad years or as a refuge in times of threatening military adventures.

Rural people who feel that their traditional self-sufficient lifestyles are being threatened by outsiders are already raising their voices in protest. In at least seventeen incidents brought to the attention of the police, Ibans, Kayans, and Kenyahs from Sarawak's Bintulu area and along the Baram River tributaries decided they had had enough. They claimed timber operations polluted rivers, caused floods through erosion, frightened away game, damaged crops, and in general disrupted their traditional lifestyles. Their opportunity to earn a living was being jeopardized by the ecological damage caused by the chain saws and tractors. They hijacked vehicles, sabotaged trucks, blocked access to logging roads, and threatened Chinese timber camp managers with Iban death curses and the business end of a *parang*.

Local responsibility. Cultures have been stable for long periods in the past, so the local people must have been able to enforce regulations controlling the power of individual humans to exploit nature or other humans, to the benefit of the society. Many of today's forest farmers who also hunt, such as the people on Siberut, retain some of the ancient controls on hunting which had evolved to ensure that the resource would not be depleted by overharvesting.

Once international trade has been stabilized at sustainable levels, the need for strong central government control of land and resources will be greatly reduced. The people who are most directly dependent on nature will once again assume their custodianship.

Potentially dangerous or threatening wild animals, such as crocodiles and tigers, will help the community enforce the necessary restraints on human excesses, at least partially replacing the relatively ineffective national systems of law and regulation with an older, self-regulating law that touches people's psyches.

Symbolism. By symbolizing certain fundamental beliefs about reality, animals will continue to help people maintain their balance with nature. The ultimate truths of nature will endure and will appear through animal symbols in art, ritual, ceremony, dance, literature, and religion. These symbols, and the accompanying literature, such as the *Mahabharata* and the *Ramayana*, will continue to give traditional knowledge greater value and prestige by tracing it back to a supernatural origin in nature. Naga, Garuda, Ganesh, Hanuman, and Loro Kidul will continue to be symbolic heroes who illustrate society's values about people and nature.

The successful leaders of the fifth revolution will build on the age-old foundations of nature, and use nature's symbols to enhance their power. They might well resemble the ancient god-kings more closely than the current crop of rational technocrats who flourish because they are efficient in meeting the needs of the world system of trade. But as people become more self-reliant, they will need systems of government which are better able to meet psychological and spiritual needs rather than primarily material ones. In the challenging times ahead, the new charismatic leaders will find it useful to claim traditional ancestors, including the powerful animals which symbolize the forces of nature. They will associate themselves with historical figures who consolidated their power by enlisting nature as an ally, including people like Kaundinya, Joyoboyo, Rama Khamhaeng, Senopati, Diponegoro, Sukarno, Surin, and Sam Bram.

Spiritualism. People of the fifth revolution will wish to maintain, even strengthen, their ties to the natural world, and communication with nature through spirits will remain one of the best psychological tools for doing so. Irrespective of the dominant major religion, the entire region is teeming with spirits—*Nat* in Burma, *Phii* in Thailand, and *Jin* in Indonesia and Malaysia. Societies have always found spiritual forces useful for enforcing community solidarity and helping to discourage people from taking more from nature than nature can continue to produce. Spirits and other deeply held religious beliefs have been a powerful force for building the sense of community, so various forms of spiritualism will continue to thrive and help people deal with the unexpected and uncontrollable.

Thai farmers near Chiengmai conduct a ceremony to appease the guardian spirit of Mae On River in order to ensure enough rain for a good harvest. For the past five years, they have also evoked a curse on log poachers in the area, because deforestation has led to reduced rainfall. According to Thong Kantha, the provincial councilor who led the 100 farmers in the cursing ceremony, "Anyone who fells trees will be punished by the spirits with misfortune or death." The 1986 ceremony was held in pouring rain.

Dr. Boonsong, a good Buddhist, was convinced that the sin of killing animals—hunting big game in his youth for sport, and later collecting specimens for scientific study—had affected his fate and that he would suffer a lingering death as a result. We tried to argue that his good works had saved far more wildlife than he had killed, so the balance between merit and sin was surely heavily in his favor. After all, he had won the prestigious J. Paul Getty Wildlife Conservation Prize, conservation's Nobel Prize, "for his 30-year commitment to nature education and national parks," and is still the only Southeast Asian to have been so honored.

"No," he told us, with a resigned smile when we visited him from Indonesia in 1979. "I will have to pay for my sins by suffering. I have just come back from America, where I received the Getty Prize, and had a pacemaker installed in my chest. My body has been tampered with, just like the bodies of all the animals I've stuffed. That little machine will help me live longer, I suppose, but that's not always a blessing."

But Dr. Boonsong was reasonably content. One of his sons had returned to take over the clinic, and had quickly established himself as Thailand's leading ear, nose, and throat specialist. Following in his father's footsteps, he was developing new ways of bringing medical care to the country's most remote villages. And for the first time, Dr. Boonsong had the financial means to carry out his work; he was using the $50,000 that came with the Getty Prize to publish more books and spread more widely the conservation message he had preached all his life.

"I have been working for conservation for over forty years," he reflected, "and now there is almost no nature left." He said this with an ironic smile, as if recognizing his own folly in persisting with such a hopeless mission. "I remember how when I was a boy, the skies would be black with migrating ducks, elephants seemed to be everywhere, the forests teemed with wildlife, and Bangkok was a small city. Nobody had much money, but we all had enough to eat, we respected our religion, and we were happy. Now we are much more modern, much more numerous, and much more wealthy, but we have lost our serenity. We have sold our natural heritage to buy things that we don't really need, as if we believe that we can overcome the fundamental laws of nature. I *must* continue to fight to save whatever nature is left. It is the only thing I can do."

When we saw Dr. Boonsong six years later, in 1985, his conservation work had ended. He had suffered a stroke and was comatose, requiring around-the-clock nursing care. A hole had been cut in his throat to help him breathe, and his body had wasted away to a skeleton. We choked back tears. Although we weren't sure he could hear us, we told him that Thailand had just established its fifty-second national park. People *had* been listening to his advice. His eyes lit up, and he seemed to smile. We didn't have the heart to tell him that all of the parks suffer from poaching, conflicts with nearby villages, insufficient budgets, and a shortage of trained personnel.

When we visited him again late in 1986, Dr. Boonsong had slightly improved and could raise his right arm to greet us, although he still could not speak. Despite everything he had done to prevent the global marketplace from totally consuming Thailand's nature, his prophecy of personal suffering was coming true—he was paying for his sins of killing animals.

Karan Singh provided another perspective on spiritualism and eternity. "While terrestrial destruction is inevitable, there is ample cause for optimism," he told us. "Each of us can hasten our inner spiritual development so that we can achieve a state which *transcends* space and time. *Within* the space-time continuum everything must ultimately change and all forms sooner or later disappear, whether they last a billionth of a second or a billion centuries. However, the real miracle is that each one of us embodies a spark of consciousness which can in some way transcend the throbbing abyss of existence itself."

Spiritual forces which are strong enough to move men such as Dr. Boonsong and Karan Singh will surely guide the fifth revolution.

◆ ◆ ◆

The accuracy of Joyoboyo's prediction of the ultimate prosperity of the rural villagers depends on how well nature is able to survive the pressures of the global marketplace. How can nature conservation successfully address the needs of both wildlife and people in Southeast Asia in the coming decades?

Some of the most successful Balinese painters work in a manner similar to that used by several famous European Renaissance painters; the "name" artist conceives the design and paints the outline sketches while others fill in the blanks. Our outline for conservation action follows; we hope it will be fleshed out like a Balinese painting, by those with the necessary local knowledge, resources, and sensitivity. Conservation action will need to be custom-designed for each specific situation, as no universal panacea is likely to work.

One major concern is that the conservation business is not always run in a business-like manner. Western-oriented conservationists often sell what they are interested in rather than market projects that meet the needs of the "consumers," in this case rural people. Projects are funded which address the needs and desires of people in distant cities, seldom the needs of the people who rely on nature. We have seen many well-intentioned but locally irrelevant conservation projects succeed for brief moments, then sputter and die when external funding or the interest of the university scientist disappears.

Conservation projects have tended to be oriented to animals rather than to people. But conservation in Southeast Asia is far more a *social* challenge than a *biological* one. Most large animals will survive only if humans wish them to do so. Biologists and ecologists, to their credit, have led the conservation movement, but it is now time to enlist a far broader army, including anthropologists, sociologists, theologians, politicians, economists, historians, and communicators.

National parks, however well they might be managed, will never be sufficient by themselves to conserve nature in Southeast Asia. Rather than being fenced-in natural museums, natural areas should instead be managed to support social and economic development.

Some major national parks established for the good of a nation, or indeed for the world at large, may require outside assistance. But even these most important national parks should be designed and managed to contribute to the well-being of the people who live around them. Local people should serve on the advisory boards of the parks, have priority for park-related jobs, and be given opportunities to develop goods and services required by the park. People around the boundaries should be given preference for schools, health centers, family planning programs, public health schemes, and small hydroelectric facilities in recognition of the contributions the people are making to maintain the natural areas for the future welfare of humanity.

Building on self-sufficiency and local responsibility does not mean isolating people from the rest of the world; we are not "people who spend most of their time looking forward to the past," as playwright John Osborne put it. Outsiders will always want access to and influence in the rural areas for a variety of reasons, and local people will want some goods that can come only from distant markets.

But we also think that once oil no longer provides the energy for the global marketplace, regardless of what might replace it, the level of international trade will be significantly reduced. Judging from the rate at which nature has been plundered in Southeast Asia, it appears that a sustainable level of exploitation has already been exceeded. National governments are unlikely to find this sufficient justification to reduce their participation in the international marketplace, and will surely try to increase international trade and to convince international aid agencies to fund projects which are aimed at promoting such trade.

So development money continues to pour in to Southeast Asia, often laying waste to nature in the process and rarely contributing to conservation. In seeking to ensure the maximum sustainable benefit from this powerful outside influence, government officials and development promoters should reread their history books and resist the urge to construct grandiose Angkor Wat-type projects. They should insist instead on small-scale local developments which are not dependent on continuing major outside contributions of money, materials, or expertise. They should think small, enhance rather than destroy natural ecosystems, promote local adaptations to local environmental conditions, insist on at least some local funding, and involve local people so that the projects evolve from discussions and interchanges with people from the villages.

In the long run, the local communities must retain a vested interest in managing living resources in a manner which benefits both village and nation. When local people earn money from the forest in their backyard, they can be expected to do a better job of ensuring that the exploitation is done in a sustainable manner. Timber operators might think twice about indiscriminately felling trees if they live in the adjacent village.

Today, even the most remote people are tied into the global marketplace through the mass media. We watched television one night in a new settlement populated by about eighty Badui, who had somehow been seduced by the Indonesian government to leave behind their more determinedly isolationist neighbors and resettle near their remote ancestral homelands southwest of Jakarta. While living in their previous forest homes, the Badui were forbidden by local custom to have any contact with outsiders or to purchase anything not made locally. We sat quietly in a rustic community center while the curious Badui villagers watched the news of antinuclear demonstrations in England, a space-rocket launch in Florida, and a football game in Singapore. When a commercial we had made to convince people to buy a certain brand of candy was broadcast, we felt uneasy about the role we had played in enticing the Badui to become part of the international marketplace. They no longer controlled their own destinies.

But the right to buy manufactured candy is not the main point. Communicators have power and talent, and have a responsibility to use them for the public good. The communications abilities found in the advertising, publishing, journalism, and marketing worlds should be channeled toward reawakening interest in traditional conservation knowledge in Southeast Asia.

Already imaginative communicators are using traditional heroes to convey social messages. The Indonesian family planning board has successfully used the *Ramayana* characters to promote the idea that two children are enough. Similar tactics could help save the forests and wildlife. Naga, Garuda, Ganesh, Hanuman, and Loro Kidul are symbolic heroes who illustrate fundamental truths about people and nature. They could be used in place of Hollywood starlets, Chinese kung-fu fighters, and British rock heroes to promote new ideas, and could be effective images to convey the responsibility people have toward the creatures of jungle and plain.

Interest in traditional conservation knowledge needs to be reawakened in Southeast Asia. Research on traditional means of conservation should be a high priority, before these cultural elements are washed away by the temporary high tide of the global marketplace.

Cultural diversity parallels ecological diversity. The examples in this book demonstrate ways and means of relating people to wildlife that are interwoven into the fabric of rural cultures throughout the region. People and animals are integrated elements of healthy, functioning, evolving societies. Any development programs, conservation projects, laws, or regulations emanating from central governments should be adapted to take advantage of local predispositions, such as the use of *pawang harimau* to control problem tigers in Sumatra. Traditional cultural approaches to conservation should be employed where they still exist, or rekindled where they have receded.

◆ ◆ ◆

Most of the world's great religions have flourished in Southeast Asia, supported by sophisticated literature, art, and philosophy. But it would be wrong to consider the region a Shangri-la; rural life has always been subject to the vagaries of xenophobic jealousies, weather, volcanoes, marauding animals, pestilence, epidemics, and military adventures. But in the turmoil, people and animals have lived in reasonable balance, and it is likely that this productive balance will work again in the future. Cycles turn. A fifth revolution will come. It is likely that the people of Southeast Asia will be among the leaders, and the prime beneficiaries.

Scientific Names of Species

THESE NAMES are presented in alphabetical order in their English form, categorized into reptiles, birds, mammals, and plants, followed by any local names used in the book (I = Indonesian; M = Malay; T = Thai), then the Latin binomial.

REPTILES
American alligator; *Alligator mississipiensis*
Asian python; *Python molurus*
Chinese alligator; *Alligator sinensis*
Common cobra; *Naja naja*
Estuarine (saltwater) crocodile; buaya (I, M) all crocs; *Crocodylus porosus*
False gavial; *Tomistoma schlegeli*
Gavial; *Gavialis gangeticus*
King cobra; *Ophiophagus hannah*
Komodo dragon; *Varanus komodoensis*
Leatherback turtle; *Dermochelys coriacea*
Malayan pit viper; *Agkistrodon rhodostoma*
Many-banded krait; *Bungarus multicinctus*
Monitor; bewak, biawak (I, M); *Varanus* spp.
New Guinea crocodile; *Crocodylus novaeguineae*
Philippine crocodile; *Crocodylus philippinensis*
Russell's viper; *Vipera russellii*
Siamese crocodile; *Crocodylus siamensis*

BIRDS
Banded kingfisher; embuas (M); *Lacedo pulchella*
Brahminy kite; *Haliastur indus*
Brown shrike; ketik (M); *Lanius cristatus*
Common coucal; *Centropus sinensis*

Crested jay; bejampong (M); *Platylophus galericulatus*
Diard's trogon; papau, kalabu (M); *Harpactes diardii*
Dusky thrush; *Turdus naumanni*
Edible-nest swiftlet; *Collocalia fuciphaga*
Fruit pigeons; *Ptilinopus* spp.
Hornbills; Bucerotidae
Maleo fowl; *Macrocephalon maleo*
Maroon woodpecker; pangkas (M); *Blythipicus rubiginosus*
Munia, Javan; *Lonchura leucogastroides*
Red jungle fowl; ayam hutan (M); *Gallus gallus*
Rhinoceros hornbill; kenyalang (Iban, I); *Buceros rhinoceros*
Ruddy shelduck; *Tadorna ferruginea*
Rufous piculet; ketupong, kikih (M); *Sasia abnormis*
Sarus crane; *Grus antigone*
Scarlet-rumped trogon; beragai (M); *Harpactes duvaucelli*
Sparrow hawk; lang (M); *Accipiter gularis*
White-eyed river martin; *Pseudochelidon sirintarae*
White-rumped shama; nendak (M); *Copsychus malabaricus*
Yellow wagtail; beras-beras (M); *Motacilla flava*

MAMMALS

Anoa; *Anoa depressicornis*
Asian black bear; *Selenarctos thibetanus*
Asian elephant; chang (T), gajah (I, M); *Elephas maximus*
Asian two-horned or Sumatran rhinoceros; krasoo (T); *Dicerorhinus sumatrensis*
Babirusa; *Babyrousa babyrussa*
Banded linsang; *Prionodon linsang*
Banded palm civet; *Hemigalus derbyanus*
Bandicoot rat; *Bandicota indica*
Banteng; banteng (M, I); *Bos javanicus*
Barking deer; kijang (M); *Muntiacus muntjak*
Beaked whale; *Mesoplodon* sp.
Clouded leopard; rimau dahan (M); *Neofelis nebulosa*
Common treeshrew; *Tupaia glis*
Dugong; *Dugong dugon*
Eld's deer; *Cervus eldi*
False killer whale; *Pseudorca crassidens*
Ferret-badger, Burmese; *Melogale personata*
Gaur; *Bos gaurus*
Greater Asian one-horned; or Indian rhinoceros; *Rhinoceros unicornis*
Hog deer; *Cervus (Axis) porcinus*
Hog-nosed bat, Kitti's; *Craseonycteris thonglongyai*
Javan rhinoceros; badak Jawa (I); *Rhinoceros sondaicus*

Kloss gibbon; bilou (I); *Hylobates klossi*
Kouprey; *Bos sauveli*
Langur; *Presbytis* spp.
Leopard; kuching batu (M); *Panthera pardus*
Leopard cat; *Felis bengalensis*
Long-tailed macaque; kera (M); *Macaca fascicularis*
Malay civet; *Viverra tangalunga*
Malayan tapir; badak murai (M); *Tapirus indicus*
Mentawai langur; joja (I); *Presbytis potenziani*
Mentawai macaque; bokkoi (I); *Macaca pagensis*
Moonrat; *Echinosorex gymnurus*
Mouse deer; kancil, pelandok (M); *Tragulus* spp.
Norway rat; tikus (M) all spp.; *Rattus norvegicus*
Orangutan; maias, mawas (I); *Pongo pygmaeus*
Otter civet; *Cynogale bennetti*
Pangolin; tenggiling (M); *Manis* spp.
Pig-tailed langur; simakobu (I); *Simias concolor*
Pig-tailed macaque; berok (M); *Macaca nemestrina*
Pilot whale; *Globicephalus* sp.
Porcupine; *Hystrix* spp.
Rhesus macaque; *Macaca mulatta*
Rice field rat; *Rattus argentiventer*
Roof rat; *Rattus rattus*
Sambar deer; rusa (M); *Cervus unicolor*
Schomburgk's deer; *Cervus schomburgki*
Serow; *Capricornis sumatraensis*
Sperm whale; *Physeter catodon*
Stump-tailed macaque; *Macaca arctoides*
Sulawesi macaque; *Macaca maurus*
Sumatran hare; *Nesolagus netscheri*
Sun bear; beruang (I, M); *Helarctos malayanus*
Tiger; harimau (I), rimau (M); *Panthera tigris*
Wild pig; babi hutan (I, M); *Sus scrofa*
Wild water buffalo; khwai paa (T); *Bubalus bubalis*

PLANTS
Blowpipe-dart poison; *Antiaris toxicaria*
Phallus lily; *Amorphophallus titanum*
Stinking corpse lily; *Rafflesia arnoldi*
Tuba root/Derris; tuba (M, I); *Derris elliptica*

Local Terms
and Mythological Figures

adu domba (Indonesian): Ram fight.

Airavata (Sanskrit): Four-tusked white elephant and mount of Indra, god of the heavens. Airavata represents rain clouds, lightning, and the rainbow; he is a forerunner of *Ganesh*.

air mata duyung (Indonesian): Dugong's tears, thought to have medical and aphrodisiac properties.

amerta (Balinese): See *amrita*.

amrita (Sanskrit): The ambrosia that bestows immortality, created by the gods by churning the Sea of Milk.

apasara (Thai); *apsara* (Sanskrit): An entrancing celestial nymph.

arak (Malay, Indonesian): Homemade distilled rice liquor drunk in vast quantities in Borneo.

ayam (Malay, Indonesian): Chicken.

barong (Balinese): The lion/dragon-like hero in Balinese mythology.

Bhinneka Tunggal Ika (Indonesian): Unity in Diversity, the Indonesian national motto.

Boddhisatva (Hindi): "Essence" *(sattva)* is "illumination" *(bodhi)*. Incarnate Buddha; one of the forms the Buddha took before he was incarnated in human form as the Lord Buddha.

bomoh (Malay): Malay healer/magician.

Brahma (Hindi); *Phra Phram* (Thai): Creator of the universe and first god in the supreme Hindu triad which includes *Vishnu* and *Siva*.

Brahmin (Hindi): A worshiper of *Brahma*, of the highest caste in Hinduism and generally of the priestly order.

Buddha: Lit., "the enlightened one." An historical personage named Siddhartha Gautama (died c. 483 B.C.); the founder of Buddhism.

burii (Thai): Cigarette, hand-rolled cheroot.

Burong Apui (Iban): Lit., Fire bird, a mythological hornbill capable of great magic.

chang (Thai): Elephant.

chang pheuak (Thai): White or albino elephant.

chapati (Hindi): Wheat pancake/bread.

dalang (Indonesian): The puppeteer and narrator of the *wayang kulit* shadow plays.

Dayak (Malay): Refers to all the indigenous tribes of Sarawak, including Iban, Kayan, Kelabit, etc.

demit (Javanese): A spirit, often benevolent; sometimes used by a magician to refer to himself.

dharma (Sanskrit): Moral and religious duty; ethical doctrine developed by Buddhism and adopted by Hinduism.

dukun (Indonesian): Indonesian healer/magician/fortune-teller.

Erawan (Thai, from *Airavata):* Three-headed elephant.

esok (Malay, Indonesian): Tomorrow.

eyang (Javanese): Grandmother.

gado-gado (Indonesian): Vegetable salad with peanut sauce.

gajah (Sanskrit, now Malay, Indonesian): Elephant.

gamelan (Indonesian): Javanese or Balinese percussion orchestra, with tonal systems entirely different from western tuning systems.

Ganesh (Hindi); *Pra Khanek* (Thai); *Prah Kenes* (Cambodian); *Maha-Pienne* (Burmese); *Kuan-Shi Tien* (Chinese): Hindu/Buddhist elephant-headed god of wisdom, humor, and new ventures.

gap khao (Thai): Thai cuisine, lit., "with rice."

Garuda (Sanskrit); *Krut* (Thai): Mount of Vishnu; mythical figure that is part bird, part man; symbol of the sun and destroyer of serpents.

Gawai Kenyalang (Malay): Hornbill festival, celebrated in great style by the Iban of Sarawak.

Gerebeg Maulud (Indonesian): Celebration honoring birth of Prophet Mohammed.

halak (Malay): Magician-healer of the Orang Asli.

Hanuman (Sanskrit, now Thai, Malay, Indonesian): Monkey general; king of monkeys; important character in the Ramayana.

harimau (Malay, Indonesian, also *macan*): Tiger, sometimes any big cat.

ho-ting (Mandarin): Hornbill ivory.

hti (Burmese): Cap; sacred ornament at the tip of a pagoda.

Iban (Malay): The most numerous hill tribe group in Sarawak, also called Sea Dayak although they live inland.

ikat (Indonesian): Tie-dye technique in which segments of the thread are dyed before weaving begins.

Jataka Tales (Sanskrit): Animal fables about the Buddha's earlier incarnations.

kaiko (Papua New Guinea, local): Year-long pig festival celebrated by Maring tribe.

kaja (Balinese): "Towards the mountain," the Balinese concept of facing inland, toward the positive power of the holy volcanoes, and away from *kelod*, "toward the sea," a negative and disorienting direction.

karapan sapi (Indonesian): Bull racing held on island of Madura off eastern Java.

Karei (Malay, traditional): Supreme being of Orang Asli.

karma (Sanskrit): In Buddhism and Hinduism, the force generated by a person's actions; the motivating power for the cycle of deaths and re-births until *nirvana* is reached.

kawok (Indonesian): Euphemism for rats used in cooking, from Menado, Sulawesi.

kecak (Balinese): The famous monkey dance.

kekayon (Indonesian): The cosmic mountain symbolizing the harmony of nature, generally presented at the beginning of *wayang kulit* perfor-mance. Also called *gunungan*, or mountain.

kelod (Balinese): See *kaja.*

kenyalang (Malay, Indonesian): "Guided hornbill" used by the Iban to at-tack the spirits of their enemies. Also refers to all hornbills in general.

khwan nag (Thai): "Gift of the Naga," the ordination of new Buddhist monks.

kraton (Indonesian): Palace, generally, but not exclusively, for Javanese royalty.

kris (Malay, Indonesian): Wavy- or straight-bladed ceremonial dagger, often with magical powers.

lingam (Sanskrit): Hindu religious symbol generally in monumental phallic form. A symbol of Siva and virility, the opposite of the *yoni*.

Mahabharata: One of the two classic Hindu epics (see *Ramayana),* its 100,000 couplets (eight times the length of the combined *Iliad* and *Odys-sey)* may make it the longest epic poem in the world. Tells of a tremen-dous eighteen-day battle between the five Pandawa brothers (good guys) and their hundred cousins, the evil Kurawas. Contains the *Bha-gavad Gita.*

mahout (Hindi): Elephant trainer.

maias, also *mawas* (Malay, Indonesian): Local name in Borneo for orang-utan.

mai pen rai (Thai): "Never mind, it's not important."

mantra (Sanskrit): Generally Buddhist, a spoken formula of great magic power.

mautouw (Thai): Master mahout.

maw phii (Thai): Thai magician/healer.

mondop (Thai): Seven-tiered Buddhist temple.

mupakat (Indonesian): Discussion, usually part of the process of *musjawarat.*

musjawarat (Indonesian): Prolonged deliberation at the end of which con-sensus is reached; the traditional Javanese way of settling thorny issues.

Naga (Sanskrit); *nag* (Thai): Wise serpent; the female counterpart is *nagini*.

Refers to the gods of the underworld which control water; also refers to the king cobra.

nasi padang (Indonesian): "Rice from Padang," brain curry, rendang, chili-fried chicken, other goodies served in great, heart-burning quantities. A significant cuisine.

nenek (Indonesian): Grandmother, ancestor, epithet for tiger.

nirvana (Sanskrit): Lit., "extinction," but in Buddhism expanded to mean the dissolution of all individual desire, the attainment of supreme knowledge.

om mani padme hum (Sanskrit): "Hail to the jewel in the lotus," the classic Buddhist mantra; among the pious the first words taught a child and the last uttered on the deathbed. The lotus symbolizes universal being, the jewel referring to the individuality of the utterer.

onom (Sundanese): Spirits, generally pre-Islamic.

Orang Asli (Malay): Lit., "original people." The isolated groups found in the forests of peninsular Malaysia. The term Orang Asli is preferred to the commonly used but derogatory "Sakai."

orangutan (Malay, Indonesian): "Man of the forest," the large red ape found in Borneo and Sumatra, usually called *maias* by locals.

pak (Indonesian): Father. Honorific for most people older than yourself.

palang (Malay, Indonesian): Lit., "crossbar," but in Sarawak describes natural crosspiece on rhino's penis and similar, surgically implanted joy stick in men.

parang (Malay, Indonesian): Long-bladed bush knife; machete.

pawang manangkok harimau (Indonesian): Practitioner of magical arts who specializes in capturing man-eating tigers.

pete (Indonesian): Long, broad bean; has odor that lingers.

phon andung (Sumba, Sumbawa): Skull tree found in royal villages in Sumba and Sumbawa, and a well-known pattern on woven textiles of these islands.

prahu (Malay, Indonesia): Dugout canoe.

puliaijat (Indonesian-Siberut): Ceremony, usually involving sacrifices.

punden (Javanese): Holy place.

Raja Gamiling (Malay): Borneo lord of fish.

Rama (Hindi, now many others): A Hindu hero-god, the seventh incarnation of Vishnu, whose story is told in the *Ramayana;* a relation to the current Thai royal family.

Ramayana: One of the two classic Hindu epics (see *Mahabharata)* and the most influential piece of literature/mythology throughout Southeast Asia. Major characters include virtuous Prince *Rama,* his beautiful wife Sita, the villainous Rawana, and the loyal, mischievous monkey general *Hanuman.*

rendang (Malay, Indonesian): Spicy beef cooked for hours in coconut milk.

rumbin (Papua New Guinea, local): Small sacred tree planted by Maring to indicate start of period of pig-rearing.

sambal belachan (Indonesian): Powerful condiment made from rotten prawns and chili.

sampur (Indonesian): Long, thin, Isadora Duncan-like scarf.

sapeh (Malay): A homemade three-stringed guitar-like instrument played by some of the hill tribes of Borneo.

Sarutana (Indonesian): Magical sword presented to Diponegoro by Loro Kidul.

sate torpedo (Indonesian): Grilled brochettes of ram's testicles; thought to give men propulsion like a submarine rocket.

sawah (Malay, Indonesian): Irrigated rice field.

Serat Sakondar (Indonesian): Revisionist history book of Yogyakarta *kraton* origin, eighteenth century.

sikerei (Siberut): Medicine man, ritual specialist.

silat (Malay, Indonesian): Unarmed martial art, similar to karate, kung fu, etc.

Siva (Hindi); *Phra Siwa* (Thai): Complex Hindu deity, takes many forms. Member of the supreme Hindu triad, along with *Brahma* and *Vishnu;* god of destruction and creation.

songkok (Malay, Indonesian): Fez-like Indonesian cap, generally black velvet, commonly worn by Muslims (but never by non-Muslims). In Malaysia sometimes a white skullcap to signify that the wearer is a *Haji*— has been to Mecca.

sop kambing (Indonesian): Goat soup, very stimulating or "heaty," a man's meal.

Susuhunan (Javanese): Ruler, lit., "he who is above all other people," title of ruling prince of Solo, central Java.

tahi (Malay, Indonesian): Merde.

Tanah Air (Indonesian): Lit. "earth and water"; the way Indonesians describe their country of 13,600 islands.

takraw (Thai); *sepak raga* (Malay): A popular combination of volleyball and kickball played throughout Thailand, Malaysia, Indonesia; uses grapefruit-sized woven rattan ball.

than khao (Thai): Eating, lit., "to eat rice."

than khao laew ru yang (Thai): "Have you eaten rice yet?"

Traiphum: Sacred Buddhist texts.

transmigrasi (Indonesian): From the English "transmigration," the government-sponsored movement of people from Java and Bali to the outlying islands.

tuak (Malay): Home-brewed rice wine offered to visitors in excessive quantities by Sarawak hill tribes.

tuan (Indonesian): Sir.

ulu (Malay): Upriver.

Vishnu (Hindi): One of the supreme Hindu triad with *Brahma* and *Siva*. The preserver and savior of the world, he appears in an incarnation whenever needed, often riding *Garuda*.

wali (Indonesian): An Islamic religious leader.

wat (Thai): Buddhist temple.

wayang kulit (Malay, Indonesian): Lit., "leather puppet," the popular shadow play.

yoni (Sanskrit): The female reproductive organs; when joined with *lingam*, symbol of divine procreative energy.

Further Reading

This section includes the most important or generally informative publications on the subject covered by each chapter. These readings, complemented by the full bibliography, will enable the interested reader to delve more deeply into the various subjects.

SEARCHING FOR NATURAL ANSWERS

There are many good general overviews of Southeast Asia. A few we have found most entertaining or particularly useful are Wallace (1869), Raffles (1817), Bloodworth (1970), LeBar (1972), LeBar, Hickey, and Musgrave (1964), and Hall (1968). Helpful guidebooks include the Apa series and the Lonely Planet guidebooks. The numerous periodicals in the region frequently contain fascinating accounts of people and nature. The daily newspapers provide a constant stream of fresh material, while more thoughtful analyses are included in such publications as the *Journal of the Siam Society,* the *Sarawak Museum Journal, Quaternary Research in Southeast Asia, Asia Perspectives, Far Eastern Economic Review,* and *Asiaweek.* Good general introductions to the wildlife of the region are MacKinnon and MacKinnon (1974); Lekagul and McNeely (1977b); Medway (1977, 1978); Prater (1965); U Tun Yin (1967); Lekagul (1968); King, Woodcock, and Dickenson (1975); and Smythies (1960).

SEAS OF IMMORTALITY, VOICES OF FIRE

Campbell (1974) has written a book one critic calls a "philosophical *Whole Earth Catalog*," which not only includes the basic origin myths of Asia but compares them with similar tales from other parts of the world and other cultural systems. Bellwood (1985) provides an excellent overview of the geological history of Southeast Asia. The *Eka Dasa Rudra* ceremonies are described and illustrated by Fox (1982); the best firsthand account of the Gunung Agung eruption is Mathews (1983). Stommel and Stommel

(1983) provide a detailed investigation of the impact of the Tambora eruption on the weather of Europe and the United States. Simkin and Fiske (1983) have compiled a fairly complete record of the Krakatau eruption and its aftermath, including a number of the original accounts.

FLAMES AND FARMERS

Hough (1926) is the authoritative review of the role of fire in human culture. Spencer (1966) and Wharton (1957, 1966, 1968) thoroughly cover the impact of shifting cultivation in Southeast Asia. Gorman (1971) and Solheim (1972) describe their discoveries of early agriculture. Lekagul and McNeely (1977a) reconstruct the ecological history of man in Thailand, while LeBar, Hickey, and Musgrave (1964) and LeBar (1972) document the diversity of ethnic groups in mainland and insular Southeast Asia, respectively. The prehistory of Southeast Asia is thoroughly discussed by Bellwood (1978, 1985). Geertz (1963) is the definitive study of ecological change caused by changes in agriculture in Indonesia. McNeely (1978a) covers the dynamics of extinction in Southeast Asia.

RICE AND ROYALTY

The story of rice has generated a vast literature. Useful overviews include Hanks (1972), Barker, Herdt, and Rose (1985), Norlund, Cederroth, and Gerdin (1986), and Chang (1985). Covarrubias (1972) provides an excellent picture of the rice culture of Bali. The coming of the god-kings is well covered by Audric (1972), Gesick (1983), Hall (1968), Groslier (1966b), and Coedes (1968). The water buffalo, probably the most important of all domestic animals in the rice-growing cultures, is addressed by National Academy of Sciences (1981) and Cockrill (1967).

TRADERS AND INVADERS

The history of the conquest of Southeast Asia by the colonial powers is addressed by Hall (1968) and Osborne (1985). Raffles (1817) gives a complete picture of the early years of the colonization of Java, while Vlekke (1965) and Neill (1973) cover all of Indonesia; Koentjaraningrat (1975) covers Indonesia and Malaysia. McNeely (1975) and McNeely and Ludwig (1978) provide an overview of the agricultural development of the lower Mekong Basin and the ways that protected areas were proposed to be incorporated in the overall scheme. Lester Brown (1986) analyzes the state of the world's environment through economics, including trade patterns.

STAIRWAYS TO HEAVEN

Perhaps the most accessible *Ramayana* in English is by William Buck (1976). A good, but hard to find, abridged version is by Sunardjo Haditjoroko (1975); even better is the *Ramayana* comic book, one of an excellent and vast series on Indian legends and folk tales put out by Amar Chitra Katha (India Book House Education Trust, Bombay). Fraser (1966) is a good introduction to primitive art worldwide; more to our purposes, it includes the famous essay by Heine-Geldhern on the movement of people into Southeast Asia as represented by their art—Barbier (1984) tears into Heine-Geldhern's theory with bare-knuckled glee. Rawson (1967) is a compact single volume introduction to the art of the region, with an emphasis on architecture. Claire Holt (1967) provides the best overview of Indonesian art, and Zimmer (1946, 1955) puts the whole picture into the perspective of myths and symbols. Gittinger (1979) covers the varied textile arts of Indonesia. Ramseyer (1977) gives a well-illustrated account of the art of Bali and its cultural importance.

Protector of the Buddha

The role of *nagas* in early Cambodian civilization is discussed in detail by Audric (1972), Coedes (1963, 1968), and Groslier (1966). Chou Ta-Kuan (1967-1298) provides the best eyewitness account of Angkor at the height of its splendor; he spent a year in Cambodia in 1296–1297. Jung (1964) presents an excellent discussion of snakes as symbols of transcendence between the underworld and earth, representing the conflict in our lives between adventure and discipline, or evil and virtue, or freedom and security. Popular works on snakes include Minton and Minton (1973) and Morris and Morris (1965). Zimmer (1946) and Holt (1967) cover various aspects of nagas in the art of Southeast Asia. Hickey (1982b) provides detailed information on the Vietnamese python-naga messiah.

Garuda, the Power of the Sun

Sandin (1977) covers the hornbill festival in great detail, including translations of all the chants. Smythies (1960) contains a large amount of material on bird lore of Borneo, while Cammann (1951) discusses Chinese carvings in Bornean hornbill ivory. The mythology and symbolism of Garuda is covered by Zimmer (1946, 1955), and Holt (1967, 1972) discusses the role of Garuda in Indonesian art and culture; the early history is covered by Diskul (1980). For popular articles on hornbills, see McClure (1980) and Wachtel (1981a). Hose and McDougall (1912) cover many aspects of life in Borneo, including the great peacemaking of 1899. Wachtel (1972) gives a picture of the Baram regatta.

Ganesh, the Potbellied Elephant God

The standard work on Ganesh is Getty (1936); its introduction by Foucher also provides stimulating insights. Coomaraswamy and Nivedita (1967-1913) contain a full explanation of Ganesh in Hindu and Buddhist belief. Zimmer (1946) provides his usual sound explanations of the symbolic importance of Ganesh and *Airavata*. Schnitger (1964) describes his discovery of Ganesh images in Sumatra, and Geertz (1960) defines the role of Ganesh in the religion of Java. Campbell (1962) and Rawson (1967) describe Buddhist rites relating to Ganesh.

The White Elephant

Lekagul and McNeely (1977b) describe the physical characteristics of white elephants in Thailand. U Toke Gale (1967) is the best single source on white elephants in Burma and, to a lesser degree, elsewhere in Southeast Asia. Sanderson (1960) and Carrington (1958) also cover aspects of white elephants. Bock (1884) covers the white elephant in the late nineteenth century; and MacFie (1978) and Prateepchaikul (1976) describe the modern ceremonies. Jumsai (1970) and Wales (1973) are leading authorities on the white elephant wars.

Mermaid Queens and Javanese Sultans

On the history of Loro Kidul's impact on Indonesia, see Ricklefs (1974), Vlekke (1965), Fowler, Cale and Bartlett (1974), and Lee (1976). Sir Stamford Raffles (1817), the first (and only) British governor of Java, produced an excellent history of Java which contains much on Senopati, Diponegoro, and Sultan Agung. Bocquet (1980) is the best available summary on the life and impact of Loro Kidul. On dugongs, see Compost (1980), Prater (1928), and Lekagul and McNeely (1977b). Wachtel (1977b) is a popular version of the Loro Kidul story.

Messengers of the Gods

Smythies (1960) covers the use of birds in Iban augury, especially in the papers by Harrisson and Freeman; this information is updated by Richards (1972). Harrisson (1959) describes his adventures with the Kelabits during World War II, including considerable information on omens. Hose and McDougall (1912) include descriptions of bird omens in action. Data on bird omens among the Kenyah are provided by Richards (1972) and among the Dayak by Gomes (1911). MacDonald (1956), the governor-general of Malaya and Borneo immediately after World War II, has written a perceptive, and at times touching, account of life in Sarawak. He also is one of the few visitors to remark at length on the grace and beauty of the local maidens. Morrison's (1965) picture book is a fine introduction to the traditional day-to-day life in Sarawak that is fast disappearing while O'Hanlon (1984) gives an amusing and informative traveler's account of rural Sarawak life.

The Soul of the Tiger

Skeat (1900) is the classic work on Malay magic, even providing some of the chants that accompany the magic; he provides information on a wide range of animals that transform into people and vice versa. Schilling

(1957) gives several accounts of were-tigers, anecdotes that may or may not be fiction. Locke (1954), an army officer in the (then) Malayan Civil Service, is in the best tradition of English gentlemen scholars—he presents a mélange of hunting stories, anecdotes, interviews, speculation, and humor. Carey (1976) is the best single volume introduction to the *Orang Asli,* and contains information about their tiger-spirits; Schebesta (1973) contains more of the ancient lore of these australoid pygmies. Hose and McDougall (1912) recount numerous tales of metempsychosis and transmogrification from Borneo. Lee (1976), Mulder (1978), and Fowler, Cale, and Bartlett (1974) give general insights into the importance of mysticism in the Indonesian scheme of things. Eibl-Eibesfeldt (1972) is a classic on how and why human societies band together and distrust outsiders. Zoete and Spies (1938) includes a section by Spies discussing Balinese *leyaks.*

BLOOD SPORTS

More details on the various blood sports are found in Wachtel (1977a, 1977b, 1978b). The psychology of Balinese cockfighting is investigated by Geertz (1973) and Stoddart (1981). Lee (1976) discusses some of the mystical aspects of Indonesian blood sports. Head-hunting, the ultimate blood sport, is discussed by Powell (1922), McKinley (1976), Rosaldo (1980), Bock (1985), and Gomes (1911), while cannibalism—taking the blood sport to the ultimate conclusion—is covered by Powell (1922) and Davies (1981). Animal sacrifice, which takes the blood without the sport, is discussed by Campbell (1962, 1974), Condominas (1977), Baudesson (1910), and Hickey (1982a, b).

MONKEYS IN THE RAFTERS

The earliest report on Siberut is Crisp (1799). Loeb (1929) and Schefold (1972, 1979) provide good descriptions of the religious life. Whitten (1982) gives a charming account of a thirty-month stay on the island studying gibbons, while Tenaza (1975, 1976), Tilson (1976, 1977), and Tilson and Tenaza (1977) provide details on the primates and their relations with the people. Chasen and Kloss (1927) describe the mammalian fauna of the island. A conservation master plan for the island is presented by McNeely, Whitten, and Whitten (1980). Popular accounts are found in Hanbury-Tenison (1975), McNeely (1978c, 1979), and Mitchell and Weitzel (1983).

BOAR AND PEACE

Caldecott and Caldecott (1985) provide new insights into the importance of wild pigs to the economy of rural Sarawak. The aggressive behavior of wild pigs is covered by Wells (1925) and Pollock and Thom (1900). In New Guinea, the role of pigs in the ecology of highland people has been investigated by Rappaport (1968), and further explored by Harris (1974), who provides an easy-to-read explanation of pig-dom in New Guinea. The problem of pig tapeworm in Irian Jaya is reported by Desowitz (1983). Hoogerwerf (1970) discusses the early history of pig persecution in Java, as well as current ecology and behavior. The durian literature is as rich as the fruit; see especially Wallace (1962-1869), Whitney (1905), Bowring (1977-1857), Scidmore (1984-1899), and Wells (1925).

Jungle Tractors

Sanderson (1960) and Carrington (1958) are two outstanding general books on elephants, dealing with all aspects of both African and Indian species; each of these covers in much greater detail some of the matters dealt with here, though most of our material expands on their work. An extensive literature deals with working elephants: Gale (1967) is an expert writing about his own country; Marshall (1959) presents the story of an elephant worker in the teak forests of northern Thailand; Baze (1955) covers working elephants in Vietnam, concentrating on methods of capture; and Williams (1954) deals with the life of a superb working bull and his exploits in moving a column of elephants from Burma to Assam while being chased by the Japanese Imperial Army in World War II. Gale (1974), Sanderson (1960), and Carrington (1958) cover some of the capture techniques discussed in this chapter. The ceremonies involved in elephant capturing in Thailand are discussed by Giles (1929, 1931). Lekagul and McNeely (1976) present information about Thailand's elephant training school. For details of veterinary aspects of working elephants, see Evans (1910). Deraniyagala (1955) covers everything from anatomy to fossil relatives to ancient Indian lore. On ecology and behavior, Olivier (1978) presents an excellent summary of current knowledge, and includes complete information on current status and distribution throughout the range of the species. Seidensticker (1984) enumerates the ways and means of dealing with elephants as part of World Bank development projects.

Avengers in the Forest

The Minangkabau *pawang harimau* material is from Kartomi (1977). Raffles (1817) describes the tiger-banteng contests in eighteenth-century Java. By far the best study of the tiger in the wild is Schaller (1967). Mountfort (1981) recounts the genesis of Project Tiger. The fight to save the Javan tiger from extinction is summarized by Seidensticker (1977), while Hoogerwerf (1970) presents the early history of the Javan tiger. Popular books about tigers in Southeast Asia include Baze (1957), Locke (1954), Perry (1964), Schilling (1957), and Voorhoeve (1957), the last being a romanticized re-creation of a tiger's life.

HERE BE DRAGONS

Dragon lore is discussed by Allen and Griffiths (1979), Kakuzo (1940), Williams (1932), and Aero (1980). Carl Sagan (1977) presents a popular view of the collective unconsciousness based on dinosaurs and other "dragons of Eden." Guggisberg (1972) is the best general book on crocodiles and their folklore. Many of the travel and adventure books on Borneo include sections on crocodiles; the best is Hose and McDougall (1912). Descriptions of crocodile magicians are found in Bowring (1977-1857), Gomes (1911), and Powell (1922). Crocodiles on Siberut are discussed by Loeb (1929). On the colorful crocodile customs of eastern Indonesia, see Zimmerman (1863) and Minton and Minton (1973). The most interesting general book on crocodiles comes from Africa but is still worth mentioning for those interested: Graham and Beard (1963). Luxmoore, Barzdo, Broad, and Jones (1985) provide the most up-to-date directory of crocodilian "farming" operations. Fuller descriptions of Utai's crocodile farm are found in Yangprapkorn, McNeely, and Cronin (1971) and McNeely (1972). National Academy of Sciences (1983) provides an overview of crocodiles as a resource for the tropics, with particular emphasis on Papua New Guinea. Crocodile hunting in the swamps of New Guinea is described by Pinney (1976).

DRUGSTORES ON THE HOOF

The great work on Malay magic and traditional medicines is by Walter Skeat (1900, reprinted 1984), supported by Gimlette (1915, reprinted 1971) and Winstedt (1982). Krappe (1930) and Fraser (1959) provide the more general background. Esmond Bradley Martin (1979, 1981) has been the leading recent investigator on rhino horn, its trade and uses, Guggisberg (1966) provides an overview of rhino conservation, Hoogerwerf (1970) presents the situation in Java, Rookmaaker (1977) discusses Borneo, McNeely and Cronin (1972) and McNeely and Laurie (1976) cover Thailand, and Borner (1979) and van Strien (1985) deal with Sumatra. Tiger medicine among the Chinese and Malays is very well covered by Locke (1954), with other contributions made by Baudesson (c. 1912) and Perry (1964). Bock (1985-1881) discusses bezoar stones and snake fat medicines, Auffenberg (1982) deals with monitors, and Tan (1968) covers deer. See Wachtel and McNeely (1980) and McNeely and Wachtel (1981) and Wachtel (1987) for popular articles on medicinal animals. Myers (1984) provides a valuable basic reference for new discoveries with medicinal animals and deer ranching. Cousins (1977) investigates the medical mystery of the placebo.

ANIMAL BAZAAR

The most up-to-date information on the animal trade is published by the WWF-IUCN TRAFFIC offices and IUCN's Wildlife Trade Monitoring

Centre in the United Kingdom. Martin (1979, 1981) and Martin and Bradley (1982) are excellent references on trade in rhinoceros products. Nilsson (1977) examines the commercial cage bird trade. The *Sarawak Museum Journal* has published numerous articles on the importance of bird nests to local economies. The trade in bird nests is also covered by Smythies (1960).

BROWN IVORY

The International Primate Protection League is one of dozens of animal-rights groups whose newsletters serve up a regular diet of stories on the atrocities of the primate trade, and their abuses by laboratories. The Interagency Primate Steering Committee (1978) of the United States National Institutes of Health and Zimmerman (1976) present the other side of the story. The Chinese epic *Monkey*, by Wu Ch'eng-en, is available in an English translation by Waley (1942); another excellent work on Chinese primate lore is Van Gulik (1967)—Van Gulik was the Dutch ambassador to China and the author of the Judge Dee mystery series. For further information on the natural history of the Southeast Asian monkeys, see Roonwal and Mohnot (1977), Caldecott (1984), and Napier and Napier (1970). The newspaper stories referred to in the text are found in the Bibliography under "Anon."

EQUALS AMONG EQUALS

Orangutans have generated a massive literature. We feel the most innovative and insightful observer has been John MacKinnon (1974a, 1974b, 1977, 1978); he is the only one of the orang researchers to have also studied all the other apes—gibbons, siamangs, pygmy chimps, chimps, and gorillas. Competent long-term field studies have also been carried out by Rijksen (1978) and Schurmann (1982); short-term studies have been carried out by Schaller (1971) and a host of others. Biruté Galdikas (1975, 1979, 1980) holds the longevity record at fifteen years and still going strong, but her impact has been more on public relations than on science. Her work has nonetheless been important in bringing the plight of orangutans to the attention of both Indonesian government officials and the general public. In this, she follows in the footsteps of Barbara Harrisson (1963a, b). Of the early observers, Wallace (1869, reprinted 1962) is the most interesting and accessible. Yerkes and Yerkes (1929) provide an excellent summary of all that was known of orangs—in captivity as well as nature—at that time. Rijksen (1978) contains the most complete information on local orangutan lore. Morris and Morris (1966) cover the relationship between man and ape, especially in captivity. De Silva (1971) presents a view from within the region on the rehabilitation efforts in Sabah. Wachtel (1982a) is the only popular article published on Gary Shapiro's sign language project; for the original data see Shapiro (1985).

A Snowman in the Jungle

Kitti's hog-nosed bat is described in Lekagul and McNeely (1977b). The classic books on untrahoms are Heuvelmans (1965), Napier (1972), and Sanderson (1961). Shackley (1983) provides considerable information on the Chinese forms and their possible relationship with Neanderthal man. Recent popular accounts include Stephens (1971), Jaivin (1985), and Topping (1981). MacKinnon (1974a) presents the perspective of a scientist who meets untrahom evidence on the ground. McNeely, Cronin, and Emery (1973) review the yeti lore, while Blanford (1888–91) contains two eyewitness accounts of the *tua yeua*. Helton (1986) shows a fuzzy picture of what might be a yeti.

Return to the Wild

Harrisson (1963a) called the world's attention to orangutan conservation and gave birth to the rehabilitation effort; her (1963b) paper contains more details about the rehabilitation effort in Bako National Park of Sarawak. John MacKinnon (1977, 1978) made some highly original contributions to orang rehabilitation thinking, while Rijksen (1978) provided a sound analysis of the pros and cons of rehabilitation efforts. Biruté Galdikas (1975, 1980) describes some of her adventures with orangs, while De Silva (1971) presents a view from within the region on the rehabilitation efforts in Sabah. Wachtel (1979c) provides a look at the day-to-day activities at the Bohorok and Ketambe rehabilitation stations.

A Question of Breeding

Van Strien (1985b) and Borner (1979) are the only field scientists who have had the patience to study the Sumatran rhino, a large animal they hardly ever saw. Skafte (1962) gives a detailed blow-by-blow of how Sumatran rhinos are captured. The *Malayan Naturalist* issue of December 1985 has collected numerous newspaper articles, letters to the editor, and other material about the rhino capture efforts in Malaysia. Van Strien (1985a) describes the Singapore proposals and how they are being differentially implemented in Indonesia and Malaysia.

Gnawing Persistence

Frazer (1959) contains many stories on rats and people from the anthropological literature. Zinsser (1934) has written the classical work on how rats have affected history, while Hendrickson (1983) provides a social history of rats and people. The role of rats in art and mythology is covered by Williams (1932) and Zimmer (1946). Tales of rats and their depredations in Southeast Asia are included in Monteiro (n.d.), Mathews (1983), Shuyler and Ratanaworabhan (1970), Diamond (1985), Deoras (1966), Kurylas (1980), Fulk and Akhtar (1981), and Singh (1979). Canby

(1977) presents an outstanding popular article about rats. Lekagul and McNeely (1977b) discuss the ecology, behavior, and taxonomy of the thirty-six species of rats that occur in Thailand. Numerous anonymous newspaper articles cover beauty contests, rats as food, and problems farmers have with rats—they are listed in the Bibliography.

MONUMENTS TO FOLLY

The history of the Dumoga scheme is included in Sumardja, Tarmudji, and Wind (1984), Wind (1984), and Binnie and Partners (1976). Goldsmith and Hildyard (1984) extensively cover the problems of big dams in general; their work is a standard reference. The *International Dams Newsletter* highlights current dam problems. The case of the Bakun Dam is recounted by Apin (1986), Mohun and Sattaur (1987), and numerous Survival International publications. Our work for the Mekong Committee is reported in McNeely (1975) and McNeely and Ludwig (1977). Audric's (1972) description of the fall of Angkor is chillingly similar to the fall of Phnom Penh over 500 years later. Myrdal and Kessle (1970) cover the social implications of early Khmer policies. Christie (1983) provides a good picture of the classical state in early Java and why the great period of monument building was so short. McNeely (1986) presents an overview on how dams and wildlife can coexist in Asia. Check any regional news magazine or local newspaper for regular stories about the inappropriateness of "mega-development projects."

THE CYCLE OF PROGRESS

The Hindu version of the earth's destruction and rejuvenation, and calculations of the time spans of the various cycles, are covered in Campbell (1974). The *World Conservation Strategy* of IUCN (Anon., 1980) is a broad and widely accepted plan that argues predominantly economic reasons to save wildlife. Myers (1984) is an excellent general reference on tropical rain forest problems and possibilities. *The State of the Ark* (Durrell, 1986) and *The Gaia Atlas of Planet Management* (Myers, 1985) look at many of the current man-made influences on nature and conservation efforts. Hembree (1980), Barnes (1974, 1980), Tobing (1980), and Badil (1986) provide details on the sperm whale hunt in Lamalera.

THE FIFTH REVOLUTION

Many authors have tried to depict the future, but few of them take reasonable account of ecological reality. The exceptions tend to be novels, such as the classic *Earth Abides*, written in 1949 by George R. Stewart; others include *The Navigator*, by Morris West (1976), and *The Birth of an Island*, by Francois Clíment (1975). Schumacher (1973) is the classic defense of Buddhist economics. Many publications examine the status of nature conservation today: *International Wildlife, IUCN Bulletin, WWF News,*

The Ecologist, Environmental Conservation, Biological Conservation, Malayan Nature, National Geographic, Natural History Bulletin of the Siam Society, Suara Alam, and many others. Publications of Survival International and Cultural Survival examine the impact of development projects on local people.

Bibliography

Adams, M. J. 1980. "Myth, Ritual, and Textile." *Sawaddi*, November–December.

Adams, W. H. Davenport. 1880. *The Eastern Archipelago*. T. Nelson and Sons, London.

Adorno, T. W. 1950. *The Authoritarian Personality*. W. W. Norton and Co., New York.

Aero, Rita. 1980. *Things Chinese*. Doubleday & Co., Garden City, N.Y.

Ali, Abdul Kassim bin. n.d. "The Hidden Power of Shaman Masks from Sarawak." *Connaissance des Arts Tribaux* 19.

Allen, J. J. Golson, and R. Jones. 1977. *Sunda and Sahul: Prehistoric Studies in Southeast Asia, Melanesia, and Australia*. Academic Press, London.

Allen, Judy, and Jeanne Griffiths. 1979. *The Book of the Dragon*. Orbis Publishing, Ltd., London.

Andaya, L. Y. 1975. *The Kingdom of Johor, 1641–1728*. Oxford University Press, Kuala Lumpur, Malaysia.

Anon. 1966. "Filipino Beauty Contest Wipes Out 84,276 Rats." New York *Times* (UPI), February 8.

Anon. 1972. "Big Drive on Rats." Bangkok *Post*, February 3. Bangkok.

Anon. 1972. "Roasted Rats: Gourmet Way to Rid Pests." *Nation*, April 30. Bangkok.

Anon. 1972. "Rodents Are Nutritious." *Nation*, August 28. Bangkok.

Anon. 1975. *A Barefoot Doctor's Manual* (The American Translation of the Official Chinese Paramedical Manual). Running Press, Philadelphia.

Anon. 1978. "The Rats Are Winning." *Asiaweek*, June 2. Hong Kong.

Anon. 1978. "Time for Tiger Bone Wine? Shipments Prove It's Genuine." *Taiwan Trade Trends*. Taiwan.

Anon. 1980. "Beauty Queen Contest Turns Into a 'Rat Race.'" *Straits Times* (AFP), June 25. Singapore.

Anon. 1980. "Hama Tikus Menyerang Ribuan Hektar Tanaman Padi di Purbalingga." *Kompas*, May 29. Jakarta, Indonesia.

Anon. 1980. "Orang Utan, Kok Jadi Manja." *Tempo*, March 1. Jakarta, Indonesia.

Anon. 1980. "10,000 Jam Meneliti Orangutan di Hutan Kalimantan." *Kompas*, March 16. Jakarta, Indonesia.

Anon. 1980. "Why So Many Mice?" *Science Digest*, September/October. New York.

Anon. 1980. *World Conservation Strategy.* IUCN, with WWF, UNEP. Gland, Switzerland.

Anon. 1980. "The Youth Who Led a Monkey's Life." *Straits Times* (UPI), April 24. Singapore.

Anon. 1981. "Big Ulu Group Sought Logging Compensation." *Borneo Bulletin,* December 26. Brunei.

Anon. 1981. "Loggers Broke Water Pipes, Villagers Claim." *Borneo Bulletin,* October 24. Brunei.

Anon. 1981. "Police Move Against Ulu Extortionists." *Borneo Bulletin,* September 13. Brunei.

Anon. 1981. "Policemen Confront Longhouse Folk." *Borneo Bulletin,* September 5. Brunei.

Anon. 1981. "Threat of a Death Curse." *Borneo Bulletin,* December 5. Brunei.

Anon. 1981. "Timber Camp Trio for Marudi Court." *Borneo Bulletin,* April 11. Brunei.

Anon. 1982. *Elephants: Distribution, Status and Conservation in Burma.* Socialist Republic of the Union of Burma, Ministry of Agriculture and Forests, Working Peoples' Settlement Board, Rangoon.

Anon. 1983. *Human Plague in 1982.* Weekly Epidemic Record No. 35. WHO, Geneva, 265–66.

Anon. 1985. "The Rhino Export Deal." *Malayan Naturalist* 39(1&2):11–22. Kuala Lumpur, Malaysia.

Anon. 1985. "Timber Gang Foils BPP Raiding Team." Bangkok *Post,* November 23. Bangkok.

Anon. 1986. "Should Malaysia Build Bakun?" *Asiaweek,* March 30. Hong Kong.

Anon. 1987. "Placebo's Chemical Effect," *International Herald Tribune,* 22 January.

Anon. 1987. "India to Enlist Crocodiles in Ganges Cleanup." *International Herald Tribune,* 29 September.

Appell, G. N. (ed.). 1976. *Studies in Borneo Societies: Social Process and Anthropological Explanation.* Special Report 12, Center for Southeast Asian Studies, Northern Illinois University.

Apin, Teresa. 1986. "Southeast Asia's Biggest Dam Threatens to Displace 5,000 Natives." Third World Network Features, Penang, Malaysia.

Attenborough, David. 1986 (1957). *Zoo Quest for a Dragon.* Oxford University Press, Kuala Lumpur, Malaysia.

Audric, John. 1972. *Angkor and the Khmer Empire.* Robert Hale, London.

Auffenberg, Walter. 1978. "Social and Feeding Behaviour in Varanus komodoensis." In *Behavior and Neurology of Lizards,* ed. N. Greenberg and P. D. MacLead. NIMH, Washington, D.C.

———. 1981. *The Behavioral Ecology of the Komodo Monitor.* University of Florida Press, Gainesville, Fla.

———. 1982. "Catch a Lizard, Use a Lizard." *International Wildlife* 12(6). Washington, D.C.

Aung, Maung Htin. 1954. *Burmese Folk-Tales.* Oxford University Press, London.

Aung-Thwin, Michael. 1983. "Divinity, Spirit, and Human: Conceptions of Classical Burmese Kingship." In Gesick 1983.

Badil, Rudy. 1986. "Baleo . . . Pikul Tali! Mari tikan ikan raksasa," *Kompas.* Jakarta, Indonesia. 27 July.

Baker, H. G. 1978. *Plants and Civilization*. Wadsworth Publishing Co., Belmont, Calif.

Barbier, Jean Paul. 1983. *Tobaland: The Shreds of Tradition*. Barbier-Muller Museum, Geneva.

———. 1984. *Indonesian Primitive Art*. Dallas Museum of Art, Dallas, Tex.

Barker, Randolph, Robert W. Herdt, and Beth Rose. 1985. *The Rice Economy of Asia*. Resources for the Future, Washington, D.C.

Barnes, R. H. 1974. "Lamalera: A Whaling Village in Eastern Indonesia." *Indonesia* 17:137–59.

———. 1980. "Cetaceans and Cetacean Hunting, Lamalera, Indonesia." Unpublished report to WWF/IUCN. Gland, Switzerland.

Barnett, S. A., and Ishwar Prakash. 1976. *Rodents of Economic Importance*. Heinemann Educational Books, Ltd., London.

Bastin, John, ed. 1960. *The Journal of Thomas Otho Travers 1813–1820*. Government Printer, Singapore.

Baudesson, Henry. c. 1912. *Indochina and Its Primitive People*. E. P. Dutton, New York.

Bayard, D. T. 1970. "Excavation at Non Nok Tha, Northeast Thailand." *Asian Perspectives* 13:109–43.

Baze, William. 1955. *Just Elephants*. Elek Books, London.

———. 1957. *Tiger! Tiger!* Elek Books, London.

Bellwood, Peter. 1978. *Man's Conquest of the Pacific: The Prehistory of Southeast Asia and Oceania*. Collins, Auckland.

———. 1983. "Some Ancient Peoples of North Borneo." *Hemisphere* 28(1):48–52.

———. 1985. *Prehistory of the Indo-Malaysian Archipelago*. Academic Press, Sydney.

Belo, J. 1949. *Bali: Rangda and Barong*. American Ethnological Society Monographs 22:1-148. Washington, D.C.

Bernatzik, H. A. 1958. *The Spirits of the Yellow Leaves*. Robert Hale, London.

Binnie and Partners. 1976. *Report on the Economic Appraisal of the Toraut Irrigation Scheme, Dumoga Project, North Sulawesi*. Directorate General of Water Development, Jakarta.

Blacker, Carmen. 1978. "The Snake Woman in Japanese Myth and Legend." In *Animals in Folklore*, ed. J. R. Porter and W. M. S. Russell. D. S. Brewer, Ltd. and Rowman and Littlefield, London.

Blanford, W. T. 1888–91. *The Fauna of British India*. Taylor and Francis, London.

Bloodworth, Dennis. 1970. *An Eye for the Dragon*. Lancer Books, New York.

Bock, Carl. 1884. *Temples and Elephants: The Narrative of a Journey of Exploration Through Upper Siam and Laos*. Sampson Low, Marston, Searle, and Rivington, London.

———. 1985 (1881). *The Head-Hunters of Borneo*. Oxford University Press, Singapore.

Bocquet, Margaret. 1980. "Goddess Indubitable . . ." *Hemisphere* 25(1):58–63.

Bodley, John H. 1982. *Victims of Progress*. Mayfield Publishing Co., Palo Alto, Calif.

Boelaars, J. H. M. C. 1981. *Head-Hunters About Themselves: An Ethnographic Report from Irian Jaya, Indonesia*. Martinus Nijhoff, The Hague.

Bontius, Jacob. 1658. *Historiae Naturalis et Medicae Indiae Orientalis*. Amsterdam, the Netherlands.

Boon, James A. 1977. *The Anthropological Romance of Bali 1597–1972*. Cambridge University Press, Cambridge.

Borner, Marcus. 1979. *A Field Study of the Sumatran Rhinoceros*. Juris Druck and Verlag, Zurich.

Bowring, Sir John. 1977 (1857). *The Kingdom and People of Siam*. Oxford University Press, Kuala Lumpur.

Bradley, Neville. 1945. *The Old Burma Road*. William Heinemann, Ltd., London.

Bray, J. R. 1977. "Pleistocene Volcanism and Glacial Initiation." *Science* 197:251–54.

Broinowski, Alison. 1978. "Taungbyon." *Hemisphere* 24(12):34–40.

Brooks, J. E., and F. P. Rowe. 1979. *Commensal Rodent Control*. WHO, Geneva.

Brown, Lester. 1986. *The State of the World*. W. W. Norton and Company, New York.

Brown, Paula. 1978. *Highland Peoples of New Guinea*. Cambridge University Press, Cambridge.

Buck, William. 1976. *Ramayana*. University of California Press, Berkeley.

Bull, John O. 1973. "Rodents and Food Spoilage." *Chemistry and Industry*, November 17, pp. 1056–57.

Burden, W. Douglas. 1927. *Dragon Lizards of Komodo*. G. P. Putnam's Sons, New York.

Burgess, J. 1972. *Buddhist Art in India*. S. Chand and Co., New Delhi.

Burke, Kevin, and Peter Francis. 1985. "Climatic Effects of Volcanic Eruptions." *Nature* 314:136.

Burton, Robert E. 1969. "The Meows of Northern Thailand." *Explorer's Journal*, March.

Caldecott, Julian. 1984. "Coming of Age in Macaca." *New Scientist*, February 9.

———. 1986. "Hunting and Wildlife Management in Sarawak." Report to WWF. Kuching. May.

———, and Serena Caldecott. 1985. "A Horde of Pork." *New Scientist*, August 15.

Cameron, Nigel. 1976. "The Shwedagon Pagoda." *Hemisphere* 22(5):32–35.

———. 1981. "A Chinese Bestiary." *Hemisphere* 25(4):194–98.

———. 1983. "Indonesian Ikat." *Hemisphere* 28(2):66–71.

Cammann, Schuyler. 1951. "Chinese Carvings in Hornbill Ivory." *Sarawak Museum Journal*. 5(18):394–99.

Campbell, Joseph. 1962. *Oriental Mythology: The Masks of God*. Penguin, London.

———. 1974. *The Mythic Image*. Princeton University Press, Princeton, N.J.

———. 1985. *Myths to Live By*. Paladin Books, London.

Campbell, Margaret, Nakorn Pongnoi, and Chusak Voraphitak. 1978. *From the Hands of the Hills*. Media Transasia, Ltd., Hong Kong.

Canby, Thomas Y. 1977. "The Rat: Lapdog of the Devil." *National Geographic*. 152(1) July.

Caras, Roger A. 1975. *Dangerous to Man*. Penguin Books, London.

Carey, Iskandar. 1976. *Orang Asli*. Oxford University Press, Kuala Lumpur.

Carlyon, Richard. 1981. *A Guide to the Gods*. William Heinemann, Ltd., London.

Carpenter, C. R. 1940. "A Field Study in Siam of the Behavior and Social Relations of the Gibbon." *Comparative Psychology Monographs* 16(4):1–212.

Carrington, Richard. 1958. *Elephants: A Short Account of Their Natural History, Evolution and Influence on Mankind*. Chatto and Windus, London.

Casey, Robert J. 1929. *Four Faces of Siva: A Detective Story of a Vanished Race*. Blue Ribbon Books, New York.

Caulfied, Catherine. 1982. *Tropical Moist Forests*. Earthscan, London.

Chandler, David. 1983. "Going Through the Motions: Ritual Aspects of the Reign of King Duang of Cambodia (1848–1860)." In Gesick 1983.

Chang, K. C. 1983. *Art, Myth, and Ritual: The Path to Political Authority in Ancient China.* Harvard University Press, Cambridge.

Chang, Te-Tzu. 1985. "Crop History and Genetic Conservation: Rice—A Case Study." *Iowa State Journal of Research* 59(4):425–55.

Chasen, F. N. 1940. "A Handlist of Malaysian Mammals." *Bulletin of the Raffles Museum* 15:1–209.

———, and C. B. Kloss. 1927. "Spolia Mentawiensia—Mammals." *Proceedings of the Zoological Society of London* 53:797–840.

Cheesman, Evelyn. 1949. *Six-Legged Snakes in New Guinea.* George G. Harrap and Co., Ltd., London.

Chin, Lucas. 1980. *Cultural Heritage of Sarawak,* Sarawak Museum, Kuching, Sarawak.

Chou Ta-Kuan. 1967 (1298). *Notes on the Customs of Cambodia.* Social Science Association Press, Bangkok.

Christie, Jan Wisseman. 1983. "Raja and Rama: The Classical State in Early Java." In Gesick 1983.

Ciochon, Russell L., D. E. Savage, Thaw Tint, and Ba Maw. 1985. "Anthropoid Origins in Asia? New Discovery of *Amphipithecus* from the Eocene of Burma." *Science* 229:756–59.

Clark, James. 1969. *Man Is the Prey.* Panther, London.

Clark, Kenneth. 1977. *Animals and Men.* Thames and Hudson, London.

Clifford, Hugh. 1897. *In Court and Kampong.* Grant Richards, London.

———. 1898. *Studies in Brown Humanity.* Grant Richards, London.

Cockrill, W. Ross. 1967. "The Water Buffalo." *Scientific American* 217(6):118–25.

Coedes, G. 1963. *Angkor: An Introduction.* Oxford University Press, London.

———. 1966. *The Making of Southeast Asia.* University of California Press, Berkeley, Calif.

———. 1968. *The Indianized States of Southeast Asia.* University of Hawaii Press, Honolulu.

Cole, Fay-Cooper. 1945. *The Peoples of Malaysia.* Van Nostrand Co., Inc., Princeton.

Collis, Maurice. 1965. *Siamese White.* Faber, London.

Comber, Leon. 1972. *Favourite Stories from Malaysia.* Heinemann Educational Books (Asia), Ltd., Hong Kong.

———. 1975. *Favourite Stories from Borneo.* Heinemann Educational Books (Asia), Ltd., Hong Kong.

Committee for Vietnam Resources and Environmental Research. 1985. *Vietnam National Conservation Strategy (Draft).* IUCN, Gland, Switzerland.

Compost, Alain. 1980. *Pilot Survey of Exploitation of Dugong and Sea Turtle in the Aru Islands.* Yayasan Indonesia Hijau. Bogor, Indonesia.

Condominas, Georges. 1977. *We Have Eaten the Forest: The Story of a Montagnard Village in the Central Highlands of Vietnam.* Hill and Wang, New York.

Coolidge, Harold. 1940. "The Indochinese Forest Ox or Kouprey." *Memoirs of the Museum of Comparative Zoology, Harvard* 54(6):421–531.

Coolidge, Harold, and Theodore Roosevelt. 1933. *Three Kingdoms of Indochina.* Thomas Y. Crowell Co., New York.

Coomaraswamy, Ananda K. 1965 (1927). *History of Indian and Indonesian Art.* Dover Publications, Inc., New York.

————, and Sister Nivedita. 1967 (1913). *Myths of the Hindus and Buddhists.* Dover Publications, Inc., New York.

Corbett, Jim. 1946. *Man-eaters of Kumaon.* Oxford University Press, London.

Cousins, Norman, with Schiefelbein, Susan. 1977. "Medical Mystery of the Placebo," *Saturday Review,* October 1. New York.

Covarrubias, Miguel. 1972. *Bali.* Oxford University Press, London.

Crawfurd, John. 1820. *History of the Indian Archipelago.* Constable, Edinburgh.

————. 1971 (1856). *A Descriptive Dictionary of the Indian Islands and Adjacent Countries.* Oxford University Press, London.

Crisp, J. 1799. "An Account of the Inhabitants of the Poggy or Nassau Islands." *Asiatic Research* 6:77–91.

Crosette, Barbara. 1986. "An Oil City Stumbles; Is Its Future in the Jungle?" New York *Times,* January 20.

Dasmann, Ray. 1975. "Difficult Marginal Environments and the Traditional Societies Which Exploit Them." *Survival International News* 11:11–15

Davies, Nigel. 1981. *Human Sacrifice.* Macmillan London, Ltd., London.

Davis, D. Dwight. 1962. "Mammals of the Lowland Rain-Forest of North Borneo." *Bulletin of the National Museum, State of Singapore* 31:1–129.

Day, Anthony. 1983. "The Drama of Bangun Tapa's Exile in Ambon." In Gesick 1983.

Debeck, Hermann. 1965. *Animals and Men.* Natural History Press, New York.

De Boer, Leobert E. M., ed. 1982. *The Orang Utan.* Dr. W. Junk Publishers, The Hague.

DeLeeuw, Hendrik. 1956. *Java Jungle Tales.* Arco Publishers, London and New York.

Dentan, Robert K. 1968. *The Semai: A Non-Violent People of Malaya.* Holt, Rinehart and Winston, New York.

Deoras, P. J. 1966. "Some Observations on the Probable Damage Caused by Rats in Bombay." *Indian Journal of Entomology.* December:543–47.

Deraniyagala, P. E. P. 1955. *Some Extinct Elephants, Their Relatives, and the Two Living Species.* Government Press, Colombo.

Desowitz, Robert S. 1983. "On New Guinea Tapeworms and Jewish Grandmothers." *Natural History.*

Diamond, Jared M. 1966. "Zoological Classification System of a Primitive People." *Science* 151:1102–4.

————. 1985. "Rats as Agents of Extermination." *Nature* 318:19/26.

Dickerson, Roy E. 1928. *Distribution of Life in the Philippines.* Bureau of Printing, Manila.

Dimmitt, Cornelia, and J. A. B. van Buitenen. 1978. *Classical Hindu Mythology: A Reader in the Sanskrit Puranas.* Temple University Press, Philadelphia.

Diong, C. H. 1973. "Studies of the Malayan Wild Pig in Perak and Johore." *Malayan Nature Journal* 26(3–4):120–51.

Diskul, M. C. Subhadradis, ed. 1980. *The Art of Srivijaya.* Oxford University Press, Kuala Lumpur.

————, and C. S. Rice. 1982. *The Ramakian Mural Paintings Along the Galleries of the Temple of the Emerald Buddha.* State Lottery Bureau, Bangkok.

Dove, Michael R. 1984. "Man, Land and Game in Sumbawa: Some Observations on Agrarian Ecology and Development Policy in Eastern Indonesia." *Singapore Journal of Tropical Geography* 5(2):112–24.

————. n.d. "Pig-Humans and Human-Pigs: Transformation and Sacrifice in Melaban Kantu Ritual." Stanford University, Calif. Unpublished paper.

Drucker, Charles. "Dam the Chico: Hydro Development and Tribal Resistance in the Philippines." In Goldsmith and Hildyard 1984.

Dubois, Cora. 1944. *The People of Alor: A Social-Psychological Study of an East Indian Island.* Harper and Bros., New York.

Dumarcay, Jacques. 1978. *Borodudur.* Oxford University Press, Kuala Lumpur.

————. 1986. *The Temples of Java.* Oxford University Press, Singapore.

Dunbar, Robin. 1985. "How to Listen to the Animals." *New Scientist,* June 13.

Durrell, Lee. 1986. *The State of the Ark.* Doubleday, Garden City, New York.

Dwivedi, V. P. 1974. "Elephant God of the Hindus." *Orientations,* March.

Dye, Joseph M. 1981. "A Stunning New Show Defines the Hindu God of Many Guises. *Asia,* March/April.

Earl, G. W. 1971 (1837). *The Eastern Seas.* Oxford University Press, Singapore.

Eibl-Eibesfeldt, Irenäus. 1970. *Ethology: The Biology of Behavior.* Holt, Rinehart and Winston, New York.

————. 1972. *Love and Hate: The Natural History of Behavior Patterns.* Holt, Rinehart and Winston, New York.

Eliade, Mircea. 1972 (1951). *Shamanism: Archaic Techniques of Ecstasy.* Princeton University Press, Princeton, N.J.

Ellerman, J. R., and T. C. S. Morrison-Scott. 1951. *Checklist of Palaearctic and Indian Mammals,* 1758–1946. British Museum (Natural History), London.

Endicott, K. M. 1970. *An Analysis of Malay Magic.* Oxford University Press, Singapore.

Errington, Shelly. 1983. "The Place of Regalia in Luwu." In Gesick 1983.

Evans, G. H. 1910. *Elephants and their Diseases.* Government Printing Press, Rangoon.

————. 1912. *Big-Game Shooting in Upper Burma.* Longmans, Green, and Co., London.

Evans, I. H. N. 1923. *Studies in Religion, Folk-lore and Custom in British North Borneo and the Malay Peninsula.* Cambridge University Press, Cambridge.

————. 1937. *Negritos of Malaya.* Cambridge University Press, Cambridge.

Evans, Ivor H. 1981. *Brewer's Dictionary of Phrase and Fable.* Harper and Row, New York.

Evans-Pritchard, E. E. 1965. *Theories of Primitive Religion.* Oxford University Press, London.

Farb, Peter. 1978. *Humankind.* Jonathan Cape, Ltd., London.

Ferro-Luzzi, Gabriella Eichinger. 1980. "The Female Lingam: Interchangeable Symbols and Paradoxical Associations of Hindu Gods." *Current Anthropology* 21(1):45–68.

Foenander, E. C. 1952. *Big Game of Malaya.* Batchworth Press, Ltd., London.

Forbes, Kathleen. 1978. *More Favourite Stories from Burma.* Heinemann Educational Books (Asia), Ltd., Hong Kong.

Forrest, Thomas. 1969 (1780). *A Voyage to New Guinea and the Moluccas 1774–1776.* Oxford University Press, Kuala Lumpur.

Forty, C. H. 1929. *Bangkok: Its Life and Sport.* H. F. and G. Witherby, London.

Fowler, George A., Jr., Roggie Cale, and Joe C. Bartlett. 1974. *Java: A Garden Continuum.* Amerasian, Ltd., Hong Kong.

Fox, David J. Stuart. 1982. *Once a Century: Pura Besakih and the Eka Dasa Rudra Festival.* Sinar Harapan, Jakarta.

Fox, James J. 1977. *Harvest of the Palm: Ecological Change in Eastern Indonesia.* Harvard University Press, Cambridge.

Francis, Charles M. 1984. *Pocket Guide to the Birds of Borneo.* The Sabah Society and WWF Malaysia, Kuala Lumpur.

Francis, Peter. 1983. "Giant Volcanic Calderas." *Scientific American* 248(6):46–56.

Frantz, S. C. 1976. "The Web of Hunger: Rats in the Granary." *Natural History.*

Fraser, Douglas. 1966. *The Many Faces of Primitive Art.* Prentice-Hall, N.J.

Frazer, James George. 1939. *The Native Races of Australasia.* Percy Lund Humphries and Co., Ltd., London.

————. 1959 (1890). *The New Golden Bough.* ed. T. H. Gaster. S. G. Philipps, Great Meadows, N.J. 738 pp.

Freeman, J. D. 1960. "Iban Agury." In Smythies, 1960.

Freud, Sigmund. 1950. *Totem and Taboo.* W. W. Norton and Co., New York.

Frey, Edward. 1986. *The Kris: Mystic Weapon of the Malay World.* Oxford University Press, Singapore.

Fulk, G. W., and M. T. Akhtar. 1981. "An Investigation of Rodent Damage and Yield Reducation in Rice." *Tropical Pest Management* 27(1):116–20.

Galdikas, Biruté M. F. 1979. "Orangutan Adaptation at Tanjung Puting Reserve: Mating and Ecology." In *The Great Apes,* eds. D. A. Hamburg and E. R. McCown. Benjamin Cummings, Menlo Park, N.J.

————. 1980. "Living with the Great Orange Apes." *National Geographic* 157(6). June.

Galdikas-Brindamour, Biruté, and Rod Brindamour. 1975. "Orangutans, Indonesia's 'People of the Forest.' " *National Geographic* 148(4).October.

Gale, U Toke. 1967. *Elephants in Burma.* Government Press, Rangoon.

Galvin, A. D. 1972. "Kenyah Omen Birds and Beasts." *Sarawak Museum Journal* 20(40–41):53–62.

Gardner, Robert, and Heider, Karl G. 1968. *Gardens of War.* Random House, New York.

Garrison, Lloyd. 1986. "Forest War." *Time,* March 17.

Geddes, W. R. 1957. *Nine Dayak Nights.* Oxford University Press, Melbourne.

Geertz, Clifford. 1960. *The Religion of Java.* University of Chicago Press, Chicago.

————. 1963. *Agricultural Involution: The Processes of Ecological Change in Indonesia.* University of California Press, Berkeley, Calif.

————. 1973. *The Interpretation of Cultures.* Basic Books, New York.

————. 1980. *Negara: The Theatre State in Nineteenth Century Bali.* Princeton University Press, Princeton, N.J.

Gesick, Lorraine, ed. 1983. *Centers, Symbols, and Hierarchies: Essays on the Classical States of Southeast Asia.* Yale University Press, New Haven.

Getty, Alice. 1936. *Ganesa: A Monograph on the Elephant-faced God.* Clarendon Press, Oxford.

Ghazarbekian, Bonnie. 1973. "The Durable Elephant." *Sawaddi,* January.

Giles, Francis H. 1929. "Adversaria of Elephant Hunting." *Journal of the Siam Society* 23(2):61–96.

————. 1931. "An Account of the Rites and Ceremonies Observed at Elephant Driving Operations in the Seaboard Province of Lang Suan, Southern Siam." *Journal of the Siam Society* 25(2):153–214.

————. 1934. "An Account of the Hunting of the Wild Ox on Horse Back in the

Provinces of Ubol Rajadhani and Kalasindhu, and the Rites and Ceremonies Which Have to Be Observed." *Journal of the Siam Society* 27(1):39–59.

Gillsäter, Sven. 1961. *We Ended In Bali*. George Allen and Unwin, Ltd., London.

Gimlette, John D. 1971 (1915). *Malay Poisons and Charm Cures*. Oxford University Press, Kuala Lumpur.

Girish, G. K., K. K. Arora, and K. Krishnamurthy. 1974. "Studies on Rodents and Their Control." *Indian Grain Storage Institute* 12 (2).

Gittinger, Mattiebelle. 1979. *Splendid Symbols: Textiles and Tradition in Indonesia*. The Textile Museum, Washington, D.C.

Golden, Janet. 1980. "In Search of Monkeys." *Orientations,* February.

Goldsmith, Edward, and Nicholas Hildyard. 1984. *The Social and Environmental Effects of Large Dams*. Sierra Club Books, San Francisco.

Gomes, Edwin H. 1911. *Seventeen Years Among the Sea Dyaks of Borneo*. J. B. Lippincott Co., Philadelphia.

Gorer, Geoffrey. 1936. *Bali and Angkor*. Little, Brown, and Company, Boston.

Gorman, C. F. 1971. "The Hoabhinian and After: Subsistence Patterns in Southeast Asia During the Late Pleistocene and Early Recent Periods." *World Archeology* 2(3):300–21.

Gorstin, Crosbie. 1928. *The Dragon and the Lotus*. William Heinemann, Ltd., London.

Govinda, Lama Anagarika. 1976. *Psycho-cosmic Symbolism of the Buddhist Stupa*. Dharma Publishing, Emeryville, Calif.

Graham, Alistair, and Peter Beard. 1963. *Eyelids of Morning: The Mingled Destinies of Crocodiles and Men*. A&W Visual Library, New York.

Graves, Robert. 1959. *Larousse Encyclopedia of Mythology*. Paul Hamlyn, London.

Gray, Denis D. 1978. "A School for Elephants." *International Wildlife,* June.

Green, Martyn. 1985. "Rare Tigers Butchered for Sale." *Straits Times,* May 20. Singapore.

Green, Michael, and Richard Taylor. 1986. "The Musk Connection." *New Scientist,* June 26.

Groslier, Bernard. 1966a. *Angkor: Art and Civilization*. 2d ed. Thames and Hudson, London.

Groslier, Bernard P. 1966b. *Indochina*. Frederick Muller, Ltd., London.

Guggisberg, C. A. W. 1966. *S.O.S. Rhino*. André Deutsch, London.

———. 1972. *Crocodiles: Their Natural History, Folklore, and Conservation*. David and Charles, Ltd., London.

Hall, D. G. E. 1968. *A History of Southeast Asia*. 3d ed. Macmillan, London.

Hall, K. R., and J. K. Whitmore. 1976. *Explorations in Early SE Asian History: The Origins of SE Asian Statecraft*. University of Michigan Press, Ann Arbor.

Halpern, J. M. 1967. *Economy and Society of Laos*. Yale University Press, New Haven.

Hamilton, Alexander. 1930 (1727). *A New Account of the East Indies*. The Argonaut Press, London.

Hampden-Turner, Charles. 1981. *Maps of the Mind*. Mitchell Beazley Publishers, Limited, London.

Hanbury-Tenison, Robin. 1975. *A Pattern of Peoples*. Angus and Robertson, London.

———. 1980. *Mulu: The Rainforest*. Weidenfeld and Nicolson, London.

Hanks, Lucien M. 1972. *Rice and Man: Agricultural Ecology in Southeast Asia*. Aldine-Atherton, Chicago.

Hansen, James E., Wei-Chyung Wang, and Andrew A. Lacis. 1978. "Mount Agung Eruption Provides Test of a Global Climatic Perturbation." *Science* 199:1065–67.

Hardjono, J. 1970. *Indonesia, Land and People.* Gunung Agung, Jakarta.

Harner, Michael. 1980. *The Way of the Shaman.* Harper and Row, New York.

Harris, Marvin. 1974. *Cows, Pigs, Wars and Witches: The Riddles of Culture.* Vintage Books, New York.

———. 1977. *Cannibals and Kings: The Origins of Culture.* Vintage Books, New York.

Harrisson, Barbara. 1963a. *Orang-utan.* Doubleday & Co., Garden City, N.Y.

———. 1963b. "Education to Wild Living of Young Orangutans at Bako National Park, Sarawak." *Sarawak Museum Journal* 9(21–22):222–58.

Harrisson, Tom. 1955. "Maias v. Man." *Sarawak Museum Journal* 6(21):600–32.

———. 1959. *World Within: A Borneo Story.* The Cresset Press, London.

———. 1966. "The Gibbon in West Borneo Folklore and Augury." *Sarawak Museum Journal* 14(28–29):132–45.

———. 1970. *The Malays of Southwest Sarawak before Malaysia.* Michigan State University Press, East Lansing.

———, and Loh Chee Yin. 1965. "To Scale a Pangolin." *Sarawak Museum Journal* 12(25–26):415–18.

Hartmann, Fred. 1978. "The Fierce and Fatherly Siamese Fighting Fish." *Natural History* 87(5):69–70.

Hatley, Tom, and Michael Thompson. 1985. "Rare Animals, Poor People, and Big Agencies: A Perspective on Biological Conservation and Rural Development in the Himalaya." *Mountain Research and Development* 5(4):365–77.

Hayden, B. 1981. "Research and Development in the Stone Age: Technological Transitions Among Hunter-Gatherers." *Current Anthropology* 22:519–48.

Heider, Karl G. 1970. *The Dugum Dani: A Papuan Culture in the Highlands of West New Guinea.* Viking Fund Publications in Anthropology 49, New York.

Heine-Geldern, Robert. 1966. *Some Tribal Art Styles of Southeast Asia: An Experiment in Art History.* In Fraser 1966.

Helton, David. 1986. "The Creature from the Avalanche." *BBC Wildlife,* September.

Hembree, E. D. 1980. "Biological Aspects of the Cetacean Fishery at Lamalera, Lembata." Unpublished report to WWF/IUCN; Gland, Switzerland.

Hendrickson, Robert. 1983. *More Cunning Than Man: A Social History of Rats and Men.* Stein & Day, New York.

Hervey, Harry. 1927. *King Cobra: An Autobiography of Travel in French Indo-China.* Cosmopolitan Book Corporation, New York.

Herwaarden, C. van. 1924. "Een Ontmoeting Met Een Aapmensch." *Tropische Natuur* 13:103–6.

Heuvelmans, Bernard. 1965. *In Search of Unknown Animals.* Hill and Wang, New York.

Hickey, Gerald Cannon. 1982a. *Sons of the Mountains: Ethnohistory of the Vietnamese Central Highlands to 1954.* Yale University Press, New Haven and London.

———. 1982b. *Free in the Forest: Ethnohistory of the Vietnamese Central Highlands, 1954–1976.* Yale University Press, New Haven and London.

Higham, C. F. W. 1975. "Aspects of Economy and Ritual in Prehistoric Northeast Thailand." *Journal of Archeological Science* 2:145–48.

Hillman, A., and Walter W. Skeat. 1938. *Salam the Mouse-Deer: Wonder Stories of the Malayan Forest.* Macmillan, London.

Hitt, Russell. 1962. *Cannibal Valley.* Harper and Row, New York.

Hoefer, Hans. 1970. *Guide to Bali.* Hotel Bali Beach Corp., Singapore.

Hogan, D. W. 1972. "Men of the Sea: Coastal Tribes of South Thailand's West Coast." *Journal of the Siam Society* 60(1):205–35.

Hollands, Martin. 1982. "The Crocodiles That Count." *New Scientist,* August 19.

Holt, Claire. 1967. *Art in Indonesia: Continuities and Change.* Cornell University Press, Ithaca and London.

———, ed. 1972. *Culture and Politics in Indonesia.* Cornell University Press, Ithaca and London.

Hong, Evelyne. 1987. *Natives of Sarawak.* Institut Masyarakat, Pulau Pinang, Malaysia.

Hoogerwerf, Andries. 1970. *Udjung Kulon.* E. J. Brill, Leiden.

Hose, Charles. 1985 (1929). *The Field-book of a Jungle-Wallah.* Oxford University Press, Singapore.

———, and William McDougall. 1912. *The Pagan Tribes of Borneo.* Macmillan, London.

Hough, Walter. 1926. *Fire as an Agent in Human Culture.* Smithsonian Institution Bulletin 139, Government Printing Office, Washington, D.C.

Hubback, T. R. 1905. *Elephant and Seladang Hunting in the Federated Malay States.* Rowland Ward, London.

Hutchingson, E. W. 1940. *Adventurers in Siam in the Seventeeth Century.* Royal Asiatic Society, London.

Hutton, Peter. 1978. *Java.* Apa Productions, Singapore.

Huxley, Anthony. 1984. *Green Inheritance.* Collins, London.

Huyghe, Rene, ed. 1970. *The Larousse Encyclopedia of Prehistoric and Ancient Art.* 2d ed. Paul Hamlyn, London.

Ingersoll, Ernest. 1928. *Dragons and Dragon Lore.* Payson and Clarke, Ltd., New York.

Interagency Primate Steering Committee. 1978. *National Primate Plan.* U.S. Department of Health, Education, and Welfare Publication No. (NIH)80–1520, Washington, D.C.

Ions, Veronica. 1967. *Indian Mythology.* Paul Hamlyn, London.

Iten, Oswald. 1986. "Die Tasaday—Ein Philippinischer Steinzeitschwindel." *Neue Zürcher Zeitung,* April 12.

Jackson, Peter. 1985. "Man-Eaters." *International Wildlife,* November.

Jaivin, Linda. 1985. "Is There a Wildman?" *Asiaweek,* May 24.

Jeanloz, Raymond, T. J. Ahrens, H. K. Mao, and P. M. Bell. 1979. "Can Rapid Climatic Change Cause Volcanic Eruptions?" *Science* 206:826–28.

Jensen, Adolf E. 1963. *Myth and Culture Among Primitive Peoples.* University of Chicago Press, Chicago.

Johnson, Osa. 1965. *Last Adventure: The Martin Johnsons in Borneo.* Jarrolds, London.

Jones, Gwilym S., and Diana B. Jones. 1976. *A Bibliography of the Land Mammals of Southeast Asia 1699–1969.* Bishop Museum, Honolulu.

Judd, J. W. 1889. "The Earlier Eruptions of Krakatoa." *Nature* 40:365–66.

Jumsai, M. L. Manich. 1970. *History of Thailand and Cambodia.* Chalermnit, Bangkok.

Jung, C. G. 1938. *Psychology and Religion.* Yale University Press, New Haven.

———. 1977. *Psychology and the Occult.* Routledge and Kegan Paul, London.

———, ed. 1964. *Man and His Symbols.* Aldus Books, Ltd., London.

Kahlenberg, Mary Hunt. 1977. *Textile Traditions of Indonesia.* Los Angeles County Museum of Art, Los Angeles.

Kahlke, H. D. 1972. "A Review of the Pleistocene History of the Orangutan." *Asian Perspectives* 15:5–15.

Kakuzo, Okakura. 1940. *The Awakening of Japan.* Tokyo.

Kamma, Freerk C. 1975. *Religious Texts of the Oral Tradition from Western New Guinea.* E. J. Brill, Leiden.

Kartomi, Margaret. 1977. "Tigers into Kittens." *Hemisphere* 22(6):23–29.

Kavanaagh, Michael. 1981. "Sexual Behavior in Orangutans." *Laboratory Primates Newsletter* 20(1):1–3.

Keeton, Charles L. 1974. *King Thebaw and the Ecological Rape of Burma.* Manohar Book Service, Delhi.

Kempers, A. J. Bernet. 1976. *Ageless Borobudur.* Servire, Wassenaar.

———. n.d. *Monumental Bali: Introduction to Balinese Archaeology.* Van Goor Zonen, Den Hag.

King, Ben, Martin Woodcock, and E. C. Dickenson. 1975. *A Field Guide to the Birds of Southeast Asia.* Collins, London.

King, V. T. 1976. "Migration, Warfare, and Culture Contact in Borneo: A Critique of Ecological Analysis." *Oceania* 46:306–27.

Kingdon-Ward, Frank. 1956. *Return to the Irrawaddy.* Andrew Melrose, London.

Kipling, John Lockwood. 1981. *Man and Beast in India.* Macmillan, London.

Kloss, C. Boden. 1903. *In the Andamans and Nicobars.* John Murray, London.

Kluckhohn, Clyde. 1942. "Myths and Rituals: A General Theory." *Harvard Theological Review* 35:45–79.

Knappert, Jan. 1977. *Myths and Legends of Indonesia.* Heinemann Educational Books (Asia), Ltd., Singapore.

Koentjaraningrat. 1975. *Anthropology in Indonesia: A Bibliographic Review.* Mantinus Nijhoff, The Hague.

Konner, Melvin. 1982. *The Tangled Wing: Biological Constraints on the Human Spirit.* Holt, Rinehart and Winston, New York.

Krappe, Alexander. 1930. *The Science of Folklore.* Methuen and Co., Ltd., London.

Kriss, M. 1972. *Werewolves, Shapeshifters, and Skinwalkers.* Sherbourne Press, Los Angeles.

Kunstadter, Peter. 1970. "Subsistence Agricultural Economics of Lua and Karen Hill Farmers of Mae Sariang District, Northern Thailand." In *International Seminar on Shifting Cultivation and Economic Development in Northern Thailand,* Land Development Department, Bangkok, Thailand.

———, ed. 1967. *Southeast Asian Tribes, Minorities, and Nations.* Princeton University Press, Princeton.

Kurylas, Hans. 1980. "Socioeconomic and Ecological Aspects of Field Rat Control in Tropical and Subtropical Countries." *Proceedings 9th Vertebrate Pest Conference,* Fresno, Calif.

Laderman, Carol. 1983. "Trances That Heal." *Science Digest,* July.

Landon, Margaret. 1944. *Anna and the King of Siam.* John Day Co., New York.

Leach, E. R. 1960. "The Frontiers of Burma." *Comparative Studies in Society and History* 3:49–68.

Leakey, Richard E., and Roger Lewin. 1977. *Origins.* Dutton, New York.

LeBar, F. M., G. C. Hickey, and J. K. Musgrave. 1964. *Ethnic Groups of Mainland Southeast Asia*. Human Relations Area Files Press, New Haven.

Lebar, Frank M., ed. 1972. *Ethnic Groups of Insular Southeast Asia*. Human Relations Area Files Press, New Haven.

Lee Khoon Choy. 1976. *Indonesia: Between Myth and Reality*. Nile & Mackenzie, Ltd., London.

Leeuw, Hendrik de. 1931. *Crossroads of the Java Sea*. Garden City Publishing Co., Inc., Garden City, N.Y.

Legendre, Sidney J. 1936. *Land of the White Parasol and the Million Elephants: A Journey Through the Jungles of Indochina*. Dodd, Mead and Co., New York.

Lekagul, Boonsong. 1952. "On the Trail of the Kouprey or Indochinese Forest Ox." *Journal of the Bombay Natural History Society* 50(4):623–28.

———. 1968. *Bird Guide of Thailand*. Association for the Conservation of Wildlife, Bangkok.

———, and J. A. McNeely. 1976. "Elephants in Thailand: Importance, Status and Conservation." *Conservation News of Southeast Asia* 10(4):12–18.

———, and J. A. McNeely. 1977a. "Thailand's Disappearing Forests." *Tigerpaper* 3(3):12–16.

———, and J. A. McNeely. 1977b. *Mammals of Thailand*. Association for the Conservation of Wildlife, Bangkok.

———, and J. A. McNeely. 1979. "The Conservation of Wilderness in Thailand." In *Voices of the Wilderness*, ed. Ian Player. Jonathan Ball Publishers, Johannesburg.

Levi-Strauss, Claude. 1978. *Myth and Meaning*. Routledge and Kegan Paul, London.

Lewis, Norman. 1951. *A Dragon Apparent: Travels in Indochina*. Jonathan Cape, Ltd., London.

Lewis, Paul, and Elaine Lewis. 1984. *Peoples of the Golden Triangle: Six Tribes in Thailand*. Thames and Hudson, London.

Lim Boo Liat. 1974. "Snakes as Natural Predators of Rats in an Oil Palm Estate." *Malayan Nature Journal* 27(2):114–17.

Littauer, Raphael, and Norman Uphoff, eds. 1971. *The Air War in Indochina*. Beacon Press, Boston.

Locke, A. 1954. *The Tigers of Trengganu*. Museum Press, Ltd., London.

Loeb, Edwin M. 1929. "Mentawei Religious Cult." *University of California Publications in American Archaeology and Ethnology* 25(2):185–247.

———. 1972 (1935). *Sumatra: Its History and People*. Oxford University Press, Oxford.

Logan, J. R. 1855. "Ethnography of the Indo-Pacific Archipelagoes: The Chagalelegat, or Mantawe Islands." *Journal of the Indian Archipelago and Eastern Asia* 9:273–305.

Lonsdale, Steven. 1981. *Animals and the Origins of Dance*. Thames and Hudson, London.

Lore, Richard, and Kevin Flannelly. 1977. "Rat Societies." *Scientific American* 236(5):106–16.

Lowry, John. 1974. *Burmese Art*. Her Majesty's Stationery Office, London.

Lubis, Mochtar. 1969. "Mysticism in Indonesian Politics." In *Man, State, and Society in Contemporary Southeast Asia*, ed. R. O. Tilman. Praegar Publishers, New York.

Luxmoore, R. A., J. G. Barzdo, S. R. Broad, and D. A. Jones. 1985. *A Directory of Crocodilian Farming Operations*. IUCN, Cambridge, UK.

Luxmoore, Richard. 1985. "Exploitation of the Saltwater Crocodile in Indonesia." *Traffic Bulletin* 7(5):78–80.

McClure, H. Elliott. 1980. "Hornbills—Forest Clowns." *Hemisphere* 24(1):32–39.

McConnell, R. B., ed. 1983. *Art, Science and Human Progress*. Universe Books, New York.

MacDonald, Malcolm. 1956. *Borneo People*. Jonathan Cape, Ltd., London.

Macfie, D. F. 1978 (1926–27). "An Elephant That Chiangmai Will Never Forget." Bangkok *Post*, July 2.

McKinley, Robert. 1976. "Human and Proud of It: A Structural Treatment of Headhunting Rites and the Social Definition of Enemies." In *Studies in Borneo Societies: Social Process and Anthropological Explanation*, ed. G. N. Appell. Center for Southeast Asian Studies, Northern Illinois University.

MacKinnon, John R. 1974a. *In Search of the Red Ape*. Collins, London.

———. 1974b. "The Behaviour and Ecology of Wild Orang-utans." *Animal Behaviour* 22:3–74.

———. 1977. "The Future of Orangutans." *New Scientist,* June 23.

———. 1978. *The Ape Within Us*. Holt, Rinehart and Winston, New York.

———, and Kathy MacKinnon. 1974. *Animals of Asia*. Peter Lowe, London.

McNeely, J. A. 1972. "In Thailand Wurden 15,500 Krokodile Gexuchtet." *Das Tier,* August.

———. 1975. *Wildlife and National Parks in the Lower Mekong Basin*. ESCAP, Bangkok.

———. 1976. *Wildlife and the Mekong Project*. ESCAP, Bangkok.

———. 1977a. "Mammals of the Thai Mangroves." *Tigerpaper* 4(12):10–15.

———. 1977b. "The Post-Impoundment Effects on Wildlife of the Nam Phong Dam and Reservoir." SEATEC, Bangkok.

———. 1978a. "Dynamics of Extinction in Southeast Asia." In McNeely, Rabor, and Sumardja 1978, 137–55.

———. 1978b. "Management of Elephants in Southeast Asia." In McNeely, Rabor, and Sumardja 1978, 219–28.

———. 1978c. "Saving Siberut: Conservation of Indonesia's Island Paradise." *Tigerpaper* 5(2):16–20.

———. 1978d. "Vanishing Species of Thailand." *International Wildlife* 8(6):52.

———. 1979. "Siberut: Reconciling the Interests of Man and Animal." *Oryx* 15(2):159–65.

———. 1980a. "Conservation Opportunities in Burma." Report to the IUCN Commission on National Parks and Protected Areas, Gland, Switzerland.

———. 1980b. "Distribution, Diversity, and Abundance of Indonesian Mammals." Biotrop, Bogor.

———. 1980c. "Java's Vanishing Animals." *International Wildlife* 10(2):38–39.

———. 1980d. "The Giant Civet: A Photo First." *International Wildlife* 10(3):2.

———. 1980e. "Wildlife, Conservation and Land-use Planning in Southeast Asia." In *Tropical Ecology and Development,* ed. J. I. Furtado, 333–38. International Society of Tropical Ecology, Kuala Lumpur.

———. 1981a. "Conservation of Endangered Large Mammals in Sumatra." *Elephant* 1(4):33–38.

———. 1981b. "Quiet Hunters of the East." *International Wildlife* 11(6):20–24.

———. 1981c. "The Importance of Elephants in Burmese Forestry: A Proposal for World Bank Support." *Elephant* 1(4):29–32.

————. 1986. "How Dams and Wildlife Can Co-exist: Natural Habitats, Agriculture, and Major Water Resources Development Projects in Tropical Asia." Paper presented to Fourth International Congress of Ecology, Syracuse, N.Y.

————, ed. 1982. *The World's Greatest Natural Areas: An Indicative Inventory of Natural Sites of World Heritage Quality.* IUCN, Gland.

————, and E. W. Cronin. 1972. "Rhinos in Thailand." *Oryx* 11(6):457–66.

————, E. W. Cronin, and H. B. Emery. 1973. "The Yeti—Not a Snowman." *Oryx* 12(1):65–73.

————, J. E. Hill, and K. Thonglongya. 1975. *The Bats and Bat Parasites of Thailand.* Applied Scientific Research Corporation of Thailand, Bangkok.

————, and A. W. Laurie. 1976. "Rhinos in Thailand: 1976." *Oryx* 15(3):237–38.

————, D. S. Rabor, and E. A. Sumardja. 1978. *Wildlife Management in Southeast Asia.* BIOTROP, Bogor.

————, and J. Seidensticker. 1974. "Huay Kha Khaeng: A Preliminary Ecological Survey." Association for Conservation of Wildlife, Bangkok.

————, and M. K. Sinha. 1981. "Protected Areas for Asian Elephants." *Parks* 6(1):4–7.

————, and E. A. Sumardja. 1979. *National Parks and Protected Areas of Indonesia.* 15th Meeting of IUCN's Commission of National Parks and Protected Areas, Canberra, Australia.

————, and P. S. Wachtel. 1981. "They Use Everything But the Cat's Meow." *International Wildlife* 11(3):14–19.

————, and P. S. Wachtel. 1986. "The Cobra King." *International Wildlife* 16(1):38–41.

————, and H. Ludwig, eds. 1978. *Agriculture in the Lower Mekong Basin.* ESCAP, Bangkok.

————, and Kenton R. Miller, eds. 1984. *National Parks, Conservation, and Development: The Role of Protected Areas in Sustaining Society.* Smithsonian Institution Press, Washington, D.C.

————, and David Pitt, eds. 1984. *Culture and Conservation: The Human Dimension in Environmental Planning.* Croom Helm, London.

————, A. J. Whitten, and J. Whitten. 1980. *Saving Siberut: A Conservation Master Plan.* WWF, Bogor.

Marasinghe, M. M. J. 1974. *Gods in Early Buddhism.* University of Sri Lanka, Colombo.

Marsden, William. 1976 (1811). *The History of Sumatra.* Oxford University Press, Kuala Lumpur.

Marshall, H. N. 1959. *Elephant Kingdom.* Robert Hale Ltd., London.

Martin, Esmond Bradley. 1979. *The International Trade in Rhinoceros Products.* IUCN, Gland.

————. 1981. "Rhinoceros Products: Use and Trade in Indonesia, Malaysia and Burma." A report for WWF/IUCN. Gland, Switzerland.

————, and Chryssee Bradley. 1982. *Run Rhino Run.* Chatto and Windus, London.

Mathews, Anna. 1983. *The Night of Purnama.* Oxford University Press, Kuala Lumpur.

Maxwell, George. 1960. *In Malay Forests.* Eastern Universities Press, Ltd., Singapore.

May, Reginald le. 1926. *An Asian Arcady.* W. Heffer and Sons, Ltd., Cambridge.

———. 1962. *A Concise History of Buddhist Art in Siam*. Charles E. Tuttle Co., Rutland, Vt.

Medway, Lord. 1976. "Hunting Pressure on Orangutans in Sarawak." *Tigerpaper* 3(4):24.

———. 1977. *Mammals of Borneo*. Malaysian Branch of the Royal Asiatic Society, Kuala Lumpur.

———. 1978. *The Wild Mammals of Malaya and Singapore*. Oxford University Press, Kuala Lumpur.

Miller, Charles. 1950. *Cannibal Caravan*. Museum Press, Ltd., London.

Miller, Peter. 1980. "Bali Celebrates a Festival of Faith." *National Geographic* 157(3).

Milner, G. B. 1978. *Natural Symbols in Southeast Asia*. University of London, London.

Milroy, A. J. W. 1927. "Elephant Catching in Assam." *Journal of the Bombay Natural History Society* 29(4):803–11.

Mims, Bob. 1986. "Deadly Snail May Yield Clues to Neurological Ills." *International Herald Tribune*. April 24.

Minton, Sherman A., and M. R. Minton. 1973. *Giant Reptiles*. Charles Scribner's Sons, New York.

Missen, G. J. 1972. *Viewpoint on Indonesia: A Geographical Study*. Nelson, Melbourne.

Mitchell, Arthur, and Vern Weitzel. 1983. "Monkeys and Men in the Land of Mud." *Hemisphere* 27(5):308–14.

Mitchell, K. W. S. 1928. *Tales from Some Eastern Jungles*. Cecil Palmer, London.

Moebirman. 1967. *Wayang Purwa: The Shadow Play of Indonesia*. Yayasan Pelita Wisata, Jakarta.

Mohun, Janet, and Omar Sattaur. 1987. "The Drowning of a Culture." *New Scientist*, January 15.

Mole, Robert L. 1970. *The Montagnards of South Vietnam: A Study of Nine Tribes*. Charles E. Tuttle Co., Rutland, Vt.

Monteiro, E. S. n.d. *The Rat and Man*. Quins Pte., Ltd., Singapore.

Moore, Omar K. 1957. "Divination: A New Perspective." *American Anthropologist* 59:69–74.

Morauta, Louise, John Pernetta, and William Heaney, eds. 1982. *Traditional Conservation in Papua New Guinea: Implications for Today*. Institute of Applied Social and Economic Research, Boroko.

Morgan, Dan. "Timber Firm Bucks Trend in E. Borneo." Washington *Post*, November 26, 1978.

Morris, Ramona, and Desmond Morris. 1965. *Men and Snakes*. Hutchinson, London.

———. 1966. *Men and Apes*. Hutchinson, London.

Morrison, Hedda. 1965. *Sarawak*. Donald Moore Press, Ltd., Singapore.

Mouhot, H. 1966 (1864). *Travels in the Central Part of Indochina*. John Murray, London.

Mountfort, Guy. 1981. *Saving the Tiger*. Michael Joseph, London.

Mowbray, Scott. 1985. "Heart of the Matriarchate." *Discovery*, February.

Mulder, Niels. 1978. *Mysticism and Everyday Life in Contemporary Java*. Singapore University Press, Singapore.

Muller, Kal. 1981. "A Look at Lombok." *Silver Kris* 6(3):57–62.

———. 1985. "Sumbawa's Islam and Magic." *Hilton Horizon*, winter.

Mulyono, Sri. 1981. *Human Character in the Wayang Javanese Shadow Play*. Gunung Agung, Singapore.

Muth Alibasah, Margaret. *Adventures of Mouse Deer*. Penerbit Djambatan, Jakarta.

Myers, Norman. 1982. *The Sinking Ark*. Pergamon Press, Oxford.

————. 1983. *A Wealth of Wild Species*. Westview Press, Boulder, Colo.

————. 1984. *The Primary Source*. W. W. Norton and Company, New York.

———— (ed.). 1985. *The Gaia Atlas of Planet Management*. Pan Books, London and Sydney.

Myrdal, Jan, and Gun Kessle. 1970. *Angkor: An Essay on Art and Imperialism*. Random House, New York.

Naiwen, Chen, and Zhang Guoying. 1984. "More Evidence on 'Abominable Snowman'?" *China Reconstructs*, June.

Nance, John. 1975. *The Gentle Tasaday: A Stone Age People in the Philippine Rain Forest*. Harcourt Brace Jovanovich, New York.

Napier, John. 1972. *Bigfoot*. E. P. Dutton, New York.

————, and P. H. Napier. 1970. *Old World Monkeys: Evolution, Systematics, and Behavior*. Academic Press, New York.

National Academy of Sciences. 1981. *The Water Buffalo: New Prospects for an Underutilized Animal*. National Academy of Sciences Press, Washington, D.C.

————. 1983a. *Crocodiles as a Resource for the Tropics*. National Academy of Sciences Press, Washington, D.C.

————. 1983b. *Little-Known Asian Animals with a Promising Economic Future*. National Academy of Sciences Press, Washington, D.C.

Newman, Barry. 1980. "Nanyang Family Firms: As Flexible as a Plate of Noodles." *Asian Wall Street Journal*. May 1.

Newman, Philip. 1965. *Knowing the Gururumba*. Holt, Rinehart and Winston, New York.

Nha, Trang. 1978. *Favourite Stories from Vietnam*. Heinemann Educational Books (Asia), Ltd., Hong Kong.

Niekisch, Manfred. 1985. "The International Trade in Frogs' Legs." *Traffic Bulletin* 8(1):7–11.

Neill, Wilfred T. 1973. *Twentieth Century Indonesia*. Columbia University Press. New York.

Nilsson, Greta. 1977. *The Bird Business: A Study of the Commercial Cage Bird Trade*. Animal Welfare Institute. Washington, D.C.

Norland, Patricia. 1986. "Vietnam's Ecology: Averting Disaster." *Indochina Issues* 66:1–5.

Norlund, Irene, Sven Cederroth, and Ingela Gerdin. 1986. *Rice Societies: Asian Problems and Prospects*. Curzon Press, London.

Nyandoh, R. 1966. "Man Weds Sow." *Sarawak Museum Journal* 14 (28–29):124–31.

O'Hanlon, Redmond. 1984. *Into the Heart of Borneo*. Penguin Books, London.

Olivier, Robert. 1978. *On the Ecology of the Asian Elephant*. Doctoral Dissertation, University of Cambridge, England.

Osborne, Milton. 1975. *River Road to China: The Mekong River Expedition 1866–1873*. George Allen and Unwin, Ltd., London.

————. 1985. *Southeast Asia*. George Allen and Unwin, Ltd., London.

Passingham, Richard. 1982. *The Human Primate*. W. H. Freeman and Company, Oxford.

Patanne, E. P. 1972. "The Wonderful Maranao Rooster." *Orientations*, August.

Payne, Junaidi, Charles M. Francis, and Karen Phillipps. 1985. *A Field Guide to the Mammals of Borneo*. The Sabah Society and WWF Malaysia, Kuala Lumpur.

Peacock, E. H. 1933. *A Game-book for Burma and Adjoining Territories*. Witherby, London.

Peranio, Roger. 1959. "Animal Teeth and Oath-taking Among the Bisaya." *Sarawak Museum Journal* 9(13–14):6–13.

Perry, Richard. 1964. *The World of the Tiger*. Cassell & Co., Ltd., London.

Perti, S. L., Y. C. Wal, and C. P. Srivastava, eds. 1968. *Proceedings of International Symposium on Bionomics & Control of Rodents*. Science & Technology Society, Kanpur, India.

Pinney, Peter. 1976. *To Catch a Crocodile*. Angus and Robertson, London.

Pires, Tome. 1944. "The Suma Oriental of Tome Pires: An Account of the East, from the Red Sea to Japan, Written in Malacca and India in 1511–1515 and the book of Francisco Rodrigues" (Trans. and Edited by Armando Cortesao), *The Hakluyt Society*, London, Second Series, No. 89, Vol. 1 & 2.

Plion-Bernier, Raymond. 1973. *Festivals and Ceremonies of Thailand*. Assumption Press, Bangkok.

Pollock, C., and W. S. Thom. 1900. *Wild Sports of Burma and Assam*. Hurst and Blackett, Ltd., London.

Polo, Marco. 1958 (1301). *The Travels*. Penguin Books, New York.

Ponder, H. W. 1937. *Java Pageant*. Seeley Service and Co., Ltd., London.

Powell, E. Alexander. 1922. *Where the Strange Trails Go Down*. Charles Scribner's Sons, New York.

Powell, Hickman. 1982 (1930). *The Last Paradise*. Oxford University Press, Singapore.

Prateepchaikul, Veera. 1976. "A Day This Elephant Will Never Forget." *Bangkok Post*, May 9.

Prater, S. H. 1928. "The Dugong or Sea Cow." *Journal of the Bombay Natural History Society* 33(1):84–99.

———. 1965. *The Book of Indian Animals*. Bombay Natural History Society, Bombay.

Pritchard, Chris. 1980. "Endangered Darwinites Shed Few Tears for Crocodiles." *Asian Wall Street Journal*, September 30.

Radcliffe-Brown, A. R. 1933. *The Andaman Islanders*. Cambridge University Press, Cambridge.

Raffles, Thomas Stamford. 1978 (1817). *The History of Java*. Oxford University Press, Kuala Lumpur.

Ramseyer, Urs. 1977. *The Art and Culture of Bali*. Oxford University Press, Oxford.

———. 1979. *Indonesien*. Museum für Völkerkunde und Schweizerisches Museum für Volkskunde, Basel.

Rappaport, Roy A. 1968. *Pigs for the Ancestors: Ritual in the Ecology of a New Guinea People*. Yale University Press, New Haven.

Rasid, Gadis. 1982. "Minangkabau—a Feminist's Paradise?" *Hemisphere* 27(1):38–43.

Ratnam, Perala. 1982. *Laos and Its Culture*. Tulsi Publishing House, New Delhi.

Rawson, Jessica. 1977. *Animals in Art*. British Museum, London.

Rawson, Phillip. 1967. *The Art of Southeast Asia*. Thames and Hudson, London.

Reid, A., and L. Castles, eds. 1975. *Pre-colonial State Systems in Southeast Asia*. Monographs of the Malayan Branch of the Royal Asiatic Society 6, Kuala Lumpur, Malaysia.

Rensch, Bernhard. 1967. "The Intelligence of Elephants." *Scientific American*, February.

Ribu, Lu'un, and Tom Harrisson. 1955. "Agan Plandok, the Noble Mouse-deer." *Sarawak Museum Journal* 6(21):573–79.

Richards, Anthony. 1972. "Iban Augury." *Sarawak Museum Journal* 20(40–41):63–81.

Ricklefs, M. C. 1974. *Jogjakarta under Sultan Mangkubumi 1749–1792*. Oxford University Press, London.

Rijksen, H. D. 1978. *A Field Study on Sumatran Orangutans*. H. Veenman and Zonen B.V., Wageningen, the Netherlands.

Ripley, S. Dillon. 1964. *The Land and Wildlife of Tropical Asia*. Time-Life Books, New York.

Rock, J. F. 1952. *The Na-Khi Naga Cult and Related Ceremonies*. Pt. 1. Istituto Italiano per il Medio Ed Estremo Oriente, Rome.

Rogers, Susan. 1985. *Power and Gold: Jewelry from Indonesia, Malaysia and the Philippines*. Barbier-Muller Museum, Geneva.

Rookmaaker, L. C. 1977. "The Distribution and Status of the Rhinoceros in Borneo." *Bijdragen tot de dierkunde* 47(2):197–204.

Roonwal, M. L., and S. M. Mohnot. 1977. *Primates of South Asia: Ecology, Sociobiology, and Behavior*. Harvard University Press, Cambridge.

Roper, Tim. 1984. "A Question of Taste." *New Scientist*. March 29.

Rosaldo, Renato. 1980. *Ilongot Headhunting 1883–1974: A Study in Society and History*. Stanford University Press, Stanford, Calif.

Rutter, Owen. 1985 (1929). *The Pagans of North Borneo*. Oxford University Press, Singapore.

Sagan, Carl. 1977. *The Dragons of Eden*. Ballantine Books, New York.

Sahi, Jyoti. 1980. *The Child and the Serpent: Reflections on Popular Indian Symbols*. Routledge and Kegan Paul, London.

St. John, Spenser. 1974 (1862). *Life in the Forests of the Far East*. Oxford in Asia Historical Reprints, Kuala Lumpur.

Sanderson, Ivan. 1960. *The Dynasty of Abu*. Alfred A. Knopf, New York.

———. 1961. *Abominable Snowmen: Legend Come to Life*. Chilton, Philadelphia.

Sandin, Benedict. 1959. "Cock-fighting: The Dayak National Game." *Sarawak Museum Journal* 9(13–14):25–32.

———. 1977. *Gawai Burong: The Chants and Celebrations of the Iban Bird Festival*. Penerbit Universiti Sains Malaysia, Pulau Pinang, Malaysia.

SanDubock, A. C. 1978. "Rodent Control in Crop Stores." *Outlook on Agriculture* 9(5):220–24.

Sangermano, Father. 1843. *The Burmese Empire a Hundred Years Ago*. Archibald Constable and Co., London.

Sather, Clifford. 1986. "Iban Agricultural Augury." *Sarawak Museum Journal* 24(55):1–35.

Sawaddi, ed. 1979. *The Artistic Heritage of Thailand*. Sawaddi Magazine/National Museum Volunteers, Bangkok.

Schaefer, Juergen. 1976. "Crop Gains—Crop Losses." *Plant Protection News*. IV (3&4).

Schaller, George B. 1961. ""The Orang-utan in Sarawak." *Zoologica* 46:73–82.

————. 1967. *The Deer and the Tiger.* University of Chicago Press, Chicago.

————. 1977. *Mountain Monarchs: Wild Sheep and Goats of the Himalaya.* University of Chicago Press, Chicago.

Schebesta, Paul. 1973. *Among the Forest Dwarfs of Malaya.* Oxford University Press, Kuala Lumpur.

Schefold, Reimar. 1972. "Religious Conceptions on Siberut, Mentawai." *Sumatran Research Bulletin*: 12–24.

————. 1979. *Speelgoed Voor de Zielen: Kunst en Cultuur van de Mentawai-Eilanden.* Volkenkundig Museum Nusantara, Delft.

Schilling, Ton. 1957. *Tigermen of Anai.* George Allen and Unwin, Ltd., London.

Schnitger, F. M. 1964. *Forgotten Kingdoms in Sumatra.* E. J. Brill, Leiden.

Schot, Wim E. M. van der. 1986. *The Batek of Taman Negara.* Doctoral Thesis, University of Amsterdam, Amsterdam.

Schultz, A. H. 1944. "Age Changes and Variability in Gibbons." *American Journal of Physical Anthropology* 2:1–129.

Schultz, Adolph H. 1969. *The Life of Primates.* Weidenfeld and Nicolson, London.

Schumacher, E. F. 1973. *Small Is Beautiful: A Study of Economics as if People Mattered.* Blond and Briggs, Ltd., London.

Schurmann, C. 1982. "Mating Behaviour of Wild Orangutans." In Leobert E. M. de Voer (ed.). *The Orangutan: Its Biology and Conservation.* Dr. W. Junk Publishers, The Hague, Netherlands.

Schuyler, H. R. 1972. "Rodents in the Tropics: Their Effects and Control." *PANS* 18(4).

Schwartz, Jeffrey H. 1984. "The Evolutionary Relationships of Man and Orangutans." *Nature* 308:501–5.

————. 1987. *The Red Ape.* Houghton Mifflin. Boston.

Scidmore, Eliza B. 1984 (1899). *Java: The Garden of the East.* Oxford University Press, Singapore.

Scott, Sir Peter. 1981. "20 Years of Achievement," speech made at WWF's 20th anniversary, Wembley Conference Centre, London, 27 May 1981. Published in *Celebration,* WWF, Gland, Switzerland.

Segaller, Denis. 1976. "Worshipping Brahma, Lord of the Heavens." Bangkok *World*, February 13.

Seidenfaden, E. 1967. *The Thai Peoples.* Siam Society, Bangkok.

Seidensticker, John. 1977. *The Javan Tiger and the Meru Betiri Reserve: A Plan for Management.* World Wildlife Fund, Bogor, Indonesia.

————. 1984. *Managing Elephant Depredations in Agriculture and Forestry Projects.* World Bank, Washington, D.C.

————, and J. A. McNeely. 1975. "Observations on the Use of Natural Licks by Ungulates in the Huai Kha Khaeng Wildlife Sanctuary, Thailand." *Natural History Bulletin of the Siam Society* 26(1&2):25–34.

Sen, Asis. 1972. *Animal Motifs in Ancient Indian Art.* Firma K. L. Mukhopadhyay, Calcutta.

Shackley, Myra. 1983. *Wildmen: Yeti, Sasquatch, and the Neanderthal Enigma.* Thames and Hudson, London.

Shapiro, Gary Louis. 1985. "Factors Influencing the Variance in Sign Learning Performance by Four Juvenile Orangutans *(Pongo pygmaeus)."* Unpublished Ph.D. dissertation presented to University of Oklahoma, Norman.

Shelford, Robert W. C. 1916. *A Naturalist in Borneo*. T. Fisher Unwin, Ltd., London.

Shuttleworth, Charles. 1965. *Malayan Safari*. Phoenix House, London.

————. 1981. *Malaysia's Green and Timeless World*. Heinemann Educational Books (Asia), Kuala Lumpur.

Shuyler, Harlan R., and Sawart Ratanaworabhan. 1970. "Rats as Pests of Rice in Thailand." *International Rice Commission Newsletter* 19(2):20–24. Manila, the Philippines.

Siek, Marguerite. 1972. *Favourite Stories from Indonesia*. Heinemann Educational Books (Asia), Ltd., Hong Kong.

————. 1975. *Favourite Stories from Burma*. Heinemann Educational Books (Asia), Ltd., Hong Kong.

Silva, Anslem de. 1980. "The Impact of Buddhism on the Conservation of Flora and Fauna in Ancient Sri Lanka." *Tigerpaper* 7(4):21–25.

Silva, G. S. de. 1971. "Notes on the Orang-utan Rehabilitation Project in Sabah." *Malay Nature Journal* 24:50–77.

Simkin, Tom, and Richard S. Fiske. 1983. *Krakatau 1883: The Volcanic Eruption and Its Effects*. Smithsonian Institution Press, Washington, D.C.

Singh, A. J. 1979. "The War Against King Rat." *Financial Times News Features*, June.

Sinha, B. C. 1979. *Serpent Worship in Ancient India*. East-West Publications, London.

Skafte, Hakon. 1962. "A Contribution to the Preservation of the Sumatran Rhinoceros." *Journal of the Siam Society* 20(2):85–94.

Skeat, Walter W. 1984 (1900). *Malay Magic*. Oxford University Press, Singapore.

————, and C. O. Blagden. 1906. *Pagan Races of the Malay Peninsula*. Macmillan, London.

Smith, Huston. 1958. *The Religions of Man*. Mentor Books, New York.

Smyth, H. W. 1898. *Five Years in Siam*. John Murray, London.

Smythies, B. E. 1960. *Birds of Borneo*. Oliver and Boyd, London.

Soedarsono. 1974. *Living Traditional Theaters in Indonesia*. Akademi Seni Tari Indonesia, Yogyakarta.

Solheim, W. G. 1972. "An Earlier Agricultural Revolution." *Scientific American* 266(4):34–41.

Solyom, Garrett, and Bronwen Solyom. 1979. "Java's Sacred Daggers: Fusion of Art and Spirit." *Perspectives*, winter.

Sowerby, Arthur de Carle. 1940. *Nature in Chinese Art*. John Day Company, New York.

Spencer, J. E. 1966. *Shifting Cultivation in Southeast Asia*. University of California Press, Berkeley, Calif.

Srisavasdi, Boon Chuey. 1967. *The Hill Tribes of Siam*. Nai Sura Saranakhom, Bangkok.

Stanford, Barbara. 1972. *Myths and Modern Man*. Washington Square Press, New York.

Stephens, Harold. 1971. "Abominable Snowmen of Malaysia." *Argosy*, August.

Steubing, Robert. 1985. "Batang Lupar Crocodiles: Happy Bachelors, Lovesick Behemoths, or Nasty Brutes?" *Malayan Naturalist* 39 (1–2):43–46.

————, Ghazally Ismail, and Kusaudi Sallih. 1986. "The Ecology of Crocodile Attacks in Batang Lupar, Sarawak." *Sarawak Musuem Journal* 24(55):195–214.

Stevenson, H. N. C. 1943. *Economics of the Central Chin Tribes*. Times of India Press, Bombay.

Stoddart, Brian. 1981. "Bali and Survival." *Hemisphere* 26(3):188–94.

Stommel, Henry, and Elizabeth Stommel. 1983. *Volcano Weather: The Story of the Year Without a Summer.* Seven Seas Press, Newport, R.I.

Stothers, Richard B. 1984. "The Great Tambora Eruption in 1815 and Its Aftermath." *Science* 224:1191–98.

Stutley, Margaret, and James Stutley. 1977. *A Dictionary of Hinduism.* Routledge and Kegan Paul, London.

Sumardja, Effendi, Tarmudji, and Jan Wind. 1984. "Nature Conservation and Rice Production in the Dumoga Area, North Sulawesi, Indonesia." In McNeely and Miller 1984, 224–27.

Swettenham, Frank. 1895. *Malay Sketches.* John Lane, London.

Tambiah, S. J. 1970. *Buddhism and the Spirit Cults in Northeast Thailand.* Cambridge University Press, Cambridge.

Tan, Vu Ngoc. 1968. "The Raising of Deer, an Attractive Resource for Developing Countries in Southeast Asia." *IUCN Publications* 10:132–34.

Tate, D. J. M. 1971. *The Making of Modern Southeast Asia.* Oxford University Press, Kuala Lumpur.

Tate, G. H. H. 1947. *Mammals of Eastern Asia.* Macmillan, New York.

Taylor, K. D. 1972. "The Rodent Problem." *Outlook on Agriculture* 7(2):60–67.

Tenaza, R. R. 1975. "Territory and Monogamy Among Kloss' Gibbons in Siberut Island, Indonesia." *Folia Primatolgica* 24:60–80.

———. 1976. "Songs, Choruses and Countersinging of Kloss' Gibbons in Siberut Island, Indonesia." *Z. Tierpsychol.* 40:37–52.

Thom, W. S. 1933. "Some Experiences Amongst Elephant and Other Big Game of Burma 1887 to 1931." *Journal of the Bombay Natural History Society* 36:321–33.

Thompson, V. 1937. *French Indochina.* Macmillan, New York.

Ti, Ji. 1981. "China Has Its Yeti Too." *International Wildlife* 10:1.

Tilson, R. L. 1976. "Infant Coloration and Taxonomic Affinity of the Mentawai Islands Leaf Monkey." *Journal of Mammalogy* 57(4):767–69.

———. 1977. "Social Behaviour of Simakobu Monkeys and Its Relationship to Human Predation." *Journal of Mammalogy* 58(2):202–12.

———. and R. R. Tenaza. 1977. "The Evolution of the Long-distance Alarm Call in Kloss' Gibbons." *Nature* 268:233–35.

Tisdell, C. A. 1985. *Wild Pigs: Environmental Pest or Economic Resource?* Pergamon Press, Sydney.

Topping, Audrey. 1981. "Hairy Wild Men of China." *Science Digest,* August.

Trier, Jesper. 1981. "The Khon Pa of Northern Thailand: An Enigma." *Current Anthropology* 22(3):291–92.

Tweedie, M. W. F., and J. L. Harrison. 1954. *Malayan Animal Life.* Longman Malaysia Sdn. Bhd, Kuala Lumpur.

Tylor, Edward B. 1873. *Primitive Culture.* John Murray, London.

Van Gennep, J. L. 1896. "A Note on the Kangean Archipelago." *Tijdschrift voor Nederlandsch-Indie* 46:101.

Van Gulik, R. H. 1967. *The Gibbon in China.* E. J. Brill, Leiden.

Van Strien, Nico. 1985a. "Report on a Preparatory Mission for the Implementation of the 'Singapore Proposals' for Captive Breeding of Sumatran Rhinoceros as Part of a Conservation Strategy for the Species." Report to IUCN, Gland.

————. 1985b. *The Sumatran Rhinoceros in the Gunung Leuser National Park, Sumatra, Indonesia.* Privately published, Wageningen, the Netherlands.

Vietmeyer, Noel. 1984. "Hog Wild." *International Wildlife* 14(3):35.

Vlahos, Olivia. 1976. *Far Eastern Beginnings.* Viking Press, New York.

Vlekke, Bernard H. M. 1965. *Nusantara: A History of Indonesia.* W. Van Hoeve, Ltd., The Hague.

Voorhoeve, Rudolf. 1957. *Harimau.* Elek Books, London.

Wachtel, Paul Spencer. 1972. "Baram Regatta," *Asia Magazine.* January 10.

————. 1977a. "Adu Domba: Java's Holy Gladitorial Rams." *Orientations,* February.

————. 1977b. "Gunung Merapi: Fire Mountain." *Silver Kris,* May.

————. 1978a. "Sarawak." *InnAsia,* summer.

————. 1978b. "Karapan Sapi: Bull Racing of Madura." *Seasons,* winter.

————. 1979a. "Hornbills: Southeast Asia's Startling, Sacred Bird." *Silver Kris,* April.

————. 1979b. "Badui: Touch Not the Dirty Hands of Civilization." *Silver Kris,* May.

————. 1979c. "Return to the Wild." *Silver Kris,* October.

————. 1980a. "Indonesia's Shrinking Legacy." *Reader's Digest,* March.

————. 1980b. "Java: Treasures Past Telling." *Sawasdee,* November-December, pp. 65–75.

————. 1980c. "Dog Fights Boar, Man Wins." *Asia Magazine,* November.

————. 1981a. "Hornbills." *International Wildlife,* January–February.

————. 1981b. "Leatherback Turtles." *Silver Kris,* February.

————. 1982a. "Can We Talk to the Animals?" *Silver Kris,* July.

————. 1982b. "Malaysia's Rainforest. A Journey of Discovery." *Reader's Digest,* July.

————. 1983. "Jungle Tentacles." *Discovery,* March.

————. 1987. "The Unlikely Superstar: The Medicinal Leech Makes a Comeback." *International Wildlife,* September–October.

————, and J. A. McNeely. 1980. "The Universal Apothecary." *Winds* 2(2):12–16.

————, and J. A. McNeely. 1985. "Oh, Rats." *International Wildlife,* January–February.

————, and J. A. McNeely. 1986. "Man Against Nature." *International Wildlife* 16(1):12–15.

————, J. A. McNeely, and T. Moss. 1983. "Can we talk to the animals?" *Silver Kris.* July.

Wagner, Frits A. 1959. *Indonesia: The Art of an Island Group.* McGraw-Hill, New York.

Wales, H. G. Quaritch. 1969. *Dvaravati: The Earliest Kingdom of Siam.* Bernard Quaritch, Ltd., London.

————. 1973. *Early Burma—Old Siam: A Comparative Commentary.* Bernard Quaritch, Ltd., London.

————. 1983. *Divination in Thailand.* Curzon Press, London.

Walker, Katherine Sorley. 1978. "Voice and Shadow." *Hemisphere* 22(6):34–39.

Wallace, Alfred Russel. 1962 (1869). *The Malay Archipelago.* Dover Publications, Inc., New York.

————. 1879. *Australasia.* Edward Stanford, London.

Warren, William, and M. R. Priya Rangsit. 1986. *Thailand.* Apa, Singapore.

Watson, Jenny. 1976. *Favourite Stories from Thailand.* Heinemann Educational Books (Asia), Ltd., Hong Kong.

Wavell, Stewart. 1965. *The Naga King's Daughter.* Atheneum, New York.

Wells, Carveth. 1925. *Six Years in the Malay Jungle.* William Heinemann, Ltd., London.

Wharton, Charles. 1966. "Man, Fire and Wild Cattle in North Cambodia." *Proceedings of the Annual Tall Timbers Fire Ecology Conference* 5:23–65.

———. 1968. "Man, Fire and Wild Cattle in Southeast Asia." *Proceedings of the Annual Tall Timbers Fire Ecology Conference* 8:107–67.

Wharton, Charles H. 1957. *An Ecological Study of the Kouprey, Novibos sauveli.* Institute of Science and Technology, Manila.

Wheatley, Paul. 1980. *The Golden Khersonese: Studies in the Historical Geography of the Malay Peninsula Before A.D. 1500.* Penerbit Universiti Malay, Kuala Lumpur.

Whitehead, George. 1924. *In the Nicobar Islands.* Seeley, Service and Co., Ltd., London.

Whitmore, T. C. 1975. *Tropical Rain Forests of the Far East.* Oxford University Press, Oxford.

Whitney, Caspar. 1905. *Jungle Trails and Jungle People.* Charles Scribner's Sons, New York.

Whitten, A. J. 1982. *The Gibbons of Siberut.* J. M. Dent and Sons, Ltd., London.

———, and Johanne Ranger. 1986. "Logging at Bohorok." *Oryx* 20:246–48.

Wilcox, Harry. 1949. *White Stranger: Six Moons in Celebes.* Collins, London.

William, H.R.H. the Prince of Sweden. 1915. *In the Lands of the Sun.* Eveleigh Nash, London.

Williams, C. A. S. 1932. *Outlines of Chinese Symbolism and Art Motives.* No Publisher (pirated version, Taiwan).

Williams, J. H. 1960. *In Quest of a Mermaid.* Rupert Hart-Davis, London.

Williams, Leigh. 1954. *Jungle Prison: Twenty Years in Siam.* Andrew Melrose, London.

Williams, Thomas Rhys. 1966. *The Dusun: A North Borneo Society.* Holt, Rinehart and Winston, New York.

Williams-Hunt, P. D. R. 1952. *An Introduction to the Malayan Aborigines.* Government Press, Kuala Lumpur.

Wind, Jan. 1984. *Management Plan 1984–1989. Dumoga National Park.* Report for IUCN/WWF, Bogor, Indonesia.

Winfrey, Laurie Platt. 1979. *The Unforgettable Elephant.* Walker and Co., New York.

Winstedt, R. O. 1925. *Shaman, Saiva, and Sufi: A Study of the Evolution of Malay Magic.* Constable and Co., London.

Winstedt, Richard. 1982. *The Malay Magician.* Oxford University Press, Kuala Lumpur.

Wittfogel, Karl A. 1981 (1957). *Oriental Despotism: A Comparative Study of Total Power.* Vintage Books, New York.

Wood, W. A. R. 1965. *Consul in Paradise: Sixty-nine Years in Siam.* Souvenir Press, Ltd., London.

Wouden, F. A. E. van. 1968. *Types of Social Structure in Eastern Indonesia.* Martinus Nijhoff, The Hague.

Wray, Elizabeth, Claire Rosenfield, Dorothy Baily, and Joe Wray. 1972. *Ten Lives of the Buddha: Siamese Temple Paintings and Jataka Tales.* Weatherhill, New York.

Wright, Leight, Hedda Morrison, and K. F. Wong. 1972. *Vanishing World: The Ibans of Borneo*. Weatherhill, New York.

Wu Ch'eng-en. 1942. *Monkey*. Trans. Arthur Waley. George Allen and Unwin, London.

Yan Ming. 1986. "The Experimental and Clinical Studies on the Anti-inflammatory and Anti-ulcer Activity of Elephant Skin." Unpublished manuscript.

Yangprapakorn, U., J. A. McNeely, and E. W. Cronin. 1971a. "Status Report on the Crocodiles of Thailand." *IUCN Publication* (new series) 32:83–85.

———. 1971b. "Captive Breeding of Crocodiles in Thailand." *IUCN Publication* (new series) 32:98–101.

Yerkes, Robert M., and Ada W. Yerkes. 1929. *The Great Apes: A Study of Anthropoid Life*. Yale University Press, New Haven.

Yin, U Tun. 1967. *Wild Animals of Burma*. Rangoon Gazette, Ltd., Rangoon, Burma.

Zainul-Abidin bin Ahmad. 1922. "The Tiger-breed Families." *Journal of the Straits Branch of the Royal Asiatic Society* 85:36–9.

Zegwaard, Gerard A. 1959. "Headhunting Practices of the Asmat of Netherlands New Guinea." *American Anthropologist* 61(6):1020–41.

Zieseniss, Alexander. 1963. *The Rama Saga in Malaysia: Its Origin and Development*. Malaysian Sociological Research Institute, Ltd., Singapore.

Zimmer, Heinrich. 1946. *Myths and Symbols in Indian Art and Civilization*. Princeton University Press, Princeton.

———. 1955. *The Art of Indian Asia, Its Mythology and Transformation*. 2 vols. Pantheon Books, New York.

Zimmerman, David R. 1976. "Monkeys and Medicine." *International Wildlife* 6(2).

Zimmerman, W. F. A. 1863. *Die Inseln des Indischen und Stillen Meeres*. Berlin.

Zinsser, Hans. 1934. *Rats, Lice and History*. Little, Brown and Company, New York.

Zoete, Beryl de, and Walter Spies. 1938. *Dance and Drama in Bali*. Faber and Faber, London.

Index